McHenry's Stories for the Soul

Raymond McHenry

HENDRICKSON
PUBLISHERS

McHenry's Stories for the Soul

McHenry's Stories for the Soul

Copyright © 2001 by Raymond McHenry
Published by Hendrickson Publishers
P.O. Box 3473
Peabody, Massachusetts, 01961-3473

Printed in the United States of America

ISBN 1-56563-631-7

First printing — August 2001

Cover design by Veldheer Creative Services, Byron Center, Michigan
Interior design and typesetting by Booksetters, White House, Tennessee
Edited by Deneen Sedlack and Shannon Goode

DEDICATION

This book is dedicated to
my parents
Al and Martha McHenry
and
my parents-in-law
Loyd and Shirley Fannin

TABLE OF CONTENTS

FOREWORD

In 1996 I was privileged to write the Foreword for Dr. McHenry's Book, *The Best of . . . In Other Words* (now entitled, *McHenry's Quips, Quotes & Other Notes*). I did so because I found his work to be so extraordinarily helpful to me. At least once each month in my Sunday School class I have used examples, illustrations, or stories from his research. In addition, in my newspaper columns I periodically make use of his efforts, and in my public seminars I do the same. In short, Dr. McHenry saves me a great deal of time.

If you're a pastor or Sunday school teacher, this is a "must read" book for you. If you're a wanna-be speaker, perhaps just getting started in Toastmasters, or if you're the president of a civic or social club—or even just a participant—here's something that will be of tremendous help to you. If you are none of the above, you can use many of the stories and examples to enrich family discussions at the dinner table.

The stories are real, the examples are usable, the data is helpful, and the humor is funny. You'll find stories and illustrations in this book that will bring you to tears and will do the same for your audiences. These anecdotes and illustrations will help you to inspire your audiences and encourage your listeners to become involved in your ministry or other mission in life. I encourage you to not only read it, but to use it on a daily basis. Once you've read all the way through the book, start over. You will be amazed how a second reading of some of the stories will touch your life in a significant way.

Zig Ziglar,
Author/Motivational Teacher

ACKNOWLEDGMENT

The Poetry of John Donne reminds us, "No man is an island." This truth becomes increasingly evident when writing a book. For this reason I express my gratitude to . . .

My beautiful wife, Michelle—for your constant love and consistent support.

My two wonderful children, Meagan and Myles—as I say each night at bedtime, "I love you and I'm proud of you!"

My loving church family, Westgate Memorial Baptist Church—what an honor it is to be your pastor.

INTRODUCTION

How many times have you found yourself clarifying a point by using the phrase, "In other words?" We've all been in conversations where we wanted to help the listener better understand our message. As a result, we've painted a word picture after introducing it with, "In other words. . . "

In 1991, this little phrase took on a new meaning when we began the publication, *In Other Words...* Since that time ministers, teachers, and motivational speakers throughout the world have used this quarterly publication. This book is the second volume of stories, quotes, interesting facts, and jokes used by *In Other Words . . .* The first book is entitled, *McHenry's Quips, Quotes, and Other Notes.*

To receive the greatest benefit from this book, it is helpful to know the layout. The contents consist of four main sections. The *first section* contains stories, quotes, and facts of a more serious nature. The *second section* is devoted exclusively to humor. The *third section* is the Source Index. It contains documentation for each entry. The *final section* is your Master Index. Each entry has been cross-referenced to help the reader more easily locate items by key words or topics.

The mission statement of my life is simply . . . "move people toward God." It is my prayer this book will help all of us accomplish that singular goal.

Best Wishes Always,
Raymond McHenry

Publishers note: Included in the back of the book is a CD-ROM (with the full text of *McHenry's Stories for the Soul*) providing convenient cut-and-paste opportunities to move quotes directly from the CD-ROM into actual manuscripts, talks, sermons, and lessons. The CD-ROM is designed as a database to help you develop your own electronic reference file wherein you can add additional quotations, quips, illustrations, and stories.

Motivational Stories, Quotes, Facts, and Anecdotes

❖

Abortion An interesting statement against abortion surrounds the Advent of Christ. In Luke 1:44, the gospel-writing physician used the Greek word *brephus* to describe the baby (John the Baptist) who leaped for joy in Elizabeth's womb when Mary shared the news that she was pregnant. Just one chapter later in Luke 2:12, 16, the good doctor uses the same word *brephus* to describe the newborn Savior lying in a manger. Through the inspiration of Scripture, God has provided another reminder that life in the womb is nothing less than life outside of the womb.[1]

Abortion Every three days, more African-Americans are murdered by abortion than were lynched from 1882–1968.[2]

Abortion In America, nearly one in four pregnancies end in abortion.[3]

Abortion On a graduation platform in New London, Connecticut, two very unusual hands came in contact with each other. One hand belonged to a woman who doctors said should have been aborted. The other hand was used in signing our nation's partial-birth abortion bill. In May of 1996, Jessica Brown received a handshake of congratulations from President Bill Clinton. Their chance meeting is an amazing story. Just eleven months after the legalization of abortion, Jessica Brown was born three and one-half months early on January 1, 1974. She was only twenty-four weeks old and the doctor said, "The baby's chances are zero. It won't be a live birth. Even if she survives, she'll probably be physically and mentally handicapped, blind, or worse." The attending physician then asked, "Do you want to try and save her or dispose her?" There was no question in her parents' minds, "Save her!" At just two pounds, she was too small to nurse, so they inserted a feeding tube and gave her one-half teaspoon of formula at each feeding. The hospital band wouldn't even stay on her tiny ankles. Jessica was much smaller than many that are aborted, but she was allowed to live. Twenty-two years later she graduated from the U.S. Coast Guard Academy, a college that accepts only 5 percent of its applicants based on a formula of academic, athletic, and leadership achievement. The child, who doctors said would never survive, much less thrive, graduated from one of our nation's most prestigious institutions. On that May afternoon, the hand of a survivor clutched the grasp of another hand. One embodied life, the other called for death. It was truly a strange encounter.[4]

Abortion On October 23, 1996, NBC's *Today* show was forced into making a point for pro-life even though the now retired host, Bryant Gumbel, is an outspoken opponent of this position. He was interviewing Albert and Angela Valencia along with their four-year-old daughter, Priscilla. National attention had come to this family because little Priscilla had saved her mother's life by calling 911 when Angela fell to the floor and became unconscious while bleeding internally. Gumbel asked the little girl a few questions, interviewed the 911 operator, and spoke with the father. The interview then took an interesting twist when Mrs. Valencia said, "I do want to add, when I was lying in the hospital, I could only remember thinking back because I had Priscilla pretty young, at fifteen." Counselors told her, "Have an abortion; you're too young." Gumbel responded by noting, "Instead she turns around and saves your life." Angela replied, "Yeah, and I think that's important; I think young girls today, even if you're pregnant, you need to think twice; it could save your life." I wonder how many additional lives have been lost because we aborted the babies who would have lived to save them.[5]

Abortion The abortion advocates suffered a setback when Norma McCorvey accepted Christ and recanted her beliefs on abortion. McCorvey was "Jane Roe" in the 1973 landmark decision of Roe vs. Wade that legalized abortion. "I think abortion's wrong. I think what I did with Roe vs. Wade was wrong and I just have to take a pro-life choice." She was baptized on August 8, 1995, in the Dallas, Texas suburb of Garland. Reverend Flip Benham baptized McCorvey not long after leading her to Christ. His strategy should be followed, lead abortionist to Christ.[6]

Abortion Though we are frightened of nuclear war, frightened of this disease called AIDS, we are not frightened to kill an innocent child. Abortion has become the greatest destroyer of peace. —*Mother Teresa*[7]

Abortion Two-thirds of all abortions are obtained by never-married women.[8]

Abundant Life "The proper function of man is to live, not to exist." —*Jack London*[9]

Abuse Every day in America, three children die of injuries inflicted by abusive parents.[10]

Abuse The Department of Health and Human Services estimates that 2.8 million children are abused each year in the United States.[11]

Acceptance There is a Pakistani folktale that addresses a common problem in our society, adult child/parent relationships. An elderly woman lived with her daughter and grandson. With the aging process came less control of her faculties and she became an irritant to her daughter. Rather than help clean and care for the house as she had once done, the older woman now made messes and broke things. One day after she broke a precious plate, the daughter erupted in anger and sent her son out to buy a wooden plate. The boy hesitated because he knew the wooden plate would humiliate and shame his grandmother. Nonetheless, his mother insisted so the boy left for the purchase. When he returned, his mother was surprised to learn he had purchased two plates. She said, "Why did you buy two plates? I only told you to buy one!" The boy replied, "I understood what you wanted, but I bought the second plate so there would be one for you when you get old." Millions of American adults are in the position of caring for their aging parents. The task is frequently hard, but we must never approach this responsibility with anything less than love and compassion. It's what we all hope our children will provide us when physical limitations come our way.[12]

Accomplishments "Some of the world's greatest feats were accomplished by people not smart enough to know they were impossible." — *Doug Larson* [13]

Accountability Centuries ago, a man conned his way into the Chinese emperor's orchestra. He could not play the flute, but he dramatically mimicked the characteristics of a seasoned flutist. His charade afforded him a modest salary and a comfortable place to live. He enjoyed the trappings of his deception until the emperor decided he would like to hear a private solo from each musician in the orchestra. In a state of panic, he took flute lessons but he couldn't learn fast enough. In desperation, he feigned illness but the court physician couldn't find anything wrong with him. On the eve before his presentation, this con artist took poison and committed suicide. The Chinese language was impacted by this historical event and it has impacted the English language as well. Because of that situation we now have the phrase, "He refused to face the music." We must all face the music in our lives and realize that each of us will be held accountable for every moment of our lives. One day, God will call every person to individually face the music.[14]

Accountability Most of us hate to be held accountable, but the Bible teaches that we all need it to mature and develop. Researchers at Michigan State University have also found accountability to be beneficial. These data crunchers discovered that 97 percent of the dieters who bet someone they would stick to a weight-loss plan for six months actually succeeded in their pursuit. Conversely, over 80 percent of those who didn't make such bets failed to stay with the dieting regimen. For these dieters, accountability gave them nearly a four-to-one edge toward success. Now the Bible doesn't suggest we bet on diets, but it does counsel us to use accountability as an effective tool for discipleship. If you haven't already made yourself accountable to a fellow Christian, try it out and see if it doesn't enhance your spiritual growth.[15]

Accountability Poor Rachel Kovac! After being ticketed twice for speeding, the seventeen-year-old resident of St. Joseph, Missouri, received a special bumper sticker from her parents in March of 1999. Concerned over their daughter's driving record, Dennis and Cindy Kovac attached a powerful note to Rachel's car which read, "If I'm Speeding, Call My Parents!" It then listed the family phone number. This accountability sticker garnered the results Mr. and Mrs. Kovac desired because Rachel quit speeding. Like that despised bumper sticker, accountability isn't usually very pleasant but it does help us do the right thing.[16]

Action "No one would remember the Good Samaritan if he had only had good intentions." —*Margaret Thatcher* [17]

Action Three frogs sat on a log and one decided to jump off. How many frogs were left on the log? Three, just because we decide to do something doesn't mean we will actually do it.[18]

Activism "The activist is not the one who says the river is dirty. The activist is the one who cleans up the river." —*H. Ross Perot* [19]

Adversity A gentleman once wrote Marilyn vos Savant with a question about life. Ms. vos Savant is listed in the *Guiness Book of World Records* Hall of Fame for highest IQ, and has a regular column in *Parade*. This particular inquirer said his life was "more exhausting than he ever imagined" and wanted to know, "Is this normal?" Marilyn told him his life was indeed normal and then gave the following analogy about life.

She said, "Much of the time, life is like going through the airport steering a loaded luggage cart with one bad wheel. Sometimes you just feel ridiculous, sometimes you actually look ridiculous, and sometimes all you can do is just try to push it in generally the right direction." She's right, life is often hard so don't waste your time wondering if it's that way for others, or wishing it wasn't that way for you. Just stay close to Christ and he will meet your every need (Philippians 4:19).[20]

Adversity In 1996, Michael Jordan took home two MVP trophies—one for the regular season and one from the championship series—and led the Chicago Bulls through a record-setting season of seventy-two wins and only ten losses, plus a championship against Seattle. It was the crowning jewel of his comeback after an eighteen-month stint in the minor leagues of baseball. Most people will remember that Jordan gave up on baseball and rejoined the Chicago Bulls during the last portion of the 1995 season. He was confident that his game would quickly return to the caliber with which everyone was acquainted, but it didn't. He struggled and wasn't the dominant force he once was. He even took his old number 23 jersey out of retirement, but that didn't make much difference. His, and the Chicago Bulls's return to glory was routed by the Orlando Magic in the semifinals. Frustration ruled the day for Jordan while the rest of the world wondered if he had become just another sensational "has been." Of the sad and humiliating experience Jordan said, "The disappointments of last year motivated me to bounce back. I thank Orlando for giving me that incentive." Jordan used the adversity of defeat as a catalyst to train harder, spend more time in the gym, and relearn the necessary skills of the game. The strategy worked. He got back on top of his game and stayed there until he retired in 1998. And for his successful comeback he gives full credit to those earlier defeats. When adversity strikes, we can crawl in a corner and quit, or we can recommit ourselves to be "more than conquerors through Christ" (Romans 8:37).[21]

Adversity "In the middle of difficulty lies opportunity." —*Albert Einstein*[22]

Adversity J. C. Penney, the founder of the store that bears his name, once said, "I am grateful for all my problems. As each of them was overcome, I became stronger and more able to meet those yet to come. I grew in all my difficulties." His words are paralleled by a recent study of religious faith in America. When adults were asked what milestones strengthened their faith, 42 percent noted the experience of a personal problem. The two closest responses were childbirth or adoption (15 percent), and joining a place of worship (14 percent). Marriage was mentioned 8 percent of the time. Adversity is often the anvil on which strength is created (2 Corinthians 12:7–10).[23]

Adversity Paul Orfalea was a kid with dyslexia, and had a school track record that included the repetition of several grades, expulsions, and a stint with a school for retarded children. Plenty of Paul's teachers were convinced he was as dumb as a stump. One junior high school administrator told his mother, "Maybe he could enroll in a good trade school and learn to lay carpet." In addition to all of this, kids called him "Kinko" because of his curly hair. From an outsider's point of view, Paul didn't have much going for him. He managed to graduate from high school with what he classified, "a low D average." He then made his way through the University of Southern California with a similar lack of distinction. Rather than learning to lay carpet, in 1970, Paul started a small copy shop at an old hamburger stand. From that humble beginning, he turned a goofy nickname into an internationally known chain of stores. In 2000, Paul Orfalea, at the age of fifty-two, stepped down from his position as CEO of Kinko's. With multiple millions of dollars in his portfolio, Orfalea credits his parents for encouraging him through such great adversity. He has said, "Without my parents, I'd be a skid-row bum right now." To fellow dyslexics, Orfalea says, "God gave you an advantage. So work with your strengths." When facing adversity, we often worry about what we don't have (our weaknesses) rather than using what we do have (our strengths).[24]

Adversity "The ultimate measure of a man is not where he stands in moments of comfort, but where he stands at times of challenge and controversy." —*Martin Luther King*[25]

Advertising In the United States, the advertising industry spends $6 billion a day.[26]

Advice "If it's free, it's advice. If you pay for it, it's counseling. If you can use either one, it's a miracle." —*Clara Null*[27]

Affirmation "It takes nine affirming comments to make up for each critical comment we give to our children." —*Abraham Maslow*[28]

Age "By the time you're eighty, you know everything, but the problem is you just can't remember it." —*George Burns*[29]

Age "Plan your life, budgeting for seventy years, and understand that if your time proves shorter that will not be unfair deprivation but rapid promotion." —*J.I. Packer*[30]

Age The sixty-plus age group is growing three times faster than the general population in America. There are now more people over age sixty-five than under eighteen.[31]

Age Women lie about it and men pretend it doesn't matter, but age is seen much differently in Nepal. When ABC's *20/20* cohost, Hugh Downs visited Nepal, he discovered it is "polite" to ask a person's age and to call someone old is a compliment in Nepal. Someone in their mid fifties typically seems embarrassed about their immature age, but they are usually comforted if the inquirer encouragingly says, "Don't feel bad, you're getting there." In Nepal they take heed to Proverbs 16:31, "Gray hair is a crown of splendor."[32]

Aging Baby boomers are turning fifty at the rate of one every 7.5 seconds.[33]

Aging The number of people in the United States over age sixty-five is larger that the entire population of Canada. Two thirds of all the people who have ever lived to age sixty-five are alive today.[34]

Aging The years of preretirement can be challenging. Sometimes there is a feeling of being caught between the retirees and the "younger" generation. Ironically, though, this can be one of the most rewarding stages of life. The Japanese seem to understand this reality because they classify fifty-five to retirement as the "age of fruition." It can be a time of reaping the rewards of earlier work while using the wisdom of experience to be extremely productive.[35]

AIDS Adolescents account for half of the forty thousand people diagnosed with HIV each year.[36]

Alcohol Alcohol-related highway deaths are the number one killer of fifteen-to-twenty-four-year-old Americans.[37]

Alcohol Alcohol-related traffic accidents killed 17,126 Americans in 1996.[38]

Alcohol Each year in America, junior and senior high school students drink 35 percent of all wine coolers and 1.1 billion cans of beer.[39]

Alcohol In America, over 40 percent of all traffic fatalities are alcohol related. This averages out to one alcohol-related death every thirty-one minutes.[40]

Alcohol On June 21, 1998, Silas Caldwell shot and killed his best friend, Larry Slusher. Both men had been drinking when Slusher, age forty-seven, put a beer can on top of his head and told his lifelong buddy to shoot it off. Caldwell obliged, but missed the can and mortally wounded his friend. "Wine is a mocker and beer a brawler; whoever is led astray by them is not wise" (Proverbs 20:1).[41]

Alcohol The effects of alcohol might take on new meaning when you consider what it can do to rats. During the spring of 1999 in New Delhi, India, a couple of rats got into some confiscated moonshine in storage at the police station. The culprits were soon found outside in a back alley trying to attack several cats. Whether it's consumed by rats or people, alcohol can cause delusional thinking that leads to potentially deadly behavior.[42]

Alcohol The *Journal of the American Medical Association* recently released a study on drunken driving. Researchers believe this study provides the first estimate of how extensive this problem has become. In their findings, it was revealed that Americans drive under the influence of alcohol 123 million times a year. That averages out to 14,000 times per hour. When researchers compared this information with law enforcement arrest records, it was discovered that for every one arrest, eighty-two drunken drivers continue down the road. These statistics help us understand why seventeen thousand people die each year due to alcohol-related accidents.[43]

Alcohol The median age at which children begin drinking alcohol is thirteen.[44]

Alcohol The risk of a fatal car crash is eleven times greater for a person with 0.8 blood alcohol content (drunk) than a nondrinking driver.[45]

Alcohol The women most likely to drink heavily (sixty or more drinks a month) have incomes above $75,000 or below $15,000.[46]

Alcohol Twenty percent of those over age sixty-five have some problem with alcohol, and nearly one-fourth of all those hospitalized over age sixty are diagnosed with alcoholism costing $60 billion in treatment.[47]

Alcohol "We have killed more people celebrating Independence Day than we lost fighting for it." —*Will Rogers* [48]

America "America has lost its sense of shame." —*Colin Powell*[49]

America "Imagine what would happen to the drug problem in America if our country was as determined to keep drugs out of schools as they are the Bible." —*Anonymous* [50]

America In July of 1893, Katharine Bates stood on the top of Pikes Peak and found the inspiration for, "America the Beautiful." This experience came at the culmination of a tremendous journey. She was an English professor at the Wellesley College for women near Boston. During the summer of 1893, she accompanied several other professors to teach a three-week summer session at Colorado College in Colorado Springs. In route to Colorado, they traveled by train across the vast expanse of America. Along the way, they stopped in Chicago for the World's Fair and were amazed by all of the exhibits. The intellectual exhilaration of the fair and the teaching assignment in Colorado, combined with the unique beauty of open plains and the majestic Rockies left Bates overwhelmed with emotion. At the end of their brief teaching tenure, the professors went to the top of Pikes Peak in a horse-drawn wagon. At the precipice of fourteen thousand feet, she felt the words rush into her heart. That evening, when she returned to the hotel, she wrote down the immortal words. Two years later she ran across the words in her notebook from Colorado and submitted this poem to *The Congregational* magazine. It was then published in their July 4, 1895 issue. The poem attracted immediate attention and was set to various melodies. Years later, Samuel Ward gave it the current music and "America the Beautiful" has been sung countless times since. This minister's daughter, who never received more than a few dollars for her words, caught the essence of America's beauty by defining its natural majesty within the confines of God's centrality. May we never forget the true beauty of America is contingent on the shed grace of God.[51]

America *The People vs. Larry Flynt* opened at the box office in December 1996. This movie chronicled the life of pornography magnate,

Larry Flynt. The film put a glossy shine on the publisher of *Hustler* magazine and attempted to hoist him on a hero's pedestal. Ironically, people of his own industry didn't buy the expensive Hollywood makeover. Mark Kernes, who reviews thousands of X-rated films every year for a pornography industry trade publication, said , "I'm not really a fan of *Hustler* humor. It's a little too nasty for me." The movie is directed by Milos Forman, an old friend of Vaclav Havel, president of the Czech Republic. This connection led to the unlikely lunch engagement of Havel with Flynt. During their luncheon, Flynt asked Havel for his critique of the movie. Havel's response said more about the degeneration of our country than the film itself. He simply said, "Very American." Worse than the content of this movie is the assessment of a world leader that glamorizing pornography is "Very American."[52]

America The title of a recent editorial blared, "One Nation, Over God." The article was well written, but the title communicated more than the ideas that followed. Has our nation already become a nation that believes we are "Over God?" For many years we have been headed in that direction even though we say "under God" when reciting "The Pledge of Allegiance." Protection and blessing are only found "under God."[53]

Anger Among psychiatrists, one of the most common terms used today is LFT. This abbreviated term addresses a prevalent problem in our society. LFT stands for "low frustration tolerance." Many Americans are walking time bombs just waiting to explode. They have allowed circumstances, situations, schedules, and people to crowd out their ability to tolerate frustrations. For this reason they are living on the edge and quickly erupt with anger when frustrations arise. To avoid this syndrome we would do well to schedule time for interruptions and frustrations so that they do not affect us so adversely. We would also do well to settle the issues that anger us before "the sun goes down" (Ephesians 4:26).[54]

Anger Each year in America, an average of fourteen men are killed by soft drink vending machines. After not receiving a drink or due change, these men shook the machines until they tipped over and crushed them to death. Each man became the victim of his own anger. Inappropriate anger is a dangerous weapon.[55]

Anger In a discussion on anger, Dr. James Dobson writes, "There is no greater opportunity to influence our fellowman for Christ than to respond with love when we have been unmistakably wronged and assaulted. On those occasions, the difference between Christian love and the values of the world are most brilliantly evident" (See Philippians 2:5).[56]

Anger On May 1, 2000, the American Heart Association released the results of an exhaustive study on anger through their periodical, *Circulation.* Dr. Janice Williams led the study while serving at the University of North Carolina at Chapel Hill. Part of their research included monitoring thirteen thousand adults for six years. These extensive profiles revealed that a person with a propensity for anger is nearly three times more likely to have a heart attack than their calmer counterparts. This ratio was maintained even after researchers took into account other major risk factors such as high blood pressure, high cholesterol, smoking, and obesity. Coupled with this information is the research done by Duke University psychiatrist Dr. Redford Williams, which notes that 20 percent of American adults have a susceptibility to anger high enough to threaten their health. Of course anger threatens far more than just our physical health. In the opening line of Amy Tan's book, *The Kitchen God's Wife,* the author writes, "Whenever my mother talks to me, she begins the conversation as if we were already in the middle of an argument." For the well-being of our bodies and souls, may we petition God's ongoing help in managing our anger without sin.[57]

Anger On Mother's Day of 1987, Percy Washington killed the wrong woman. Washington and his wife, Corene, had been married for twenty-nine years before separating the previous year. The sixty-one-year-old retiree became angry with his estranged wife and accused her of taking advantage of him. He bought a shotgun the day before and went to her church with the intent of murder. When the morning worship service ended, Washington waited for his wife to get in her car. He then leveled his shotgun and fired through the windshield. But because Washington wasn't wearing his glasses, he shot a woman who he mistook for his wife. Fannie Watson was driving a similar car so he just assumed she was his wife. After being arrested, Washington said, "I'm sorry about the other woman. I meant to kill my wife, but I forgot my glasses." Anger leaves us blinded to reality regardless of whether or not we wear corrective lenses, and it will ultimately hurt innocent people.[58]

Anger Pastor Chester Miller experienced one of the most bizarre benedictions when closing out a morning worship service in March of

1999. One of his church members, Victoria Smith, pulled a gun on Pastor Miller during the closing prayer because he had not preached from the book of Revelation that morning. The fifty-eight-year-old woman in Saddle, Arkansas, said a sermon from Revelation was "important for her feud with another church member." Poorly managed anger leads to some very irrational decisions and actions.[59]

Anger Some people believe you should just "kick it and cuss" when you get mad at something. Guy Boos took it a step further when his washing machine broke down in September of 1999. Police were dispatched to the Wisconsin resident's home after neighbors reported gunfire. Boos, age thirty-seven, got mad at the washer so he pushed it out the door and down a flight of stairs. He then got his .25-caliber pistol and fired three rounds into the machine. Boos's display of anger led to his subsequent arrest. Whether it's road rage or appliance rage, anger continues to present itself as an emotion we must learn to manage more effectively. (Additional research by Gallup reveals nearly one-fourth of the American workforce admitted to being "somewhat angry at work." One in six employees acknowledged being so angry with a coworker that he or she felt like hitting the person.)[60]

Anger "When you are in the right, you can afford to keep your temper, and when you are in the wrong, you cannot afford to lose it." —*Mahatma Gandhi*[61]

Answers In one of the *Peanuts* comic strips, Peppermint Patty came to grips with a shocking truth. She was turning to Marsha for a few answers in school. Marsha exhorted Patty to stop asking her for answers and she said, "I don't have all the answers. Sometimes I just guess." Peppermint Patty became very distressed and replied, "You guess? You've been giving me answers that you just guessed?!!" Unfortunately, Peppermint Patty's predicament doesn't just exist in the fantasy world of comics. Every day, countless people depend upon others to give them answers that may be nothing more than a guess; quite possibly a bad guess. We don't have to bank our eternity on somebody's guess, we can find the answer for ourselves in the truth of God's Word.[62]

Anxiety Approximately twenty-four million Americans suffer from panic attacks and related disorders.[63]

Anxiety In case you need anything else to worry about, the June 1996 issue of *Pediatrics Journal* reported on an experiment that hypothesizes anxious girls can end up as much as two inches shorter than their nonanxious peers. Dr. Daniel Pine, a psychiatrist with the New York Psychiatric Institute, studied seven hundred children from 1983 through 1992. The nine-year study began with the children averaging 13.7 years of age. Psychiatric tests were conducted to determine which children suffered from anxiety and chronic worrying. Girls with high levels of anxiety and worry were twice as likely as nonanxious girls to end up less than five feet, four inches as adults. The authors of this study theorize that anxiety inhibits the body's production of growth hormone. Such findings were not discovered in boys and the doctors speculate this is due to the reality that boys tend to handle their stress differently—not necessarily better.[64]

Anxiety When walking through the rural roads of India, you will occasionally come across a post with a sturdy shelf about shoulder height. These posts are called *Soma Tonga*, which means "resting place." As people travel on foot, they can stop at a *Soma Tonga* and place their heavy load on the shelf for relief. Once rested, they can continue their journey. One can easily see why Christians in India call Jesus "My *Soma Tonga*." He has told us to "cast our burdens upon him" (1 Peter 5:7) and "you shall find rest for your souls" (Matthew 11:28–30).[65]

Apathy In November of 1996, Ted Turner told a roomful of television executives to raise the standards for on-air programming. He said, "People are beginning to realize the total effect of watching so much stupid, sleazy, lousy, violent, exploitive television." Later, though, he conceded a level of apathy on his part. He acknowledged, "My networks run a lot of programming that I'm not happy with and that bothers me. But does it bother me enough to do something about it? No, not really." Turner's experience represents a mirror of our culture. We are all sickened and disturbed by many of the trends in our society, but unfortunately, an honest confession for most of us would be a duplication of Turner's quote: "Does it bother me enough to do something about it? No, not really."[66]

Apathy On May 16, 1998, Christopher Sercye died, and his death has left many people shaking their fists in angry frustration. In the early evening of that Saturday, Sercye was playing basketball with some friends. Their game was tragically terminated when gang members jumped out of a car and fired two shots into the fifteen-year-old boy's chest. His friends quickly carried him about one hundred yards toward Chicago's Ravenswood Hospital. They set him down in the alley about thirty-five feet from the emergency room and dashed inside for help. To their unbelievable surprise, the hospital personnel said it was against policy to leave their duties to treat people outside. Friends, neighbors, and police officers pleaded with the ER staff to come outside and treat the dying teenager. Some of the staff were outside smoking just thirty-five feet from Sercye, but they said it was against hospital policy for them to get involved until the boy was inside the building. Although police officer James Maurer had been trained not to move a seriously wounded person, he commandeered a wheelchair and brought the boy inside after an ambulance failed to arrive within twenty minutes of being called by those trying to help. Sercye died about an hour later from the bullet wound that had perforated his aorta. John Blair, president and CEO of Ravenswood, initially stood by the actions of his employees but later had the policy rescinded because of Sercye's death. Such scenarios are not limited to bureaucratic hospital policies. Many churches are surrounded by those mortally wounded from the smoking barrel of our adversary, yet there seems to be an unwritten policy that says we cannot leave the building to help. Comforted by the complacent resolve that we will help them if they can get through the door, we leave them to die just feet from the place that is supposed to stand as a citadel of help and hope. May we learn from this great tragedy and dispense with practices that are void of Christlike compassion.[67]

Apologetics Dr. Harry Ironside was a great Christian leader in the first half of last century. On one occasion, he was involved with a Salvation Army meeting in San Francisco. Ironside shared his testimony with the gathering then returned to his seat on the platform. Soon after sitting down, Ironside was handed a note. A well-known agnostic was in the crowd and he had written a brief note on his business card, then had someone hand it to Ironside. The agnostic challenged Ironside to a public debate and offered to pay all expenses. Ironside then returned to the podium and publicly accepted the debate on the following conditions: that the agnostic would bring one man and one woman who had both fallen into some type of vice that had caused them to experience great loss and cost them favor within society, but who were now back in the graces of their respective families and society at large because of the positive changes and transformation caused by their newfound belief in agnosticism. Ironside then acknowledged that he would have one hundred such people whose lives have been radically changed by their commitment to Jesus Christ. Upon hearing these conditions the agnostic waved his hand in polite surrender and exited the building. A transformed life is one of the most indisputable pieces of apologetic evidence.[68]

Apologies Do you ever struggle with the words, "I'm sorry?" Kathy Warman staked her claim on the difficult nature of apologizing. The former telephone operator started a home-based business called *An Apology Service.* For just $6.00 she will use her soothing, Southern accent to call an offended party and offer your apology. Of her business, Warman says, "My service is to help you get it done, and save a friendship or a relationship."[69]

Appearance "Even I don't wake up looking like Cindy Crawford." —*Cindy Crawford*[70]

Arguments A young, married man expressed frustration over an ongoing argument with his new bride. He told a close friend, "I know there are two sides to every argument, I just wish there was an end." How true. It's important to see both sides, but it is also necessary to see the end.[71]

Arguments "Nothing is as frustrating as arguing with someone who knows what he's talking about." —*Sam Ewing*[72]

Arguments "The strongest words are usually used in the weakest arguments." —*Bernice Haliburton*[73]

Arrogance Don Shula, the legendary coach of the Miami Dolphins, has told a humorous story about himself. Coach Shula is a very humble man, but he remembers a day when he let his humility slip. He and his wife had retreated to a small town in Maine to avoid being noticed on their vacation. While there, they went to see a movie on a messy, rainy night. When Shula and his wife walked into the theater, the people began to applaud. The famous coach whispered to his wife, "I guess there's no place we can go where people won't recognize me." When they sat down, Shula shook hands with the man on their row and said, "I'm surprised that you knew who I am." The man looked at him and replied, "Am I supposed to know who you are? We're just glad you came in because the manager said he wasn't going to start the movie unless there were at least ten people here." Just about the time we think we're something, somebody reminds us we're not![74]

Assisted Suicide Dr. Jack Kevorkian forced the American people to take a stand on the controversial issue of assisted suicide. Although Kevorkian was not the only person in favor of active euthanasia, he became the single most influential person in America due to his involvement in nearly one hundred deaths. For this reason it is of value to examine a few lesser known facts about this man and his work. For starters, in December of 2000, the *New England Journal of Medicine* reported on an analysis of sixty-nine suicides supervised by Kevorkian. They noted 75 percent of his patients were not terminally ill when he helped them die. In five cases there was no physical illness whatsoever. Before his imprisonment, Kevorkian, a pathologist who deals with dead bodies, was stripped of his medical licenses and declared "unfit to practice medicine" by the California Attorney General's office. Kevorkian insisted he is not obsessed with death but his life speaks to the contrary. During his medical residency, he was nicknamed Dr. Death because of his work and fascination with dead patients. He was an accomplished artist whose paintings contain detached organs, severed heads, maggots, blood, bullets, skulls, cannibalism, and suffering. In a painting titled *Give Us This Day*, a half-man/half-baby is shown eating the flesh of a decomposing corpse. He has even mixed cadaver blood with his own blood and used it to paint the frame for one of his paintings. He once tried to organize an exhibit of Adolf Hitler's artwork. Kevorkian even said Jesus Christ would have been better off dying in the back of his rusty van. This is the man who almost single-handedly convinced 75 percent of Americans to favor physician-assisted suicide (Gallup poll). After his third acquittal, Kevorkian said the only way to stop him would be to burn him at the stake. Fortunately, prison slowed him down because legally assisted suicide for the terminally ill was not his goal. He said he'd eventually like to see people who are suffering from depression to be able to decide on life or death. May we not end up like the Netherlands where more patients are killed by their doctors without their consent than are killed with their consent.[75]

Atonement Max Lucado tells of a young man who approached his pastor at the close of a worship service and asked, "What can I do to find peace in my life?" The wise minister replied, "I'm sorry, but you're too late." The distraught man was perplexed. He said, "You mean I'm too late to find peace? You mean I'm too late to be saved?" The pastor answered, "No, you're just too late to do anything about it. Jesus did everything that needed to be done two thousand years ago." The beauty of God's gracious atonement is that Christ did it all (1 Peter 3:18). We must simply embrace it.[76]

Attention Six days a week, regular mail service is delivered by the United States Postal Service. Annually, they handle 170 billion pieces of mail. Yet, in this huge sea of mail, postal officials say personal letters account for less than 4 percent of the total. That means for every one hundred pieces of mail we receive, only four will contain a personal word. Churches could capitalize on this shortfall and start a personal letter writing campaign to members and guests alike because everybody likes a little personal attention.[77]

Attitude Are you allergic to anything? Jerry was an eternal optimist who was allergic to bullets. His philosophy of life was quite simple. "Each morning I wake up to two choices; I can choose to be in a good mood or a bad mood." As he frequently said, "The bottom line is, it's your choice how you live life." Jerry had the opportunity to live out that philosophy on the most difficult and extreme level. He was in the restaurant business when three armed men robbed and shot him. While laying on the restaurant floor in a pool of blood, he said, "I remembered that I had two choices; I could choose to live, or I could choose to die. I chose to live." That choice seemed to be in jeopardy though when he saw the faces of those in the emergency room. He recalled how all of the attending medical team seemed to look at him as a man with no hope for survival. At that point he decided he must do something fast. He immediately seized an opportunistic moment while a big, burly nurse was shouting questions at him. When she asked if he was allergic to anything, Jerry replied, "Yes." His response got the attention of everyone in the room. He took a deep breath and yelled, "Bullets!" As the doctors and nurses started laughing, Jerry said, "I am choosing to live. Operate on me as if I am alive, not dead." Jerry survived the experience and was soon giving his normal response to the question, "How are you?" "If I were any better, I'd be twins." A positive attitude can't always save your life, but it sure can improve whatever life you've been given. Just ask Jerry![78]

Attitude During his first day on the job, an employee asked one of his new colleagues what it was like working in this office. The seasoned employee responded with a question of his own. He asked, "What was it like working at the place from which you came?" The new recruit quickly spit out his disdain for the former place of employment. He replied, "It was a terrible job. I didn't enjoy the work or the people for whom I worked." The wise colleague then responded, "Well, unfortunately, I'm afraid you'll find it pretty much the same here." We may change places and faces, but unless we change our attitude, life will remain much the same.[79]

Attitude "I discovered I always have choices and sometimes it's only a choice of attitude." —*Abraham Lincoln* [80]

Authority Terry Nichols was convicted as the accomplice to Timothy McVeigh in the Oklahoma City bombing. During Nichols's trial, an alarming letter was presented by the team of prosecutors. Just thirteen months prior to that fatal explosion, he mailed an affidavit to county officials where he was living in Marion, Kansas. Through that March 16, 1994, postmarked letter, Nichols gave notification that he was not subject to laws of the United States government, which he called a "fraudulent, usurping octopus." Such disregard for authority gave rise to his rationalization that he was justified in killing 168 innocent people on April 19, 1995. Nichols's philosophy about authority is not only deadly, but very prevalent in American society. Although such thinking does not always lead to terroristic actions, it does cause people to live as they did during the times of Judges. In those dark and chaotic years, "everyone did what was right in his own eyes" (Judges 21:25). It led to disaster then, and it's still destructive today. For that reason, God has commanded all of us to live under human authority (Romans 13:1) and is authority (Romans 13:2).[81]

Balance "Truth without love is too hard; love without truth is too soft." —*John Stott* [82]

Baptism A recent survey has raised grave concern over baptisms among Southern Baptists. The Home Mission Board's research department in cooperation with the evangelism division discovered that of all the recently recorded baptisms by Southern Baptists only about 40 percent involved spiritual conversions. The remaining baptisms dealt with rededications or a transfer of membership from another denomination.

Such statistics are a sobering reminder that Southern Baptists are converting fewer people to Christ than initially thought.[83]

Baptism On May 15, 1959, Vergilia Polland was taken under the baptismal waters in Salt Lake City, Utah. This particular baptism in the Mormon temple was not for her, though. It was administered by proxy for a well-known deceased woman. The priest said, "I lay hands on you in behalf of Charlotte Diggs Moon, who is dead." Baptists know this woman by her less formal nickname, "Lottie" Moon. Miss Moon served as a missionary in China for nearly forty years, and she died of starvation after giving away her food to provide for the Chinese people whom she had come to tell about Jesus' love and forgiveness. After whispering the words of the song, "Jesus Loves Me," she died on Christmas Eve 1912. Her faith, and the faith she shared with the people of China was not based upon the baptismal waters of a Mormon church, but upon the salvation that comes through Jesus Christ alone.[84]

Beauty "Just standing around looking beautiful is so boring, really boring."—*Michelle Pfeiffer* [85]

Behavior One of the biggest concerns in Japan is blood type. It is not uncommon for a man and woman to meet for the first time and quickly move to the topic of blood type. In publications about celebrities, the most vital information about up-and-coming stars is their blood type. The Japanese have a strong belief that a person's blood type dictates their character. Type A blood is thought to produce nit pickers, B types tend to be carefree, and O types are driven. Although medical experts have insisted there is no scientific correlation between character and blood type, Japanese people hold firm to the belief that a person's blood impacts their character. It may not be true in our physical makeup but it's certainly true spiritually. When we are washed by the cleansing blood of Jesus Christ, the Bible says we become "new creatures" (2 Corinthians 5:17). The blood type of Christ causes our character to be transformed into the image of God's own Son. Without that change in blood type, we wallow in the depravity of sin. If you think about it, that question about blood type might be a great lead-in for an evangelistic conversation.[86]

Beliefs "A belief is not merely an idea the mind possesses; it is an idea that posseses the mind." —*Robert Bolton* [87]

Beliefs "It's not that Americans no longer believe anything. It's that they believe everything." —*George Gallup* [88]

Bible A recent article titled, "178 Seconds to Live," chronicled the results of twenty pilots in a simulator. Each of the pilots were skilled aviators but had not taken instrument training. As long as the weather was good, they were all experts in flight. In this study, these pilots were placed in a simulator and asked to keep their plane under control as they flew through simulated clouds and bad weather. All twenty of the pilots lost control of their planes and crashed in an average of just 178 seconds. Twenty pilots who were very capable at keeping a plane aloft in good weather couldn't survive three minutes in bad weather. Although they were seasoned pilots with exceptional intuition, when rough weather hit, they lost control and crashed. Most of us can handle life when the conditions are good, but when the storms come we need much more than conventional wisdom and gut-level intuition. Whether the skies are bright and blue, or the clouds are beginning to brew, God's Word is the treasured flight manual that always leads the right way.[89]

Bible Charles Schulz consistently provided helpful and humorous insights through his *Peanuts* comic strip. In one run he showed Charlie Brown's sister, Sally, struggling with her memory verse for Sunday. She was lost in her thoughts trying to figure it out when she recalled, "Maybe it was something from the book of Reevaluation." She never did find her memory verse but she sure gave us something to remember when it comes to studying the Bible. We should always read it with the intent of reevaluating our attitudes and actions to make sure they are squaring up with the truth of God's Word.[90]

Bible Have you ever wished you hadn't clicked "send" on a piece of email? Disappearing Inc., has developed a process that may change the way email is handled in the future. This start-up company has devised a method for putting time bombs in email so the message will be readable only as long as the sender desires. This system, which was expected to hit the market in 2000, encrypts every message with an electronic key. The sender utilizes that key to make the message last anywhere from just a few seconds to many years. At the encoded time, the message simply becomes unreadable. In the near future our most widely used source of written communication may become timesensitive, but the certainty of God's Word will last forever (Isaiah 40:8).[91]

Bible In 1864, Abraham Lincoln was honored by the Committee of Colored People. On this special occasion, he was presented with a Bible. He responded to this gift by declaring, "In regard to this Great Book, I have but to say, it is the best gift God has given to man. All the good the Savior gave to the world was communicated through this book. But for it we could not know right from wrong. All things most desirable for man's welfare, here and hereafter, are to be found portrayed in it."[92]

Bible In 1992, the Associated Press evaluated fourthousand self-help books that had been written over the last year. They concluded the best self-help manual was not penned that year or any year recently. AP put the Bible on the topshelf for self-help.[93]

Bible "It is impossible to govern rightly without God and the Bible." —*George Washington* [94]

Bible Many Christians have either heard or sung, "Lord, I Lift Your Name on High." It was written by Rick Founds in 1989 and has since become one of the best-known and well-loved praise songs in the world. This beautiful chorus provides a clear summary of the gospel and offers a natural response of adoration for what God has done. Although Founds has written nearly five hundred praise songs, this song has one of the most interesting stories. He developed a unique habit of playing his guitar while reading the Bible. He just plunks along a tune that seems to go along with whatever he's reading. On this particular morning he was marveling at God's love for rebellious, fallen humanity. Suddenly, the now famous chorus emerged: "You came from heaven to earth to show the way . . . From the earth to the cross my debt to pay . . . From the cross to the grave . . . From the grave to the sky . . ." Now people around the world give musical expression to their love for God because a guy who does research and development at a fiber optics company took the time to let God's Word become living and active.[95]

Bible Noah Webster's name is synonymous with his most famous work, *Webster's Dictionary*. His dictionary graces the shelves of countless libraries, offices, and schoolrooms. Even though Webster is remembered for his book of definitions, he did not believe his dictionary was the preeminent project of his life. He also produced, The *Noah Webster Bible*. He called this edition of the Bible "the most important enterprise of my life." The man of many words claimed there is no word more important than the Word. Maybe that is why he said, "Education is useless without the Bible."[96]

Bible Officials at Indiana University School of Medicine added a new course to their medical curriculum in the fall of 1998 called Penmanship. The Indianapolis medical school added the writing class to help future doctors improve their treatment of patients. Antoinette Hood, the assistant dean, said poor penmanship can lead to mix-ups in medication, or improper treatment if the orders are misread. Hood noted that you can't successfully practice medicine if your prescriptions aren't legible. How comforting to know that the Great Physician doesn't need a refresher course in writing. He has clearly written the prescription for eternal life so that even a child can understand it.[97]

Bible The International Baptist Lay Academy serves as a training ground for church leaders in Eastern Europe. This Hungary-based ministry has trained numerous believers who have known oppression and persecution. In one particular class, a professor suddenly stopped his lecture after realizing he had taught into the break time. He apologized for holding them over into the break, but was interrupted by a student who said, "Professor, don't stop. We've had forty years of break." Oh, that all of us would have a similar hunger for God's Word.[98]

Bible The Michigan Lawsuit Abuse Watch organization holds an annual Wacky Warning Label Contest. Through this event people submit actual warning labels found on merchandise. The entries help support their premise that lawsuit abuse has pushed companies to take excessive and needless precautions with warning tags. First prize went to Bonnie Hay who submitted a phrase found on an iron. It read, "Never iron clothes while they are being worn." Second place was offered to a Michigan resident who saw this warning on his thirteen-inch wheelbarrow tire: "Not for highway use." Rounding out the top three came from a Texan who discovered an unusual warning on a bathroom heater. It declared, "This product is not to be used in bathrooms." Such warnings can give us a new appreciation for God's Word. It's pages are not filled with ridiculous warnings and rules, but truth that leads to eternal life.[99]

Bible The New International translation of the Bible now accounts for 40 percent of the new-sales market, King James 20 percent, New King James 10 percent, Living Bible 7 percent, New American Standard 5 percent, and all others account for less than 5 percent each.[100]

Bible There are 6,528 languages in the world. Of these languages, 4,564 do not have any portion of the Bible.[101]

Bible There is a very good reason the Psalmist compared God's Word to honey (Psalm 19:10). It's the only food that does not spoil. Philosophies and trends will come and go, but the Word of God will always remain fresh, relevant, and true. If we hide its words in our heart, it will keep us from spoiling (Psalm 119:11).[102]

Bible When the Barna Research Group completed a study for the Tyndale House Publishers, they discovered the following. More than 90 percent of American households contain a Bible and better than three out of four have two or more copies. 80 percent of Americans said the Bible is the most influential book in world history. Unfortunately, much of this respect for God's Word is superficial. Barely one-third of adults read the Bible in a typical week and just one in five will read every page of Scripture in the course of their lifetime. Additionally, the most popular strategy for choosing a passage to read is simply flipping through the pages until spotting something that sounds intriguing, relevant, or interesting. This method of random selection is used by nearly half of all adults who read the Bible. These findings may explain why 56 percent of Americans think the Bible teaches that taking care of one's family is the most important task of life (See Deut 6:5 and Matt 22:37), 72 percent believe that people are blessed by God so they can enjoy life as much as possible (see Gen 12:1–3), 42 percent claim the Bible says Jesus sinned while on earth (See Heb 4:15), and four out of ten people think "all individuals will experience the same outcome after death, regardless of their religious beliefs." In America, the Bible seems to be widely respected, but not seriously studied.[103]

Biblical Application In the spring of 1998, David Fleigelman had to be treated for a stab wound. The forty-year-old resident of New York was stabbed at the Sephardic Center synagogue in Brooklyn. According to police reports, Fleigelman and another man were arguing about which one knew more about the Torah. It's unclear who won the argument, but Fleigelman obviously lost the ensuing fight. Knowledge of Scripture is useless if we don't allow it to transform our lives.[104]

Biblical Application Reading the Bible without applying it to your life can be downright dangerous. On August 3, 1996, Melvin Hitchens sat on his front porch and read the Bible. After his Bible-reading, this sixty-six-year-old New Orleans resident went in his house and retrieved a .45 caliber handgun. He then went back outside and shot his neighbors. He killed Donna Jett as she swept her sidewalk, and injured Darryl Jett while he was mowing. Family members and neighborhood residents testified that Hitchens and the Jetts had a running feud over the care of their yards and the cleanliness of the gutters. Positive transformation requires the application of God's Word.[105]

Biblical Comfort James Hannington was the first Bishop of Equatorial Africa. In October of 1885, he was attacked and imprisoned. This horrible experience was recorded in his journal. Hannington wrote, "Consumed with fever, and at times delirious with pain, devoured by vermin, menaced every moment by the prospect of death." On October 29th, he became a martyr for his faith. The day before his death, Hannington made this entry in his journal: "I am quite broken down and brought low. Comforted by Psalm 27." Regardless of our circumstances, God's Word can bring comfort to our heart.[106]

Biblical Interpretation Talk-show host, Larry King, has recounted a childhood experience in Brooklyn, New York. He and his friends loved to play stickball, but finding a makeshift field wasn't easy. Many owners of vacant lots had posted signs that read: "Private No Stickball Playing Allowed." King and his buddies were not deterred by these signs because they had their own interpretation of what the sign implied. Their rendering was: "Private? No! Stickball Playing Allowed." The obvious signposts of God's Word are not to be twisted to our own satisfaction, but obeyed for our own good.[107]

Biblical Truth Madonna wants her daughter, Lourdes Maria, to grow up reading the Bible instead of watching TV. The celebrity said, "TV's poison. To be plopped in front of a TV instead of being read to, talked to, or encouraged to interact with other human beings is a huge mistake. I want my daughter to read the Bible, but I will explain to her that these are stories that people made up to teach people—it's not the rule." Contrary to the opinion of Madonna and many others, the Bible is far more than a good bedtime storybook.[108]

Blame Ron and Mary Hulnick are psychologists at the University of Santa Monica. They have done extensive research on the dynamic of blaming others or events for misfortunes and frustrations. These scholars concur that "blaming others or events for how you feel is one of the most common obstacles to good mental health and to satisfying relationships." Stop the blaming and you will start experiencing better health and better relationships. So the next time you want to blame somebody for "making you mad," realize the choice for anger belongs to you, not somebody else. Like Abraham Lincoln said, "We are just about as happy in life as we decide to be."[109]

Blame "The reason people blame things on previous generations is that there's only one other choice." —*Doug Larson* [110]

Busyness "Maintaining a complicated life is a great way to avoid changing it." —*Elaine St. James* [111]

Busyness "People who are often in a hurry imagine they are energetic, when in most cases they are simply inefficient." —*Sydney Harris*[112]

Busyness The busyness of business can easily and subtly take us further and further away from our families. This became very evident for an anonymous CEO of a start-up software business in Texas. *Inc.* magazine quoted him as saying, "I knew my travel schedule was out of control when my wife and three-year-old were standing outside. An airplane flew overhead, and my wife said, 'Do you know what that is?' 'Yes,' my daughter replied. 'It's Daddy's office." If you're in the busyness business, change jobs before you bankrupt your home.[113]

Busyness "We are the only nation with a mountain named Rushmore." —*Max Lucado* [114]

Butterfly Kisses In 1996, a musician named Bob Carlisle was preparing to release a new album entitled, *Shades of Grace*. The producers realized this album was one song short so they sent Carlisle digging for another piece of music. He knew of one song but had no intentions of putting it on an album. It was a song he had written a year earlier for his sixteen-year-old daughter, Brooke. Until that time, the only place it existed was on an audiocassette that she carried around as an expression of her father's love. Putting it on that album to fill an empty spot seemed like the right thing to do, so with Brooke's consent, the world was introduced to "Butterfly Kisses." By 1997, it was one of the most requested songs in America and became Bob Carlisle's signature song. Isn't it amazing how some treasures are found? The success of "Butterfly Kisses" was primarily an accident. It was accidentally moved from a teenager's backpack to the top of nearly every music chart in the land. Although very few of us will ever have a similar type of experience in our particular field of service, the unusual history of this single song can be a reminder that God is still full of wonderful surprises.[115]

Calling Pulpits come in all shapes and sizes. Any connoisseur of church furniture knows this, but Steve Smith is helping others see the huge variety that is actually out there. Smith is Baylor University's baseball coach. During his years prior to coaching at Baylor, Smith wrestled with a call to preach. He told God he would do anything, but begged not to preach. Ironically, God did call him to preach. As Smith says, "The Lord did call me to preach. He just did not call me to pastor a church." The coach is right, whether or not we enter the vocational ministry of pastoring, we are all called to preach. Our pulpit may not resemble the one in a church sanctuary but it is a pulpit nonetheless. It may look like a baseball diamond, a kitchen, a board room, or a check-out counter, but it's the pulpit from which we preach. May we claim it as such, respect it as such, and preach the best sermons we can with both our lips and our lives.[116]

Calvary In 564 B.C., the spectators at the Olympic games saw the most incredible athletic victory of all time. Arrichion was competing for his third consecutive championship in *pankration*, an event that combined boxing and wrestling. During the match, Arrichion's opponent got him in a suffocating stranglehold. In a desperate attempt to escape the life-threatening choke hold, Arrichion dislocated his opponent's ankle. In great pain, Arrichion's opponent released him from the death hold and raised his hand in defeat. Just as the rival conceded defeat, Arrichion died. Due to the sequence of events, Arrichion was ruled the winner and he became the only Olympic athlete who has ever won by dying. On that first Good Friday, Jesus pulled off a similar type of victory. When in the throws of death, he dealt his opponent a decisively defeating blow and then died the victor. Unlike Arrichion, Jesus also defeated death and arose three days later with the victor's crown on his head.[117]

Change Although we frequently look for major things to change in our lives, there are plenty of small things that could produce major benefits. In 1992, Delta Airlines decided to quit using a single leaf of lettuce to dress up their in-flight meal trays. Passengers still got the same meals, they just didn't have the lettuce decor. They never received a single letter of complaint for this minute change, but that forgone piece of lettuce is saving Delta Airlines $1.5 million a year. Within all of our lives there lurks some small changes that just might contain some very significant rewards.[118]

Change "Don't ever take a fence down until you know the reason why it was put up." —*G.K. Chesterton* [119]

Change In 1998, Christopher Cerf and Victor Navasky wrote, "The Experts Speak: The Definitive Compendium of Authoritative Misinformation." In this work they shared some rather erroneous predictions. Concerning electric lights, the British Parliament declared in 1878 ". . . good enough for our transatlantic friends . . . but unworthy of the attention of practical or scientific men." President Rutherford Hayes said of the telephone in 1876, "That's an amazing invention, but who would ever want to use one of them?" Darryle Zanuck, head of 20th Century Fox in 1946, suggested TV had a very limited future: "People will soon get tired of staring at a plywood box every night." In 1977, while serving as president of Digital Equipment Corporation, Ken Olson said, "There is no reason for any individual to have a computer in their home." In the area of aviation, Harvard astronomer William Pickering made this 1908 comment: "The popular mind often pictures gigantic flying machines speeding across the Atlantic and carrying innumerable passengers. It seems safe to say such ideas are wholly visionary." Alex Lewyt was manufacturing vacuum cleaners in 1955 when he observed, "Nuclear powered vacuum cleaners will probably be a reality within ten years." In 1837, John Erichsen was a leading British surgeon who declared, "The abdomen, the chest, and the brain will be forever shut from the intrusion of the wise and humane surgeon." As Brad Herzog wisely said, "Reverence for the past is important, but so is regard for the future."[120]

Change Occasionally, we struggle with change, and some of us wrestle with change more than just "occasionally." If you have a hard time accepting, adapting, or tolerating change, take a lesson from yourself. You change more often than the circumstances around you. Now you may be set in your ways and would never win a "Gumby" award for flexibility, but you are truly a person of change. You look pretty much the same each month but every turn of the calendar catches you changing your skin. The fact is, you get a whole new layer of skin about once a month. Doesn't it stand to reason that a person who so frequently changes his or her skin shouldn't get all that bothered about other change?[121]

Change Take a look at these letters and see if you recognize them: QWERTYUIOP. They're more familiar than might initially think. They comprise the top row of letters on a standard keyboard. Their positioning is known as the QWERTY configuration. In 1870, Sholes & Company was the leading manufacturer of typewriters but they were getting a lot of complaints about keys sticking together if the typist went too fast. Management brought together their engineers to find a solution for "slowing down the operator." After vigorous debate, they came up with an inefficient keyboard design. The QWERTY configuration requires weaker fingers to strike frequently used keys. Consequently, they resolved their problem by making the task of typing more cumbersome. Today, typing speed is not an issue. Although faster and more efficient configurations exist, the QWERTY layout is the accepted norm. Few changes are eagerly embraced, but a wise person will be open to consider the benefits of proposed adjustments while also evaluating the original goal and purpose of any endeavor.[122]

Change The average person eats about 1,417 pounds of food per year. How a lot of that food makes it to your mouth has an interesting past. The fork, as we know it today, has not always been a popular utensil. Its first ancestor appeared in Tuscany during the eleventh century, but these tiny forks were very rare. In 1611, Thomas Coryate brought several of these oddities to England after he ran across them in Italy. People were not interested. In fact, they were vehemently opposed to the fork. It was not unusual for ministers to preach against forks, and they often used funerals to declare death was God's way of showing displeasure over the use of such a novelty. It was not until the end of the eighteenth century that forks found favor. French nobility began using forks as a statement of refinement, and the use of fingers started getting frowns. So if you've got a good idea that people just won't embrace, pull out a fork and enjoy a piece of cake while you remember, change takes time.[123]

Change "The past is a foreign country; they do things differently there." —*L. P. Hartley* [124]

Change "There are only two constants in the world: Christ and change." —*Lyle Schaller* [125]

Change "Too often we change jobs, friends, or spouses instead of changing ourselves." —*Akbarali Jetha* [126]

Chaos George Peabody said, "Our task is not to bring order out of chaos, but to get work done in the midst of chaos." It is easy to become frustrated by the normal chaos that accompanies life. Your desk becomes more cluttered than you prefer, you spot a book that you haven't had time to be read, your filing system isn't as efficient as it should be, you remember an illustration but can't remember where you saw it, and in the midst of all that, your water pump goes out on your way to the doctor's office. The temptation is to believe a day is coming when life won't be chaotic and you will finally have a chance to get some things done. It's an optimistic but unrealistic thought. Chaos is an inevitable aspect of life that will never be permanently vanquished from our lives. So rather than spend our best energy trying to eradicate chaos, let's try to apply George Peabody's truth to our schedules and accomplish our work even when chaos surrounds us. [127]

Character An Amish man was asked if he had accepted Jesus Christ as his Lord and Savior. The wise gentleman responded, "Why do you ask *me* such a thing? I could tell you anything. Here is the name of my banker, my grocer, and my farm hands. Ask them if I am saved." True character is revealed in our treatment of others. [128]

Character Few people have forgotten the gut-wrenching memory of Korean Air Lines flight KE007 being shot down by Soviet fighter jets on September 1, 1983. On that fateful night, 240 unsuspecting passengers and crew members were shot down like an innocent sparrow in flight. The trigger man for the Soviet Union was Major Osipovich, a pilot who wasn't originally scheduled to be in the air during this international travesty. The Major was slated to give a talk about peace at his children's school so he volunteered for night duty to free enough time to speak during school hours. This adjustment in flight time put him in the position of patrolling the eastern skies when that Korean passenger jet strayed into Soviet air space. In the end, Major Osipovich followed orders and shot down the commercial airliner. How tragic that 240 lives were lost, and world powers were pushed dangerously close to catastrophic results because military missiles were fired at a civilian airplane by a pilot who was preparing to teach children about peace. Character can only be supported by actions, not merely words. [129]

Character "Live so that the preacher won't have to lie at your funeral." —*Bumper Sticker* [130]

Character "The measure of a man's real character is what he would do if he would never be found out." —*Thomas Macauley* [131]

Character The term "attitude adjustment" has taken on new meaning for several aging Disney characters. The year 1998 marked the seventieth birthday for Mickey Mouse so his character was reevaluated and a complete makeover came for the trademark mouse. He no longer acts the part of a cute, carefree character. According to the focus group who suggested the reworking of his persona, "these characters did not have enough attitude." They believe he, and other Disney characters, should reflect the harried 1990s and take on an edgier demeanor. Roberts Gannaway, the executive producer who's in charge of the makeover, said, "These characters were born in the Great Depression with a simple, optimistic outlook that now looks outdated." Having "more attitude" may be viewed as an improvement in the entertainment world, but in the real world progress depends on less "attitude." [132]

Character "You can't tell how much spirit a team has until it starts losing." —*Rocky Colavito* [133]

Children During the Christmas holidays, ten-year-old Lawrence Shields was with his family at a commercial gem mine in North Carolina. He was picking through a bucket of dirt when he discovered an interesting rock. Lawrence said, "I just liked the shape of it." His interesting rock turned out to be a 1,061-carat sapphire worth more than $35,000. Children unearth great value every day, but adults are often too preoccupied to notice these treasures. Take ample time to let your children show you their great discoveries. [134]

Chivalry Most people can recall the chivalry that existed when the *Titanic* sank in April of 1912. Out of honor and respect for the courageous men who declared, "Women and children first," an organization was created in 1997 called The Christian Boys' and Men's *Titanic* Society. These men gather once a year for a dinner in San Antonio, Texas, on April 14 and in Washington, D.C. on April 15. The two events are set up in conjunction with the dates of the iceberg collision and the actual sinking. At these dinners men are encouraged to be courageous, Godly protectors of their families, and to practice old-fashioned chivalry. May we join these men in reinstituting the exercise of chivalry. [135]

Christian Behavior Rex Horne pastored President Clinton's home church in Little Rock, Arkansas. His position at Immanuel Baptist Church caused many people to unfairly criticize him and the church because they disagreed with Clinton's policies. On one such occasion a very vocal group of Christians were protesting in front of the church. Across the street, pro-Clinton gays and lesbians gathered peacefully. Horne's little son, Truett, saw the scenario from a child's eye. He pointed to the gays and asked, "Those are the Christians. Aren't they, Daddy?" In similar fashion, when Chuck Colson was awarded the Templeton Prize, he received many letters of hostile criticism from Christians. Even though he gave away the $1 million prize, they condemned him for accepting it. Upon reflection, Colson said the secular press treated him better during Watergate than these Christians who chastised him about the Templeton issue. Christlike behavior, not high-octane anger, accomplishes God's will and desires.[136]

Christian Fellowship Benjamin Franklin told the founding fathers, "We must indeed all hang together, or, most assuredly, we shall all hang separately." What was true for our revolutionary heroes is also true for fellow believers. If Christians fail to hang together, they will end up hanging alone.[137]

Christian Influence Who's Who is a perennial publication that produces the names of people who have risen above the norm to make a positive impact on society. Research shows it takes 25,000 families of unskilled laboring background to produce one person in the annual Who's Who, it requires 10,000 skilled laboring families to put one person in Who's Who, 2,500 professional families are necessary to accomplish the same task, but only seven missionary families are needed to produce one member of Who's Who. Christian influence definitely adds salt to society (Matthew 5:13).[138]

Christianity Contrary to the impression that is often conveyed about Christianity in the United States, Americans view Christianity as having a more positive impact on society than any other religious tradition. According to a new survey by the Barna Research Group, 85 percent said they perceive Christianity as exerting a positive influence on society. In reality, most Americans think Christianity is an asset to this country.[139]

Christianity In the late 1800s, Charles Bladlock was a well-known atheist in London. H. R. Hughes, a man of great faith, was one of Bladlock's contemporaries and represented a stark contrast. Hughes was a zealous evangelist who stood up to the debates of Bladlock. On one occasion, Hughes challenged the claims of Bladlock by suggesting they both recruit one hundred people who espouse their beliefs. He told Bladlock to bring one hundred people who will give testimony to the fact that they are better off for not believing in God. Hughes guaranteed he would have one hundred people to tell how their life had been transformed by the power of Christ. On the assigned day, Hughes arrived as promised with one hundred people ready to tell their story. Bladlock didn't even show up, much less have anybody enlisted to speak. Hughes seized the moment as many had gathered for the great debate. He utilized the testimonies of these Christians and had them share their experience of knowing Christ. As a result, hundreds of spectators came to know Jesus Christ as their Redeemer. Our experiences of being transformed by the love and power of Christ are mighty resources in God's economy.[140]

Christianity Ken Blanchard, best known for his book, *The One-Minute Manager*, is now a Christian but it hasn't always been that way. During his investigation of Christianity, he had the opportunity of meeting the guru of business, Peter Drucker. Drucker is a Christian. So upon their first encounter Blanchard curiously asked, "Peter, why are you a Christian?" Drucker replied, "There's no better deal." This man, who knows business like no other, openly admits that Christianity is the best deal of all.[141]

Christianity Some information from the Barna Research Group raises deep concern about the influence of Christianity in America. According to their research, "the people who believe Christianity is losing its influence in our society outnumber those who say it is gaining influence by more than a three-to-one margin." Likewise, the Barna Group discovered "born-again Christians were virtually indistinguishable from nonbelievers on all sixty-five of the nonreligious variables" they examined. As Christians, it is important for us to realize three-fourths of our nation believes Christianity is losing ground, and that a large percentage of Christians are living virtually the same as those without Christ. Jesus' admonition to be salt and light must be taken more seriously by his followers if we hope to have an impact on the society in which we live.[142]

Christianity Three-fourths of all Christians live outside the Western World.[143]

Christian Living Most people think of Johann Sebastian Bach as a classical musician, but as historian Mark Galli notes, "he was a theologian who just happened to work with a keyboard." Bach was orphaned by age ten, and bounced around until finally, at the age of thirty-eight, he settled down in Leipzig. It was there that he served as musical director and choirmaster of Saint Thomas's church and school. These were not necessarily happy years because the town council regularly criticized him for stubbornly clinging to obsolete forms of music. Ironically, it was in this setting that Bach created his most enduring works. Although he is remembered for classical music, nearly three-fourths of his one thousand compositions were written for worship. On each score he would write "S.D.G." It stood for *Soli Deo Gloria*, Latin for, "To God alone be the glory." During his lifetime he labored for poor wages and little recognition. After his death, some of his music was sold and some was reportedly used to wrap garbage. It would be another eighty years before the world would come to know Bach, because it was not until 1829 that Felix Mendelssohn, the great German composer, arranged a performance of Bach's, *The Passion of Saint Matthew*. During a lifetime of relative obscurity that was punctuated by ongoing criticism, Johann Sebastian Bach lived for the glory of God.[144]

Christlike Behavior A Christian woman experienced a most unusual dream. While sleeping, she dreamed that Christ was coming to visit her the next day at 4:00 P.M. Her dream then carried her through a time warp to the coming day. On the day of her Lord's expected arrival, she feverishly worked to clean and prepare her house. At four o'clock, she heard a knock at the door. Quickly, the woman examined her appearance in the mirror, then swiftly walked to the door. In shock and horror, she saw a grotesque, dirty figure standing on the other side of the threshold. She feared this emaciated and disheveled individual would ruin her visit with Christ so she rudely demanded, "Who are you?" The man answered, "I am the One you are expecting." She quickly stated, "You're not the Jesus I know!" To which he replied, "No, but I'm the Jesus others see in you!" Whether we like it or not, our behavior paints a picture of the Lord. What image do others see on the canvas of your life?[145]

Christmas About 5:00 A.M. on Christmas morning, a minister walked through the dimly lit sanctuary. The church looked beautiful and was majestically set up for the Christmas services that would soon take place. In anticipation of the day, he went to the nativity display and prepared to say a prayer. To his chagrin, the little Christ child figurine was missing. He momentarily looked around the immediate vicinity to see if it had been misplaced. When he didn't find it he began a full-scale investigation of the entire building. Unfortunately, the nativity piece was never found and it greatly troubled the minister. He was so upset by the seemingly callous behavior of some prankster or thief, the minister brought up the incident in each of the services. With his agitation evident to all, he declared, "The Christ child must be returned to the crèche before this Christmas Day is over." Sadly, nighttime fell with no sign of the piece, so the minister set out for a meditative stroll in the wintry dark. Along the way he encountered a little boy, Johnny Mullaney, who belonged to his church. Johnny came from a very poor family but his spirits couldn't have been any higher on this Christmas evening. He was inadequately dressed for the cold, but that didn't stop him from pulling his prized new gift, a bright red wagon. The minister knew such a gift was a major sacrifice for Johnny's parents so he hurried across the street to speak with little Johnny about his special gift. His demeanor radically changed when he saw the Christ child riding in the wagon. The furor of the day seemed to erupt as he lectured Johnny about the severity of stealing things from the church. The little boy began to cry as he replied, "But I didn't steal the Christ child. I've been praying for a red wagon and I promised him that if I got it, I'd take him out for the first ride." Throughout the bounty of gifts that are exchanged at Christmas, may we each remember the source of our blessings as completely as did little Johnny Mullaney.[146]

Christmas According to a Roper Survey conducted for the Quicken financial software company, the average American spends $816 on Christmas gifts.[147]

Christmas Bil Keane's comic strip, *Family Circus*, has communicated a beautiful truth about Christmas. As the children were setting up their nativity set, little Dolly held up the baby Jesus and declared, "Here's the star of Bethlehem!" May you and your family experience the majesty of gazing on the Star of Bethlehem during each and every Christmas season.[148]

Christmas Each year at Christmas, Jeannie Williams pulls out a partial nativity set and lets it remind her of a deeper truth about our Savior's birth. It all started years ago when Williams was doing some last-minute Christmas shopping. She had previously spotted a crèche spilled out over the floor before hearing a mother scold her daughter for putting something in her mouth. The little girl said it was a little baby Jesus and she wasn't putting it in her mouth, she was kissing it. Her mother didn't care, she just wanted the child to put it down. Oblivious to her mom's concerns, Sarah kept talking about the figurine. "But look, Mommy, it's a little manger and the baby Jesus got broked off." Her mother was focused on other things until little Sarah asked, "Mommy, can we buy this here little baby Jesus?" With that, the lady lost her temper and yelled, "I told you to put that thing down!" She moved toward the child and Williams fully expected something ugly to occur. But rather than an outburst of rage, the woman crumpled in her daughter's arms and began to weep. The little girl tried to console her mother by apologizing for her behavior. "I'm sorry, Mommy. I promise I won't ask for nothin' else. I'll put baby Jesus back in the manger." The mother apologized as well. She expressed sorrow for their impoverished plight and told Sarah how much she wished she could buy something extra. She then tried to boost her daughter's confidence for the future by saying, "Maybe next year we can get us a real Christmas tree." The little girl simply said, "You know what Mommy? I don't need this here little baby Jesus doll anyhow 'cause my Sunday school teacher says Jesus really lives in your heart! I'm glad he lives in my heart, aren't you, Mommy?" They quietly walked to the checkout counter and bought their handful of necessities. Overcome by what she had just witnessed, Williams scrambled to pick up the broken nativity set and rushed to the front. Sarah and her mother were walking out so she motioned for a clerk to come take the baby Jesus to the girl while she paid for the remaining pieces. That precious child graciously accepted the gift, then gave the doll another big kiss. Now, when guests see the nativity set at Jeannie Williams's house and ask, "Where's the baby Jesus?" she remembers the words of that beautiful little girl, and says, "He's in my heart!"[149]

Christmas From Thanksgiving to Christmas, Americans charge more than $120 billion worth of goods and services.[150]

Christmas In 336 A.D., the first recorded celebration of Christmas on December 25 took place in Rome.[151]

Christmas In 1949, Johnny Marks wrote "Rudolph the Red-Nosed Reindeer." He asked Gene Autry to record it but he wasn't interested. Autry's wife finally talked him into singing it for the flip side of another song from which he expected great things. Now, nobody remembers that other "big hit."[152]

Christmas In England, an elementary school teacher let her students construct a nativity scene in the corner of their classroom. They had a model barn, real straw, and clay figurines for all of the characters and animals. In the middle of the cluster was a small crib and a tiny doll that represented the Christ child. After it was all finished, one boy seemed troubled about the way it all turned out. Sensing a problem, his teacher asked the boy if there was a problem. With his eyes glued on the crowded scene, the little boy exclaimed, "I just want to know where does God fit in?" Before the Christmas season starts crowding too much of your money and time, take the necessary measures to make sure there's plenty of room for God to fit in.[153]

Christmas More heart attacks occur during December and January, peaking between Christmas and New Year's Day.[154]

Christmas On December 17, 1903, Orville and Wilbur Wright finally succeeded in keeping their homemade airplane aloft for fifty-nine seconds. They were ecstatic! As part of their excitement, they rushed a telegram to their sister in Dayton, Ohio. Their simple message was, "First sustained flight today fifty-nine seconds. Hope to be home by Christmas." She was so enthralled with their success that she immediately took the telegram to the newspaper and gave it to the editor. The following morning the Wright brothers' name was splashed across the front page. The headline read, "Popular Local Bicycle Merchants to Be Home for Holidays." That newspaper editor missed the main point of this historic telegram. Each December millions of people are equally oblivious. God's telegram of love and forgiveness is eclipsed by the seasonal trappings that allure us from the true meaning of Christmas. May we each take the time to reread God's December telegram to make sure we see the most important element of his beloved message.[155]

Christmas One school in Florida thinks they have beat the problem of taking religious sides during the Christmas season. Rather than have parties for Hanukkah or Christmas, in 1989 they started a tradition of having a birthday party for Steven Spielberg each year. Nautilus

Middle School in Miami Beach marks the famous director's December 18th birthday by singing "Happy Birthday," providing treats, studying his life, and showing one of his films on a closed circuit TV. Just because something is "politically correct" doesn't mean it's right.[156]

Christmas The average weight gain between Thanksgiving and New Year's Day is seven pounds.[157]

Christmas The history of our mistletoe tradition is worth noting. It dates back to the Druids in Northern Europe. They believed mistletoe had curative power and thought it could even cure broken relationships. When two enemies found themselves under a tree with mistletoe above, they saw it as a sign from God that they should lay down their weapons and be reconciled. When missionaries moved into Northern Europe, they realized this was a perfect symbol for what occurred on that first Christmas. Christ's birth ushered in the opportunity of reconciliation between man and God, so the mistletoe offered a powerful tool for communicating this truth. Although today we associate the greenery with romance, it's deeper meaning provides a rich reminder of what God has done through the birth of his Son.[158]

Christmas Wally Purling was a big, clumsy boy who struggled mentally. At age nine he was in second grade rather than fourth. Fortunately, Wally was well-liked by his classmates even though he was often prevented from playing in games where each team hoped to win. Ironically, Wally was a defender of underdogs even though he didn't realize that's exactly who he was—an underdog. When the Christmas pageant rolled around, Wally desperately wanted to be a shepherd with a staff. Instead, Miss Lumbard used his imposing size to cast him as the stern innkeeper. Wally was elated about his role and was completely mesmerized by the whole play. On the night when their whole town gathered for the play, Wally was so enthralled that Miss Lumbard had to make sure he didn't just wonder onto the stage before his time. Finally, the moment arrived. Wally took his position and Joseph started knocking on the set door. Wally threw open the door and demanded, "What do you want?" The familiar lines were repeated while Wally stood stiff, staring straight ahead. He forcefully told Joseph the inn was full. When the young characters portraying Mary and Joseph turned to walk away, Wally was supposed to close the door. Instead, he watched them walk off. His countenance changed from the stiff innkeeper to a compassionate young boy. He suddenly responded as only Wally could. He yelled out to the young couple, "You can have my room!" Wally Purling rewrote the Christmas story from his tender heart and gave the world an excellent model to follow.[159]

Church According to George Gallup, America's churchgoing populace has hovered at 40 percent throughout this century. On any given Sunday, 60 percent of the U.S. population does not attend church. At Christmas and Easter, church attendance swells so *USA Today* made this phenomenon their headline story on December 24, 1996. The article shared two interesting labels for these seasonal attenders: C&Es (Christmas and Easter), and Church Tourists. As the report noted, the same God they worship on these two Sundays is also available for worship the other fifty weeks. In a corresponding article, the following statistics were presented: 33 percent of Americans said the birth of Jesus makes the holiday important compared with 44 percent who believe family time is the most significant aspect of Christmas. Other findings revealed: 97 percent buy Christmas presents, 85 percent have a Christmas tree at home, 68 percent attend parties, 65 percent go to church. All of this seems to support the unusual but real statistic that one in eleven Americans suffer from "ecclesiophobia," the fear of church.[160]

Church After World War II, church officials began the process of rebuilding the bombed-out cathedral in Coventry, England. One of the architects involved in this project was Basil Spence. He was a dedicated Christian who fully supported the expensive undertaking. Those in opposition to such an expense asked him how they could justify spending that much money when there were so many human needs in the world. His response was challenging. He noted there are two kinds of hunger: physical and spiritual. He went on to say physical hunger was not necessarily the most important. He said, "I believe that there is a hunger of the soul, and that lies at the root of the world's troubles. I believe Coventry Cathedral can remind men of God and their hunger for him. If that can be put right, then the other hunger will be well on the road of being overcome." It could be justifiably debated that some places of worship are created with too much extravagance, yet we must exercise caution and not swing to the opposite extreme by insisting on miserly facilities. Spence's point is well taken and finds an element of support in Jesus' affirmation of his anointing (Mark 14:3–9).[161]

Church An elderly saint had lost the bulk of his hearing and his eyes had grown dim with age. Even though he could not experience the worship as he once had, he never stopped attending church. One intrigued individual finally asked the obvious, "Why do you continue attending church when you cannot hear or see what's going on?" The old man replied, "I want to show everybody whose side I'm on!" Whether or not you like the music or care for the preaching, your presence in church affirms whose side you're on.[162]

Church Are you raising another "unabomber?" Theodore Kaczynski was convicted for two decades of "unabomber" activity. The term "unabomber" came from the FBI after they noticed a trend toward targeting universities and airlines with bombs. When Kaczynski was taken into custody, the media uncovered more information about his life than most of us were interested in knowing. They let us know about the square footage of his home, his diet, who he played with as a kid, plus a truckload of additional trivia. While scanning through some of this stuff, one fact caught my eye. Neighbors recalled the Kaczynski family's Sunday regimen when Theodore was growing up. Church was not the place for them. Mrs. Kaczynski believed, "The Bible and the Christian story were a myth." In their pursuit of excellence and cultural aptitude, they used their Sundays to visit museums and other sights of educationally redeeming value. In that respect, their efforts paid off. Kaczynski has an impressive academic record, he earned his undergraduate degree from Harvard and later obtained his doctorate from Michigan. He became a very talented math professor with the University of California at Berkley, and yet, he left this environment of scholarship for a reclusive life in the mountains of Montana. Kaczynski even wrote his mother a scathing letter accusing her of having "been only interested in his brilliance." Don't you wonder if things might have turned out differently had the Kaczynski family spent their Sundays in church? I'd like to think history would not be the same had all the museums and cultural experiences been supplemented with spiritual development as well. Today, many parents are making sure their kids get the best in education, athletics, diet, culture, technology, and family togetherness but are not providing their offspring with the best in spiritual development. All of the above pursuits are worthy, but they should never take precedence over spiritual needs. A busy schedule of extracurricular activities isn't a valid excuse for shortchanging spiritual growth—even if it's only a "temporary" busyness. You may not be raising another "unabomber," but one thing is for sure, if you don't give your child, or yourself, more spiritual provisions than Theodore Kaczynski received, you could be doing more harm than the bombs that exploded on those twenty-three unfortunate victims.[163]

Church A survey by the Barna Research Group revealed that church attendance in America significantly declined during the last decade of the twentieth century. In 1991, 49 percent of Americans reported going to church on Sundays. In 1992, that figure dropped to 47 percent. A year later it went to 45 percent. The percentage stayed at 42 percent during 1994 and 1995. By 1996, only 37 percent acknowledged that they attended church.[164]

Church "Churches can be like Noah's Ark, if it were not for the storm outside, you could not stand the stench inside." —*Howard Hendricks* [165]

Church Eighty percent of church growth in the United States results from transfer of membership.[166]

Church Eighty percent of regular churchgoers gravitate toward the same seat every Sunday.[167]

Church "Every church should have a membership drive every once in while to drive out all of the troublemakers." —*Frank Harrington* [168]

Church Growing churches rely primarily on word-of-mouth advertising.[169]

Church In 1900, there were twenty-seven churches for every one hundred thousand people. In 1950, America had seventeen churches for the same number of people. At the dawning of a new century, that number has decreased to eleven churches per one hundred thousand people. Church growth depends on the intentional reversal of this unhealthy trend.[170]

Church In 1997, Americans spent $6 billion constructing and renovating religious facilities. New construction reached its highest level in three decades with forty-one billion square feet being built.[171]

Church In September of 1999, more than four hundred Christian leaders gathered from fifty-four countries to discuss the international problem of sagging discipleship. The International Consultation on Discipleship met in England to address better strategies for maturing believers throughout the world. One of their concerns involved church attendance. They cited a recent international survey which revealed more than 40 percent of the people who identify themselves as Christians are neither members, or frequent attenders, of any church. Such concerns are certainly legitimate in America. In the United States, church attendance has declined from 60 percent in 1981 to 55 percent in 1998. Overall, the Fourth Commandment is not being taken very seriously.[172]

Church Most Americans can recall what they were doing on January 28, 1986. On that historic date, the space shuttle *Challenger* exploded just seventy-three seconds into flight. Seven families were robbed by death and an entire nation was racked with grief. All of this loss was ultimately blamed on one inexpensive O-ring. Records revealed that the space shuttle was comprised of one million components. In this sea of mechanical makeup, it took just one part to destroy the whole. One million parts did their job, but one failed and disaster occurred. Most people feel their role within the church is not only small and insignificant, but inconsequential as well. This erroneous doctrine of the church causes individuals to believe their behavior can't hurt the church. But like that small and seemingly insignificant O-ring, one failed performance can produce catastrophic results.[173]

Church On July 29, 1999, Mark Barton stormed two office complexes in Atlanta and killed nine people. He had earlier killed his two children and his wife, then ultimately took his own life. As the people of Atlanta tried to cope with this senseless destruction of thirteen lives, a memorial service was held a week later at the Peachtree Road United Methodist Church. Mayor Bill Campbell organized the citywide service in hopes of helping his city begin the healing process. Appropriately, he made a strong statement concerning the location of this service in a church. He said it was right for them to meet in a church because it is "a place where heaven and earth meet." God does indeed want heaven and earth to meet in the church. We all know and experience the harsh reality of walking on this earth so we need a place where we know our life on earth can intersect with heaven. "Lord, help us to provide places of worship where heaven and earth truly meet."[174]

Church Research of the *Inc.* 500 companies revealed that among fast-growing companies, "95 percent of the failures are due to internal problems." The same dynamic that hamstrings industry also cripples church growth. Although there may be the perception that some external source is preventing growth, it is usually internal problems that impede growth and create a stagnant congregation.[175]

Church Sandra Bullock is a well-known actress. In an interview she told about her response to the news that her ninety-two-year-old grandmother had died. She told the reporter, "My grandmother just died, and I've been out searching for a church. I thought the thing to do was to find a church and say a prayer." Bullock represents a large segment of our population who find themselves without a church in times of crisis, but they sense the need to turn toward God. They're "searching for a church." May our churches be beacons of bright light's that are compelling and inviting to those out looking for God.[176]

Church "Seventy percent of the population is unchurched. Christians are not working to get people to come back to the church; they are working with generations who have never been to church." —*Kennon Callahan*[177]

Church "The church is not here to be popular, but to proclaim the good news of the gospel to those who like it and to those who don't." —*Humberto Medeiros*[178]

Church "The function of management is to make the church more church-like, not to make the church more business-like." —*Peter Drucker*[179]

Church The giant sequoias of California have very shallow root systems. A tour guide pointed out that their roots extend just barely below the surface. It sounds impossible because we all know trees need deep roots to withstand drought and wind, but sequoias are most unique. They grow only in groves and their roots intertwine with each other. When the strong winds blow, they hold each other up. Sounds a lot like the Church, doesn't it? We find support for ourselves in times of need, and we provide strength when others are calling for help. Like the sequoias, we grow tall when we hang with each other in the context of the church.[180]

Church The Heritage Foundation recently compiled all of the studies it could find on religion's link to health and social stability. Here are some of their findings: Regular church attendance is the most critical factor in marital stability, regardless of denominational or doctrinal teaching on divorce. Blood pressure is reduced an average of five millimeters of pressure by regular church attendance. A twenty-eight-year study of five thousand adults found that frequent churchgoers are almost 25 percent less likely to die than those persons who attend services less frequently. Persons who attend church frequently have stronger immune systems than less frequent attendees. Better mental and physical health are characteristics of frequent church attendees. Just from a physiological and sociological standpoint, frequent church attendance is a smart investment. Couple that with the spiritual advantages and you'd be a fool not to regularly attend church (Psalm 14:1).[181]

Church The next time you, or someone else feels nonessential, take a minute to read the following lines. Xvxn though my typxwritxr is an old modxl, it works vxry wxll xxcxpt for onx kxy. You would think that with all thx othxr kxys functioning propxrly, onx kxy not working would hardly bx noticxd, but just onx kxy out of whack sxxms to ruin thx wholx xffort. You may say to yoursxlf, "Wxll, I'm only onx pxrson, no onx will xvxn noticx if I don't quitx do my bxst." But it doxs makx a diffxrxncx bxcausx to bx xffxctivx an organization nxxds activx participation by xvxryonx to thx bxst of his or hxr ability. So thx nxxt timx you think you arx not important, rxmxmbxr my old typxwritxr. You arx a kxy pxrson![182]

Church What would keep you away from church . . . hypnotizing rain on a Sunday morning, a mild headache, weather that's too hot or too cold? Our faithfulness to be active in worship each week should be bolstered by the determination of a thirty-seven-year-old bull rider named Johnny Chavez. When he arrived at the Houston Rodeo in February of 2000, he had two broken ankles. Four months earlier, Chavez broke his right ankle in six places during a rodeo in Washington. Less than three months later, he cut off the cast so he could get back on a bull. That freed him up to break his left ankle in three places while participating in the Fort Worth rodeo. That cast lasted just a week. So with nine breaks between two ankles, Chavez took his place in the chutes at Houston. He told reporters that riding the bull was the easy part, it's the getting off that's a killer. "I almost want to land on my head because my ankles hurt so bad." In 1996, he broke his neck and missed six months so he's not about to let a few broken ankles stop him now. "It's been tough, but I'm going to stick it out, because despite everything, it's still been fun." May

Chavez's tenacity inspire us all to be more dependable members of our church.[183]

Church "While we need to be a learning organism, we also need to be an unlearning organism." —*Leonard Sweet* [184]

Citizenship Dwight Moody had a good thought on Christian citizenship: "Heaven is my home, but I vote in Cook County, Illinois."[185]

Cohabitation The rate of cohabitation before marriage is seven times higher among people who seldom or never attend religious services.[186]

Commencement In 1993, the senior class of River Valley High School in Three Oaks, Michigan, found an interesting way to acknowledge God. Aware of all the threats about openly praying to God at their graduation, these seniors devised a unique plan. Once the diplomas were received, an unidentified graduate deliberately sneezed very loudly. In unison, all ninety-five graduates exclaimed, "God bless you!" The ACLU is probably still trying to figure out if that's legal.[187]

Commitment According to data collected by the Barna Research Group, "only four out of ten people who claim to be a Christian also claim they are 'absolutely committed' to the Christian faith."[188]

Commitment American's have a national colloquialism which is frequently used when signing documents. This common practice of asking for a person's "John Hancock" comes from the most obvious signature on our Declaration of Independence. John Hancock's name is the only signature that can be easily identified by the casual observer . . . and that's exactly what he intended. The Declaration was approved on July 4, but it was not signed until August 2. After its initial approval, Jefferson's words were hand printed on parchment in preparation for being sent to the king. This gave Hancock nearly a month to contemplate his actions in signing. As president of the Congress, he felt responsible to make a clear statement to not only the king, but to his fellow countrymen as well. Consequently, he was the first to sign, and as all Americans know, he artistically scrawled his name in large, flowing letters. His expressed intent was to make certain King George III could read his name without the aid of glasses. It was a bold declaration of his personal commitment to the cause for which he was willing to die. John Hancock's overly legible signature hit the target at which he aimed. During the Revolutionary

War, King George offered amnesty to all of the Americans who were willing to stop the war. Hancock and a few select others were intentionally omitted from this proposition. His zealous signature informed the king there was no turning back, and the British empire clearly heard that strong message of commitment. All of us have been asked to give our "John Hancock" in a variety of settings. Among those settings should be the local church. Our "John Hancock" should be next to a specific job in the ministry of our church home. Fifty-six delegates signed the Declaration of Independence, but only one name stands out above the others because John Hancock wanted the king to know where he stood with his country. Has your signature let *the king* know where you stand with his church?[189]

Commitment During the Olympic marathon race in 1968, the world saw a clear picture of true commitment. John Akhwari was running for Tanzania, and although he didn't win the race, he won the hearts of all who saw him run. Akhwari was injured by a fall early in the race. Most runners would have conceded defeat and dropped out of the race to receive proper medical attention, but on this cool night in Mexico City, John Akhwari picked himself up and quickly bandaged his bleeding leg. The injury took its toll, but this determined Tanzanian wasn't going to quit. He kept running even though he was miles behind the main pack. Finally, more than an hour after all of the other runners had finished, John Akhwari limped into the stadium that was now almost completely empty of spectators. Slowly, he jogged the final lap and crossed the finish line in virtual solitude. Bud Greenspan, a respected commentator, watched the spectacle from a distance. He was so intrigued by the heroic finish that he walked over to this physically depleted young man and asked why he continued the race after sustaining such an injury. John Akhwari replied, "My country did not send me nine thousand miles to start the race. They sent me to finish the race." Commitment means giving your best until the job is done, even when the conditions are harsh.[190]

Commitment In 1519, Hernando Cortes landed at the present site of Veracruz, Mexico. This Spanish explorer came with the commitment to conquer the land for his country. Two previous Spanish expeditions had been unable to establish a settlement in Mexico. Cortes was determined to succeed, so to make certain that his men shared similar zeal for the task, he set fire to their fleet of eleven ships. Retreat was no longer an option as they were forced to move toward conquest. This whole-hearted devotion of Cortes has been described by historians as one of the most important elements in his success. With such zeal, he led 110 sailors and 553 soldiers to conquer five million people. (Ironically, his zealous pursuit began on Good Friday . . . reminiscent, though not comparable, with another Conqueror who nailed his possibilities for retreat to a cross). Cortes's determination provides Christians with a picture of commitment, and serves as a reminder that if men will yield themselves to such earthly goals how much greater should be our commitment to conquer spiritual darkness with the Light of the world. (Cortes claimed to fight under the banner of Catholicism but history suggests his intentions were far more self-serving.)[191]

Commitment Jim Denison is pastor of Park Cities Baptist Church in Dallas, Texas. While in college, Denison served as a summer missionary in East Malaysia. During one of their worship services, a teenage girl shared her faith in the small warehouse that was used for a church. She was baptized that day in their baptistry, which was a bathtub, and glowed with the love of Christ. While all of this was going on, Denison noticed some worn-out luggage leaning against the wall. He asked a church member for an explanation of the suitcase. He pointed to the girl who had been baptized and said, "Her father said that if she was baptized as a Christian she could never go home again. So she brought her luggage." What a challenge for greater commitment.[192]

Commitment "No one gives at all until he has given all." —*A. W. Tozer*[193]

Commitment The government of Mexico added the "double nationality amendment" to their constitution in March of 1998. This amendment allows citizens of Mexico, who live in the United States, to retain Mexican nationality rights even when they adopt citizenship in the United States. There are obviously some very strong political opinions surrounding this practice of allowing people to receive benefits from two countries. Regardless of your political views, such an amendment can help us understand our own tendency to straddle the fence spiritually. Although Mexico has joined the ranks of Britain, France, and Israel, where dual nationality is also permitted, we must all decide whether our citizenship will be in Satan's kingdom or God's. Dual nationality does not and cannot exist in the spiritual realm.[194]

Commitment The pastor of an underground Chinese church told a group of Southern Baptists about the precautions they must take to avoid government persecution. Each time their church reaches ten to fifteen members, they split to reduce attention. They also alternate meeting places for the same reason. Because phone lines are monitored, members meet with a volunteer on a downtown street to find out where the church will meet next. One such volunteer was discovered by the government, arrested, beaten, and put in prison. He lost his job, house, and medical benefits. Another man stepped in and took his place and he too suffered the same fate. One of the visitors said, "I suppose you have difficulty filling that job." The Chinese pastor replied, "No. We have a waiting list."[195]

Commitment While attending college, Robert Short told his mother he had become an atheist. She became very upset and cried for weeks. Sometime later, his life was transformed when he made a commitment to Christ. The next time he came home to visit, he told his mother he was now a Christian and had decided to become a minister. His mother again became upset. This time she thought he'd become a fanatic. Mrs. Short's reactions to her son illustrates the distorted perception of commitment that is espoused by so many. We want to be included in the "roll call of the saints" but don't wish to "go overboard" with zeal. Such mediocre "commitment" is described as "lukewarm" and is repulsive to the Savior who has given nothing less than his all.[196]

Committees "To get something done, a committee should consist of no more than three people, two of whom are absent." —*Robert Copeland*[197]

Communication A recent article noted that illegible handwriting costs businesses $200 million a year. Such hieroglyphics account for Kodak being stuck with nearly four hundred thousand unreturnable rolls of developed film each year. Poor writing results in the U.S. Postal Service annually sending thirty-eight million pieces of mail to its dead letter office at a cost of $4 million. It was also recorded that "Secretaries say they spend more time trying to figure out what the boss intended for them to do than doing the chore itself." It's truly amazing how much trouble careless writing can produce. Communication is prevented, frustration is created, and monetary loss is sustained because someone didn't have the time to make it clear. God obviously understood man's propensity to get lazy with his letters so he wrote his own. Encased in sixty-six books, we have God's legible message to man found most succinctly in the one verse that so many have memorized—John 3:16. No one needs to hire a professional for deciphering. It's basic enough for a five-year-old to understand yet profound enough to make a grown man weep. So the question isn't whether or not God's Word is readable. The question is whether or not.God's Word is read. God has taken the initiative to make sure you can understand his Word. Please take the time to read what he has to say.[198]

Communication "I've got nothing to say and I'm only going to say it once*!"—Casey Stengel*[199]

Communication Marriage enrichment speaker and author, Gary Chapman, cited a survey which revealed 50 percent of wives say their husband is uncommunicative. An additional study reported that 86 percent of divorces were fueled by deficient communication. As Chapman noted, "Any couple can have good communication. It's not a matter of personality, it's basically an act of the will. Communication is something we choose to do or not do." Effective communication is even more difficult during conflict. Chapman noted when a couple is in conflict the average spouse listens seventeen seconds before interrupting their mate.[200]

Communication NASA learned a hard lesson in communication during September of 1999. For ten months, the Mars Climate Orbiter had been in route to the red planet and scientists were excited that it was finally maneuvering into the sequence that would allow it to fulfill its mission of being a weather satellite on Mars. But on September 23, 1999, the $125 million project destructed just thirty-seven miles above the Martian surface. The failed mission was caused by a simple miscommunication. The Orbiter crashed because there was a mix-up in the use of English and metric units. This far-flung satellite was supposed to be hovering ninety-three miles above the surface, but the wrong system of measurements forced it down to thirty-seven miles instead. This one minor detail destroyed years of work and millions of dollars. Whether it's a satellite going to Mars, or a conversation at the dinner table, clear communication is essential for success.[201]

Communication Researchers at Case Western Reserve University in Cleveland have discovered the impact of passive-aggressive behavior.

Such behavior is generally known as "the silent treatment." In a comparative study of those who communicated and those who did not, Dr. Kristin Sommer found that those who remained silent showed dulled brain activity after an episode of opting for silence. Their mental edge was lost and their persistence was diminished. Sommer noted, "consciously ignoring people requires a lot of mental energy." Ignoring others is scientifically proven to make us more ignorant.[202]

Communication Research shows you have about eighteen seconds to talk before your doctor interrupts with a question.[203]

Communication "Some people speak from experience while others, from experience, don't speak." —*Anonymous* [204]

Communication The average person speaks at a rate of 125 words per minute. People listen at about 600 words per minute.[205]

Communication Verbal content accounts for 7 percent of communication's impact, voice tone is responsible for 37 percent, and body language has a 56 percent effect.[206]

Communication We all talk to ourselves at a rate of about 1,200 words a minute. This activity is called "self-talk" or thinking.[207]

Compassion "Hardening of the heart ages more people than hardening of the arteries." —*Anonymous* [208]

Compassion Joseph Stowell, president of Moody Bible Institute, heard a powerful story about compassion from a Jewish/Christian friend who had recently returned from a trip to Denmark. Having never been there himself, Stowell was deeply interested in hearing about the trip. There was obviously much to tell, but the highlight of the trip took place on their tour of the palace where each of Denmark's kings have lived. The guide told of the time when Hitler took over their country and required King Christian X to read the edict concerning an armband that all Jews must wear. The Danes listened to their king read these words from the palace balcony as tears brimmed from his eyes. When he finished delivering Hitler's edict, King Christian X reached into his pocket and pulled out a yellow armband. He then slid it up his arm. Those present to witness this moving declaration of compassion were inspired to do the same. Throughout Denmark, many non-Jews acquired yellow armbands of compassion to help hide the Jews from Hitler's henchmen. Compassion occurs when another's problem is embraced as our own.[209]

Compassion Through the atrocities of World War II came an unmistakable lesson on compassion. A young Jewish boy from Poland was rounded up by the Nazi troops to be shot with his family and neighbors. They were forced to dig a common grave then the soldiers gunned them down. The bullets ripped through all those around him, but he miraculously escaped injury. In trauma, he collapsed among the corpses and was buried as dead. The shallow grave provided just enough air to sustain him until nightfall. He then clawed his way out and ran for safety. His dirty, naked body was covered with blood and did not solicit a welcome from the homes he encountered. In the shivering cold he begged for help, but each resident turned him away for fear of the Germans. In desperation, he tried a different approach. He timidly knocked at the door and cried, "Don't you recognize me? I am the Jesus you say you love." A compassionate woman embraced the little boy, took him in, and raised him as her own. Compassion is best realized when we recognize others as the Jesus we say we love.[210]

Compassion While walking home from school, Mark noticed the boy ahead of him had stumbled to the ground and dropped everything he was carrying. Mark hurried to the boy's side and helped him collect his belongings. Surprisingly, the boy was carrying an especially hefty load. There was a baseball glove and bat, a couple of sweaters, a small tape recorder, and an armful of books. Mark helped him carry the things home and his new friend, Bill, was most appreciative of his compassion. During the walk home, Mark discovered Bill was struggling in school and had just broken up with his girlfriend. When they arrived at Bill's house, he invited Mark in for a Coke and they spent the rest of the afternoon talking, laughing, and watching TV. Although the two boys never became real close friends, they kept up with each other throughout the rest of junior high and high school. Several weeks before graduation, Bill approached Mark and asked him if he remembered that day they met when Mark helped him with all of his stuff. Mark nodded as he remembered. Bill then asked, "Did you ever wonder why I was carrying so many things that day?" Without pausing for an answer, Bill explained he had cleaned out his locker and was going home to take his life. He had been storing away sleeping pills and was headed home to end it all when Mark happened along to help him out. Bill told Mark how that simple act of compassion inspired him to go on living. He said, "Mark, when you picked up my books that day, you saved my life!" Imagine how many times our small, seemingly insignificant gestures of concern may reignite the flame of life and inspire someone to continue on. Thankfully, compassion has a way of doing that.[211]

Complaining During game four of the 1996 World Series, Ted Turner bought a hot dog while the Braves were hosting the Yankees in Atlanta. To see him carefully count out three $1 bills you would have never thought he actually owned the Atlanta Braves. When he went over to the condiment table he was overheard commenting to a stranger, "Three dollars for a hot dog. Can you believe it?" A fan who heard the complaint and recognized Turner said, "Then do something about it!" If we have the means to make things better, let's "do something about it" instead of just voicing our complaints.[212]

Compliments "Some people pay a compliment like they expect a receipt." —*Kin Hubbard*[213]

Compromise Compromise is often pictured as a watered-down method for reaching a resolve, but it can be the perfect component for finding a winning solution. That's what people discovered in two small Texas towns. KSHN-FM serves the cities of Liberty and Dayton, but that posed a problem when trying to cover local football games. If both teams were playing at the same time, either a choice must be made, or a new solution would have to be discovered. Ingenuity and compromise developed an idea that seems to work well for everybody. By using stereo capabilities, listeners in Liberty can turn the balance control on their radios all the way to the left and hear their game. Those in Dayton listen to their game by throwing the balance to the right. Nobody gets stereo, but everybody gets to cheer for their home team. A small radio station in Southeast Texas has shown us that compromise can be a great tool for solving seemingly impossible situations.[214]

Compromise In Matthew 26, Jesus declared a day of Judgment is coming when his sheep will be separated from the goats. Strangely enough, some scientists at the Institute of Animal Physiology in Cambridge, England, have added a new twist to Jesus' classification of sheep and goats. These lab-coat intellects have crossed a sheep with a goat in test-tube experiments and they call their new hybrid a "geep." Although it's a new reality in the laboratory, it's nothing new in the church. For centuries people have been trying to walk the barnyard fence and enjoy the benefits of being a sheep while maintaining the unruly liberty of roaming like a goat. Unfortunately for such compromising individuals, Jesus did not reserve a spot for "geep." You're either following the Shepherd as one of his sheep, or you're part of the goat herd.[215]

Compromise The preacher wasn't going to allow any Sunday school teachers to compromise the standards of God's Word so he called one of his teachers into the pastor's study. It was the late 1950s and the teacher was none other than Willie Nelson. The pastor said, "Willie, either you quit playing in beer joints or else you quit teaching Sunday school." Nelson replied, "You must be nuts." But the minister didn't back down. Nelson recalled, "he had to choose between satisfying the congregation—including the hypocrites—or siding with a musician who drank and smoked and cussed and picked his guitar and sang in dance halls. I decided to stay with the beer joints." Nelson also said, "The preacher sounded so wrong to me that I quit the Baptist Church." Willie Nelson's decision to choose the beer joints over the church led him to other avenues of religious thought. He noted, "I discovered a world full of people who believed in reincarnation. The King James version of the Bible was later written to cover up the fact that Jesus had discovered reincarnation. The Aquarian Gospel had a great impact on me. It explained everything to my satisfaction." Compromise never leads to an oasis, it just deceives you with a myriad of mirages.[216]

Concern Calvin Miller, a popular author and preaching professor, recently told about a little girl who didn't think anybody cared whether she lived or died. Her body was fished out of the river in Kansas City and the rescue team found a note pinned to her dress. The washed-out ink revealed the thoughts she had written down before ending her life. The note read, "I don't have a friend in the world. Nobody cares for me." What a plight when little lives are self-destructed because they don't feel concern stemming from those around them. May we let every child know we care about them.[217]

Confession On September 22, 1998, Daniel Crocker confessed to a murder he committed nineteen years prior. Nobody had tracked him down, it just came from the conviction God had placed on his heart. At the age of thirty-eight, with a wife and two young children, Crocker practiced what he had read in Proverbs 28:13, "He who conceals his transgressions will not prosper, but he who confesses and forsakes them will find compassion." Nineteen years earlier, Crocker had been on a three-day LSD high when he killed nineteen-year-old Tracy Fresquez after meeting her briefly at a convenience store. Few clues were left behind, and detectives admitted the case would have never been solved had Crocker not made his confession. Not long after that murder on October 6, 1979, Crocker realized he had to make serious changes in his life. He quit using drugs and returned to the teachings of his Christian parents. He got involved in a church and started studying God's Word. By 1986, he married a woman from his church and they started a family. During the summer of 1998, Crocker and his wife came to a consensus agreement that he needed to confess his crime. He said good-bye to his two children and wife, then boarded a flight from his home in Virginia and flew to Kansas City. A prearranged meeting with prosecutors took place shortly thereafter and now Crocker is serving time in prison. He will not be eligible for parole until 2008. His lawyer, Tom Bath, is amazed at Crocker's confession. He said, "I have never seen anybody willing to risk so much to take responsibility for what he's done." District Attorney Paul Morrison admitted, "I've never seen anything like this." Crocker simply says, "It is hard for me and my wife and our children, but it is the right thing to do." Daniel Crocker understands that the Truth himself uses the truth itself to set us free, even if it means suffering the consequences of our deeds. (John 8:32).[218]

Confession Thomas Martin is the former manager of a Jack in the Box restaurant in Oroville, California. During 1996, he reported a robbery in which the crook took $307 as the store was closing. When questioned about the suspect, Martin provided police sketch artist, Jack Lee, with a detailed description of the assailant. After Lee completed his sketch, he observed how the drawing looked just like Martin. When investigators noted the similarity, Martin confessed to the crime. Confession occurs when we clearly identify ourselves as the culprit.[219]

Confidence During the 1970s, when Dan Fouts was just beginning his march to the Hall of Fame, the San Diego Charger's star quarterback was having a bad day. With just two minutes remaining in the game, San Diego was behind 14-0. Frustrations were running high so the coach pulled Fouts and put in his backup quarterback, Bobby Douglas. Douglas was thrilled about the opportunity to play so he strapped on his helmet and bolted onto the field. On his way to the huddle, he stopped and looked back to the sidelines. He yelled, "Coach, do you want me to win the game, or just tie it?" The tension between being confident and cocky can be tricky to balance, but the Church sure needs more Christians to enter the game with a confident perspective like Bobby Douglas.[220]

Conflict Although Mary Carney and her husband arrived at church in the same car, they were miles apart. They had engaged in one of those arguments before church and did not get their problem resolved. Humorously, God's sovereignty was reflected in a secretary's typographical error. As Mary sat stewing in church, she glanced down at her bulletin. She and Gary were scheduled to sing a duet during the worship service. Next to their name was typed the word "duel." She smiled then looked at her husband. The decision was theirs to make a duet or duel. Through the quietness of that Sunday service she reached for his hand and the "duet" began. In all of our relationships, marriage or otherwise, we make daily choices to participate in either a duet or a duel. Those decisions will dictate whether we build bridges or bombs.[221]

Conflict August 17, 1998, was a tough day for Kenneth DeLeon. The resident of Boca Raton, Florida, was out enjoying a walk while reflecting on his recent law school graduation from Berkeley, California. His thoughts were rudely interrupted when twenty-two-year-old Adam Blumhof lost control of his car and jumped the curb. DeLeon was hit by the car and thrown through the windshield. He landed in the passenger's seat but was too dazed to realize what had so quickly happened. The confusion didn't last long though. DeLeon was violently revived by the fist of Blumhof. The guy who had just hit him was now beating on him and ordering him to get out of the car. DeLeon, who suffered a broken arm and leg, was punched repeatedly while Blumhof screamed, "Get out! Get out!" The driver was finally able to push him out of the car, then sped away. Authorities arrested the madman shortly thereafter. Does this bizarre scenario sound strangely familiar? There are days when you feel like people have not only run over you, but they've pummeled you and yelled at you while you were still reeling from their initial blow. Fortunately, that's not generally a daily occurrence, but when it does happen it can surely set you back. When those unfair episodes transpire, may you weather the experience with the hope of Christ and the support of Christian friends.[222]

Conflict How do you handle problems? If running from adversity is your style, pay attention to the plight of Patricia Christy. After Hurricane Andrew devastated Florida in 1992, this South Florida resident was standing in line waiting for food. She decided then and there that she was going to run as far away from this problem as possible. She boarded the first available flight and headed for a restful vacation on the Hawaiian island of Kauai. She arrived just in time to experience Hurricane Iniki. Running from your problems usually just leads to more problems.[223]

Conflict Studies demonstrate that 70 percent of complaining customers will continue doing business with an organization that favorably resolves their problem. Loyalty jumps to 95 percent if you resolve their situation immediately. This simple piece of datum reconfirms what we already know; it pays to resolve conflicts quickly.[224]

Conflict *The Jerry Springer Show* has been notorious for on-the-air fights and brawls. The producers of this show once tried to alter their reputation by making, what they called, improvements. Henry Schleiff, executive vice president of USA Networks Studios, said, "We have heard the criticism and . . . we're responding to it." Schleiff said they would deal with the problem by prompting their security guards to move more quickly to diffuse fights. Conflicts are one of the variables that tragically moved Jerry Springer to the top of daytime dysfunctional TV, but equally disheartening is the reality that many of us deal with conflicts in similar fashions. Rather than address the issues that are causing conflict, we simply push for faster security guards. Swift bouncers don't resolve conflicts, but humble and contrite people can reach a mutual accord.[225]

Conflict "Where there is friction between two people, a smile is a good lubricant." —*Anonymous*[226]

Conformity "A man knocked down by an opponent can get up again. A man flattened by conformity stays down for good." — *Thomas Watson*[227]

Conformity Conformity is a big social issue even if it's not always verbalized. Dr. Ben Carson grew up in one of Detroit's poverty-stricken neighborhoods. The rule of conformity there challenged him to do destructive things with his life. He eventually saw the futility of conforming to the wrong crowd and broke away to become a well-respected neurosurgeon at Johns Hopkins. Carson illustrates this pressure of negative conformity with a crab tank. He says, "They never have to put a lid on it because if one crab starts to crawl out, the others will grab onto him and pull him back down." To overcome such pressure to stay down in the mire of sin we must rely upon the Holy Spirit to not only inspire us, but strengthen us. Likewise, we would do well to keep our distance from believers who are "crabby."[228]

Conformity During an interview with a group of astronauts, the crew was asked, "What do you think is the single most important key to successful space travel?" One astronaut offered the following response: "The secret of traveling in space is to take your own atmosphere with you." This observation from space helps us better understand Paul's admonition for Christians to not be conformed to the world. By carrying the atmosphere of Christ with us, we can thrive in the hostile environment of this sinful world.[229]

Congeniality A recent study of more than 800,000 people revealed that just 2 percent of the population viewed themselves as below average in their ability to get along with other people. In essence, virtually everyone was claiming to be a congenial person. Reality would certainly shrink the elevated opinions of many, but the concept of everyone wanting to be congenial is a great goal to pursue.[230]

Consequences In Texas, football is a very big deal. That's why the consequences of this story are so profound. On Friday, December 18, 1998, the football team from Katy High School, in a suburb of Houston, boarded a bus bound for Irving while the marching band belted out their school fight song. The Katy Tigers were preparing to defend their Class 5A Division II state title. They were the defending state champs with a good shot at repeating that feat. While sitting on the bus in anticipation of playing on the same field as the Dallas Cowboys, Coach Mike Johnson instructed the players to get off the bus and meet him in the field house. With tearful eyes, Johnson told his team they would not be going to the championship game. For the first time in Texas high school football history, they were disqualified from participating on the eve of their title game. Two weeks previously, a senior, whose name was not released, played in the final three plays of Katy's 40-0 victory over Clear Brook High School. During the week after Thanksgiving, this senior had falsified grades and forged a signature on his progress reports to hide the fact that he was failing two classes. According to the University Interscholastic League (UIL), a player cannot participate in sports if he is not passing all of his classes. When a teacher saw this young man preparing to travel with the team, while knowing he was failing her class, the violation was reported to the principal who in turn informed the UIL. Just a brief time before the team was scheduled to leave for the championship game, the verdict of complete forfeiture was made and the Katy Tigers were forced to stay home and watch the game on TV. The team they had beaten the week before went and played in their place. Although many people felt the penalty was too harsh, the verdict stood because the rules and penalties are clearly stated and every school is required to comply with all of the regulations. Only one player broke the rules, and he alone knew what he had done. He was a marginal player who was on the field for just three plays during the playoffs, but when his deeds were discovered, a host of innocent people were hurtfully impacted by what he had secretly done. We seldom believe that the consequences of our private lives will hurt others, but this lesson from Katy, Texas, reminds us otherwise.[231]

Consequences "The reputation of a thousand years may be determined by the conduct of one hour." —*Japanese proverb* [232]

Consistency Craig Davison has been known as a consistent man. The Phoenix, Arizona resident began running regularly in 1978 and hadn't missed a single day since then when an article was written about him in 1997. By May of 1997, at age forty-three, he calculated he had logged in 120,000 miles (nearly five laps around the world). His regimen of running is an example of consistency by itself, but what he's done traveling all of those miles is an equally impressive lesson in consistency. While running, Davison keeps his eyes open for loose change and doesn't pass up a single penny. This consistent vigilance has paid off. Over the years he has collected $5,170. All those dimes, nickels, and pennies paid for a second honeymoon to Hawaii in 1991. Consistency pays off but we frequently neglect it because the dividends come in slower than we desire. We'd all like to find $5,000 but are we willing to run 120,000 miles to get it? Whether it's finances, meaningful relationships, spiritual maturity, or physical fitness, consistency is the best route to take.[233]

Consistency Everybody likes a "clutch hitter." You know, the guy who wins the game with a crucial hit when the score is close in the last few innings. We tend to think of certain great ballplayers who seem to pull the game out of the fire on a regular basis, but statistics reveal such players only exist in our minds. Studies done by pioneer baseball analyst Bill James and researchers for Stats Inc. have determined the phenomenon of clutch hitters is simply a myth. Allen Barra and Alan Schwarz, sports writers for the *Wall Street Journal,* have noted, "what a hitter does in most clutch situations is pretty much what he does all the rest of the time." The statistics even reveal the top hitters in baseball actually average a thirteen-point drop in their overall batting average when the game is close in the late innings. What occurs on the baseball diamond is no different than what happens in every aspect of life. When things are tough, the person who comes through is generally the same person who consistently comes through day in and day out when things aren't so tough. By practicing consistent excellence every day we will not only get the job done when life is mundane, but we'll have a far greater likelihood of coming through in the clutch.[234]

Contentment Erma Bombeck has humored people for years with her satirical outlook on life. Her battle with cancer took her on a journey through emotions she was unaccustomed to feeling. Humor didn't cover the emotional pain that was tearing her apart. Ironically, she had labored for two years on a book about children with cancer, *I Want to Grow Hair, I Want to Grow Up, I Want to Go to Boise.* Now she had the dreaded disease. Solace came from plenty of soul-searching, surgery, a supportive family, and a bit of reflection from those cancer-ridden children she had been with for two years. One little voice that comes to visit her when she struggles with contentment and gratitude for her current survival from cancer is that of eight-year-old Christina. This little girl had cancer of the nervous system. When she was asked what she wanted for her birthday, she thought it over for a long time and finally answered, "I don't know. I have two sticker books and a Cabbage Patch doll. I have everything!"[235]

Contentment "I'm still convinced that if you have to move even ten inches from where you are now in order to be happy, you never will be." —*Tim Hansel*[236]

Contentment "If not completely satisfied...learn to live with it. — *Ziggy comic strip*[237]

Contentment Wayne Watson is a well-known Christian vocalist. His perspective on life has served him well through the ups and downs which have come his way: "There's always going to be something to whine about. We have to be thankful for what we've got. Gratitude helps to take a lot of the edge off."[238]

Contentment "While it takes courage to achieve greatness, it takes more courage to find fulfillment in being ordinary." —*Marilyn Thomsen*[239]

Cooperation "Have you ever noticed how many people are willing to carry the piano bench when it comes time to move a piano?" — *Anonymous*[240]

Cooperation Margaret Patrick and Ruth Eisenberg have taught the world a great lesson in cooperation. In 1982, both of these ladies were partially paralyzed by strokes. Prior to paralysis, they each had been accomplished pianists. Patrick began playing the piano at the age of eight. She stayed with the piano and taught countless children how to play. Eisenberg learned to play the piano as an adult. Her husband devised a method of teaching the piano to adults and insisted that she learn the technique. She became her husband's prize pupil and toured the country demonstrating her acquired talent. After their strokes, neither of them attempted the piano until they met Millie McHugh at the Southeast Senior Center for Independent Living in Englewood, New Jersey. McHugh introduced them and suggested they put together their piano talent. Patrick could still play with her left hand and Eisenberg was able to use her right hand. They started cooperating on the keyboard and the duet of "Ebony and Ivory" was born. Beautiful music started flowing through the hallways of the senior center and concerts began happening all over New Jersey. At the ages of seventy-five and eighty-six, these two cooperative ladies produced some of the most beautiful music of their lives.[241]

Cooperation The late Jimmy Durante was a world-class entertainer. After World War II, he was asked to perform in a show for our country's veterans. He consented but under the condition that they realized his busy schedule would only permit a brief monologue. The show's director eagerly agreed and Durante was booked. He went on stage and did his short monologue, but something happened. He didn't stop at the appointed time. He moved into other material and the crowd was ecstatic. His brief appearance grew into a thirty-minute performance. After his final bow, he was questioned about his extended stay. Everyone was thrilled that he stayed, but they all wondered why. Mr. Durante pointed to the front row and said, "There's the reason I stayed." Seated next to each other were two war heroes who had both lost an arm in battle. One had lost his right arm, the other his left. Together they were creating lively applause that motivated a compassionate entertainer to adjust his schedule and extend his stay. Cooperation not only helps us to more thoroughly enjoy life, it motivates others to do the same.[242]

Corporate Tithing The Bible clearly teaches the principle and command for Christians to tithe. A small bank in Midland Park, New Jersey, has taken this Biblical mandate to the board room as well. In 1985 the Atlantic Stewardship Bank was formed with a unique twist - it would donate 10% of its pretax profits. In 1992 it gave away $80,000 that went to help everything from missions in Africa to the local YMCA. Their rationale for this activity is best summarized in a promotional brochure they produced. It says, "As every man hath received the gift, even so minister the same one to another, as good stewards of the manifold grace of God." (1 Peter 4:10) Many corporate executives might question this practice but every year their assets have grown and profits have increased.[243]

Coupons In the United States, each household receives an average of twenty-five-hundred coupons per year. With these coupons Americans save $3 billion a year.[244]

Creation In January of 1996, the Hubble telescope led astronomers to estimate there are fifty billion galaxies in the universe. Previously they had estimated just ten billion galaxies.[245]

Creation Sometimes our limited view of God's creation actually contributes to a limited view of God himself. The following realization is a good antidote when we start reducing the Creator to someone we can easily comprehend. Our solar system has a diameter of seven hundred light minutes, or eight billion miles. The galaxy that contains our solar system has a diameter of one hundred thousand light years, not minutes. Yet our galaxy, the Milky Way, is but one of over ten billion galaxies in the universe. The God we serve is he who created it all with but the sound of his voice.[246]

Creation The moon is approximately 240,000 miles from earth (238,852 miles). The sun is about 93 million miles from earth (92,956,000 miles). Scientists have concluded that if either one of these astronomical bodies was 100 miles closer or further away from the earth, life on this planet would not be possible. Likewise, the earth spins at 1,000 mph while orbiting the sun at 60,700 mph. Just a 2 mph difference would prevent life on earth. The amazing handiwork of God is not only perfect, but perfectly balanced.[247]

Creativity Ralph Samuelson was a very creative teenager who seldom hesitated to take a risk. In the summer of 1922, this daredevil from Lake City, Minnesota, found himself longing for the adventure of snow skiing. In an attempt to satisfy this craving, he strapped on his snow skis and headed for the lake. Nobody had ever tried such a feat so most people wrote it off as another one of his crazy ideas. He tied a rope to the back of his friend's speedboat and jumped into the water. His snow skis didn't work very well but that didn't stop young Samuelson. He tried other types of skis with little success, so eventually he made a pair of "water" skis out of pine. These enabled him to glide across the water and a new sport was discovered. Creativity is an unlimited natural resource that unlocks countless doors. May we unleash this valuable commodity for the glory and honor of God.[248]

Credit Cards Americans are mailed three billion credit card solicitations each year.[249]

Crime It's not in my thesaurus, but it should be. Next to "crime" should be the synonym "stupidity." On May 27, 1996, James Lertola and Brian Witham escaped from the Marble Valley prison in Rutland, Vermont. The two crooks didn't want to forget anything in their master scheme so they made a to-do list. It read, "Drive to Maine, get safer place to stay, buy guns, get Marie, get car in Dartmouth, do robbery, go to New York." Six days after their escape, the pair ran from a stolen car in Dartmouth, Massachusetts, when they saw a police officer approaching. They left their to-do list in the stolen car. Police learned that Lertola's girlfriend, Marie, had boarded a bus to New York. Law officials then located Lertola waiting at the New York bus station and arrested him after a brief chase. He willingly told police that his partner was at a nearby bar and now both are back in jail. These organized criminals have presented a very telling truth—crime has a predictable agenda and it's never good.[250]

Crime Shaun Tomson is the former world champion of surfing. After gaining all of his accolades on a surfboard, he decided to escape the high crime rate of South Africa by relocating to Montecito, California. On December 17, 1999, the forty-four-year-old Tomson returned from dinner to find his home had been burglarized. The intruders took $50,000 worth of jewelry and his prized surfing medals. The surfing champ said, "This really hits us hard. I was going to pass the medals on to my son. These things were very precious to us." There is no escaping the reality and consequences of crime. We can only soften its blow by taking heed to Jesus' admonition, "Don't lay up for yourselves treasures upon earth where . . . thieves break in and steal. But lay up for yourselves treasures in heaven"(Matthew 6:19–21).[251]

Criticism "Any fool can criticize, condemn, and complain...and most of them do." —*Dale Carnegie* [252]

Criticism Have you ever imagined living without criticism? Maybe you've thought greater success would usher in a life free of criticism. If either, or both, of these fantasies have crept through your mind, just think of Dr. Billy Graham. The good that God has delivered through this man is hard to fathom. Nonetheless, he has known criticism all of his life. In 1993, one fundamentalist leader said Dr. Graham "has done more harm to the cause of Christ than any other living man." Doesn't that make you feel better about the criticisms you've received lately?[253]

Criticism M. A. Gruder said, "To be successful in Washington you must have the ability to lay a firm foundation with the bricks others throw at you." What was true for this administrator in the Department of Transportation is true for any believer. Regardless of our position or role, we must be able to take any type of criticism, even that which is unfounded, and use it to improve our usefulness for God.[254]

Criticism "Most people don't mind criticism as long as it's about someone else." —*Suzan Wiener* [255]

Criticism "Most people find fault like there's a reward for it." —*Zig Ziglar* [256]

Criticism Psychologists monitored a select group of businessmen to determine the ratio of negative-to-positive remarks they received in their respective jobs. The final analysis revealed that 67 percent of their daily input was negative. Like these businessmen, most people are living with a greater influx of criticism than affirmation.[257]

Criticism "The man who says it can't be done should never interrupt the man who is actually doing it." —*Anonymous* [258]

Criticism "The trouble with most of us is we would rather be ruined by praise than saved by criticism." —*Norman Vincent Peale* [259]

Criticism "Wanted: Christians who overlook the faults of others as easily as they do their own." —*Anonymous* [260]

Crying Everybody knows the shortest verse in the Bible, "Jesus wept," but few really understand human tears. Men try to refrain, children are encouraged not to, and it's somewhat expected of women. In 1964, a sixteen-year-old boy named William Frey saved the life of a two-year-old girl. He was traumatized by the event but didn't cry. That experience began Frey's journey toward becoming an expert on crying and stress. In 1985, he released his groundbreaking book on the subject called *Crying: The Mystery of Tears.* Dr. Frey is a leading neuroscientist and head of the Ramsey Foundation Alzheimer's Treatment and Research Center in St. Paul, Minnesota. He is one of the world's leading proponents of the theory that men die younger than women in part because they don't deal well with emotions. His twenty-five years of researching tears have provided some interesting findings: Women average 5.3 crying episodes per month, men just 1.4. Men's eyes tear up, women's tears run down their face. Tears for emotional reasons are chemically different from tears caused by eye irritation. 85 percent of women and 73 percent of men report feeling better after they have cried about a stressful situation. Boys and girls under the age of twelve cry the same amount. The difference begins developing in puberty. Generally, boys stop crying between ages thirteen and sixteen, due primarily to societal expectations. *Human tears contain a unique mix of chemicals. They have thirty times more manganese than human blood, endorphin hormones, which provide a natural lift to the body; and prolactin which is a hormone that helps nursing mothers produce milk. Frey has stated, "The only physiological mechanism we have to alleviate stress that is different from every other animal is the ability to cry emotional tears." In John 11:35, Jesus showed that God has provided a unique way for us to experience natural relief from the sadness of life. [261]

Cynicism Are you cynical? It could land you in the Coronary Care Unit. According to Dr. Redford Williams, an internist and behavioral medicine researcher at Duke University Medical Center, "A cynical,

mistrusting attitude is a driving force that makes people most suscep-
tible to heart disease." Of course any cynic worth his weight would dispute this research.[262]

Death Death is a process that never ceases to function, yet we seldom
believe it will happen to us. Lance Foster certainly wasn't thinking about
it when he broke from his dormitory desk to get a soft drink in March of
1988. The twenty-three-year-old student at the University of Kansas
encountered a vending machine that took his money but didn't deliver
his drink. Foster aggressively shook the machine and it ended up tipping
over on top of him. He died of internal injuries shortly thereafter. Ali-
Asghar Ahani never dreamed he would die by a gun-firing snake, but
that's exactly how he met death in 1989. When he came across a snake in
Iran, he attempted to capture it rather than shoot it. He pressed the butt
of his shotgun behind the snake's head. The snake immediately coiled
around the gun and its tail activated the trigger. Ahani died of a single
shot to the head. William Curry believed life was just beginning in 1990
when he won $3.6 million in the lottery. But just two weeks after strik-
ing it rich, the thirty-seven-year-old Curry died of a heart attack. His sis-
ter-in-law told reporters the stress of winning is what killed him. Death
doesn't always call the way we believe it should, so we need to be prepared
for its inevitable arrival.[263]

Death Dustin Hoffman is the Academy award-winning actor who has
amazed audiences with some incredible characters. In a recent interview,
Hoffman revealed his plans for the epitaph on his tombstone. He says it
will simply read, "I knew this was going to happen." Death is something
we all know is going to happen, but too often we think of it happening
to someone else. It will happen to each of us and we need to be spiritually prepared when it comes.[264]

Death Dying is a grave offense, literally, in Le Lavandou, France. The
Riviera town's only cemetery is full and ecologist are holding up their
proposal for another one along the coast. Because the dispute may continue for some time, Mayor Gil Bernardi passed a law on September 21,
2000, stating, "It is illegal for anyone without a cemetery plot to die
within the town limits." The mayor readily acknowledged the new law is
"absurd," but insisted it was "enacted because of an absurd situation." He
also noted they would not punish those who broke this law. Death is a

reality that does not respond to legislation. "It is appointed for all men to die once and after this comes judgment" (Hebrews 9:27).[265]

Death Nothing hurts quite like the loss of a loved one. When such pain occurs, it can be helpful to remember what happens at airports every day. Travelers from all types of backgrounds crowd onto jets, then taxi out to the runway. Frequently you will see remaining family members pressed against the glass as they watch the plane take off. They will watch the aircraft shrink into the sky until it vanishes from sight. At that point, someone generally says, "Well, he's gone." Yet the truth is they're gone from our sight . . . not gone. In a distant place that plane will be spotted by a welcoming committee who will likewise be gazing out the window. As they see the jet approach the runway and touch down, someone will invariably say, "He's here." Death's pattern is much like a one-way airline ticket. It takes a person from our sight and we say he's gone, but God is waiting on the other side to usher him into eternity.[266]

Death On November 1, 1989, John Michael Cox killed his step-grandmother and two other relatives. Consequently, he received the death sentence for his ruthless crime. Cox sat on death row for nearly a decade and claimed he might be immune to the lethal injection used for executions. This three-time murderer felt he might cheat death when his date in the chamber arrived. On February 16, 1999, he had the opportunity to prove his claim as he was administered a lethal injection in the Varner, Arkansas, death chamber. Less than fifteen minutes later, Cox's lifeless body was wheeled out on a gurney. In some ways, many of us are like Cox in that we're secretly hoping we are immune to death. Actuaries prove otherwise and confirm the reality that we will all die (Hebrews 9:27). Therefore, we would be wise to prepare for this certain event.[267]

Death Richard Lederer is now a famous teacher because Ann Landers recently reprinted a humorous article he composed on the history of the world. The entire essay is made up of lines from student papers that were collected by history and English teachers throughout the country. The following lines are highlights of that essay. "Jacob, son of Isaac, stole his brother's birthmark. Socrates was a famous Greek teacher who died from an overdose of wedlock. The Magna Carta provided that no free man should be hanged twice for the same offense. Gutenberg invented the Bible. Sir Walter Raleigh invented cigarettes. John Milton wrote *Paradise Lost*, then his wife died and he wrote *Paradise Regained*. Abraham

Lincoln's mother died in infancy. Bach and Handel were famous composers. Handel was half-German, half-Italian, and half-English. Bach died from 1750 to the present. Benjamin Franklin died in 1790 and is still dead." These student errors do at least reveal the truth about death. Like Franklin and Bach, when we die we remain dead. Only Christ can resurrect us to a new life. Couple this with the true story of a letter returned to the post office on which the recipient had written, "He's dead." An oversight caused the same letter to be sent back to the original destination. It was returned again with the additional remark, "He's still dead!"[268]

Death Seventy percent of Americans die intestate, that is, without a will.[269]

Death Tony Campolo attends an African-American Church. Each year they have a very special day between Christmas and New Year's when the home-for-the-holidays college students report on their experiences at school. On one such Sunday after half a dozen students had shared, the pastor got up and delivered the following exhortation about life. He said, "Children, you're going to die! You may not think you're going to die, but you're going to die. One of these days, they're going to take you out to the cemetery, drop you in a hole, throw some dirt on your face, and go back to the church and eat potato salad. When you were born, you alone were crying and everybody else was happy. The important question I want to ask is this: When you die are you alone going to be happy, leaving everybody else crying? The answer depends on whether you live to get titles or you live to get testimonies. When they lay you in the grave, are people going to stand around reciting the fancy titles you earned, or are they going to stand around giving testimonies of the good things you did for them? Will they list your degrees and awards, or will they tell about what a blessing you were to them? Will you leave behind just a newspaper column telling people how important you were, or will you leave crying people who give testimonies of how they've lost the best friend they ever had? There's nothing wrong with titles. Titles are good things to have. But if it ever comes down to a choice between a title or a testimony—go for the testimony."[270]

Debt Americans owe $384 billion on credit cards alone, and 70 percent of credit card holders carry an average balance of $3,900?[271]

Debt At $1.16 trillion, consumer debt is growing at twice the rate of wages.[272]

Debt Between 75percent and 80 percent of American households owe $15,000 in consumer debt.[273]

Debt In the United States during 1998, the number of people filing for bankruptcy exceeded the number of people who graduated from college.[274]

Debt More than one million Americans file for bankruptcy each year.[275]

Debt The average American household is $12,500 in debt and holds seven credit cards.[276]

Deception In the last quarter of 1999, a new British company opened its doors under the name, The Alibi Agency. This business was created to provide elaborate alibis for married people who want assistance in hiding an extramarital affair from their spouse. For $32 to $40 per use, they will send a falsified invitation to a convention, an imaginary hotel room, and a prearranged phone number, which is monitored by an operator who screens all incoming calls. Alibi's director said, "Our clients tell us they'd cheat with or without us, so we provide a necessary service that lets them get away with a casual dalliance without risking the love of their long-term partner." It is telling and tragic that a company can operate under the expressed intent of deceiving marriage partners about marital unfaithfulness.[277]

Deception The horrors of war are accentuated by the use of deception. In World War II, one of the German ploys was that of switching road signs. The pursuing Allied forces could not depend on the signage because it generally pointed in the wrong direction. The same spiritual craftsman of that worldwide crisis continues to use his dated tactic. Satan is the angel of light (2 Corinthians 11:14) who still intentionally changes the guideposts of life to confuse and hurt anyone who will fall for his deadly deceptions.[278]

Deception The movie rage of 1999 was that traditional battle between good and evil, *The Phantom Menace*. This *Star Wars* prequel had people losing their ability to reason as they camped in long lines for a chance to be one of the first to see . . . colored Q-tips. One of the big draws for this movie was its special effects, but one great irony was how these high-tech gurus duped the public into believing colored Q-tips were actually people in a stadium. In a scene where there's a pod race, a miniature model of a stadium was created and then colored Q-tips were put in place to look like a crowd. Fans were blown at the "crowd" to give it movement, and the audio of a San Francisco 49ers football game was laid over it for sound. For this reason you can hear someone yell "Niners!" when Anakin Skywalker flies past the stands in his fast-moving pod. If Hollywood technicians can make us think Q-tips are people, how much greater caution must we take to prevent the master of special effects (2 Corinthians 11:14) from feeding us spiritual deception.[279]

Decisions In the National Basketball Association draft of 1984, the Houston Rockets had the number one pick. They opted for Akeem Olajuwon, who led them to two consecutive NBA championships in 1994 and 1995. The Portland Trailblazers took Samuel Bowie as the number two draft pick for that year. Unfortunately, Bowie was injury-prone and did not reach the potential for which Portland had hoped. The Chicago Bulls had the third pick and they selected a young man who was passed over by both Houston and Portland. It was none other than Michael Jordan, the round-ball legend who took his team to the top of the basketball world in 1991, 1992, 1993, 1996, 1997, and 1998. Ironically, the only two years that Houston won was during Jordan's stint in baseball. Speculative historians can only imagine what would have happened had Jordan not taken a sabbatical in 1994 and 1995, or retired after the championship in 1998. The Biblical statesman, Samuel, was involved in a another draft that held some surprising similarities. The Hebrew leader was in charge of anointing a new king for Israel, but he missed the best candidate until God opened his eyes to see David's enormous potential (1 Samuel 16). When making decisions, the obvious answer isn't always the best, so it's imperative that we stay in tune with God for guidance.[280]

Decisions Justin Rose gained international attention as a teenager in the summer of 1998 because of some decisions he made. In July of 1998, this seventeen-year-old British golfer turned pro and became the youngest man to join the tour. Although his professional career did not begin with a sensational win like Tiger Woods, he has nonetheless been compared to America's youngest golfing celebrity. At the press conference where he spoke about his decision to become a pro golfer, Rose stated,

"Since my early childhood, I've always wanted to play professional golf and every decision I've taken has been with that in mind." What if every decision we made was done with Christ in mind? Every day we face a multitude of decisions. Psychologists estimate that we make about twelve hundred decisions per day when every minute decision is calculated into the equation. How many of those decisions are made with Christ in mind? It's a good question because the answer provides a good reading of our spiritual condition. Every believer is a servant of our Lord, and a good servant consistently makes sure his decisions are in keeping with his master's desires.[281]

Decisions We have all struggled with decisions. Sometimes it's a major decision that will impact the balance of our life. Other times it may be a fairly minor decision, but we wrestle with it nonetheless. During those decision-making times when we seem to get stuck and can't decide one way or the other, management expert Warren Bennis has a helpful suggestion. He says, "toss a coin." If while the coin is in the air, you find yourself hoping it lands on heads, you have shown which choice you think is best. Obviously you wouldn't allow the fate of a simple coin toss determine what you do, but it can help you discover the desire of your heart, and through prayer you can evaluate whether or not your desire is the same as God's (Psalm 37:4).[282]

Decisions "When you come to a fork in the road...take it." —*Yogi Berra* [283]

Delayed Gratification We've all paid ridiculous prices for a coke at a movie or ball game, but can you imagine paying $5 for just a cold drink out of a machine? That's actually what it costs you in lost earnings. If you passed on the coke and invested that dollar instead, it would be worth $5 in twenty years. Using a very conservative return of just 8.38 percent, the rule of thumb is $1 equals $5 if it is invested rather than spent. Translated to a larger scale, this means a $20,000 car ultimately costs you $100,000 in lost investment earnings. A simple upgrade of just $10,000 on a newer car takes $50,000 out of your future pocket. Obviously some expenses are necessary and you don't want to always squelch the present by only looking at the future, but having this basic insight might help you save more than you thought possible. If you can find just an extra $50 per week to invest, you will amass an additional $52,000 toward investments in twenty years (this doesn't even include your profit through interest earnings). So the next time you rent a movie, remember that $3.50 late fee is actually costing you $17.50.[284]

Delegation Do you ever struggle with delegation? In 1996, Kinko's spent a ton of money addressing the problem of delegation in a two-page ad targeted at the business community. The tag line read, "Trying to do it all yourself doesn't always make you look like a hero." Adjacent to these words was a full-page picture of an impeccably dressed CEO who looks as though he's posing for a boardroom portrait. Although he has a "no nonsense" expression on his face, he is wearing a large, conspicuous, red, clown's nose. Pastors and church leaders who fail to appropriately delegate responsibilities can not only hurt the effectiveness of their church, but can make themselves look rather foolish as well. Heed the words of Jethro (Exodus 18:17–27) and delegate appropriate tasks.[285]

Demographics Only 25 percent of Americans now live in rural areas.[286]

Demographics The world's population increases by 220,000 per day with 365,000 babies being born every day and 140,000 people dying each day.[287]

Denial In Lincoln, England, authorities suspected a man named Wayne Black of theft. The police apprehended a man who had a tattoo on his forehead that read, "I'm Wayne Black." When confronted about his identity, the man insisted he was not Wayne Black. Frequently our denials of guilt are just as lame as Black's. Although "guilt" may not be tattooed across our forehead, we know we're wrong.[288]

Depravity During the middle of July 2000, a shrimp boat sank off the coast of Louisiana. Severe weather took down a skiff named Bandit and the two men onboard. Alvin Latham, aged forty-six, survived, but his captain, Raymond Leiker, aged thirty-four, did not. Latham was rescued by a fishing boat on July 17 and told a remarkable story. He said the two men prayed together before the boat sank. Just after the prayer, Leiker got his foot caught in a fishing net and Latham tried to help free him. When he couldn't get the captain loose, Latham tried to swim for help. Unfortunately for Latham, Leiker's body was found and a much different story developed. An autopsy revealed stab wounds and severe blows to the head and arms. When confronted with this new information, Latham opted for the truth. He confessed to stabbing Leiker and hitting him with a pipe as they fought for the only life jacket on board. In the brawl for survival, the life jacket got washed overboard and Leiker fell into the water and died. Latham salvaged enough debris from the boat to keep him afloat until rescued. He was charged with second-degree murder. Depravity will lead us to kill for our own well-being then cover our actions with self-exalting fabrications.[289]

Depravity "Total depravity means not that at every point man is as bad as he could be, but that at no point is he as good as he should be." — *J.I. Packer*[290]

Depression An international health study revealed some startling information about depression. On September 15, 1996, the World Health Organization and the World Bank released their findings on the world's greatest health problems. Christopher Murray, professor of health economics at Harvard University, was the study's chief author. One of the most significant findings was their prediction that "major depression will become the second-leading cause of disability in 2020." Major depression was the fourth-leading cause of disability in 1990. On October 10, 1996, the sixth annual National Depression Screening Day was held. Dr. Douglas Jacobs, the Harvard psychiatrist who founded this program for free, annual screenings, said, "Over the last five years, we have screened two hundred thousand people. Seventy percent were ill and needed some kind of treatment." He pointed out that about seventeen million Americans agonize with this illness to varying degrees, and about thirty thousand take their own lives each year. The perceived progress of society is not diminishing depression. Technological advancements cannot provide the peace that only comes through Jesus Christ.[291]

Depression At any given moment, up to 5 percent of the United States population is depressed.[292]

Depression Residents of the United States spent $6.3 billion on antidepressants in 1998. The cost of depression-caused absenteeism and productivity loss is $23.8 billion.[293]

Depression While standing on the precipice of a new millennium, psychologists took the time to look back over the twentieth century and evaluate the mental health of Americans. In so doing, they discovered there has been a 300 percent increase in depression over the last one hundred years.[294]

Determination From 1960 to 1981, Walter Cronkite anchored the *CBS News*. It's a position he might have never attained had he let an earlier experience tarnish his determination. At the age of twenty-one, Cronkite was doing what he dreamed of, reporting the news. At KCMO in Kansas City, Missouri, Cronkite was the entire news department of the then small radio station. When he did not handle a story the way his program director insisted, Cronkite was fired. Determination kept him from quitting and he eventually found great success in the newsroom.[295]

Determination "If you think you are too small to be effective, you have never been in bed with a mosquito." —*Betty Reese* [296]

Diet Americans consume ten billion ounces of ketchup per year. That's about three bottles per person.[297]

Diet Americans drop $36 billion into vending machines each year.[298]

Diet Americans have one hundred tons of fat surgically removed each year.[299]

Diet Americans received 230,000 liposuction procedures in 1999.[300]

Diet French fries are ordered more often than any other restaurant food in America. In 1960, the average American ate 3.5 pounds of french fries per year. By 1997, that average rate of annual consumption had risen to 30 pounds.[301]

Diet Habitually skipping breakfast may shorten your lifespan by three to five years.[302]

Diet Humans chew more than one hundred tons of gum every year.[303]

Diet In the United States, over 50 percent of the adult population can be classified as obese.[304]

Diet On average, Americans consume thirty-six to forty hundred milligrams of sodium per day. That's the equivalent of two teaspoons of table salt or twenty times more than the human body needs.[305]

Diet The average American consumed 27.3 pounds of candy and gum in 1997. To accomplish this feat we spent $23.1 billion on 7.3 billion pounds of candy and gum.[306]

Diet The average American eats thirty-five thousand cookies in a lifetime.[307]

Diet The average American eats out 271 times per year, and each day Americans spend $970 million dining out.[308]

Diet The chances of an American woman eating her next restaurant meal at a McDonald's are one in eight.[309]

Diet Two baked potatoes, without all of the trimmings, have the same fat content as two french fries.[310]

Dieting Hopefully you aren't participating in a joint diet with your spouse because dieting couples are three times more likely to argue than those not watching their weight.[311]

Digital Enhancement When Britain's Prince Edward married Sophie Rhys-Jones in June of 1999, Prince William wasn't wearing his best smile. Princess Diana's eldest son couldn't quite muster a smile for the family photo so Prince Edward had his photographer do some digital magic. They simply scanned in a smile from another picture and made the seventeen-year-old prince look quite happy in the official family photo. The Royal Family's use of modern technology isn't that unusual, Hollywood does that kind of stuff all the time. But such behavior does remind us of how blurred the lines have become between reality and illusion, truth and fiction. Just like the Royal Family photo, we tend to believe we can simply alter things if they don't turn out like we want. Such delusional thinking will lead to the belief that we can easily alter the consequences of our actions and turn any predicament around to our preferred end. Digitally enhanced photos aren't that big of a deal, but when you cross the line and start trying to do the same thing in real life, you've taken the bait of deception and someone will get hurt.[312]

Diligence Each year one professional team walks away with the most prestigious trophy in football, the Vince Lombardi trophy, which is awarded to the Super Bowl champs. This $10,000 trophy represents the best of football. Its presence at the pinnacle of football achievement is a tribute to the man for whom it is named. Lombardi was the legendary Green Bay Packers's coach who led his team to victory in Super Bowl I and II. Ironically, he was an unlikely success. One expert predicted nothing but failure for the young coach. He said, "Vince Lombardi possesses minimal football knowledge . . . lacks motivation." Interestingly enough,

Hall of Fame quarterback, Bart Starr, remembers the following Lombardi quote as catalyst for his own success: "Perfection is not attainable, but in chasing it you could catch excellence."[313]

Dining Americans now consume nearly half of their calories away from home.[314]

Directions It started off as an unbelievable email, but that story about shooting dead chickens through windshields is actually true. NASA developed a gun to launch dead chickens nineteen thousand miles per hour at windshields of space shuttles to test their strength. Britain borrowed the gun to test it on their high-speed trains. When they fired it, the chicken smashed the windshield, ripped off the engineer's backrest, and embedded itself in the back wall of the cabin. The British went to the Americans and asked, "What went wrong?" The American scientists simply replied, "Thaw the chicken." NASA spokesman Mike Braukus confirmed the story is indeed true. He said, "That happened a year ago (1999)." We all know the drill . . . "when all else fails read the directions." With God's Word, we demonstrate wisdom by reading the directions first so "all else" won't fail.[315]

Disappointment The sixty-seven-year-old man stood on a curb as he watched his life's work burn up in December of 1914. Adding insult to injury, his property was only insured for $238,000, far less than the $2 million worth of damage. His twenty-four-year-old son, Charles, said, "My heart ached for him. He was sixty-seven, no longer a young man, and everything was going up in flames." When Charles found his father, he was surprised by his dad's request. He said, "Find your mother and bring her here. She will never see anything like this as long as she lives." The next morning the old man gathered his employees at the charred ruins and said, "There is great value in disaster. All of our mistakes are burned up. Thank God we can start anew." Three weeks later, Thomas Edison delivered his first phonograph. Disaster and disappointment can destroy us or refine us. The choice is ours to make.[316]

Discipleship "Christ is not looking for part-time followers." — *Anonymous* [317]

Discipleship Earthquakes seem to have become a regular part of the news. With each report on destruction there is usually a story of hope about a survivor who beat the odds and is found alive days after the big collapse. Tragically, many of these incredible survivors die soon after being unearthed from the rubble because of a rare phenomenon known as "rescue death." While trapped in debris, the circulation is greatly reduced. The crushed muscles produce a toxin called myoglobin, which surges to the vital organs when circulation is restored and throws the body into terminal shock. Doctors now know these survivors must be handled far more carefully after their rescue or they will most likely die. A simple solution of saline, bicarbonate, and artificial sugar retard the leakage of myoglobin from the muscles and greatly increase their potential for lasting survival. Discipleship should be viewed in much the same way. Those who have been trapped and crushed by the toxins of sin still need vital attention after they have been rescued from Satan's rubble. Left to their own they may not make it, but with proper care and attention they can be given the resources and help to let them thrive in their new-found freedom through Christ.[318]

Discipleship Every year, General Motors, AT&T, and IBM each spend more on the education and training of their employees than the combined educational budgets of all eight Ivy League universities. Just as a business depends on the continuing development of its workers, so too the Church needs its members to be continually sharpening and improving their discipleship skills.[319]

Discipleship Five out of six active churchgoers do not engage in discipleship.[320]

Discipleship Lazaro Orpusongu walked three days from his village in Tanzania to meet Tim and Annie Tidenberg. The couple were newly appointed missionaries with the Southern Baptist International Mission Board. Lazaro greeted the new missionaries with these words: "We are so glad you are here, because we are a hungry people." Tim assumed the man was looking for food so he told him their primary purpose in Longido was to train pastors, not to provide food. This headman of a Maasai settlement replied, "Oh, you misunderstand me. I am not asking for food. I am asking for the Bread of Life. We are hungry for God's Word." May such hunger define our level of commitment to ongoing discipleship.[321]

Discipleship Only 5 percent of the people living in the United States will either buy or read a book this year.[322]

Discipleship Spiritual development and growth can frequently seem frustrating and discouraging when we, or someone we are discipling, progresses at a much slower pace than desired. Patience and perseverance are good words to remember when this happens. That's exactly what is required to successfully grow a Chinese bamboo tree. This unique tree demands patience from its grower because all it visibly develops in the first four years is a little bulb and a small shoot. Although you've planted a tree, it appears you are growing nothing more than a big weed. Nonetheless, a mighty tree is taking shape because the first four years are devoted to the development of a massive root system. Then, in the fifth year, the Chinese bamboo tree uses that incredible foundation to launch as much as eighty feet of new growth in just one year. Growth that can be seen and measured often doesn't occur until there is a strong foundation upon which it can be built. There appears to be great wisdom in picturing discipleship like the development of a Chinese bamboo tree.[323]

Discipleship Two quotes from Tiger Woods speak to the subject of discipleship. Of his earlier days in junior golf, Woods said, "I really didn't know where the ball was going, except forward and a long way." Discipleship is not about finding seasoned pros who have mastered the Christian life, but about helping each other refine and improve our lives so we can experience clearer direction and greater control. It's also about encouraging one another with the reality that even though you might not be doing so well today, you may really excel in the years to come. When asked about improving his swing, Tiger Woods said, "I don't believe that there is such a thing as perfection. But I have always been a big believer of professional excellence, and that is what I try to achieve." Discipleship helps Christians realize they aren't perfect, and won't be this side of heaven, but they can and should be moving toward spiritual excellence. Even though he was talking about golf, Tiger Woods said a lot about discipleship as well.[324]

Discipline "God will deal with us as gently as he can and as harshly as he must." —*Jim Denison* [325]

Discipline UCLA sociologist, James Wilson, has observed an interesting fact about city life: The crime rate escalates on those streets where broken windows are not repaired. His study showed that the failure to replace windows makes an announcement to the public by saying the standards have been lowered and authority has been abandoned. Wilson sees such practices of disrepair as an invitation for further crime without the threat of adverse consequences. What is true on the street is also true in our personal lives. If we allow bad habits, inappropriate behavior, or unacceptable practices to go unchecked, we will be inviting further destruction into our lives. When we exercise the discipline needed to stop and change our damaging behavior, we will erect a fence of protection that will prevent further personal erosion.[326]

Discouragement Martin Luther's masterful piece, "A Mighty Fortress Is Our God," has been called the "Battle Hymn of the Reformation." James Moffatt described it as the "greatest hymn of the greatest man of the greatest period of German history." This triumphant song, taken from Psalm 46, has inspired legions of Christians for nearly five centuries. A significant twist to this victorious hymn is that Luther wrote it during a season of great depression. In 1527, Martin Luther experienced nearly a year of sickness and intense depression. It was a year of struggle, and one from which he wished he could have escaped, but in the depths of that pain and sadness, God brought forth a majestic hymn that has fortified the faith of millions. Martin Luther, like all of us, hoped for escape from his discouraging experience, but God used that difficult time to shape a mighty message of hope. Although none of us would run to discouragement, we might do well to spend less time trying to shake it and more time searching for the truths God wants to show us when discouragement comes our way.[327]

Distractions Do you have a cellular phone? If you do, your chances of being in an auto accident are 35 percent higher than non-phone-toting Americans. This discovery by the Rochester Institute of Technology is not surprising. When you talk on a phone while driving, your attention is distracted. The same happens to each of us spiritually. Talking on a phone is not inherently bad and neither are many of the activities we involve ourselves with each day. Yet, when we get too many of these things going at the same time, we can become distracted and thus put ourselves in a dangerous position. Like physical travel, spiritual journeys also require undistracted drivers.[328]

Divine Appointments In the summer of 1996, Pastor Bob Stewart was driving down a Texas highway in the church van. He was returning from a church-related function on a rather lazy summer night. While listening to the Texas Rangers baseball game on the radio, two young men pulled alongside his van and waved with great enthusiasm. Stewart waved back while guessing they were probably Christians who saw the church name emblazoned on the van. He continued down Interstate-35 as normal when the same two young men again pulled beside him. This time the passenger rolled down his window and shouted, "Where do you find the sinner's prayer?" Pastor Stewart pulled off to the shoulder and struck up a conversation with these two young men. He learned that one of the guys had been a Christian for just a few days and was telling his friend about Christ. The other young man was convinced and ready to receive Christ, but the new convert felt he needed some help. On the shoulder of I-35, Bob Stewart took this young man down another road, the Roman Road, and helped him pray to receive Christ. Pastor Stewart's encounter with two strangers on a summer night along I-35 remind us of God's passion for none to perish (2 Peter 3:9). May we always be available when he provides divine appointments for us to share his indescribable love.[329]

Divorce A 1998 study in Minnesota found that the majority of those who have gone through a divorce wish they had tried harder to work through their differences. This study, by the nonprofit Minnesota Family Institute, discovered 66 percent of those divorced look back with regret that they didn't give their marriage a better effort.[330]

Divorce A recent newcomer to the magazine stand reflects a true American tragedy. *Divorce Magazine* launched its inaugural issue in Chicago during the week of August 15, 1996. It was billed as the only publication catering to the divorcing and divorced. Publisher Dan Couvrette said readership is virtually guaranteed because more than one million divorces take place each year in America. Noted in the premiere issue was the mess of Prince Charles and Princess Diana. The routine court proceedings for the prince and princess to divorce was just $31. Prince Charles's final bill, however, was a lump-sum settlement of $26 million to his former (now deceased) wife. What a significant example of how easy a divorce initially appears, but how expensive (not just monetarily) it ultimately becomes.[331]

Divorce "Children tear up a house. Adults break up a home." —*John Drybred*[332]

Divorce In the Bible, God clearly states, "I hate divorce" (Malachi 2:16). Research continues to unveil why God despises the breakup of families. It has been a long-determined fact that children of intact families are better adjusted and have a higher level of satisfaction in life. Most recently, though, an international study by sociologists at the University of Illinois discovered another dynamic surrounding the issue of divorce. Many have contended that children of divorced parents don't fare as well because of the social stigma that has been associated with divorce. In essence, they were saying children do equally well in nations where divorce rates are high and there isn't a stigma attached to divorce. This study found the exact opposite. It revealed that children of divorced parents do best in countries where divorce is less common. Regardless of a nation's divorce rate or social views of it, divorce hurts and hampers its victims. God simply hates divorce because of the pain and problems it brings to those he loves.[333]

Divorce Of great concern to the Church is this fact that for the first time in history, the divorce rate among Christians is higher than the divorce rate among the general population" (27 percent versus 24 percent). In the midst of this tragedy we must redouble our efforts to shore up marriages by encouraging, training, and exhorting couples to make and uphold a lifelong commitment to one another.[334]

Domestic Violence In the United States, domestic violence is the leading cause of injury to women between the ages of fifteen and forty-four. The frequency of such violence is calculated to occur every nine seconds in America. Tragically, animals appear to receive better treatment than women in that there are over thirty-eight hundred shelters for abused and homeless animals, but only fifteen hundred shelter programs for battered women and children.[335]

Dope There is an obvious reason illegal drugs are referred to as dope. In March of 1997, Rosie Hill called the police to her home in Pensacola, Florida. Her complaint was about as strange as they come. She told the police officers that someone sold her fake crack. When the policeman arrived, Hill showed him two crack cocaine rocks that she had just purchased for $50. She said they tasted like baking soda. The officer tested the drugs and discovered that even if it wasn't good crack, it was real. He then returned to the police station with the dope— the two rocks of crack.[336]

Driving "Most people who drive like they own the road don't even own the car." —*Sam Ewing*[337]

Driving The average American car travels 11,000 miles per year. Cars and light trucks travel 2.2 trillion miles each year. Freight trucks and buses add another 206 billion miles. The total distance navigated on U.S. roads every year equals 300 round trips to Pluto.[338]

Drowsiness Drowsiness is a significant problem. In fact, it has become such a common problem that in 1990, "Insufficient Sleep Syndrome" was added to the International Classification of Sleep Disorders. It is blamed for thirty-eight thousand deaths per year. The National Highway Traffic Safety Administration has declared that two thousand of these deaths occur each year because of drowsy drivers. The direct cost of drowsiness is $16 billion per year, and the indirect annual cost (lost productivity) is estimated at $150 billion. Drowsiness affects seventy million Americans in large part because the populous is getting less and less sleep. In 1910, Americans averaged nine hours of sleep per night. Today, the average is only seven hours. We tend to idolize and seek to emulate such heroes as Thomas Edison who survived on brief naps. Unfortunately, this trend is not adding to our overall productivity and it's having a negative impact on our ability to be alert at school, work, home, and church. In 1979, drowsiness played a role in the Three-Mile Island nuclear power plant accident, and ten years later it contributed to the Exxon Valdez oil spill in Alaska. Max Hirshkowitz, research director of the sleep lab run by Baylor College of Medicine in Houston, Texas, says sleep deprivation began with the Industrial Revolution when machines started taking over. It was aggravated by Edison's invention of the light bulb, and has been accelerating with our increasingly competitive global economy. Significantly, Dr. Hirshkowitz notes, "People can grow accustomed to being tired, but they don't actually begin to need less sleep. We're fooling ourselves. We're running on half a battery, and we think we're OK. We don't even know what it's like to be alert anymore." That might explain why worldwide, four hundred billion cups of coffee are consumed every year. Maybe before we all try to make it on as little sleep as Edison, we should take time to consider another genius, Albert Einstein. This great scientist developed amazing thoughts after logging in eleven hours of sleep every night.[339]

Drug Abuse In 1996, a *U.S. News & World Report* cover story asked, "Can the church save America?" In this special report, their writers noted the impact churches are having on both individuals and communities. One notable fact was, "The two most reliable predictors of teenage drug avoidance is optimism about the future and regular church attendance." In an interview with John DiIulio, this political scientist from Brookings Institution said, "It is remarkable how much good empirical evidence there is that religious belief can make a positive difference." This statement was supported by a survey conducted by John Gartner of Loyola College of Maryland and David Larson of Duke University Medical Center. They found "over thirty studies that show a correlation between religious participation and avoidance of crime and substance abuse." Saying yes to church can help you say no to drugs.[340]

Drugs Every day in America eight thousand young people will try an illegal drug for the first time.[341]

Drugs In 1995, Americans spent $57.3 billion on illegal drugs of which $38 billion of that went for cocaine. That same $57.3 billion could have provided a four-year college education for one million American students.[342]

Drugs More people are carrying drugs than you might expect. The fact is, you've probably got some cocaine with you right now. Lee Hearn, chief toxicologist for the Dade County Medical Examiner Department in Miami, Florida, and Jay Poupko, a consulting toxicologist, sampled 135 bills from twelve American cities. Traces of cocaine turned up on all but four, and those four bills had just been printed. Hearn explained, "We know people use bills rolled up to snort cocaine, or folded into a packet to carry it." He went on to say that whenever contaminated bills come in contact with clean bills, little flakes of cocaine are transferred. The monetary fibers then absorb and trap tiny fragments of the drug. For this reason the money can be many times removed from the drug use but still contain traces of the powder. Knowing cocaine is in your pocket is a strong reminder that illegal drug use has reached epidemic proportions in America.[343]

Easter A study by the Barna Research Group revealed that 90 percent of Americans know the Bible teaches "Jesus was crucified, died, rose from the dead, and is spiritually alive today; that Jesus was born to a virgin; and that eventually all people will be judged by God." Easter brings large numbers of people who already know the facts, they just haven't embraced the faith.[344]

Easter The fact that Jesus died during Passover causes Easter to be filled with rich symbolism. One aspect of this symbolism involves the choosing and sacrificing of the Passover lamb. On the tenth day of the month, the Passover lamb was chosen (Exodus 12:3). This selection process caused each family to hope and pray for the coming of their Messiah. It was on this day that Jesus arrived in Jerusalem. It was God's perfect timing for communicating this was his Passover lamb. Traditionally, the daily sacrifice took place at 3:00 p.m. This would have also occurred on the day of Passover. At that time, the priest stood at the pinnacle of the temple (remember it was from this precipice that Satan sought to have Jesus miraculously attract a following) and blew the shofar, a ram's horn. Scripture records that Jesus died at 3:00 P.M. While hanging on the cross as God's sacrificial lamb, Jesus heard the shofar announcing that the lamb's throat had been slit and the sacrifice was complete. Upon hearing this, the Lamb of God triumphantly announced, "It is finished!"[345]

Eating Habits According to a 1996 report on dietary habits in the Archives of Adolescent and Pediatric Medicine, "Nearly one-quarter of all vegetables consumed by children and adolescents were french fries."[346]

Eating Habits Psychologists at Georgia State University have discovered that when you dine with other people, the amount of food you eat increases by as much as 44 percent. The bigger the group at your table, the more food you are likely to eat. Researchers at Johns Hopkins University have learned that people eat less while listening to classical music. Those who listen to rock music eat more and wolf it down more quickly. *Bon appetit!* [347]

Education High school seniors often want nothing more than to graduate and move into the world of high finance. For many graduates, getting started in a career seems more valuable than the energy and expense of college. Yet statistics reveal a college graduate will earn, in the course of his or her lifetime, $1.2 million more than a student who does not pursue an undergraduate degree. Just as there are significant financial advantages for continuing one's academic education, there are numerous advantages to believers who continue their education of God's Word.[348]

Effort Frank Sonnenberg is the author of *Managing with a Conscience*. From a recent edition of *Industryweek*, he cites the results of a study in which it was determined that "75 percent of American workers say they can be significantly more effective on their jobs." Three-quarters of our workforce acknowledges they could "do better." What is happening in the workplace is also occurring in the church. The majority of us could improve our productivity at work, at church, and at home if we would just make a better effort.[349]

Emotions As a young boy, the late John Kennedy, Jr. would go skiing with his family and relatives. On one particular slope he took a nasty fall. His uncle, Bobby Kennedy, skied down to the hurt young boy and found him crying. The senior Kennedy told his nephew, "Kennedys don't cry." John Kennedy looked up and replied, "This Kennedy cries." Little JFK showed superior wisdom to his uncle's stoic philosophy. It is a far healthier man who isn't afraid to reveal his emotions.[350]

Emotions Dr. Michael Jacobson cited a recent study in which patients were asked to recall various types of emotionally charged experiences while doctors monitored their physiological reactions. The first recalled experience was to be in an argument in which they became very angry or frustrated. The patient was to relive the experience in their mind for five minutes. The physicians noted that these patients' immune systems became depressed and the antibody levels dropped 55 percent. Six hours later, their immunity system was still depressed. Conversely, patients were told to reexperience an event involving love, care, compassion, or appreciation for someone. This emotional reaction caused the antibody level to rise 40 percent and it was still elevated six hours later. Emotions can provide very powerful ammunition for our demise or our deliverance.[351]

Emotions Edmund Muskie died on March 26, 1996. The Democratic politician from Maine served as a senator, governor, secretary of state, and in 1968, he was paired with Hubert Humphrey on the Democratic presidential ticket. As political analysts have evaluated his career, they consistently go back to a snow-covered day in February of 1972. This is the day on which many think Muskie experienced the turning point of his political future. He was campaigning for a run at the presidency just before the New Hampshire primary. On the back of a flat-bed truck he addressed a crowd in heavy, falling snow. In his speech,

Muskie commented on an article in the *Union Leader* newspaper that attacked his wife. In defense of his wife, the presidential hopeful became choked up and displayed his emotions. Even to this day there is debate as to whether or not he actually cried or that melting snow dripped down his face. Regardless of where the water started, the perception (or reality) of tears caused political experts to think he was unstable and might crack under pressure. Muskie himself would write of that day, "It changed people's minds about me. They were looking for a strong, steady man, and here I was weak." George McGovern won the Democratic nomination for president and Muskie never got another chance. During his presidency, Bill Clinton reminded some chiding reporters, "Presidents have feelings too." It is unfortunate that tears of sensitivity are seen as a weakness and a stern demeanor is interpreted as strength. Of the strongest man to walk this earth it was succinctly said, "Jesus wept."[352]

Encouragement A poverty-stricken boy in Kenya was blessed to not only receive some financial support from a British schoolteacher, but encouragement as well. When John Ngugi was young, he exchanged letters with a schoolteacher from Great Britain. This teacher was part of an organization that sought to provide financial relief through the sponsorship of children. John's letters to the teacher reflected a low opinion of himself. He described himself with phrases like, "I'm not smart, I'm not handsome, and I don't have many friends." He did include one positive though. He said, "But I am the fastest runner in my class." The teacher keyed in on that phrase and wrote back, "I'm proud of you. If you're a good runner, be the best runner you can be." He took her counsel to heart and in 1988 it paid off. As a member of Kenya's Olympic team, John Ngugi won the five thousand-meter run in Seoul, Korea. On his return trip to Kenya, he was routed through England and made his way to that caring teacher's house and gave her his gold medal. He told her, "I never would have run if you hadn't believed in me as a child." Maybe this British teacher had been impacted by what the Duke of Wellington said near the end of his life. When asked what one thing he would change if he could live his life again, he replied, "I would give more praise." Encouragement is a powerful and necessary tool in everyone's life.[353]

Encouragement Have you ever wondered whether or not you should offer a word of encouragement? Some people are worried their encouragement might give the recipient a big head. Others convince themselves that the person in question really doesn't need encouragement. Doug

Fields has proposed a helpful litmus test for determining if a person truly needs encouragement. He says, "If the person is breathing, they need encouragement."354

Encouragement Jaime Escalante became a well-known man after the movie, *Stand and Deliver*. This cinematized biography told the story of his creative and passionate teaching career in the barrio of East L.A. One of his most memorable teaching experiences never made it into the script of this popular movie. At the beginning of a school year, Escalante was stopped by a parent after a PTA meeting. The woman asked how her son, Johnny, was getting along in the classroom. The brilliant teacher thought she was the mother of another boy named Johnny. One boy was an excellent and compliant student, the other Johnny spent most of his time goofing off and disrupting the class. Assuming that her son was the better student, Escalante said, "I can't tell you how much I enjoy your son. I'm so glad he's in my class." The next day that problem child approached him and said, "My mom told me what you said about me last night. I haven't ever had a teacher who wanted me in his class." The boy made a complete turn around. Within a few weeks he was one of Escalante's hardest-working students and a true joy to teach. There are many people who are much like Johnny. Their frustrating behavior could be changed by the knowledge that somebody wants them around.355

Encouragement Mark Twain said, "I can live two months on one good compliment." The legendary UCLA basketball coach, John Wooden, understood the truth of Twain's statement and had a special way of making sure his players applied it. Wooden instructed his players that whenever a basket was made, the scoring player was required to smile, wink, or nod at the player who passed him the ball. When Coach Wooden gave these instructions to the team, one new player asked, "But coach, what if he's not looking?" Wooden replied, "I guarantee he'll look." He's right, everyone is looking for encouragement and affirmation.356

Encouragement Most men don't believe there is a man good enough to marry their daughter, but occasionally a man musters some confidence in his son-in-law. In 1943, Helen Robson married a man with a big dream but very little cash. Because there wasn't enough capital to launch his new venture, Helen turned to her father for a $20,000 loan. Mr. Robson took a big risk with his son-in-law and wrote the check. This enabled Helen and her husband to open up their first variety store in Newport, Arkansas, during 1945. It turns out Mr. Robson made a wise investment. When his son-in-law died in 1992, Helen Robson Walton was left with 10 percent interest in their chain of stores named Wal-Mart. Sam Walton made good on his father-in-law's confidence and left his widow $20 billion. A little faith and encouragement can sometimes reap enormous returns.[357]

Encouragement Sister Helen Mrosla taught at St. Mary's School in Morris, Minnesota. After several years of teaching, she found herself in a strange predicament one day. Her class of junior-high students was struggling to grasp a new concept in math. By the end of the week, their frustration was becoming very evident as they were getting edgy with each other. In a moment of inspiration, she had the students clear their desks and take out two sheets of paper. She instructed them to write the names of every student in the class with a space between the names. In the space, they were to write down the nicest thing they could say about each classmate. Sister Mrosla used her weekend to put each student's name on a separate sheet of paper and then wrote all of the classmates' remarks on that page. On Monday, she gave each student their page of positive remarks. Before long, the whole class was beaming and she could hear whispers of excitement. The papers of encouragement had accomplished their task so the class was able to resume their normal routine. Sister Mrosla never again heard about the papers until years later when she learned one of her favorite students, Mark Eklund, had been killed in Vietnam. After the funeral, Mark's parents gathered with Sister Mrosla and many of Mark's former classmates. His father pulled something from Mark's wallet and said, "We want to show you something. They found this on Mark when he was killed. When Sister Mrosla saw the two pieces of notebook paper she knew exactly what they were. These pages had been folded and refolded many times. Several strands of tape held the worn pieces together. Mark's mother said, "Thank you so much for doing that. As you can see, Mark treasured it." Mark's classmates then started talking about their lists. One kept it in the top drawer of his desk. Another had the list in her diary. One lady reached into her purse and said, "I carry this with me at all times." She then added, "I think we all saved our lists." Long after the frustrations of that week in math had been forgotten, the words of kindness were still being savored. The writing was worn, but the meaning still sparkled like new.[358]

Encouragement Thanks to a milkman, Cheryl Prewitt became the 1980 Miss America. As a child, Cheryl hung around her father's country grocery store. On a regular basis, the milkman would greet her by asking, "How's my little Miss America?" As a child she just giggled at his greeting, but as time went on, she started dreaming and believing she could be Miss America. Encouragement is powerful tool for lifting us beyond our own expectations.[359]

Encouragement The support we gain from one another is far more essential than what we readily assume. To comprehend the magnitude of our need for moral support we can compare our lives to that of a human spine. When the spine is supported by surrounding muscles, ligaments, and tendons, it can serve as a mighty lever for manipulating the body and lifting heavy objects. Yet when that same spine loses the support of soft tissues, it will buckle under a load of just five pounds. Without the encouragement and support of others we will quickly crumble, but if we are surrounded by care and concern, we can withstand the enormous loads that come our way.[360]

Encouragement While traveling from Pennsylvania to the West Coast, Ray and Carol Leaman decided to host a family "kindness day." The vacation game called for each family member to have their name placed in a hat, then everyone pulled out somebody's name. The object was for each person to administer preferential treatment to the family member whose name they had drawn. It turned out to be a great idea, so much so that their son, Durelle, called for another round the next day. He passed the hat full of names, and each person in the car started looking for opportunities to unload a special dose of kindness. It wasn't long, though, until they all realized a unique peculiarity . . . everyone was being especially nice to Durelle. With good reason, he had placed his name on every piece of paper in the hat. A good laugh for one family is a good reminder for everyone. People of all shapes and sizes are longing for more attention and encouragement every single day.[361]

Encouragement "Words of comfort, skillfully administered, are the oldest therapy known to man." —*Louis Nizer* [362]

Entertainment Men tire themselves in pursuit of rest. —*Laurence Sterne* [363]

Entertainment The lure of entertainment can pull us away from many important responsibilities. Nancy Sinatra was recently reminded of this truth when her famous father died. On the night of Frank Sinatra's death, his daughter Nancy was at home watching the TV show finale of *Seinfeld*. She was planning to visit her father that evening of May 14, 1998, but she got so involved in watching the TV that she never made it over to his house. While she became enthralled with the antics of Jerry Seinfeld on TV, her father went to the hospital and died. Ms. Sinatra said she initially felt bad about letting TV keep her from saying good-bye to her dad, but later resolved, "It didn't really matter because we had so many wonderful moments together in the past year that it didn't make any difference that I didn't actually get to say, 'Good-bye daddy, I love you.'" Given the opportunity to replay this event, I'm sure Ms. Sinatra would set the VCR and drive to the hospital because it does matter, and too often entertainment robs us of the things in life that matter most.[364]

Enthusiasm Al Michaels won the honor of being named "Sportscaster of the Year" for 1995. In his acceptance speech, he made reference to a comment he received when he was just a teenager. Curt Gowdy, an older announcer, told the young Michaels, "Your biggest problem down the road will be to maintain your enthusiasm." Thirty years later, the comment was still fresh in Michaels's mind. What is true for a sportscaster is also true for a Christian. The flames of enthusiasm usually burn most fervently when our experience with Christ is new. In time, disappointments, disagreements, and discontentment can quickly quench the warmth of your spiritual fireplace. A critical spirit usually follows and cobwebs form where the embers once burned. God seems more distant than he once did, and people feel more like bothers than brothers. If your spiritual enthusiasm has been on sabbatical, be of good cheer—it can be rekindled. Enthusiasm literally means "God in-breathed." When God breathed into the nostrils of Adam, the first man became "enthusiastic." To be enthused is to be alive as God intended. Paul told Timothy to "fan the flame" within him (2 Timothy 1:6). Why not a take a minute to fan your flame of spiritual enthusiasm by asking God to breathe new life into your soul. It will not only make you feel better about every*thing*, but every*one* as well.[365]

Eternal Life Ann Landers has been offering daily advice for decades. Whether it's a marital struggle, a physical problem, or a question about human irritants, Ms. Landers readily dispenses answers.

Surprisingly, a recent question left her somewhat speechless when she was asked, "Do you believe in a heaven and a hell?" Landers only replied, "It's a subject I haven't given much thought." Ann Landers's answer speaks for many people; they haven't given eternal life much thought. When considering the reality of eternal life and one's need for salvation, we generally fall into one of two camps: those who stop to think, or those who stop thinking.[366]

Eternal Life Cartoonist Johnny Hart scripted a sobering reminder in a layout of his *Wizard of Id*. Hart, who also draws *B.C.,* frequently includes his Christian perspective on the pages of his artwork. In this particular strip he had one of the characters call into question an obituary that ended with "to be continued." How true! Death is by no means the end because every life will "be continued" in eternity. Make certain your continuation will be with Jesus Christ.[367]

Eternal Life "My hopes of a future life are all founded on the Gospel of Christ." —*John Quincy Adams* [368]

Eternal Life "Only those who are prepared to die are really prepared to live." —*Dr. Nelson Bell* [369]

Eternal Life The plan of salvation seems to be simply defined in Scripture, but so many people continue to look for eternal life through other means. Rodney Hines was a thirty-six-year-old from Chico, California, when he was arrested for stealing, eating, and snorting the cremated remains of four people. He told the police he snorted some of the ashes and sprinkled others on his food because he wanted to obtain "everlasting life." The lost need to hear and the saved need to proclaim, "Jesus is the Way, the Truth, and the Life."[370]

Eternal Security Names like Arnold Palmer, Jack Nicklaus, and Tiger Woods roll from the lips of those who talk about golf's premier event, the Masters. One name that will probably never surface in a conversation about golfing legends is Doug Ford. Few people would have any idea that Ford won the 1957 Masters. He never won another green jacket and he hasn't made the cut since 1971 (four years before Tiger Woods was born), but he is invited to play in the Masters every year. The Masters's rules include a lifetime invitation to every champion of the event. Ford only won the tournament once, hasn't qualified with his golf skills in nearly three decades, and hasn't been able to break par in the event since

1958. Nonetheless, he gets to play in the tournament every year because on one single occasion he won the jacket. Our salvation is similarly linked to a single event. If we have at one point made a commitment of our eternal security to Christ, we do not need to requalify. Regardless of our abilities and performance, the invitation of eternal and abundant life remains constant.[371]

Euthanasia One in five cases of assisted suicide occurring in the Netherlands takes place without the patient's consent.[372]

Evangelism A top salesman was interviewed to learn some of his secrets for success. In the course of this interview, the reporter asked how many calls he made on a prospect before giving up. The salesman replied, "It all depends on which one of us dies first." God has called every believer to evangelize with equally dogged determination.[373]

Evangelism Despite the widespread feelings of being evangelistically inadequate, a survey conducted by Leadership and Church Growth Institute of Lynchburg, Virginia, revealed that 97 percent of lay people believe "every Christian has the responsibility to share his or her faith with the lost."[374]

Evangelism Doug Murren is a highly respected pastor and ministry strategist. In a recent conference he exhorted Christians to share the gospel. He grievously reported that, "Only 10 percent of the people who die in the United States each year are born-again Christians." Tragically, more people will argue about the accuracy of his figures than the reality that the majority of Americans are going to hell.[375]

Evangelism During the preparations for one of Luis Palau's crusades in Latin America, a very poor, unshaven man came to one of their week-long biblical counseling courses. It was unusual to see a man of this condition attending an in-depth training session. Most often, those with a better education and social standing are the ones who take an active role in this type of intensive preparation. The illiterate man attended every class, but those in leadership didn't expect him to do much counseling. Several weeks later, all of the available counselors were busy when a physician walked in. This shabbily dressed man immediately greeted the doctor and took him into a room for counseling. Once the director discovered what had happened, he became deeply concerned. When the doctor came out, the director asked if he needed any help. The physician replied, "No, thank you. This fellow has helped me very much." The next day that same doctor showed up with two other colleagues and asked to see the shoeless man. By the end of the week, that illiterate man had led four doctors and their wives to Christ. God needs nothing more than available servants.[376]

Evangelism Ellie, an elderly Jewish woman, told a Tennessee congregation about the great price that was paid for her to find Christ. She was imprisoned in a concentration camp with no hope for survival. Convinced that her only chance hinged on an escape, she meticulously made her plans. On the night she broke for freedom, everything went well until she tried to scale the barbed-wire barrier. She was halfway up the fence when she was spotted by a NAZI SS guard. At gunpoint, he screamed for her to stop. She fell to the ground bleeding and weeping. Her only hope had vanished. Miraculously, the guard recognized her as a classmate from school. During their adolescent years they had been best of friends, but now they were on opposite sides of the war. Agonizing over her plight, Ellie cried out to her friend: "Oh, Rolf, go ahead and kill me. Please, I have no reason to live." The guard replied, "Ellie, you're so wrong. There's everything to live for so long as you know who to live for. I'm going to let you go. I'll guard you until you climb the wall and get on the other side. But would you promise me one thing?" Ellie couldn't believe what was happening. In disbelief she asked, "What is it, Rolf?" He said, "Promise me when you get on the other side and become free, that you will ask one question continuously until someone answers it for you. Ask, 'Why does Jesus Christ make life worth living?' Promise me, Ellie. He's the only reason to live. Promise me you'll ask until you get the answer." Ellie shouted, "Yes, I promise, I promise!" She then scampered over the barbed wire. As she ran for freedom she heard several gunshots. She glanced over her shoulder to see if Rolf had changed his mind and was now seeking to kill her. Instead she saw the bloodied, dead body of her friend. Upon realizing that he had aided her escape, the other guards shot him for his treason. The hasty promise she had made to gain freedom now took on new meaning. This young man gave his life for her to have a chance at discovering true freedom in Christ. Ellie told that Tennessee church, "I did exactly as Rolf told me to do. I kept asking and asking, until one day I met someone who answered his question. I am a Christian today because Rolf sacrificed his life for me." May our witness for Christ be as valiant as that brave young man.[377]

Evangelism "I'm thankful for a church that remembers that we exist primarily for those who aren't here yet." —*Bob Reccord*[378]

Evangelism In 1800, Napoleon led his troops across the Alps as they returned to Italy. The journey was hardened by the snow, but Napoleon pressed on. To keep the troops moving in sequence, a drummer played a cadence by which they marched. One of these drummers slid on some ice and went over a large precipice. He fell into a drift of snow far below the advancing troops, but was miraculously unhurt. He began to beat his drum with the signal for relief, but not a single soldier broke rank because Napoleon commanded, "March on!" When it became obvious that nobody was coming to his aid, the young drummer stopped playing the cadence of relief. Those who marched that day never forgot what they heard next. After several minutes of silence, the abandoned drummer began to beat the funeral dirge. He played for his own funeral. Countless people who are lost without Christ will be left to play their own funeral march if we as Christians don't break rank with our agendas and routines to provide spiritual relief.[379]

Evangelism In Cecil Northcott's, *A Modern Epiphany*, he tells of a discussion among Christian young people. These youths had come together at a camp where many nations were represented. On this particular night, they were talking about various ways to share the gospel. The question came to a young lady named Maria, who was from Africa. Her response was poignant. She said, "We don't have missions or give pamphlets away. We just send one or two Christian families to live and work in a village, and when people see what Christians are like, then they want to be Christians too." What a plan for evangelism—Christians living such godly lives that neighbors can't help but want to receive Christ as well.[380]

Evangelism Josh McDowell has told the story of an acquaintance who serves as an executive hirer, or as the industry says, a "headhunter." This man has spent an enormous amount of time interviewing executives. Although many words are exchanged in these interviews, his top priority is to get a clear and concise response to his most strategic question, "What's your purpose in life?" He's amazed at how often this one simple inquiry throws top-notched executives for a loop. One day while he was in the interviewing process, he got a razor-sharp answer to his loaded question. After going through his usual routine of loosening up the prospect through several minutes of disarming conversation, he asked, "What's your purpose in life, Bob?" Without blinking an eye, this schooled businessman replied, "To go to heaven and take as many people with me as I can." Regardless of profession, that's a mission statement every believer should embrace.[381]

Evangelism Many Christians can take comfort in the fact that the founder of Evangelism Explosion has not always been a soul winner. By his own admission, Dr. James Kennedy said he did not attempt to reach people for Christ because of a serious "back problem." He said the ailment involved a "wide yellow stripe that ran up his spine and connected to his jawbone." He was a shy minister who had trouble turning any conversation toward Christ. Ironically, a friend invited Kennedy to be the guest "evangelist" in a revival meeting. The majority of their time was spent visiting those who were known to be lost. During these personal visits, it became very apparent that the young Kennedy did not possess evangelistic skills. The hosting pastor assumed the evangelist's role and led over fifty people to Christ that week. Kennedy returned home both humiliated and challenged. He prayed for God to help him overcome his fears and reach out to the lost around him. The new dynamic of intentionally sharing the gospel transformed his church of seventeen people. As the senior pastor of Coral Ridge Presbyterian Church in Fort Lauderdale, Florida, his weekly messages are televised throughout America and in over fifty other international regions. He founded Evangelism Explosion and the principles of this approach to witnessing has been taught in over one hundred countries. Fear is not a legitimate reason to remain quiet about the gospel. It is something God can use to make us dependent and obedient servants of his. God used an evangelistic coward to launch a worldwide emphasis on evangelism. He could do the same through you or me.[382]

Evangelism Only 4 percent of Christians came to faith after age thirty.[383]

Evangelism On October 8, 1871, D. L. Moody made what he called the worst mistake of his life. On that particular Sunday, Moody spoke to a capacity crowd at Farwell Hall on the subject, "What then should I do with Jesus." At the conclusion of the service, Moody told the audience to "Take this text home with you and turn it over in your minds and next Sabbath . . . decide what to do with Jesus of Nazareth." That night, the terrible Chicago fire charred 3.5 square miles, destroyed eighteen hundred buildings, left ninety thousand people homeless, and claimed three hundred lives. Years later, Moody said, "I have never dared to give an audience a week to think over their salvation since." When fishing for men we mustn't fail to draw the net.[384]

Evangelism Personal evangelism is scary work for most of us. We would like to think that those who really stay involved in soul winning are unaffected by fear. Consequently, we rationalize that our fear exempts us from witnessing. Consider the following about personal evangelism. Luis Palau is an internationally known evangelist who said, "When it comes to witnessing to your neighbor, even an evangelist has problems." Leighton Ford, also a world-renowned evangelist, admitted, "I have preached to crowds of sixty thousand people and yet I still get nervous in speaking to an individual about Christ." You're not alone if you find personal evangelism frightening, so let there be strength in numbers and join the ranks of those who wrestle with their fears because they believe salvation is worth the fight.[385]

Evangelism Prunes have a bad image in the United States, so they're getting a new name. California, which produces 99 percent of the prunes in America, appealed to the Food and Drug Administration to market prunes as "dried plums." Extensive research disclosed what most of us already knew, prunes are thought to be exclusively for old people with problems. "Dried plums," however, are perceived as a healthy snack for anybody. For this reason, authorization to change their name comes as a sweet reprieve for the California Prune Board. They will begin marketing "dried plums" toward the beginning of 2001 with "prunes" on the label in small print. By 2003, "prunes" will fall from the label all together. So how does all of this relate to witnessing? Prunes are higher in antioxidants than any other fruit, but people won't buy them because of the stigma. That sounds a bit like the gospel sometimes. It's exactly what people need, but they have this negative perception about religion. Without changing the message or its content, we may need to simply change our strategy to make that which we preach more appealing. We're not talking about watering down the gospel, we're talking about improving our presentation of it (in both word *and* deed) so lost people will have a greater desire for what Christ has to offer. That's what Jesus did when he turned to some fishermen and piqued their interest by inviting them to join him in "fishing for men." With the woman at the well, he got her attention by doing more than just saying, "You need to get saved." He drew her into the Kingdom by creatively speaking about a water that was different from that which was in the well. The California Prune Board won't be changing their content, just the way it's presented. Maybe we as Christians need to consider doing the same.[386]

Evangelism Statistics show that out of every six times the gospel is presented, one person will receive Christ.[387]

Evangelism The Middle Tennessee Billy Graham Crusade was held in Nashville during June of 2000. Adelphia Coliseum, built to accommodate the Tennessee Titans, was used as a platform for the gospel and thousands responded to God's call. In the shadows of this new stadium, a small band of believers gathered every Tuesday during its construction and prayed that God would use it for his purposes. Indeed he has. One fifty-six-year-old man who accepted Christ on the second night of this crusade said, "I've been waiting for this all my life." In our communities there are countless others like that middle-aged man who are waiting to hear the good news of God's redeeming love.[388]

Evangelism Through the years, Vince Lombardi's thoughts on winning have been frequently misquoted. The legendary coach of the Green Bay Packers is purported to have said, "Winning isn't everything, it's the only thing." In reality, Coach Lombardi said, "Winning is not everything . . . but making the effort to win is." Christians, more than any other group of people, should follow this advice and make every effort to win people to Christ.[389]

Evangelism We sometimes forget that an evangelist is literally "a messenger of good news." Bob LeVitus writes a syndicated column called "Dr. Mac." In his weekly article, LeVitus shares tips for getting the most from a Macintosh computer. He provides information about software, hardware, system manipulation, shortcuts, and various other pieces of "good news" for Mac users. Ironically, his official job description is defined as "director of evangelism for Power Computing Corporation" in Austin, Texas. Thanks to this computer expert, we've been reminded that evangelism involves "good news." Let's proclaim the gospel with renewed enthusiasm and "do the work of an evangelist" (2 Tim. 4:5).[390]

Evolution "Evolution requires tremendous faith. It believes that a universe created itself in violation of its own laws." Such are the words of mathematician John Heffner. He is head of the math department at Kilgore High School and teaches on the faculty of Kilgore College. He earned his undergraduate math degree from Texas A&M University, and his master's degree was completed at Stephen F. Austin University. Heffner, who rejected all claims of Christianity as a youth, now devotes all of his extra time to pursuing a deeper understanding of biblical creation. One of his specialties involves using mathematical statistics to develop population growth and density models. Through the use of math, Heffner notes we can prove the accuracy of the biblical account of Noah and a cataclysmic flood about forty-five hundred years ago. He notes, "Both the creationist and evolutionist agree that there are currently the same number of people on the planet (about 6.2 billion). If you start with eight people and come forward from forty-five hundred years ago, you get 6.2 billion people." You don't need to be a rocket scientist to believe in creation, but it's nice to have one around who can statistically prove what we already knew to be true.[391]

Evolution To look at the complexity of this world and the people who inhabit it, it is not logical to assume that all of this just accidentally happened. To believe such an argument would require one to look down at his watch and declare, "My watch is the product of a recent explosion at a metal factory." Voltaire likewise compared our vast universe to the relationship of a watch and a watchmaker. He said, "The world embarrasses me, and I cannot think that this watch exists and has no watchmaker." Even as a non-Christian Voltaire was correct in his assessment of God when he said, "God has made thee to love him, and not to understand him." "By faith we understand that the worlds were prepared by the word of God . . ." (Hebrews 11:3)[392]

Examples "You are never completely worthless. You can always set a bad example." —*Robert Payne* [393]

Excellence "Excellence is a habit, not an event." —*Aristotle* [394]

Excellence "Excellence is the gradual result of always wanting to do better." —*Pat Riley* [395]

Excellence "Quality is a race with no finish line." —*William Johnson, CEO, Ritz-Carlton Hotels* [396]

Excellence Van Cliburn mastered the piano like very few people. His excellence at the ivory keys is known throughout the world.

In a conversation with Howard Hendricks, the famed pianist talked about his discipline in practice. After years of success he still spent eight to nine hours a day practicing the piano. During those ongoing, lengthy practice sessions he did finger exercises every day for two straight hours. Van Cliburn's excellence at the piano most certainly includes natural talent, but the bulk of his success can be attributed to the arduous price he has paid in the practice room. If we hope to likewise excel in any venture for our Lord we must be willing to exert a great deal of energy and effort in both prayer and practice.[397]

Excuses While ministering in Dublin, Ireland, Sidney Laing wrote a satirical piece in response to the various excuses he's heard for not attending church. His work is entitled, "Ten Reasons Why I Never Wash." Included on his list are the following: "I was made to wash as a child. . . . People who wash are hypocrites. . . . Those who wash think they're cleaner than other people. . . . There are so many different kinds of soap, I could never decide which one was right. . . . I used to wash but it got boring so I stopped. . . . I still wash on special occasions like Christmas and Easter. . . . None of my friends wash. . . . I'm still young, when I'm older and a bit dirtier I might start washing. . . . People who make soap are only after your money." It's amazing how ridiculous these excuses seem when thinking about a bath, but when it comes to church, some folks believe these excuses are nothing less than legitimate reasons.[398]

Exercise "Those who think they have not time for bodily exercise will sooner or later have to find time for illness." —*Edward Stanley* [399]

Exhortation The well-known author, James Michener, carried a memory that inspired him to continue being a productive writer even in his old age. When he was five years old, a neighboring farmer drove eight nails into the trunk of an aging, unproductive apple tree. The following autumn, that tired old tree produced a bumper crop of delicious apples. Little Michener asked the farmer how this "miracle" occurred. The farmer explained, "Hammering the rusty nails gave it a shock to remind it that its job is to produce apples." Like that old apple tree, there are times in our lives when we need a good jolt to get us back on course and make us productive believers once again. Encouragement is a wonderful tool that should never be discarded, but there are also times when a strong word of exhortation is needed to alter our unproductive behavior.[400]

Failure Don't give up when you fail. Learn from your mistakes and you might be surprised by what happens to your blunders. Ivory Soap wasn't supposed to float, but a manufacturing error became its top selling point. The material used to manufacture Kleenex tissues was originally invented as a gas-mask filter in World War I. It later failed as a cold cream remover, but finally hit success when it was repackaged as a disposable handkerchief. Now Americans buy nearly 200 billion tissues a year. The fact is, 80 to 90 percent of new product launches fail, so don't be afraid to try something new, and keep on trying it until you find the right mix.[401]

Failure Most people see failure as a disaster to be avoided at all costs. But failure doesn't have to be the end, sometimes it can be the means to a very successful end. Thomas Edison said, "I failed my way to success." Ken Olan is a motivational speaker who has given a new twist to the word "fail." He uses it as an acrostic for Final Attempt In Life. Failure occurs if we give up and quit. Citing a Harvard Business School study, Olan described how important a don't-quit attitude is for the equation of success. Harvard noted there are three aspects of success that can be best understood by drawing a triangle. The left side is knowledge, the right leg is skill, and the foundation on which these two rest is Attitude. That's because, as their research indicated, your attitude carries 93 percent of the weight in determining whether or not you succeed or fail. Maybe that's why Thomas Edison ended up inventing the light bulb. When asked about his numerous failed attempts with the light bulb, Edison remarked, "I never failed once. I invented the light bulb. It just happened to be a two thousand-step process." Likewise, the apostle Paul knew the power of attitude when he wrote Philippians 2:5 and 4:8.[402]

Failure One of the rich Christmas traditions is watching the classic movie, *It's a Wonderful Life*. Some people can't celebrate Christmas without watching it at least once during the holiday season. Each year consumers buy six hundred thousand copies of it on video. But you would have never thought this would be possible when it opened on December 20, 1946. Frank Capra's classic was a box-office flop. It cost $3,180,000 to make and lost $480,000 (a sizable figure back then). It didn't win a single Oscar. The film that ended up with George Bailey being played by Jimmy Stewart instead of the first choice, Cary Grant, seemed destined to become nothing more than a financial disaster. But the failure of fifty years ago is now a monumental success. When failure seems to scare you, take a minute to think about the movie and the message of this Christmas classic. As Robert Schuller has so appropriately said, "All successful people are experienced in failure."[403]

Failure Our failures in life are generally not quite as catastrophic as we first think. Failure is simply one variable in the equation of life. Michael Jordan is helping teenagers realize this truth by opening up about the failures that occurred during his illustrious career on the basketball court. In *Famous Black Quotations For Teens*, Jordan writes, "I've missed more than nine thousand shots in my career. I've lost almost three hundred games. Twenty-six times I've been trusted to take the game-winning shot and missed. I've failed over and over again in my life. And that is why I succeed." Our failures can be excellent trainers for success, and our acknowledgment of shortcomings can be a wonderful encouragement to others as well.[404]

Faith Adoniram Judson (1788–1850) served in Burma as a foreign missionary. For the first seven years of his ministry he did not see a single convert to Christ although he diligently worked to bring the message of Christ to the Burmese people. His longing was to translate the Scriptures so these people could know God. His work was viewed as hostile to the government so he became a political prisoner. His small prison cell had a little window just above the ground. Each day, his wife, Anne, would bring food to him and hand it through this small barred window. One day she told him of a letter from their supporters back home. These Christians wanted to know what the Judson's needed. From behind bars, after seven years of not reaching a single person for Christ, Judson said without hesitation, "Tell them to send a communion set. We're going to need it someday." He was later released from prison and translated the Bible. Today, more than 600,000 Baptist Christians can trace their roots to this man of faith who saw the need for a communion set.[405]

Faith A safari hunter was startled by the loud screeching of a bird. When he caught sight of the bird, it was darting back and forth around its nest. He was perplexed by all the racket until he noticed a huge snake moving up the tree. The hunter could have easily aided the bird with one shot from his gun, but he was captivated by the drama before him. As the snake slithered up the tree, the bird became silent and flew from the nest. It now seemed as though the snake would dine without resistance. But before the reptile could reach the nest, the mother bird returned with a leaf in her beak. She carefully placed the leaf over her babies then flew to another tree. The snake raised his head to strike, but then hesitated. It froze as if it had met a foe. Slowly it recoiled from the nest and wound its way down the tree. The puzzled hunter related the event to native Africans when he returned to the camp. They laughed with enthusiasm as they explained this unlikely victory of the bird. The leaf that the mother bird used to cover her nest was poisonous to the snake. What looked like nothing more than a leaf was, in fact, a life-saving shield. Our faith may at times feel as flimsy as a leaf, but God's Word reminds us that it is a shield against the attacks of our serpentine enemy (Ephesians 6:16).[406]

Faith A small congregation in the foothills of the Smokey Mountains encountered a major problem when they built their new church. A church member had willed the growing church some property so they relocated and constructed a new sanctuary. Just ten days before their dedication service, the building inspector told them their parking lot was too small for that size building. He informed the pastor they could not occupy the facility until they doubled the parking. Unfortunately, they had already used every usable square foot of their property. They backed up to a mountain so their situation seemed hopeless. Rather than lose hope, the pastor called a special prayer meeting and asked for those with "mountain-moving faith" to be present. A couple of dozen people showed up for a prayer time that lasted nearly three hours. With confidence, the pastor said, "We'll open next Sunday as scheduled." The following morning, the pastor was greeted by a contractor who came with a unique request. He explained his position as the builder of a shopping mall and told of a problem they were having in getting fill dirt. He asked if the church would be willing to sell them dirt from the mountain on the back of their property. In exchange for their prompt agreement, the contractor would level the surface and pave it at no charge. The mountain movers' prayer had been answered and their church was packed for the dedication service that next Sunday.[407]

Faith A. W. Tozer eloquently described the unusual characteristics of a Christian who lives by faith. "A real Christian is an odd number anyway. He feels supreme love for one whom he has never seen, talks familiarly every day to someone he cannot see, expects to go to heaven on the virtue of another, empties himself in order to be full, admits he is wrong so he can be declared right, goes down in order to get up, is strongest when he is weakest, richest when he is poorest, and happiest when he feels worst. He dies so he can live, forsakes in order to have, gives away so he can keep, sees the invisible, hears the inaudible, and knows that which passeth knowledge." To live by faith means embracing a lifestyle that contradicts most of life.[408]

Faith Best-selling author, Barbara Johnson, tells a light-hearted story about a man who struggled to understand the balance between faith and works. A farmer of great faith became a flood victim when an adjoining river started extending beyond its banks. Although the flood was extremely serious, the waters rose rather gradually. At first the farmer had plenty of time to vacate his place, but he chose to trust God. A neighbor drove to the farmer's house in a jeep and urged him to leave while there was a safe passage out. The farmer assured his friend that, "God will save me." The waters continued to rise and the man was forced to the second story of his house. Members of the local police department pulled alongside the farmer's upstairs balcony in a boat and told the man to get in. He graciously expressed appreciation for their concern but said, "That won't be necessary. God will save me." Within just a few hours the waters started to rise more quickly and the current began moving more rapidly. The man was forced onto the rooftop. As he sat clutching the bricks of his chimney, a helicopter swooped in for a daring rescue. The farmer waived off the dangling sling and yelled, "God's gonna save me." Shortly thereafter the man was washed away to his death. When he stood before the Lord he demanded an answer for God's negligence. God replied, "What do you mean? I sent a jeep, a boat, and a helicopter, but you wouldn't budge!" Faith is believing God will do his part while works is making sure we do our part.[409]

Faith Dr. Gordon Alles was a noted chemist who pioneered the development of insulin for treating diabetes. Alles's extensive research on insulin helped lead to its purification for human use. His daily work afforded him the luxury of knowing how to best treat diabetes, yet he died of that very disease. While at home, he collapsed in a diabetic coma and died soon after in a Pasadena, California, hospital. Alles had the knowledge and resources for treating his illness, but failed to act on it.[410]

Faith "Faith is a day by day process in which God will show us what to do moment by moment." —*Anonymous* [411]

Faith In a village near Glasgow, Scotland, you can find Harper Memorial Church. It is named after its founder, John Harper. This Baptist minister felt the call to preach at the age of seventeen. For nearly six years after his calling, he worked in a paper mill during the day and preached wherever he could find an audience at night. In his early twenties, Harper became a full-time pastor and started several churches. He later moved to London and enjoyed such success that he was invited to preach a revival at Moody Church in Chicago during the winter of 1911. The meeting went so well that he was invited back the following spring. On April 11, 1912, Harper boarded the *S.S. Titanic* to return to Moody Church. The thirty-nine-year-old widower traveled in second-class with his six-year-old daughter, Nana. When the ship's fate became evident, Harper wrapped his daughter in a blanket and made certain she got on a lifeboat. He then began calling out, "Women, children, and the unsaved into the lifeboats first!" He took off his life jacket and gave it to another man. A man who was later saved by the *S.S. Carpathia* gave even greater detail to the faith of John Harper. He said he saw Harper struggling to stay afloat. The minister called out in the dark, "Are you saved?" The man replied, "No." Harper then quoted Acts 15:31, "Believe in the Lord Jesus, and you shall be saved." This survivor gave no response and the waves soon separated the two men. Shortly thereafter, the currents brought them near each other again. Harper repeated his question, "Are you saved?" The man declared, "No, I can't honestly say that I am." Harper once again quoted from Acts before the two drifted apart in the sea. Not long afterwards, Harper sank to his death. This man who had encountered the sheer strength of Harper's unfailing faith said, "There, alone in the night, with two miles of water beneath me, I believed. I am John Harper's last convert." May such bold faith be found in us all![412]

Faith Koi are exotic fish that originated in Japan. The Japanese revere these fish and Americans are collecting them in rapidly increasing numbers. They come in at least sixty varieties, and no two fish are exactly alike. For the amateur collector, you can buy a small domestic koi for as little as $7.50. The starting price for a respectable Japanese koi is $500, and a grown Japanese koi can be sold for as much as $10,000. The most unusual aspect of these exotic fish is how they grow. Koi can grow up to three feet in length or remain just a few inches long. Their growth is determined by the size of the pond. If the pond is large, the fish will be large. If the pond is small, the fish will remain small. Regardless of their size, they can live up to seventy-five years. Faith seems to have koilike qualities in that it grows or remains small based on the environment in which we keep it. If we surround ourselves with few challenges and small aspirations for spiritual growth, then our faith will stay small. But if we stretch our faith and seek to know God in all of his fullness, then we will end up with a larger view of God and an ever-increasing faith.[413]

Faith "Our faith becomes practical when it is expressed in two books: the date book and the checkbook." —*Elton Trueblood*[414]

Faith "The future belongs to those who set their sights on what is humanly unattainable." —*Wilbur Howard*[415]

Faith Wang Ming Dao served as the pastor of Peking's largest church. During Communistic persecution, he was thrown into prison because of his testimony and ministry. At the hands of his perpetrators, he was tortured for his faith. Fearing even greater suffering, Dao recanted his belief in Christ and was released by the authorities. He quickly regretted his decision and was seen walking the streets of the city weeping and mumbling, "I am Judas! I have betrayed my Lord!" Within a few weeks, he was unable to bear the guilt and shame any longer. He returned to the Communist authorities, confessed his faith in Christ, and asked to be put back in prison. For the next twenty-seven years he suffered the abuse of prison life, but never again entertained the thought of denying his Lord. When Dao was released at the end of his life, the Chinese church considered him a hero who had given strength and assurance to the many who faced the perpetual threat of persecution and imprisonment. Enduring faith will experience doubts, struggles, and disappointment. It happened to John the Baptist (Matthew 11:2–3) and it will happen to every person who seeks to walk in Christlike obedience. In times of spiritual crisis, may we be inspired by both the success and failure of people like Wang Ming Dao (1 Peter 5:9).[416]

False Prophecy On July 6, 2000, Sylvia Mitchell received a sentence of five to fifteen years in prison for poisoning her husband, Andrew Vlasto. The thirty-five-year-old wife apparently plotted to knock off her eighty-five-year-old spouse to inherit his $500,000 estate. Within weeks of their 1993 wedding, Mitchell began feeding Vlasto powerful drug cocktails. He ultimately died in a New York hospital after being treated for a series of drug overdoses. His death came just eighty-three days after their wedding, and she is now serving time in prison for second-degree manslaughter. You'd think Mitchell would have seen all of this trouble coming her way because, after all, she made her living as a fortune-teller in Manhattan.[417]

False Prophets Actor Dean Martin died on Christmas Day, 1995. His memorial service was held three days later in Los Angeles. During the funeral, actress Shirley Maclaine was on hand to comfort the mourners. She said she talked with Martin just an hour before the service and he told her how happy he was in heaven. Ms. Maclaine sounded like a spokesperson pitching a new feature for long-distance calling. Every person's eternal destiny is determined by their response to Jesus Christ, not the whimsical speculation of a New Age channeler. False prophets are always hinting that Jesus Christ is not the only way.[418]

Family An in-depth study of American's values was completed just before President Clinton admitted sexual impropriety on August 17, 1998. The research was conducted by *The Washington Post* in collaboration with Harvard University and the Henry Kaiser Family Foundation. Among the most significant findings was the fact that 90 percent of Americans believe our country "would have many fewer problems if there was more emphasis on traditional family values." But, of these 90 percent who feel we must recapture a greater focus on traditional values, 70 percent think "we should be more tolerant of people who choose to live according to their own moral standards even if we think they are wrong." Although the democracy of America is designed to foster freedom, we must decide which ideal we are going to embrace: traditional family values that will reduce the multiplicity of problems plaguing our land, or tolerance of immorality, which now means acceptance, endorsement, and financial support. The health of our nation's families depends largely on that single choice.[419]

Family Between the ages of ten and fifteen, the amount of time children spend with their families decreases by half.[420]

Family Dr. Alvin Reid was in the middle of a very busy traveling schedule that caused him to be away from home more than usual. He called home from a hotel and as he talked with his four-year-old daughter, she said, "I miss you, Daddy." She then asked, "Why are you gone?" The seminary evangelism professor replied, "Because I'm telling people about Jesus." She repeated, "Why?" He then reminded her, "Because God told me to." His daughter then said in a most dejected voice,

"Daddy, why can't God tell you to come home?" These words led Dr. Reid to seriously rework his calendar. Just as God calls us to tell others about His love, He also calls us to go home and demonstrate that love to our families.[421]

Family Dr. Henry Cloud has a humorous method for helping people understand that, because of sin, all families have a certain level of dysfunction. During a lecture he will ask everyone who did not come from a dysfunctional family to stand. He then tells the rest of the crowd to look at those who are standing so they can see what a person in denial looks like. The ever-popular practice of blaming our families for current personal struggles would be greatly reduced if more of us would accept the reality that a perfect family is impossible this side of heaven.[422]

Family Fifty-seven percent of all children in the United States live with their mother and father. In 1960, the percentage was eighty-one.[423]

Family From all external signs it looked like a routine traffic stop. LAPD officer Kelly Benitez pulled over a blue, Ford Thunderbird on September 18, 1998, for an expired registration sticker. The twenty-nine-year-old policeman felt kind of strange when he noticed the last name on this gentleman's driver's license was the same as his own. He took a shot in the dark and asked several probing questions. The forty-nine-year-old schoolteacher saw the officer's name tag and suddenly blurted out, "Are you Kelly?" He then yelled, "I'm your dad!" The two men had not seen each other since Kelly was four months old. They immediately embraced and several cars pulled over thinking a police officer was being assaulted. Kelly assured them of his safety and waved them back into traffic. The two men, who unwittingly lived just five miles from each other, retreated to Kelly's house where they talked for hours. Paul and Debra were never married, and after he was drafted into the Army in 1969, he lost complete contact with Kelly. The younger Benitez was eventually raised by Debra's parents. Both men agreed they always had a void in their life and a fierce desire to find one another. Paul expressed remorse and said he never forgave himself for losing touch. The Los Angeles schoolteacher said, "If there's a lesson in this, it is to never give up. If you're looking for someone, don't stop until you find them." The world is filled with lost sons and daughters who have a fierce desire to be found. It is the privileged responsibility of every Christian to make sure we don't stop until we find them.[424]

Family Given the names of more than sixty sitcom families, which TV family would best describe your home life, and which would be the model for which you would wish? In a 1999 national survey by Reuters/Zogby, Americans were asked that very question. The sitcom family that most families wanted to emulate was the Huxtables *on The Cosby Show*. Second place went to *7th Heaven*, with *Home Improvement* and *The Waltons* following in third and fourth place. Fifth place went to *The Simpsons*. When asked which family is most like your own, *Home Improvement* took first with *The Cosby Show* finishing second. Third place belonged to *The Simpsons* and *7th Heaven* came in fourth. Ward and June Cleaver of *Leave It To Beaver* secured fifth place. For all of the dysfunctionality displayed on TV, it's significant that the majority of Americans see traditional TV families as that which best describes them, and that which represents the type of family they desire.[425]

Family "I just got back from a pleasure trip. . . . I took my mother-in-law to the airport." —*Henry Youngman* [426]

Family Sixty-nine percent of Americans say they are satisfied with their home life.[427]

Family Some recent statistics demonstrate the significantly different complexion of today's American family. Forty-six of every one hundred marriages is a remarriage for one or both partners. Approximately thirteen hundred new stepfamilies are formed every day. One out of every three Americans is now a stepparent, stepchild, stepsibling, or a member of a stepfamily in some other way. If this trend doesn't change, by the year 2010 there will be more stepfamilies in the United States than any other type of family.[428]

Family The Families and Work Institute monitors the level of familial satisfaction in America. Their research raises reason for concern. In 1977, 55 percent of Americans said they were "very satisfied with their family life." By 1997 that number had dropped to 39 percent. The opportunity to reach hurting families with the redemptive love of God is at an all-time high.[429]

Family We have all heard the statistics about how much TV children watch by the time they graduate from high school. Michael Medved, the chief film critic for the New York Post who has chastised the movie industry for belittling Judeo/Christian values, recently cited a jolting discovery.

Medved noted that by the age of six, an average American child has already spent more time watching TV, movies, and videos than he will spend talking with his father during his entire life. Imagine, a lifetime of father-child communication is less than the child's first six years of viewing entertainment.[430]

Fatherhood "Being a dad has no dress rehearsal. Therefore, you've got to be willing to do it well the first time or you will be paying the wages of your wrong choices for many, many years to come." —*Ronnie Floyd*[431]

Fatherhood "Fatherlessness is the engine driving our most urgent social problems, from crime to adolescent pregnancy to domestic violence." —*David Blankenhorn*[432]

Fatherhood Have you ever felt like your "daddy permit" was about to expire? Robert Fulghum tells a touching story of a gift his daughter gave him when she was seven years old. At this tender age she made her daddy's lunch one day and then gave him a second sack that was held together with duct tape, staples, and paper clips. She assured him he needed both sacks, so he gave her a kiss and headed off to work. During his hurried lunch he ate the sandwich and looked over the contents of the "other" sack. It contained two hair ribbons, three small stones, a plastic dinosaur, a pencil stub, a tiny seashell, two animal crackers, a marble, a used lipstick, a small doll, two chocolate kisses, and thirteen pennies. It brought a slight smile, but looked like nothing more than junk. By the end of the day the entire contents of both bags ended up in the trash. That evening, Molly asked for her bag. Fulghum claimed he left it at the office then asked, "Why?" She handed him a note and said, "I forgot to put this note in it. Besides, I want it back." Fulghum couldn't understand why she wanted the sack until she explained, "Those are my things in the sack, Daddy, the ones I really like. I thought you might like to play with them, but now I want them back. You didn't lose the bag, did you, Daddy?" When her eyes filled with tears, he lied again and promised to bring the sack home tomorrow. The lump in his throat metastasized as he read her note that didn't make in to the bag, "I love you, Daddy." He hustled to the office and dumped the contents of his trash can on the desk. The janitor heard his story and didn't think he was foolish. He simply said, "I got kids too." On his return from a successful salvage, Fulghum had his daughter tell him about each piece in the bag. It took her a long time to explain because each item had a story, dreams, and memories. A few days later, Molly trusted her daddy with the bag again and he saw it in a different light. Now it felt like a "daddy prize." The exchange occurred many times over until one day the game ran out and she didn't ask for its return. Two decades later, this little tattered bag is one of his most treasured possessions. It reminds him of a time when he missed the affection of his little girl and forgot to cherish what was important to her. One of Fulghum's friends has compared such parental oblivion to standing knee-deep in the river and dying of thirst. If you're a father, take the time to drink in the joy of your children—tattered lunch sacks and all.[433]

Fatherhood H. B. London closed out an edition of Focus on the Family's Pastor to Pastor with a powerful reminder for fathers. A young boy wanted to build a tree house with his father. The boy repeatedly asked his father if they could work on the tree house but the man always had an excuse for not getting involved in the project. The boy desperately wanted his father's attention, but the man was generally focused on other things. The father's perspective changed after his son was involved in a serious accident and lay dying in the hospital. This man, who had not taken the time to give his son ample attention before the accident, was now struggling with how to relate to his dying boy. His heart was broken when this little guy turned to him and spoke the final words his father would ever hear: "I'm sorry dad, it looks like we won't get around to building that tree house after all." On the surface, tree houses, ball games, and meals at McDonalds don't seem as important as balanced checkbooks and board meetings, but don't be deceived. A father who gives priority to his children has made the right choice.[434]

Fatherhood He was exhausted from a long day and his nerves were shot. As he entered the darkened room to tell his son good night, the irritations quickly erupted when the boy began to badger him about money. The little boy asked, "Daddy, how much money do you make?" The father was noticeably agitated and quickly grunted, "Enough!" But the boy wasn't satisfied so he pressed on and said, "I mean how much do you make an hour?" The man was not in the mood for games so he gave a quick lecture and finally grumbled, "They pay me $25 per hour." The boy then asked, "Can I borrow $10?" The father gruffly replied, "*No!* Now go to sleep!" The following morning brought a different perspective to the overworked man so he apologized to his son and handed him a $10 bill. The little guy lit up like a Christmas tree and ran to his room. He soon returned with his small piggy bank and spilled its contents on the table. The man watched curiously as his son excitedly pushed all of his pennies, dimes, and nickels toward him. The little boy then reached into his pocket for the new $10 bill and said, "Here's $25, Daddy. Can I buy an hour of your time?"[435]

Fatherhood In 1924, Bill Havens was one of America's best rowers and was destined to win three medals, probably gold, at the Olympic Games in Paris. But a few months before the Olympics, Havens realized his wife was due to deliver their first-born child during his trip to Paris. In the 1920s, it took two weeks to travel across the Atlantic so he would be gone a total of six weeks. He decided he would not leave his wife and forfeited his spot to another. He felt bad about deserting his fellow team-mates (one of those was Benjamin Spock, who rose to fame as the "Baby Doctor") and wondered about the medals he might have won. Twenty-eight years later he received a telegram that he treasured more than any gold medal. The following words came from his son who had just won a gold medal in the ten-thousand-meter canoeing final at the Olympics in Helsinki, Finland, during the summer of 1952: "Dear Dad, thanks for waiting around for me to be born. I'm coming home with the gold medal you should have won. Your loving son, Frank." Bill Havens knew he made the right choice![436]

Fatherhood In 1993, workers made a remarkable discovery while doing some renovations at the Baseball Hall of Fame in Cooperstown, New York. Tucked away under a display case was an old photograph of a base-ball player who had never been formally inducted into the famous museum. The picture reveals a man with a bat on his shoulder and a base-ball uniform that has "Sinclair Oil" printed across the chest. Stapled to the picture was a handwritten note. It read, "You were never too tired to play ball. On your days off, you helped build the Little League Field. You always came to watch me play. You were a Hall-of-Fame Dad. I wish I could share this moment with you. Your son, Peter." Many well-known figures grace the walls of baseball's greatest shrine, but this one anonymous father made an impression far more significant than a place in Cooperstown; he made it into his son's heart.[437]

Fatherhood On February 27, 1993, Tim Burke walked away from his career in major league baseball. The all-star pitcher gave up the glamour of professional sports to spend more time with his wife, Christy, and their five children. Unable to have their children biologically, the Burkes have adopted their children. Each child was previously an orphan in another country. When Burke left the mound for home, he told the *Los Angeles Times*, "Baseball is going to do just fine without me, but I'm the only father my children have." No wonder he's known as the "Major League Dad."[438]

Fatherhood Paul Lewis has suggested a tangible reminder for helping fathers to keep their priorities in order. He has suggested that men include their role of father on business cards. Lewis asks fathers to consider placing "Father of (children's names)" under their title or occupation on all of their business cards. Such cards will remind fathers that their vocational occupation is not their only job. In reality, all fathers should see themselves as bivocational. Likewise, wives probably would not complain if their husband added another line on that business card which states, "Husband of (wife's name).[439]

Fatherhood Recent statistics reveal that 60 percent of men have unsolved problems with their fathers.[440]

Fatherhood Sociologist, family expert, and chairman of the National Fatherhood Initiative, Wade Horn, has compiled some telling statistics that affirm the reality that "the one factor that most clearly determines the well-being and future success of children is whether or not they grow up with a father in the home." 70 percent of long-term prison inmates grew up fatherless. Girls without a father in the home are one and one-half times more likely to get pregnant before marriage. Children in families without fathers are five times more likely to grow up in poverty, are two to three times more likely to abuse drugs, and are three to four times more likely to commit suicide. Significantly, research proves that such negative effects are not present when a father's absence occurs due to death. The problems arise when the father never marries the mother of his child, and when the parents are divorced. Seemingly, permanent marriages would provide some of the best salve to our nation's most pressing problems.[441]

Fatherhood The University of Pennsylvania and Princeton University recently completed their joint research of six thousand males (ages 14–22). Their work spanned fourteen years of observation. This study discovered that "boys with absentee fathers are twice as likely to be incarcerated as those from traditional two-parent families regardless of their race, income, and parents' education." Their is no substitute for God's original design of the family.[442]

Fatherhood Two bizarre stories from recent police reports paint a somber picture of the negative influence a father can wield. In the Kerr County jail of Texas, forty-year-old Bill Wells was serving time for burglary. To his great surprise, he met up with another inmate who was also incarcerated for burglary, his twenty-two-year-old son, Corey Hillger. It was the first time they had seen each other since Corey was a small child. Sheriff deputies outside of New Orleans, Louisiana, confirmed the unlikely event of two drunken drivers colliding with each other on the road. George Francois, age seventy-two, crashed his car into another drunken driver, his thirty-five-year-old son Roland Francois. Father and son were both hospitalized for the injuries they sustained. The influence of a father is a powerful force for either good or bad.[443]

Father's Day In 1967, Eloise Shick was a seventeen-year-old candy striper who volunteered her Saturdays at the local hospital. On the Saturday before Father's Day, she was assigned to Ward 5. It was a bad assignment as that ward housed the deathly sick. On this particular day she was intrigued by a young man in a military uniform. They rode the elevator together to Ward 5, but neither of them spoke. Immediately upon exiting the elevator, a nurse grabbed the young man and said, "You must be Mr. Bates. Come with me, your father's waiting." The elderly Bates had come to the E.R. with no identification except an old letter in his pocket. The letter was from his son, Jim Bates, and it looked as though the father had read it hundreds of times. The hospital used the information from this letter to contact the Red Cross who, in turn, located Private Bates. The military flew him from the base in Kentucky to O'Hare airport. Now the young Bates was standing in Ward 5 beside Mr. Bates, senior. Nurse Jenkins turned to the seventeen-year-old candy striper and said, "I'm glad they found him. I don't think his dad will make it to Father's Day." Eloise periodically peaked through the door to see the soldier sitting next to the bed and holding the old man's limp hand. One time the teenager stopped by to offer some relief. She said, "If you'd like to take a break, I'll stay with your father." He softly replied, "Thank you, but this is where I want to be." Eloise went home with a heavy heart. The next morning she made a special trip to the hospital to see how the man was doing. When she arrived, the soldier was standing at the nurses' station. She heard him say, "He's gone." A nurse tried to offer comfort by touching his arm and saying, "I'm so sorry." To the surprise of all, the soldier asked, "Who was that man?" The nurse pulled back and remarked, "Why, he was your father, wasn't he?" The man then explained, "No, I've never seen him before. When I first saw him I knew there had been a mistake, but I realized he was too sick to tell whether or not I was his real son. I figured he needed me, so I stayed." The soldier then bid the nurses farewell and left the hospital. The love and compassion of that stranger revolutionized Eloise's relationship with her father. Until his death ten years later, she expressed a newfound love. He often asked why she wanted to kiss an old coot like him. She simply replied, "Because you're my father who aren't in heaven . . . yet!"[444]

Fatigue "Fatigue makes cowards of us all." —*Vince Lombardi* [445]

Fear "Never let the fear of striking out get in your way." —*Babe Ruth* [446]

Fear "The remarkable thing about fearing God is that when you fear God you fear nothing else, whereas if you do not fear God you fear everything else." —*Oswald Chambers* [447]

Fellowship In each cell of your body there are approximately fifty thousand genes. Scientists have discovered that in the midst of these normal genes there are about twenty genes in every cell that are classified as oncogenes. An oncogene carries the potential of causing a cancerous tumor. It is simply a latent gene that can be triggered for destruction. Amazingly, every cell of our body contains twenty of these oncogenes, but they remain inactive until they are triggered by an outside source. Unfortunately, every church also contains oncogenelike members. The temptation is to look around and try to identify these dangerous people, but a wiser approach involves examining ourselves for the purpose of making certain we are not carriers of potential death. Like the disciples at the Last Supper, we should ask, "Is it I, Lord?" If we are then found faithful, we must be cautious to not "trigger" another member into becoming an active agent of destruction.[448]

Financial Stewardship Derek headed to Sunday School with two quarters in his hand. His mother made sure he understood that one quarter was to be put in the offering plate and the other one was for him to do with as he pleased. He set out on the two-block walk with great enthusiasm and excitement. He pulled the quarters from his pocket and began tossing them from hand to hand. On one pass, he dropped a quarter and it started rolling toward a drainage pipe. He quickly raced after it, but couldn't get to it fast enough. For a few moments he was deeply saddened by the loss, but then a smile started creeping across his face. He stuck the remaining quarter in his pocket and said, "Well, God, there goes your quarter." Unfortunately, God loses a lot of quarters like that.[449]

Finishing Well The distance of the Olympic marathon was standardized in 1908 when the games were held in London. The Royal Family wanted to watch the start of the race from their home. The distance from this vantage point in Windsor Castle to the finish line in the Olympic stadium was 26 miles, 385 yards. From this point on, the marathon distance was fixed. The first winner of this newly defined marathon should have been an Italian candy maker named Dorando Pietri. He was the first to enter the stadium, but turned the wrong way. Rather than going right, he went left. When the mistake was realized, Pietri staggered and fell. Anxiety from his error triggered an onslaught of fatigue. He turned around and continued staggering toward the finish line. With just a few yards remaining, Pietri fell one final time. Sympathetic spectators and trackside officials assisted him to his feet and the tiny runner wobbled to the finish. Meanwhile, Johnny Hayes, running for the United States, was racing down the homestretch of the stadium. After a lengthy discussion by the officials, Hayes was given the gold medal because Pietri had been unfairly aided near the finish line. A wonderfully run race was ruined by a wrong turn at the end. Finishing well is as important as running well.[450]

Flexibility "Over my dead body" has taken on new meaning after the completion of a study conducted at the Ohio State University Medical School. Tilmer Engebretson and his colleague, Catherine Stoney, studied 116 middle-age pilots and discovered that those who flexibly manage stress, anger, and conflict have the healthiest cholesterol ratings. Those who tend to draw battle lines had total cholesterol levels forty points higher than their more flexible colleagues, and their LDL (bad cholesterol) was thirty points higher as well. The next time a guy tells you it will happen "over my dead body," he may be right![451]

Flexibility "The game of life is not so much in holding a good hand as playing a poor hand well." —*H. T. Leslie* [452]

Flexibility The Japanese have a great "word picture" for flexibility. In Japan, people are encouraged to be "the wise bamboo." The bamboo preserves itself by bending in the wind rather than breaking with rigidity. In life we are continuously confronted with situations that force us to decide whether we will bend or break. Sadly, we too often choose to break rather than give some ground and preserve a relationship, idea, or goal. May we pray for wisdom to know which endeavors are best served with a gentle bend.[453]

Focus In 1992, Bill Cowher became the Pittsburgh Steelers's head coach. His employment as one of the NFL's youngest head coaches was attributed in part to his razor-sharp focus. He basically does just two things, coach football and spend time with his wife and three daughters. Everything else remains outside of his focus. This became most evident several years ago when he attended a civic luncheon. He turned to the woman seated next to him and politely asked, "What is it you do?" The woman replied, "I'm the mayor of Pittsburgh." Coach Cowher's limited focus may expose him to some occasional embarrassment, but it provides great clarity for what he feels he is called to accomplish. It is easy to become so acquainted with all that is happening around us that we lose focus of our real mission in life. We all hate to admit it, but clear focus means missing out on some very interesting things.[454]

Foresight Everyone is familiar with the maxim, "Hindsight is 20/20." It's easy to look back on our past and see how we could have acted more prudently, but the primary focus of Scripture is that of providing wise foresight. When we forsake the foresight of God's Word, we end up with good hindsight but far too many regrets. It happened to Matt Groening, the creator and executive producer of, *The Simpsons*. During the onset of Bart Simpson mania, Groening couldn't understand why he was being so heavily criticized for giving kids a bad role model. In December of 1998, Groening issued a national apology through the *New York Times*. He said, "I have a seven-year-old boy and a nine-year-old boy, so all I can say is, 'I apologize.' Now I know what you were talking about." Even Solomon in all of his wisdom failed to exercise good foresight, but he, like others in Scripture, has given us great foresight through his tragic hindsight. Sam Levenson said, "You must learn from the mistakes of others. You can't possibly live long enough to make them all yourself." If we want less regretful hindsight, we must practice more consistent Biblical foresight.[455]

Foresight "Prepare and prevent, rather than repair and repent." — *Anonymous* [456]

Forgiveness A little boy was sitting on a park bench in obvious pain. A man walking by asked him what was wrong and the young boy said, "I'm sitting on a bumble bee." The man urgently asked, "Then why don't you get up?" The boy replied, "Because I figure I'm hurting him more than he is hurting me!" How many of us handle forgiveness like this little boy? We endure pain for the sadistic satisfaction of believing we are hurting them more than us. When we get off the bench of unforgiveness, both parties can begin to realize relief from their pain. [457]

Forgiveness God has promised he will remove our transgressions as far as the east is from the west (Psalm 103:12). The distance from east to west may not seem very far when you're standing on the Continental Divide and the east is right next to the west. So the scope of God's forgiveness is better explained when you think of embarking on an airline flight to the west. If you start flying west, you can continue in that direction without ever reaching the east. No matter how long you fly toward the west and no matter how many times you circle the globe you will never be heading east. If you took a flight north you would eventually hit the North Pole and then start heading south. At that point, north meets south. God didn't say our sins have been removed as far as the north is from the south. When he spoke of his unlimited love and forgiveness he used the earth's latitude, not longitude. [458]

Forgiveness Henry Ingram has struggled with forgiveness. In February of 1998, Ingram filed a deed restriction with the Jasper County Courthouse in South Carolina. This legal move placed restraints on the sale of his 1,688 acre plantation. By definition, nobody living north of the Mason-Dixon line can buy his property nor can anyone with the name of Sherman (General Sherman burned every building on that property during the war). Even though the Civil War ended in 1865, this man is still resentful some 135 years later. Resentment will always chain us to the past, but forgiveness will free us to enjoy the present. [459]

Forgiveness John Ehrlichman and Charles Colson were embroiled together in the Watergate scandal that ultimately led to President Nixon's humiliating resignation. Both men spent time in prison for the roles they played in Watergate. Colson became a Christian through this experience but Ehrlichman, a Christian Scientist, seethed in anger. For over twenty years he openly despised Colson and wrote defamatory articles against him. Less than a year before Ehrlichman's death in 1999, Colson learned of his antagonist's failing health. The former domestic affairs adviser, whose office was once immediately above the Oval Office, was now alone in a nursing home. He was dying of renal failure, his third wife had left him, and he was alienated from his children. Into this setting, Charles Colson came and not only shared the love of Christ, but also demonstrated it as well. Ehrlichman was amazed at the forgiveness and concern offered to him by a man he had so vehemently attacked. That one-hour meeting led to Ehrlichman's journey toward God. Three months later he called Colson and told him the doctors said he wouldn't live much longer. Colson was sick at the time so he sent a good friend who led John Ehrlichman to Christ. He died shortly thereafter and entered into the presence of God because one Christian decided to extend Christlike forgiveness. Genuine forgiveness is incredibly powerful![460]

Forgiveness Marjorie Holmes was struggling with some past failures in her life until she got an interesting letter from a friend. The stationery recounted a recent visit this woman had with her granddaughter when they went to see a plane write messages in the sky. The young girl loved watching the words being drawn in the air, but was puzzled when the letters started disappearing. She studied the situation for a moment then suddenly blurted out, "Maybe Jesus has an eraser!" When we find ourselves wrestling with our own fallen humanity, we can take comfort in the fact that God is able to erase all of our failures with his remarkable eraser . . . a cross.[461]

Forgiveness "Most of us can forgive and forget; we just don't want the other person to forget that we forgave." —*Ivern Ball*[462]

Friends During the Civil War, General JEB Stuart was the Confederate cavalry commander. He served as a subordinate to the Confederacy leader, Robert E. Lee. Each time Stuart wrote a letter to Lee he would close with these words, "Yours to count on, JEB Stuart." Although Stuart generally upheld these words, he failed his leader when Lee needed him most at Gettysburg. Emory Thomas, a professor of history at the University of Georgia, writes in his book, *Robert E. Lee: A Biography,* "At Gettysburg, Stuart rode off into nowhere and left Lee blind in the presence of his enemies." Faithfulness and friendship go hand in hand. Can your friends, family, and colleagues always count on you?[463]

Friendship In 1955, *Gunsmoke* began its twenty-year run on prime-time television. John Wayne was asked to star in the classic western show, but turned down the role of Marshall Matt Dillon. Instead of taking the lead, he recommended his friend for the starring role. James Arness accepted the job and the rest is entertainment history. Friendship involves spotting opportunities for your friends.[464]

Funerals When a minister speaks at a funeral, he must seek to accomplish two objectives. He needs to "comfort the disturbed and disturb the comfortable." Those who are in touch with the reality of death and eternal life can feel very vulnerable so they need to experience a message of comfort. Those who are complacent about death and the reality of impending judgment desperately need to be unsettled from their dangerous zone of comfort.[465]

Gambling Each year, Americans gamble more money than they spend on groceries.[466]

Gambling Gambling is now a $48 billion-a-year industry in the United States.[467]

Gambling In 1998, Americans lost $50 billion gambling. With gambling now legal in most every state, Americans wager nearly $600 billion a year (1999). That's at least $100 billion per year more than is spent on food. The industry is growing at an unprecedented rate and it keeps moving toward creative ways to attract participants. The latest phenomenon is the creative attachment of exercise equipment to slot machines. The Sunset Station Casino in Las Vegas now offers a Pedal'n'Play, a combination stationary bike and slot machine. Gambling aerobicizers must pedal and operate the slot simultaneously because a timer will shut off both operations if you let up on either. The other innovative thief is the Money Mill treadmill. It works likes the Pedal'n'Play except it's a treadmill. Both are the brainchild of Kathy Harris who birthed the idea while riding a stationary bike in Atlantic City. Bored with her routine in the gym, she longed for the "ambiance of the bells ringing, the decadence of the casino." Since that Christmas season in 1996, she's invested $120,000 on her creation, acquired the patents, and is taking orders for her $6,300 Pedal'n'Play and the $7,600 Money Mill. America's obsession with the illusive carrot of gambling might be adjusted if we just realized that one-third of all lottery millionaires end up filing for bankruptcy. When it comes to gambling, even if you win . . . you lose![468]

Gambling In South Carolina, Army Sergeant Gail Baker left her ten-day-old baby, Joy, in a hot car while she spent seven hours in a casino playing video poker. Baker never went to the car to check on her daughter because, as she told the police, "I thought she would be okay." Unfortunately, she wasn't okay, and the little girl's mother was charged with homicide. Gamblers tend to think that everything and everybody will be "okay," but they fail to realize how deadly gambling can become.[469]

Gambling "I think of lotteries as a tax on the mathematically challenged." —*Roger Jones, mathematician* [470]

Generosity Ray Boltz is a Christian singer/songwriter who has written a powerful song about giving entitled, "What If I Give All." Such songs should come easy for Boltz because he himself is a very generous man. During each of his concerts, he directs people's attention to a ministry called Mission of Mercy. This Christian organization is devoted to feeding hungry people throughout the world. At each concert, Ray Boltz invites people to become financial sponsors of an impoverished child. Several years ago, a three-year-old boy saw the images of hungry children being shown on the large video screens as Boltz sang. He obviously had many questions. When he pointed to the screen and asked his mother why that little boy was hungry, she explained how his parents didn't have enough money to buy food. He then reached into his pocket and pulled out a $1 bill. "How many will this feed?" he asked. His mother told him it would provide about ten meals. The little boy immediately asked, "What if I give all I have?" After learning about this child's generous perspective, Boltz cowrote "What If I Give All" with his road manager and guitarist, Mark Pay. God is moved by his children who regularly ask, "What if I give all?"[471]

Giving Chad was a young, shy outcast. At the end of the school day when other children would walk home together, Chad was left to himself. For this reason his mother was deeply concerned when Chad told her he wanted to make a Valentine for every child in his class. Nevertheless, she purchased all of the supplies for him to fulfill his desire. With paper, glue, and crayons, Chad spent three weeks making thirty-five Valentines. On the morning of Valentine's Day, Chad was overflowing with excitement. He carefully collected all of his Valentines and headed out for school, but his mother was not so enthusiastic. She knew her son might not receive a single Valentine and wondered if he could handle that level of hurt. To compensate for the pain, she baked his favorite cookies and had them ready when he walked through the door. The afternoon silence was broken by the sound of children walking down the street. As usual, the other kids were laughing as they walked together and Chad was all by himself. She noticed his hands were empty and tears started to fill her eyes. When the door opened, she choked back the emotions and said, "Mommy has some warm cookies and milk for you." He barely heard a word. His face was glowing and his chest was about to burst with pride as he said, "Not a one . . . not a one. I didn't forget a one, not a single one!" The greatest joy in life is reserved for those who are more interested in giving than receiving.[472]

Giving During the 1995 Thanksgiving season, Paul Harvey shared a true story that reflects a subtle thought about giving to the church. A lady called the Butterball Turkey Hotline with a very unusual dilemma. She had a turkey that had been in the freezer for twenty-three years. She wanted to know if the turkey was safe to eat. The Butterball specialist said the old bird would be edible only if it had remained at zero degrees all of these years. He quickly added that the turkey would have probably lost its flavor and would not recommend eating it. The caller responded to this information by saying, "That's what we thought. We'll just give it to the church." If it's of value, keep it. If it's worthless, give it to the church. This subtle mindset involves a lot more than old, frozen turkeys. This may explain why 75 percent of adult Americans gave less than $500 to both churches and charities in 1995. Within the Southern Baptist Convention, only 10.25 percent of the 15.4 million members give a tithe or more of their income.[473]

Giving In the Korean culture, people give their gifts with both hands. They do this to communicate an important aspect of giving. . . . "I'm not holding anything back. I'm giving you all that I have to offer." Such a philosophy should permeate all of our giving whether it is to God or others. Ironically, children are often taught to fold their hands together when praying. With the Korean perspective in mind, this small gesture could be a constant reminder of our commitment to give God all that we have while holding nothing back.[474]

Giving When we think of philanthropy we might picture Bill Cosby giving $20 million to Spelman College, or Ted Turner making a $1 billion pledge to the United Nations. Most of us can't comprehend making that kind of money, much less giving it away. Making large donations seems like a rite reserved for the wealthy, unless you're Matel "Mat" Dawson. In the spring of 1999, Dawson surpassed the million-dollar mark in lifetime philanthropy by giving a $200,000 scholarship grant to Wayne State University in Detroit, Michigan. Mat Dawson isn't your typical donor, though. In 1999, he was seventy-eight years old and still working with the same company that hired him in 1940. He didn't sit in the boardroom or make a commanding salary. He simply bypassed retirement so he could continue operating his forklift at Ford's Rogue Complex in Dearborn, Michigan. He worked 12-hour days and sometimes put in seven-day weeks. He was a hourly employee who snapped up all the overtime he could get while choosing to live alone in a one-bedroom apartment. His expenses were as frugal as the car he drove, a 1985 Ford Escort. When asked about all of his generosity, Dawson simply replied, "I just do this because I want to give back." Mat Dawson is living proof that extravagant giving stems more from the heart than the bank account.[475]

Giving Years ago, a monk came to the aid of a needy traveler. He opened his small pouch of belongings and offered the man a precious stone worth a small fortune. The monk had previously found it and was now giving it away. The traveler was amazed at his good fortune and quickly left to sell the valuable stone. Surprisingly, though, the man returned a few days later with the valuable jewel. He placed it in the monk's hand and said, "Now please give me something much more precious than this stone. Please give me that which enabled you to give it away." Giving begins in the heart, not the wallet.[476]

Goals A farmer in Kansas raised two sons who joined the Navy. This rarity intrigued the farmer so when his brother, a psychologist, came for a visit, the farmer asked, "Tell me how a farmer living in the middle of Kansas, where there's almost no water, can raise two sons who join the Navy and love it?" His brother was also interested in the unusual phenomenon so he agreed to pursue an answer. That night he slept in the bedroom where both boys had grown up. By the next morning he had a response. He brought his farming brother into the boys' room and had him lay down on the bed. He then asked, "What's the first thing you see when you get up?" The farmer pointed at a picture. Displayed prominently on the wall was a painting of a large ship in the middle of the ocean. It was a beautiful and captivating picture that dominated the focal point of anyone coming into the room. It was the first thing seen in the morning, and the last thing seen at night. When the psychologist asked his brother how long the picture had hung in that position, the farmer noted it had been there since the boys were very young. The visiting brother then stated the obvious, "If you think about a picture like that long enough, you might become a sailor." What we think about most will be what we most naturally become.[477]

Goals A motivational speaker recently discussed how he helps people understand the importance of clear goals. When Ken Olan is trying to communicate this thought, he divides his listeners into two groups. Both parties are given a puzzle with a certain time limit for getting all of the pieces into place. The puzzles are identical except that one group gets the box top to see what the puzzle is supposed to look like, the other group must piece it together without a picture to guide them. Without exception, enthusiasm remains high for those who can see what they are trying to accomplish, and morale plummets for those who flounder without a clear goal. Strategic leadership invariably makes certain that those who follow have a clear picture of what they are doing and where they are attempting to go. Without this visible vision, your goals, as noble as they might be, will be most puzzling to the people you are trying to lead.[478]

Goals "I visualized where I wanted to be, what kind of player I wanted to become. I knew exactly where I wanted to go, and I focused on getting there." —*Michael Jordan* [479]

Goals Karl Wallenda was the patriarch of the most daring family in tightrope history. He trained every child in the family to walk the wire without a net, and to live out his motto: "Walking the wire is living; everything else is waiting." His goal of developing a feat that could never be duplicated was fulfilled when "The Seven" was perfected. Seven members of the family created a pyramid on the wire with one of his granddaughters seated in a chair at the top. The Wallendas performed this act for sixteen years without a mishap, and without a net. Then tragedy struck. One grandson lost his balance and the whole family fell. Two were killed and several were permanently injured. The incident changed Wallenda. His wife said, "All Karl thought about for months was not falling. He put his focus on not falling instead of walking the wire." He still walked the wire and he still pushed the limits, but his focus was blurred. This lack of focus no doubt contributed to his final demise in San Juan, Puerto Rico. He stretched a wire between two ten-story buildings in downtown San Juan. With thousands watching, this seventy-year-old performer took to the wire. Unfortunately, the day would not end with success. The great Wallenda lost his focus and fell to his death. As Wallenda's widow suggested, we must focus on what we want to happen rather than what we fear will happen.[480]

Goals When establishing goals, it's wise to remember what psychologists have discovered: "commitment to a written goal is three times as high as a commitment to a goal that we have only in our head." Many times our disappointments with unrealized goals could be prevented if we simply take the time to write out our goals and refer to them regularly.[481]

God Although he ministered to a previous generation in another land (England), J. B. Phillips sounds like a contemporary prophet when he said, "The trouble with many people today is they have not found a God big enough for modern needs. While their experience of life has grown in a score of directions, and their mental horizons have been expanded to the point of bewilderment by world events and by scientific discoveries, their ideas of God have remained largely static." Modern technological advances and the information age have seemingly impacted everything except our thoughts about God.[482]

God Elie Wiesel, the Jewish Nobel Prize laureate, has written, "The Jew may love God, or he may fight with God, but he may not ignore God." How true! A person who genuinely desires truth cannot ignore the reality of God.[483]

God "For most of us, God is little more than the 911 number of our lives." —*Joseph Stowell*[484]

God In the book, *Lincoln: The War Years*, author Carl Sandburg tells of a special event during Lincoln's second inaugural reception. Frederick Douglass, a black antislavery leader, tried to enter the White House to greet the President. He was seized by the guards and escorted outside. With little hope of breaking through the security, Douglass asked an arriving guest to tell Lincoln that he was detained at the door by officers.

Upon hearing the news, Lincoln invited Douglass into the East Room. Lincoln told the journalist that he saw him in the crowd during his inaugural address. The President then asked for Douglass's opinion concerning a statement he made during the speech, "There is no man's opinion that I value more than yours." Satan's guards seek to bar us from the celebration in God's House, but our Heavenly Father won't allow us to stay outside. He invites us into his presence and says, "there is no man's opinion that I value more than yours."[485]

God "It is the duty of all nations to acknowledge the providence of Almighty God, to obey his will, to be grateful for his benefits and humbly to implore His protection and favor." —*George Washington* [486]

God Michael Jordan was one of the best basketball players of all time. He has been a worldwide hero to millions of fans and a great advertisement for God. His name is a constant reminder of God because Michael literally means "Who is like God." How fitting for the man who played basketball on a level higher than most of humanity. Every time he made an amazing shot his name declared, "This ain't nothin' compared to God!"[487]

God The picture is vividly etched in the memories of millions of Americans. Greg Louganis was standing high atop the diving platform at the 1988 Olympic games. This was to be the last dive of his illustrious career. The gold medal required a near-perfect dive to beat his Chinese competitor. He hit the three and one-half reverse somersault with gold medal precision and won the competition by less than two points. It was truly one of the greatest moments in Olympic history. In 1995, Greg Louganis's public perception was radically altered when he announced that he is a homosexual with AIDS. His announcement was followed by his autobiography, *Breaking the Surface*. In this book Louganis shares a very honest look at his struggles with being a victim of physical and verbal abuse, a low self-esteem, a learning disability, his homosexuality, and a dysfunctional family life. As a child he was taunted in elementary school for his dark Samoan skin. He took dance and acrobatics so he was often called a sissy. In the classroom he was a very slow learner because of undetected dyslexia, and his stuttering only complicated the problem. Consequently he was often beaten up by other boys and felt like his dad did not approve of him as well. On one occasion a boy made good on his promise to beat up Louganis after school at the bus stop. Word got out about the fight and Louganis's father was among the spectators who saw his son get his shirt torn and his face repeatedly pounded into the asphalt. He never lifted a finger to stop the fight and was strangely absent when his hurt and humiliated son started walking home alone. It was an experience that confirmed his father's own condemnation of him. Years later when Louganis found out he had AIDS his brother encouraged him to seek help from the church. Louganis acknowledges a turn to the church was out of the question. To him, the church would only provide further condemnation. The current lifestyle of Louganis cannot be condoned, justified, or blamed on his parents, but you can't help but wonder what might have happened if his father had been a Christian who sought to model the love of our Heavenly Father. He may have never turned to homosexuality or rejected the church if he knew the Heavenly Father who said, "I will never desert you nor will I ever forsake you." (Hebrews 13:5)[488]

God "Without God we face a hopeless end; with God we can experience endless hope." —*Anonymous*[489]

God "Without Thee, what am I but a guide to my own destruction?" —*Augustine*[490]

God You can rest more peacefully tonight because God has been found. The American Family Publishers located him in Sumter County, Florida. Via the Bushnell Assembly of God, an announcement arrived stating that God was a finalist for the $11 million sweepstakes. The letter noted, "God, we've been searching for you." Located between two round adhesive seals was a request for God to "come forward." The notice went on to declare, "What an incredible fortune there would be for God! Could you imagine the looks you'd get from your neighbors? But don't just sit there, God." Fortunately, God's location is not contingent on a publishing house's database. He can be found with nothing more than a searching heart (Jeremiah 33:3).[491]

God's Laws A very tragic story from Yosemite National Park reveals a truth we frequently resist. On October 22, 1999, Jan Davis joined four other parachutists to protest a law. The extreme sport of parachuting off the top of thirty-two-hundred-foot El Capitan was banned from the National Park because of its relative danger. This protest was designed to demonstrate that these jumps can be made safely. The first three protesters successfully completed their jumps and floated safely to the ground. Sixty-year-old Davis was the fourth to jump, but her parachute never opened. Even though she was a seasoned paratrooper with 70 such jumps and three thousand sky dives, she did not escape death. This somber and tragic event strikes a familiar chord with the way we so often approach God's laws. He has designed guidelines to protect us, but we regularly protest them and try to prove we can navigate safely through life without submitting to his laws. Unfortunately, it is often in the midst of our protests that we discover the truth and validity of his protective laws. We break God's laws at the risk of destroying ourselves.[492]

God's Love One Jewish tradition tells of the time when their ancestors walked through the Red Sea on dry ground. After safely arriving on the other side, the water crashed down on the Egyptian army. As all of Pharaoh's men perished, the tradition congers up a picture of heaven where the angels are rejoicing over the miraculous deliverance. But God silenced the heavenly hosts and said, "My creatures are drowning and you are praising me?!" God's love is so powerful and sure, that even the death of those who oppose him breaks his heart.[493]

God's Love The advancement of technology has caused one of America's most hallowed places to be disturbed. In May of 1998, the quiet place in Arlington National Cemetery known as the Tomb of the Unknowns was unearthed. The remains of one unknown were exhumed for DNA testing to determine if they were those of Air Force Lieutenant Michael Joseph Blassie. Blassie's sister, Pat, believed her brother's remains were among those interred in Arlington's sacred tomb and had campaigned for the testing. Lt. Blassie was shot down in Vietnam on May 11, 1972 while flying a bombing run on An Loc. Although his wallet and dog tags were found near the crash site, he was listed as "killed in action, no body recovered." On Memorial Day of 1984, his remains—four ribs, pelvis, and the upper part of an arm—were buried in the Tomb of the Unknowns. For fourteen years Lt. Blassie was classified as unknown. That all changed when DNA tests confirmed his identity. On July 12, 1998, he was laid to rest in the Jefferson Barracks National Cemetery in St. Louis, Missouri. An honor guard fired a twenty-one-gun salute and F-15 fighter pilots flew the honorary missing man formation. Now the name of a man who was once classified as unknown is clearly marked on the military's standard headstone of white Georgia marble. Many of us walk through life feeling as though we will live and die with the same classification as Lt. Blassie . . . unknown. Yet the truth of Scripture reminds us in the great chapter on love that we are "fully known" by a loving God (1 Corinthians 13:12). We needn't wait for some new technology to convince us that God knows and loves us, we simply need to *D*evelop *N*ew *A*ppreciation for the Book that confirms his love and concern.[494]

God's Love The Rabbis of ancient history composed an imaginary look at heaven to convey the extent of God's love. The drama unfolds when the Hebrew people were being pursued by the Egyptian army. The angels were perched on heaven's edge watching the miraculous parting of the Red Sea. When the waters came crashing in on the Egyptians, the angelic host shouted and cheered in victory. God stopped the jubilant celebration with a wave of his hand. With tears in his eyes, God rebuked the angels for their perspective on this tragedy. He said, "The very work of my hands has been destroyed and you would cheer?" God's love is extended to all men, even those who position themselves as enemies of his kingdom. This is most evident in Jesus's request of forgiveness for those who nailed him to the cross. Incidentally, a recent Gallop poll revealed that 90 percent of Americans believe God loves them.[495]

God's Presence Native Americans had a rite of passage for all boys when they turned thirteen. On the night of their first teenage birthday, they were blindfolded and taken several miles from camp. The warriors would leave this new teenager alone in a dense, dark forest. He would be forced to stay there and fend for himself throughout the night. The darkness seemed endless as wild animals would howl, the wind would make strange noises, and the rustling of leaves would sound like an approaching enemy. After enduring a night without rest or sleep, the dawn would finally begin to break. The young teen would see the forest as it really was . . . flowers blooming, tall majestic trees swaying in the breeze, wildlife scurrying for food. To his utter surprise, though, he would come to see an imposing male figure just a few yards away. Unbeknownst to the scared warrior, his father had been there the whole time and he was ready to protect his son against any wiles of the forest. No matter what experience we undergo, God stands there with us, even when we're unaware of his divine presence and protection.[496]

God's Promises Everet Storms was a schoolteacher in Kitchener, Canada, when he took the challenge to discover how many promises were in the Bible. For a year and a half he scoured the pages of Scripture and took detailed notes. During his twenty-seventh reading of the entire Bible, Storms concluded that the Bible contains 7,487 promises by God to man. We are reminded in 2 Peter 1:4 that God's promises are "precious and magnificent," and Romans 3:4 assures us that God can be trusted to deliver on his promises.[497]

God's Provision Circumstances can leave us declaring, "I'm at the end of my rope!" It's a cry of both desperation and frustration. In times like these it is good to remember "God lives at the end of our rope." Sometimes we must get to the end of what we can do before we are willing to step aside and let God meet our needs. Thankfully, He's always there to care![498]

God's Provision Marilyn vos Savant is listed in *Guinness Book of World Records* for having the highest IQ. Her brilliance was reflected in a recent column where she humorously said, "The real wealth of this country is not stored in Fort Knox. It is in 'the back.'" She noted how often the item we want is not on the self but is found "in the back." How many times have you asked an employee, "Do you have any more in the back?" Sometimes we're pleasantly surprised when the salesperson returns from the back with our desired product. But many times we learn there aren't any in the back either. Philippians 4:19 reminds us that God has an unlimited supply "in the back." What we need may not be in plain sight, but God always has our needed provision in the back.[499]

God's Will "To know the will of God is the greatest knowledge. To do the will of God is the greatest achievement." —*George W. Truett*[500]

Golden Rule A psychologist did a very unique experiment on a group of college students. He had each of the students jot down the initials of the people they disliked. Some of the students could only think of one or two people that they disliked. A few other students found the assignment much easier and listed the initials of as many as fourteen people that didn't quite suit them. After evaluating this simple piece of research, the psychologist discovered that "those who disliked the largest number of people were themselves the most widely disliked." These students demonstrated the truth of Jesus' words about the Golden Rule (Matthew 7:12).[501]

Golden Rule Florence Nyemitei received a new twist to the Golden Rule. This New York property owner was sentenced to live in the apartment building she rents to tenants. In December of 1997, the then seventy-one-year-old landlady, pleaded guilty to six violations concerning her property and was ordered to pay a $5,000 fine, plus put up $15,000 for needed repairs. She did neither. The tenants didn't have any hot water, there was no heat, and because she didn't pay the electric bill, residents had to string Christmas lights, using electricity from the next door apartment to illumine the hallways. On January 14, 1997, Judge JoAnn Friia ordered Nyemitei to spend at least four nights a week in her building for the next sixty days. The landlady protested the verdict and referred to her own building as a prison. She said, "It's not fair to put me in prison at this time of my life." One resident remarked, "At least she'll have to suffer like the rest of us." When we have little regard for the Lord's Golden Rule, we create prisons for those around us and cause them to suffer. We might more easily learn how destructive this practice is if we had to live in the prisons we build. What if we had to endure the cutting sarcasm that we throw at others? Would we want to feel the anger that we vent on other people? Could we survive the apathy that we show others? The Golden Rule calls for us to continually ask ourselves, "Would I enjoy the environment that I am creating for others?"[502]

Gossip Before you talk about someone behind their back, take a minute to ponder the results of some recent research on gossip. Dr. John Skowronski, a psychology professor at Ohio State University, was the lead author of a study that assessed the effects of gossip. They discovered that people who hear your gossip will actually associate the message with you. If you talk about someone who is dishonest, the person hearing you tell the story will associate that characteristic with you as well. Likewise, if you sing the praises of someone who is getting a degree from Harvard, you will be remembered as intellectual. Dr. Skowronski said, "It's a memory mistake. You listen to the descriptions of others' actions without thinking much about it. Later, when you search your thoughts about the person who told you, you subconsciously associate them with their description of someone else." Long before this research was unveiled, Paul wrote of an excellent safeguard to this issue in Ephesians 4:29.[503]

Gossip "Many people think it takes at least two people to keep a secret." —*Clara Null*[504]

Gossip Richard Choi is vice president of Radio Korea USA, the leading Korean-language radio station in Los Angeles. On December 19, 1997, Choi was arrested in Seoul, South Korea, for spreading rumors.

Prior to his arrest, Choi had reported on another Korean-language station saying they were experiencing financial difficulty and would be acquired by a large conglomerate. His report was shown to be inaccurate and officials placed him in jail for nearly three weeks until a trial could be secured. Under South Korean law, "anybody who makes false statements and thereby damages the credit or reputation of another person, shall be subject to imprisonment of up to five years." Richard Choi, the forty-nine-year-old U.S. journalist, was caught in the crossfire of two cultural views: the American ideal of free speech, and the Korean belief in accuracy and responsibility. His case was obviously politically charged, but it did speak to the issue of gossip. What if you lived in South Korea, would your normal routine of conversation place you under the threat of incarceration? Regardless of the country in which we reside and the laws under which we must live, Christians are commanded to abstain from gossip (Ephesians 4:25).[505]

Government Our federal government has come a long way since 1800. In that year, the nation's capital was moved from Philadelphia to Washington, D.C. All of the paperwork and records of the United States government were packed into twelve boxes and transported by just one horse and buggy.[506]

Government "The Kingdom of God is not going to arrive on Air Force One." —*Chuck Colson*[507]

Government The U. S. government has one employee for every seventeen Americans.[508]

Government You might find this quote rather amusing because it comes directly from the lips of a founding father. Thomas Jefferson said, "Were it left to me to decide whether we should have a government without newspapers or newspapers without a government, I should not hesitate to prefer the latter."[509]

Grace "I've never been surprised by God's judgment, but I'm still stunned by his grace." —*Max Lucado*[510]

Grace In an English church some years ago, the pastor was overcome by the sight at his altar. An ex-convict was kneeling beside a judge who sat on the bench of England's highest court. In a strange twist of providence, this judge had been the one who handed down a seven-year prison sentence to the man now kneeling at his side. In a conversation after the service, the judge asked the pastor if he had noticed who was praying next to him. The pastor acknowledged this remarkable sight. The judge then stated, "What a miracle of grace!" The pastor agreed and made reference to the criminal's conversion. "But I was not referring to him, I was thinking of myself," noted the judge. He went on to explain, "That man knew how much he needed Christ to save him from his sins. But look at me. I was taught from childhood to live as a gentleman, to keep my word, to say my prayers, to go to church. I went through Oxford, took my degrees, was called to the bar, and eventually became a judge. Pastor, nothing but the grace of God could have caused me to admit that I was a sinner on a level with that convict. It took much more grace to forgive me for my pride and self-righteousness, to get me to admit that I was no better in the eyes of God than the convict whom I sent to prison." Grace is necessary for all sinners to find forgiveness, regardless of how they, or the world, picture their deeds.[511]

Grace In a recent *Dennis the Menace* cartoon there was a vivid picture of grace. Dennis was shown walking away from the Wilson's house with his friend Joey. Both boys had their hands full of cookies. Joey then asked, "I wonder what we did to deserve this?" Dennis delivered an answer packed with truth. He said, "Look Joey, Mrs. Wilson gives us cookies not because we're nice, but because she's nice." My name could easily be replaced for Dennis and God could be substituted for Mrs. Wilson. The good that comes my way is not because I'm good but because God is so good. "Every good and perfect gift is from God . . . (James 1:17)[512]

Grace "Just as a mother's love is stronger than the filth on a child, the love of God toward us is stronger than the dirt that clings to us." — *Martin Luther*[513]

Grace On January 24, 2000, Goshawk Syndicate filed a suit against Buena Vista Entertainment, Inc. to end its contract for underwriting the prize money on *Who Wants to Be a Millionaire.* The London-based insurance company said the show was paying out too much prize money. Basing their profit margins on the original British version of the show where nobody has ever won the big prize, Goshawk said the questions were too easy and too many people were winning large sums of money. They declared a breech in the contract with ABC's top-rated show that frequently attracts thirty million viewers a night. Aren't you glad God doesn't work like underwriters? He never gripes about too much grace being given out, and never asks his followers to toughen up the entrance exam. He simply offers his grace to all who want it.[514]

Grace On June 16, 1989, Mohammed Shera'ie came within seconds of death. He had murdered the wife and two children of Mohammed Yehia Ali Saeed Faqihi, and was now kneeling before his executioner. The sword was already raised when Faqihi cried out before the crowd of witnesses. "Listen, I have forgiven you for the murder of my wife and children, whom you will meet before God." In accordance with Islamic law, which is enforced in Saudi Arabia, Shera'ie was released and his death sentence was revoked. He entered the square expecting justice, but found grace instead. His change of destiny parallels that of those who exchange the price of sin for the gift of God.[515]

Grace Shortly after sunrise on January 2, 2000, a noose was placed around the neck of seventeen-year-old Morteza Moqaddam. He killed a fellow Iranian in Tehran on December 13 after a quarrel about smoking in public. Now, the portable gallows was standing just thirty feet from where the crime had taken place and a large crowd was assembled for the execution. With hands cuffed and tears streaming down his ashen face, the teenager waited for the final signal to end his short life. To his utter surprise, the victim's father, Ali Mohebbi, exercised his privilege under Iran's Islamic legal system and granted the boy forgiveness. Just seconds before being hanged, he was extended grace rather than justice. The killer's mother collapsed under the strain and cried out, "I will never forget as long as I live how he gave me my son's life back." After receiving clemency, Moqaddam was ushered away from the gallows in an ambulance that was waiting to take his body to the morgue. State-run television ran footage of the teenager repeatedly thanking the father whose son he killed. Like this young man from Iran, we are all guilty of sin and worthy of spiritual execution. But God has "demonstrated his love for us in that while we were yet sinners, Christ died for us" (Romans 5:8).[516]

Grandparents "The reason grandparents and grandchildren get along so well is that they have a common enemy." —*Sam Levinson*[517]

Grandparents There will be ninety-eight million grandparents in 2002.[518]

Gratitude "I have always thought it would be a blessing if each person could be blind and deaf for a few days during his early adult life.

Darkness would make him appreciate sight; silence would teach him the joys of sound." —*Helen Keller*[519]

Gratitude "It's better to say 'thank you' and not mean it, than to mean it and not say it." —*Anonymous*[520]

Gratitude Pastor Jack Hinton had the opportunity of leading music for a worship service in a leper colony on the island of Tobago. There was time for one more song so he asked for a request. A woman who had been facing away from the pulpit turned toward him and raised a fingerless hand. The woman's nose and ears were entirely gone, and most of her lips had rotted away. Nonetheless, she asked if they could sing *Count Your Many Blessings.* Pastor Hinton was overcome with emotion and had to leave the service. A team member followed him out and said, "Jack, I guess you'll never be able to sing that song again." The pastor replied, "Yes I will, but I'll never sing it the same way again."[521]

Greatness Wayne Gretzky retired from professional hockey in 1999. When "The Great One" skated off the ice for that final time, he owned sixty-one NHL records. Most sport's enthusiasts focused on his unmatchable record of 894 goals, but that isn't the one Gretzky treasures most. He said, "Ten years from now, they won't be talking about my goal scoring. It'll just be my passing." After twenty years of skating in the pros, he was most pleased by his record number of assists to teammates. Ken Dryden said, "Gretzky is the first forward to play a true team game . . . and that will be this superstar's legacy." Imagine setting nearly every significant record, but finding your greatest fulfillment in helping others succeed. That's greatness![522]

Greed Former President Jimmy Carter has invested much of his post-White House time to serving the poor. Through research and first-hand experience, Carter has come to believe selfishness is the biggest obstacle facing Americans in the future. He said, "The greatest challenge we face in the millennium is the growing chasm between the richest people on earth and the poorest people on earth." His studies reveal the twentieth century began with the richest nations of the world being nine times richer than the poorest. By the close of the same century, they are now sixty-five times richer. Carter said, "In the process, even our generous American people have grown more and more stingy. We give less than 1 percent of our gross national product to people in need."[523]

Greed "The poorest man I know is the man who has nothing but money." —*John D. Rockefeller*[524]

Greed While serving as a pastor, Neil Knierim witnessed greed first-hand. In the town where he was serving, there were only two funeral homes. One day these two funeral directors got on the phone and started discussing ideas for saving money. They were both advertising in the Yellow Pages so one man suggested they drop their large ads and simply run line ads with their business name, address, and phone number. It was mutually agreed they would both cancel their half-page ads and invest the saved money on something more productive. Ironically, when the new phone book came out, there were two full-page ads, one for each funeral home. Apparently, both men reconsidered the agreement and saw it as an excellent opportunity to increase their share of the market. Greed is seldom far from any of us.[525]

Greed World hunger is not only a reality which claims the lives of sixty thousand people every day, but it is a constant source of anguish for concerned and compassionate people with plenty to eat. Tragically, there is no reason for any person to die of starvation. There is now more food per person available on this planet than any time in history. Even with more people than ever before, six billion, there is food enough for each person to have 4.3 pounds of food every day. Unfortunately, the driving force of greed prevents distribution, and guarantees the death of millions.[526]

Greetings Don't be too stingy with your personal greetings. In 1919, Fred Allen's will was probated and his green parrot ended up with $5,000. Allen left his bird the money because "it said 'hello' to him every day when he returned home from the office." That bird from Brooklyn was smarter than most of us because it understood the importance of a daily greeting.[527]

Grief Grief is a serious dynamic that is too often minimized. Society at large seems to think a person should be "OK" within a few weeks after the death of a loved one. A 1996 study helps us to understand the enormous stress that grief places on our bodies. This study revealed that the risk of a heart attack is fourteen times higher than usual on the day following the death of a parent, child, grandparent, or other close relative or friend.[528]

Grief John Tomlin is remembered as the first victim of the Columbine massacre to be buried. The death of this bright and ambitious young man left immeasurable hurt in the heart of his parents, John and Doreen. Mrs. Tomlin, a deeply committed Christian, shared her story of pain in *Today's Christian Woman*. The intensity of her grief is felt as she told of a two-week period where she just sat in her son's room. She left everything exactly as it had been the morning of April 20, 1999. During this time she simply held and rocked his clothes. She so longed for his return that she frequently asked herself, "Am I going crazy?" Her journey through grief obviously has not been easy, but she notes, "I've experienced God's comfort in a deeper way than ever before. He hasn't taken away the pain of grieving, but he has become my partner in it." She went on to say, "I know I face a long road ahead, but I know that God will give me what I need in abundant measure." Grief can indeed lead us down a long and difficult road that sometimes causes us to wonder if we're going crazy, but with God as our partner we will find what we need in abundant measure.[529]

Grief Leo Buscaglia told of a contest he once judged where he was to select the most caring child. The winner turned out to be a four-year-old boy. The little boy's next-door neighbor was an elderly man who had recently lost his wife. When the guy saw his neighbor crying, he walked over to his yard and climbed up in the man's lap. His mother later asked him what he told their heartbroken neighbor. He replied, "Nothing, I just helped him cry." Sometimes people just need somebody to "help them cry."[530]

Grief Many mourning families have found support in Terry Kettering's poem, "The Elephant in the Room." It is a poignant piece of prose that helps us see the need for mourning people to talk about the loved one they have lost. It reads, "There's an elephant in the room. It is large and squatting, so it is hard to get around it. Yet we squeeze by with 'How are you?' and 'I'm fine.' And a thousand other forms of trivial chatter. We talk about the weather. We talk about work. We talk about everything else—except the elephant in the room. There's an elephant in the room. We all know it is there. We are thinking about the elephant as we talk together. It is constantly on our minds. For, you see, it is a very big elephant. It has hurt us all. But we do not talk about the elephant in the room. Oh, please, say her name. Oh, please, say 'Barbara' again. Oh, please, let's talk about the elephant in the room. For if we talk about her death, perhaps we can talk about her life. Can I say 'Barbara' to you and not have you look away? For if I cannot, then you are leaving me alone . . . in a room . . . with an elephant."531

Guidance In March of 2000, the small town of Fruita, Colorado, received a unique new sculpture on a downtown corner. Lyle Nichols unveiled his four-foot masterpiece of Mike the headless chicken. It's a reminder of what happened in Fruita sixty years earlier. Lloyd Olsen, a farmer, lopped off the head of one of his chickens in the 1940s. Wanting to preserve as much of the neck as possible for dinner, he laid his ax at the base of Mike's skull. Rather than roll over and die, this chicken became a bizarre piece of history. Olsen not only didn't eat the bird, he actually started to care for it. Mike could go through the motions of pecking for the food but couldn't get anything. When he tried to crow, only a gurgle came out. The farmer fed this strange chicken with an eyedropper, and after a week of survival, he took Mike to some scientists at the University of Utah. They theorized the chicken had enough brain stem left to live without his head. Mike made it into *Life* magazine and the *Guinness Book of World Records*. He also became quite an attraction until he choked to death on a kernel of corn in an Arizona motel eighteen months after surviving the chopping block. Mike the headless chicken might describe some of us who move through the motions of life without the Head of Christ to guide us. We may have movement and life, but not much direction.532

Guidance In May of 1996, one of the greatest tragedies in mountain-climbing history took place upon the slopes of Mount Everest. In a quest to stand on the 29,028-foot summit, twelve climbers lost their lives. Jon Krakauer was apart of this expedition and has written of the experience in his best-selling book, *Into Thin Air*. Krakauer describes how the imperiled group came to this dreadful fate. On their final ascent to the top, several climbers violated clear instructions not to be on the summit after 2:00 P.M. This delay caused the entire group to remain in a dangerous sector of the mountain far too long. A murderous storm blew in on the climbers and they found themselves in a fight for their lives. The full-blown blizzard sent the wind-chill factor plummeting one hundred degrees below zero. They were enveloped in darkness and blowing snow and visibility dropped to less than twenty feet. Their oxygen was depleted and the batteries on their lights were fading. For two hours they simply staggered blindly through the snow hoping to stumble upon the camp.

Hypothermia and exhaustion were taking a terrible toll, and their floundering steps nearly took them over the precipice of a seven-thousand-foot cliff. Nothing but chaos could describe their search for safety. While the fierce wind continued to create a ground blizzard, the sky above began to clear. As the climbers looked up, they saw the silhouettes of Everest and Lhotse. From that brief glimpse of these reference points, they were able to determine the route back to camp, safety, and survival. When the landscape around us is swirling, and the winds of confusion are howling, we can always look up to God and find his reference points of dependable guidance. Likewise, our spiritual stability can be used by God to guide a lost soul to the safety of his love and forgiveness.[533]

Guidance Ken Blanchard, author of *The One Minute Manager*, is now a Christian, but prior to his conversion he needed a powerful challenge from Bill Hybels to get him thinking seriously about Christ. Hybels knew Blanchard carried a bedrock belief in the enormous value of utilizing business consultants. For this reason he gave Blanchard counsel by saying, "You need to call in three consultants that could really help you: the Father, Son, and Holy Spirit." When we need guidance in any area of our lives we can't find a better group of consultants.[534]

Guidance One of the most pronounced memories of 1997 was that of Princess Diana's death. In the early morning hours of August 31, the princess died in a Paris hospital after a violent car accident. According to her psychic, this tragedy was not supposed to be part of her future. Just a few weeks before her death, Diana went with Dodi al-Fayed to see a clairvoyant on August 12. They spent almost two hours with Rita Rogers, a psychic in Chesterfield, England. The couple sought guidance on their future and it appeared they received some great encouragement. One witness said, "Di was grinning all over her face and looked like she had received good news." Nineteen days later she was dead. Only God can truthfully declare, "I know the plans I have for you."[535]

Habits Do you need to replace a bad habit with a good one? A Princeton University study claims if you do the same thing every day for twenty-eight consecutive days it will become a habit.[536]

Happiness "If happiness could be bought, we'd be unhappy with the price." —*Anonymous* [537]

Happiness In the May 1996 issue of *American Scientific* magazine, a myth about happiness was exposed. It noted, "People have not become happier over time as their cultures have become more affluent. Even though Americans earn twice as much as they did in 1957, the number that are 'very happy' has declined from 35 to 29 percent."[538]

Happiness "The best way to cheer yourself up is to cheer everybody else up." —*Mark Twain* [539]

Hardship During the summer of 1988, Yellowstone National Park suffered the worst fire of its history. Since being established as a national park in 1872, nothing has compared to the four months of fires that charred its acreage from May to September in 1988. A severe drought set the dramatic stage for lightning strikes in May. In late June, new fires erupted on the east and west sides of the park. By late July, the roaring fires were a daily feature of the news. On July 27, Interior Secretary Donald Hodel ordered a full-scale assault on the fires. Twenty-five thousand firefighters were deployed, 117 aircraft were put into the air, and more than $120 million in government spending was invested in battling these unbelievable fires. But it was not until the first snowfall on September 10 that the fires began to wane. Then when all of the smoke had cleared, everyone mourned the fatal loss of America's oldest national park. Ten years later, though, experts were humming a different tune. In 1998, officials said, "By nearly every measure, the park is stronger now than before." The park is filled with new life and growth even though officials didn't plant any new trees. The fires that effectively removed much of the dead wood and undergrowth also left an enriched soil that has accelerated new growth. Although some of the fires burned hot enough to destroy seeds and sterilize the topsoil, John Varley, director of Yellowstone's Center for Resources said, "There is no ecological downside to this fire." Many times we are tempted to believe there can't be any advantages to our hardships and struggles, but the reality of Yellowstone's roaring fires and subsequent improved growth can teach us otherwise. When you're facing a tough time, try to remember the lodgepole pine. It's the dominant tree species in Yellowstone. This beautiful pine seals its seeds inside wax-covered cones that only open in the presence of intense heat. The fires of 1988 caused these cones to burst open and cover the nutrient-filled ashes with new seeds. Sometimes God does the same with us. He uses the intense heat of hardship to open up opportunities for new life and greater vitality.[540]

Headaches Twenty-eight million Americans suffer migraines resulting in the loss of 150 million workdays and $13 billion in lost productivity.[541]

Healing "Time doesn't heal; it's what we do with the time that heals." —*Billy Graham* [542]

Healing While serving as an associate professor at Harvard Medical School, Dr. Herbert Benson authored a book titled, *Timeless Healing: The Power and Biology of Belief.* In this work, which is the culmination of thirty years of research, Dr. Benson maintains the conviction that "human beings are wired for God." He notes that until just 150 years ago there was no separation between belief and healing. We have since begun to replace our belief systems with medical systems. Healing is now attributed to pills and surgery rather than the combined efforts of medicine and faith. Benson reminds the reader that placebos are effective in 30 to 90 percent of the cases. We've come to discount the placebo effect and say, "It's all in your head." He says, "In truth, we should be paying more attention to it." The medicine in our "head" (faith) mustn't be replaced by pharmaceuticals or surgery but returned to its position as a complementary tool in the process of healing. Benson sees belief as one of three legs on a stool with medicines and surgery comprising the other two. We should not discount the fact that Jesus told the one grateful leper, "Your faith has made you well" (Luke 17:19). Faith in the Great Physician is the best resource in your medicine cabinet.[543]

Health Americans spend $2.8 billion per year trying to relieve the symptoms of a cold.[544]

Health In America, more than five million teeth get knocked out each year.[545]

Health More than one third of all Internet searches are health related.[546]

Heaven During the evening service of Easter, 1984, Frank Cox preached a sermon on trusting God in the midst of suffering. Little did he know that the very next day he would be sitting in a neurologist's office being told his wife had a malignant brain tumor. Just two years later, Cox became a widower with a four-year-old son. On July 4, 1986, his twenty-seven-year-old wife, Debbie, lost her fight against cancer. This event led to a very difficult time of grief. At one point he demanded that

God give him back his wife. He said, "I want her back! With a full head of hair, and I don't want there to be a bum arm or a splint on her leg. I didn't bargain for this; I just want her back." In response to his demand, Cox sensed God saying, "If I opened up Heaven and said, 'Okay, Debbie, you can go back,' she wouldn't want to come, Frank. She's enjoying everything I ever prepared for her. Now get up and get on with your life." Cox then remembered the words of another man whose wife was deathly ill during his ministry: "God is too good to be unkind, he is too wise to be mistaken, and when you can't trace his hand, that's when you must learn to trust his heart." In times of grief we would do well to remember the words of these two men who have already traveled the road of sorrow.[547]

Heaven Given the opportunity, how much would you pay for a place in heaven? A recent survey asked the wealthiest 1 percent of Americans that very question. This elite group of about one million households earns at least $250,000 per year and has a net worth of at least $2.5 million. These millionaires gave the following breakdown of what they would spend on certain unique opportunities. For great beauty, the average price they would willingly pay was $83,000. For talent, they would spend $285,000. Great intellect commandeered $407,000. They said true love was worth $487,000. The highest bid on any subject went for a place in heaven. To secure their spot in eternity, these wealthy Americans said they would part with $640,000. Isn't it interesting that even if heaven could be bought, those who have the most money don't want to spend more than 25 percent of their net worth to get there. What a stark contrast to the 100 percent investment Christ made to secure our eternal destiny.[548]

Heaven "I thank God daily that I have another life to look forward to . . . a heaven filled with sights and sounds." —*Helen Keller*[549]

Heaven Martha was buried with her Bible in one hand and a fork in the other. When Martha learned that the doctors expected her to be dead within six months, she began talking with her pastor about the funeral. They talked about her favorite hymns, passages of Scripture, and the wonderful memories that had been made. After they had seemingly covered all of her desired arrangements, she said, "One more thing. When they bury me, I want my old Bible in one hand and a fork in the other." The pastor was confused. "Why do you want to be buried with a fork?"

She went on to explain her profound logic. At the real nice church dinners when everybody was just about finished with the meal, somebody would come by and pick up the dirty dishes. As they collected the dinnerware they would say, "You can keep your fork." That meant dessert was coming, but it wasn't just a bowl of ice cream or some pudding—you didn't need a fork for that. No, when they told you to keep your fork it meant the good stuff like chocolate cake or cherry pie. She said, "When they told me I could keep my fork, I knew the best was yet to come. That's exactly what I want people to talk about at my funeral. When they walk by my casket, I want them to turn to one another and ask, 'Why the fork?' I want you to tell them I kept my fork because the best is yet to come."[550]

Heaven Mining companies still work in places where the yield of gold is just one ounce for one ton of worked dirt. It takes a lot of work to find gold on this planet because there isn't much of it. If you melted down all of the gold that has ever been mined, it would fit into a cube measuring twenty yards on each side. Gold is so limited that the international monetary system is no longer based on gold but paper currencies like the dollar. In fact, the full gold standard only lasted from the 1870s to World War I. But what is scarce on earth is abundant in heaven. When John caught a glimpse of heaven he said, "The great street of the city was of pure gold" (Rev. 21:21). It's another vivid reminder that what we frequently pursue and consider to be of greatest value is nothing more than pocket change to God.[551]

Heaven One night while sharing his testimony about Christ, Paul Azinger used a profound illustration. This professional golfer, who battled back to the PGA after a life-threatening bout with cancer, told of a friend's unusual meeting with a wealthy man on an airplane. Sitting next to Paul Azinger's friend in the first-class section of an airliner was a man with some very surprising surroundings. His seat was made of beautifully fashioned leather, a fan hung above his head, his tray table was crafted from mahogany wood, and he was within arm's reach of a VCR, television, CD player, and his own computer. Azinger's friend felt compelled to ask the obvious, "Why would anyone go to the expense of having all these things installed in an airplane?" The rich traveler replied, "Because this is my home." Azinger used this story to point out the tragedy of converting into a home something that was designed just for travel. This life is but a vehicle that will one day take us to our eternal home. Try to remember that heaven is our home and earth is but a plane to help us, and others, get there.[552]

Heaven   Samuel Morrison was a faithful missionary who served twenty-five years in Africa. In failing health, Morrison returned to the United States. Also traveling home on the same ocean liner was President Teddy Roosevelt who had been in Africa for a three-week hunting expedition. As the large ship pulled into New York harbor, it looked as though the entire city had come out to welcome the President. Music filled the air, banners wafted in the wind, balloons flew to the sky, flashbulbs were popping, and confetti streamed down like snow. As Roosevelt stepped into sight, the crowd exploded in applause and cheers. It was truly a reception fit for a king. While all of the eyes were on the President, Morrison quietly disembarked and slipped through the crowd. None of the applause was for him and nobody was there to welcome him home. His heart began to ache as he prayed, "Lord, the President has been in Africa for three weeks, killing animals, and the whole world turns out to welcome him home. I've given twenty-five years of my life in Africa, serving you, and no one has greeted me or even knows I'm here." He then felt the gentle touch of God and sensed the Spirit say, "But my dear child, you are not home yet!" What a joyous thought to realize presidential receptions pale in comparison to the heavenly homecoming that awaits every child of God.[553]

Heaven   "True success is winding up in heaven." —*Bumper sticker*[554]

Hell   Do many people worry about going to hell? In America, people worry far more about their finances and medical coverage than the prospect of winding up in hell. The ratio of Americans who worry "a lot" about money and health insurance compared to those who worry about going to hell is five to one.[555]

Hell   Only 50 percent of Americans believe in hell.[556]

Holiness   After receiving an unacceptable glass of water, a restaurant patron questioned the waiter. He remarked, "Is the water always this cloudy around here?" The waiter indignantly replied, "There's nothing wrong with our water, sir. You just happen to be drinking out of a dirty glass." Sometimes we defend unholiness by blaming it on something else, but the end result is still the same. God's living water will only sparkle in a holy vessel.[557]

Holiness "Put first things first and we get second things thrown in; put second things first and we lose both first and second things." —*C. S. Lewis*[558]

Holy Spirit "A great deal of our ineffectiveness can be attributed to ignoring the Holy Spirit." —*Oswald Sanders*[559]

Holy Spirit From Acts 12:2 we know that Herod beheaded the apostle James, brother of John, but do you know the rest of this story? James was the first apostle to suffer death after the martyrdom of Stephen. Although Herod was the authority that took his head, James's fate started when a nameless individual brought charges against him before the tribunal. When the case was over and James had been condemned to death, the man who had instigated the trial was deeply moved by the behavior and continence of the apostle. James was so filled with the Spirit of God that on the way to the place of execution the one who had initiated the charges against him made a confession of faith in Christ. When he asked James to forgive him, the apostle said, "Peace be to thee, brother." James then kissed him and both men were beheaded for their faith in 36 A.D. A Spirit-filled life may lead to physical death, but more importantly, it always leads to eternal life.[560]

Holy Spirit functioning of a church without the empowering of God's Spirit has been insightfully illustrated by Jack Taylor. He has said, "To a large extent, we are going around beating on trees with bare ax handles. At intervals, under the suspicion that this is not getting the job done, we call for strategy conferences on how to make our ax handles more effective or how to improve our swing. We take a census of the trees, motivate the wood choppers, declare that this is the day for felling forests, and with polished ax handles and persuasive personnel, we embark toward the woods. But, alas, though the noise of these workmen is great, the sound of falling trees is missing. There is movement without might, energy expended without effectiveness, much doing but little dynamic! There is little to show after all is done but bruised hands, tired bodies, and wounded trees. What is missing? Why, the ax head of course—the cutting edge of it all. But what is the ax head of the Church? It is the life of God in Christ released in our world through the work of the Holy Spirit! Our bodies, the larger body, the church, with all our abilities and programs are but the handles on which swings the ax head of his life. The ax head is that which we must recover."[561]

Home Care In the United States, over seven million people are acting as unpaid caregivers for their ailing parent(s), and the estimated value of their uncompensated care is nearly $200 billion per year, which is considerably more than the cost of nursing-home care and professional in-home care combined.[562]

Homeless The average age of a homeless person is nine years old.[563]

Homeschool Home schooling now represents about 3 percent of America's fifty million children.[564]

Honesty His is a legacy of honesty, but that legacy is built on a lie. George Washington was so highly respected by his contemporaries that some felt he was divine. In an attempt to humanize the seemingly immortal founding father, an ex-minister named Mason Weems crafted many fictitious stories about Washington. His most memorable one involves a cherry tree. He wanted people to see Washington as an equal, so he made up the tale to show the fallen side of a young boy who destroyed a valued tree. The nineteenth-century fictional work of Weems backfired as people focused on Washington's honesty rather than his mischief. Mentors from history are of great value, but the best model for honesty will always be the One known simply as Truth.[565]

Honesty Larry Burkett is a well-known Christian financial advisor. From his experience, he estimates that 50 percent of those who call themselves Christians cheat on their taxes.[566]

Honesty Steven Rogers is truly an honest guy. In January of 1997, this police officer in Nutley, New Jersey, issued himself a $17 ticket for parking too close to a street corner. When questioned about it, Rogers said, "I was thinking about pleading not guilty, but I would have had to cross-examine myself in court."[567]

Honesty What would you pick as the most important trait for effective leadership? A survey of fifteen thousand people revealed honesty is the most necessary ingredient. The results were featured in *Credibility*, the work of James Kouzes and Barry Posner. These two authors noted, "Honest people have credibility and that's what gives leaders the trust and confidence of their people." Their work also cites the second, third, and fourth most important traits of effective leaders. In order of importance were the characteristics of being visionary, inspirational, and competent.

Although competency is always necessary, it is interesting to realize that people ranked three other traits as more important.[568]

Hope Charles Swindoll has written about an unusual photograph he once viewed. This picture captured the familiar sight of a yellow "Dead End" sign, but the message had been altered by someone with a can of spray paint. Underneath the words "Dead End" was the spray-painted question, "What isn't?" This question of hopelessness has also been painted on the hearts of many disheartened people who need to hear that Christ can transform their dead ends into doorways of hope.[569]

Hope Dr. Tony Evans recently shared the experience of a seasoned chess champion touring an art museum. While passing through the gallery, his attention was drawn to a painting that involved chess. The artist had painted a match between Satan and an outwitted young man. The picture frozen on canvas showed the two engaged in a chess game being played out for the man's soul. The man was in obvious panic as the adversary's hand is shown making his final move. The artist's work is simply titled *Checkmate*. The chess champion stood and observed the painting for a long time. His scowl of concentration was finally softened by a slight smile. He turned to the curator and said, "I've got good news for the man in that picture. He still has a move." The father of lies has convinced far too many people that he has placed them in checkmate, but the grace of God has provided every man with the hope that "he still has a move."[570]

Hope "One of the most important things we can give to our kids is the sense that they live in a world being born, not a world dying." —*Alvin Toffler*[571]

Hope Westley Allan Dodd was a serial child killer who met his punishment on the gallows of a Washington State Penitentiary in 1993. Before the execution was carried out he was given the customary opportunity to make a final statement. Although a lot of press was given to the seemingly outdated method of execution, hanging, little space reflected the final words of this murderer of three young boys. Dodd had previously said he would murder again and there was no hope he would ever be released from the hideous darkness within his soul. Yet in the closing moment of his life, Dodd said, "I was wrong when I said there was no hope, no peace. There is hope. There is peace. I have found them both in the Lord Jesus Christ." These words brought a hiss from the father of two boys who Dodd had murdered because he had shown no signs of remorse until the last hours of his life. The father's response is understandable but the truth remains unchanged: God can provide hope and peace to the worst of offenders even in the final hours of life. He did at Calvary and he does today. As Chuck Colson said when Jeffrey Dahmer mentioned his forgiveness by Christ: "If God can't save Jeffrey Dahmer, then he can't save you or me."[572]

Human Nature "We want to do good, but we are prepared to do evil." —*Dallas Willard*[573]

Humility "I have failed many times, and I would do many things differently." —*Billy Graham*[574]

Humility "I have more trouble with D. L. Moody than any other man I know." —*D. L. Moody*[575]

Humility "It is always the secure who are most humble." —*G. K. Chesterton*[576]

Humility "The greatest lesson in life is to know that even fools can be right sometimes." —*Winston Churchill*[577]

Humility Whenever you start feeling disproportionately bigger than you really are, take a cue from some recent photographs that were taken of you by the Voyager spacecraft. This seemingly indestructible little piece of equipment sent back pictures of Earth taken four billion miles away. From that distance, our world is nothing more than a dot on the photo, and measures just 1/72 of an inch in width. We're all in the picture, just not as big as we sometimes think.[578]

Hunger According to a USDA study, more than one-fourth of all food produced in the United States each year is thrown out (ninety-six billion pounds). Just 5 percent of that food could feed four million people a day for a year.[579]

Hunger Each day, thirty-five thousand children die from starvation and related diseases caused by malnutrition.[580]

Hunger Every week, malnutrition and related illness claim the lives of more than 118,000 children under the age of five.[581]

Hypocrisy A recent tragedy revealed some repulsive hypocrisy in our land. On November 12, 1996, two young college students birthed their child in a Delaware motel room then tossed it in a dumpster. For this action, Amy Gross and Brian Peterson were charged with murder. Reporters who covered this story accentuated our nation's hypocrisy surrounding the issue of abortion. These reporters littered their articles with such words as "tragedy, monsters, heinous." Some in the press said, "they appeared to be good kids; unusual for the affluent, educated backgrounds of the accused; a horrible act; educated people are supposed to come up with better choices." Reporters asked, "How could this happen?" and said this event "has the nation collectively shaking its head and wondering." There is no question this was a terrible tragedy, but why was all of this such a big surprise? Since 1973, our country has sanctioned and endorsed the right to kill babies. It is even legal to partially deliver a baby and abort it. "Well-educated" and "affluent people" do it all of the time. These two teenagers could have chosen to go by a New Jersey clinic where some "well-educated" and "affluent people" performed fifteen hundred partial-birth abortions last year. Then instead of attorneys talking about the death penalty, they could have earned the applause of our government for "making the right choice." Obviously, the church isn't the only place to find hypocrites![582]

Hypocrites Zig Ziglar offers some great logic to those people who shun church because "they're a bunch of hypocrites down there." To these he simply replies, "Come on down, we've got room for one more." It's true, "if a hypocrite stands between you and God then the hypocrite is still closer to God than you are."[583]

Identity According to the General Accounting Office, consumers and institutions lost an estimated $745 million to identity theft in 1997. Identity theft occurs when a person's social security number, credit card number, phone number, etc., is discovered by a thief who then uses that information for personal gain. In recent years people have begun purchasing paper shredders for their homes to help combat the potential of their private information being swiped from a trash can or dumpster. We should not only prepare for this unfortunate phenomenon, but we should also consider other ways we allow ourselves to be robbed of our true identity. Satan steals a person's potential in Christ by convincing them they are not worthy of God's forgiveness. He robs others through enormous outlays of guilt. The devil rips off some by using peers to influence them in negative ways. We allow him to pick us clean when we buy in to the belief that our true worth is tied to our net worth. Through fear he can prevent many from taking risks and discovering God's elaborate plan for their life. If he can keep you confused or apathetic about your spiritual gift, he has diluted your true identity in Christ. None of us wants to be burglarized by a sly credit card thief, but we need to look twice to make sure we aren't being robbed by an even craftier crook.[584]

Idols Archaeologists testify that throughout history there have been idols in every culture. Man is created with a need to worship, but when that pursuit for divine communion is misguided, idols are formed. Every idol reminds us of our need to worship. May we remember that there is only One who is worthy of worship.[585]

Ignorance Twenty-seven percent of American adults still believe the sun revolves around the earth.[586]

Immorality According to a poll conducted by Luntz Research, 80 percent of Americans believe immorality is our greatest problem as a nation.[587]

Immorality On March 26, 1999, thousands of computers around the world were infected by the Melissa virus. Under the guise of email which read, "important message," the virus spread around the world like an electronic chain letter. By the time it had run its course, the Melissa virus caused more than $80 million worth of damage. David Smith, age thirty-one, was arrested and charged for "total disruption of worldwide communication." The New Jersey computer programmer cleverly used a well-traveled section of the information highway to spread this "gigagerm." He admitted to launching the virus from a sexually oriented Web site. Those who took the bait in cyberporn became infected and their computer immediately sent the virus to the first fifty names on their email address book. To date, Melissa is the worst computer virus ever released and its rapid infection can be traced to the epidemic of immorality.[588]

Indecision In December of 1999, Graham Gund started building his house for the third time. The multimillion-dollar mansion in Cambridge, Massachusetts, was a work in progress as Gund struggled to decide what he really wanted. The house was near completion in the spring of 1999 when he called for bulldozers to tear it down. A second foundation was poured and construction started over. By December, Gund decided he really wanted the house to look like the first version, which he tore down eight months before. So the project was leveled and his workers began on the third edition. Gund's indecisiveness has proven to be expensive, but spiritual indecision is far more costly.[589]

Indifference "Indifference is as dangerous as fanaticism." —*Elie Wiesel*[590]

Infertility Infertility is present in 3.5 million American couples. That's one in every six couples. These couples spend about $2 billion a year trying to have a baby with the help of fertility clinics, and the vast majority of them fail.[591]

Inflation When Disneyland opened in 1955, admission was just $1.[592]

Influence A recent study revealed men six feet, two inches or taller average starting salaries 12.4 percent higher than equally qualified men who are less than six-feet tall. In contrast, Southern Baptists use the name of one female missionary, Lottie Moon, to raise over $100 million per year for international mission work. Moon carried the gospel of Jesus Christ to mainland China over a hundred years ago and radically changed the dynamics of mission work. This missionary giant stood just four feet, three inches tall. True influence has nothing to do with your size, but it has everything to do with the passion of your heart.[593]

Influence Walter Payton, the National Football League's Hall of Fame career rushing leader, died on November 1, 1999. In the brief forty-five years that he lived, Payton touched many lives. This was evidenced by the many who spoke in his honor. One of the most poignant statements came from his former Chicago Bears's coach, Mike Ditka. He said, "It's sad to me because he had a lot greater impact on my life than I had on his." Although there is nothing wrong with being on the receiving end of a relationship, Ditka's statement challenges us to live and give in such a way that we don't end up with regrets for not having provided a greater impact on those around us.[594]

Influence "What you do speaks so loudly I can't hear what you're saying." —*Ralph Waldo Emerson*[595]

Influence Whether or not you are a boxing fan, names like Muhammad Ali, George Foreman, and Mike Tyson conjure up pictures of big-fisted gladiators. C. D. Blalock is not as well known but his feat in the ring should not be forgotten. In the 1930s, Blalock stepped on the canvas to wage war against another boxer, but no opponent was needed that day. In one of the strangest moments in boxing history, Blalock took a swing at his rival and ended up hitting himself. His punch missed the intended target and collided with his own face. He staggered and then fell down for the count. He became the only prizefighter in history to score a knockout against himself. Sometimes our Christian influence suffers the same fate. We have been called to fight against the darkness of sin, but due to an uncontrolled temper, unchecked sexual passions, materialistic pursuits, or any number of other destructive patterns, we knock out our Christian influence and witness. In 1 Corinthians 9:27, Paul said, "I beat my body (not knock it out) and make it my slave so that after I have preached to others, I myself will not be disqualified for the prize."[596]

Information By virtue of reading this print, you are either a victim of, or a candidate for, information overload. The information age has left us inundated with . . . information. Here are some clear reminders of this truth. On the World Wide Web there are over fifteen thousand sites that discuss information overload. The Library of Congress contains 2,892 books with "stress" in the title. 45 percent of U.S. households watch TV and use computers simultaneously. 80 percent of information that is filed is never used. The average person spends 150 hours per year looking for lost information. The World Wide Web expands by seventeen pages every second. An executive earning $60,000 a year is being paid $25,000 just to read. The information overload is so significant that experts are now rethinking the root cause of attention deficit disorder. Although millions of Americans are thought to suffer from an inherited form of ADD, these experts are now recognizing a whole new manifestation of what they call "culturally induced ADD." It is obvious we must fight to keep from drowning in this sea of information, and we must likewise take strategic measures to make certain the most important information of all (John 3:16) is not lost amid the comparative clutter of superfluous trivia.[597]

Information The New York Times, covering everything from international news to business and local affairs, contains more information in one edition than a person in the seventeenth century would encounter in a lifetime.[598]

Initials Have you ever taken much time to contemplate your initials? A lot of people do and what they consider is not always very optimistic. The University of California at San Diego recently presented their findings from a study of five million death certificates. They looked at men (because their initials generally don't change with marriage) who died in California from 1969 through 1997. Psychologist Nicholas Christenfeld, who headed the study, said we all have either good, bad, or neutral initials. An example of "good" initials would be, ACE, VIP, JOY, WIN, or WOW. Examples of "bad" initials include, APE, BUM, DUD, RAT, or PIG. Neutral initials would be like mine, REM. When all of the research was tabulated, the results showed that men with "good" initials lived an average of 4.48 years longer than those with "neutral" initials, and 7.2 years longer than those tagged with "bad" initials. Although the results aren't conclusive, the findings do seem to support the idea that liking your name and liking yourself may be linked together. Such insight probably won't be included in the next church growth conference you attend, but it does provide a small reminder that a person's view of himself can impact his lifestyle. You can't go around changing people's initials, although Jesus did change Peter's name, but you can change the way they view themselves. And if you do get the notion to temporarily change everyone's initials for a particular Sunday, why not give them all the same set of letters, YAL. Let it stand for You Are Loved by God, and the people of this church. It's a winning set of initials![599]

Innovation "The test of an innovation is that it creates value. A novelty only creates amusement." —*Peter Drucker* [600]

Integrity Abraham Lincoln is remembered for his honesty, but have you heard the classic story about his integrity? In 1836, Lincoln agreed to marry a woman he had not seen for three years. When he saw her his heart sank. He wrote, "She did not look as my imagination had pictured her." He went on to describe his prospective bride: "I knew she was oversize, but she now appeared a fair match for Falstaff." He said she reminded him of his mother because of two features, her lack of teeth and her age. He also said, "Nothing could have commenced at the size of infancy, and reached her present bulk in less than thirty-five or forty years." "In short," he summarized, "I was not at all pleased." In today's culture the engagement would have ended, but Lincoln was a man of his word. He went through the process of courting, and then proposed to her on bended knee. Ironically, the woman rejected his proposal. He thought she was being polite so he went through the accepted rites of pressing her to reconsider. Finally, he realized she truly had no intention of marrying him. Lincoln concluded, "Others have been made fools of by the girls, but this can never be with truth said of me. I most emphatically, in this instance, made a fool of myself." True integrity willingly risks looking foolish for the intent of doing what is honorable and right.[601]

Integrity During one of the quarterfinal events at Wimbledon, Mal Washington of the United States was competing against a German opponent named Alex Radulescu. In the final set of their match, Washington made an impressive shot that got past Radulescu, but the linesman called it out. Washington protested to the chair umpire, but he would not overrule the call. Surprisingly, Radulescu approached the umpire and assured him the ball landed inbounds. The call was reversed and Washington won the point. NBC analyst, John McEnroe, then said, "Radulescu was obviously showing his inexperience on the professional circuit by giving up a point he didn't have to, one that will most likely cost him the match." Later on, Mal Washington said, "That was probably the biggest show of sportsmanship by any athlete I've ever seen. I think only one guy on the tour would have done that, and it was him."[602]

Integrity "He who is required by the necessity of his position to speak the highest things is compelled by the same necessity to exemplify the highest things." —*Gregory the Great*[603]

Integrity One man called it the best prayer he'd ever heard. "Dear God, please help me be the person my dog thinks I am." If that prayer is answered, you'll be known for your integrity.[604]

Integrity "The time is always right to do what is right." —*Martin Luther King*[605]

Integrity "The truth of the matter is that you always know the right thing to do. The hard part is doing it." —*General Norman Schwarzkopf*[606]

Internet Six percent of Internet users suffer from some form of addiction to it.[607]

Internet The Sexual Recovery Institute in Los Angeles recently disclosed some research that reveals sex is the number one topic searched for on the Internet. Dr. Robert Weiss, director of the study, noted 60 percent of all Web-site visits are sexual in nature. An estimated twenty-five million Americans visit cyber sex sites between one and ten hours per week. Seventy percent indicated they keep their pornographic habit a secret. In the March 2000 *Journal of Sexual Addiction and Compulsivity*, a study by Stanford University revealed "at least 200,000 Internet users are hooked on pornography sites, X-rated chat rooms, or other sexual materials online." These 200,000 people who were classified as "cybersex compulsives" spent more than eleven hours per week visiting sexually oriented areas. Dr. Al Cooper, leader of the research, noted their figure of 200,000 was very conservative and represents roughly 1 percent of those using the Internet.[608]

Intervention What if she had intervened and gotten involved? Lori Fortier is haunted by that thought. In the fall of 1994, Timothy McVeigh visited his army buddy, Michael Fortier and his wife, Lori, in Kingman, Arizona. During McVeigh's stay, he pulled out soup cans to demonstrate how he would create a "shape charge" in a rental truck to bomb an Oklahoma City federal building for the avengment of the 1993 raid on the Branch Davidian compound in Waco, Texas. He also shared how the scheme was being financed by robbing an Arkansas gun dealer. McVeigh wasn't just dreaming, he was sharing specific plans. When the first news reports were released after the April 19, 1995, explosion that killed 168 people, Fortier said, "I knew right away it was Tim." She feels enormous guilt because, as she said, "I could have stopped it. I was in denial that he was really capable of this. I now wish I could have stopped it." Lori Fortier received immunity from the prosecution in exchange for her testimony, but she will never know immunity from her conscience because she hesitated to intervene. Every day we have the opportunity to prevent pain, heartache, and eternal separation from God, but too often we opt for passivity rather than intervention. May we all learn from Fortier and get involved to thwart the schemes of Satan.[609]

Invocation A little girl captured the essence of invocations when she wrote the following letter to God: "Dear God, My family, the Sandersons, is pleased to invite your family, the Gods, over for dinner (I figured you might like this). Please respond in writing or on a tablet. Very truly yours, Sheila Sanderson." Every invocation should be just as personal as this little girl's invitation to God.[610]

Isolation A Japanese sculptor came to America with a unique twist on his art. At his exhibit, each statue had a small sign that read, "Please touch." He wanted people to literally feel his work. In America, we are more accustomed to signs that read, "Don't touch." Whether it's statues or people, we tend to keep our respectful distance. In reality, we are surrounded by people who want to be touched and noticed. They may not have a small sign that invites you to reach out, but you can be certain most people are hungry for the touch of a friend.[611]

Jesus Concerning the Messiah, the Old Testament contains sixty major prophecies and 270 ramifications. Jesus fulfilled every one of these predictions, and this accomplishment is beyond comprehension. The mathematical probability of Jesus fulfilling just eight of these sixty major prophecies is 1 in 100,000,000,000,000,000. To grasp the enormity of this number, Dr. Peter Stoner has provided a picture for our understanding. The entire state of Texas would be covered with silver dollars, two feet deep. One coin would be marked, then the entire sea of silver would be thoroughly mixed. A blindfolded man would be instructed to travel as far as he wished, but he must pick up the marked coin on his first try. The chances of that occurring are the same as Jesus fulfilling just eight of the sixty major prophecies. And to think, he fulfilled them all! The probability of Jesus not being the Messiah is mathematically impossible.[612]

Jesus "For an ever-changing world, there is a never-changing message: Jesus Christ is Lord!" —*Anonymous*[613]

Jesus Larry King created a lucrative career by simply asking questions. This celebrity has been interviewing people for over forty years with his mastery of probing questions. The tables were turned when he was interviewed for the fortieth anniversary of his broadcasting debut. Bryant Gumbel had the honor of asking King some very interesting questions. Possibly the most interesting question came at the conclusion of the show when Gumbel asked King, "What questions would you ask God if he were a guest on your show?" King ignited with a torrent of questions about God's level of participation in human activity, but the very first question out of his mouth was, "Do you have a son?" Although King claims to be an agnostic, he understands the importance of asking this question first. Determining Jesus' relationship to God is pivotal for salvation, but we needn't wait for God's reply. He has already answered King's question long before the brilliant interviewer was born. In Matthew 3:17, God declared at Jesus' baptism, "This is my beloved Son, in whom I am well pleased."[614]

Jesus On July 30, 1999, the *National Catholic Reporter* announced an exciting contest for artists. To aid in the celebration of a new millennium, they hosted a contest to discover a bold new image of Jesus. Everyone was welcome to enter any visual media—computer art, stained glass, silk screens, even photographs. The only criteria for winning was "there ought to be something new that we haven't seen before." The winner's artwork of a multiethnic-looking Christ graced the millennium issue's front cover on December 24, 1999. Michael Farrell, editor of the magazine, fostered the idea from his own frustration about the skewed perspective of Americans concerning the millennium. He said, "Ask anybody about the millennium and they talk about survivalists going into the mountains, or glitches on their computers. Nobody is talking about this extraordinary man who came from heaven two thousand years ago." Farrell also noted, "Until our time, this (Jesus) was the most popular subject for artists." In many ways, he hoped this contest would alter those two trends. Mr. Farrell's idea represents the sentiments of a whole host of people who are longing for a fresh, new presentation of Jesus. Although some in this camp sadly seek a God who is simply more accommodating of their lifestyle, the majority are just crying out for the Lord they have read about in the New Testament. May we as Christians live up to our name (little Christs) and our calling (Matthew 5:13–16) so people can have a fresh and accurate picture of Jesus Christ.[615]

Jesus Oprah Winfrey received a lot of criticism for her involvement with Ellen DeGeneres in April of 1997. Oprah hosted the openly gay DeGeneres on her April 15 talk show, then gave a cameo performance a week later during the hour-long show when DeGeneres's TV character, Ellen, revealed her homosexuality. Winfrey was questioned about her pro-homosexual attitude by a young woman from the audience who asked Oprah how she could say she's a Christian and then support something that the Bible says is wrong. Winfrey replied, "Well, I have a different view of 'Christian' than you do. I'm a follower of Jesus Christ, but the Jesus Christ I follow embraces and loves everybody, and the God I serve doesn't care whether you're tall or short, or whether you were born mentally retarded, or whether you were born black or Asian or gay." To such rationalized theology we would do well to heed the words of Christian authors Patrick Morley and Luis Palau. Morley notes, "There's a God we want and there's a God who is, and they are not the same God." Palau adds, "The turning point comes when we stop seeking the God we want and start seeking the God who is." [616]

Jesus Tina is a Southern Baptist volunteer missionary from Kentucky. On a recent mission trip to Asia, she worked with twenty-two other volunteers who used basketball to enter nations where open evangelism is prohibited by law. In these limited-access countries you can only talk about your faith if someone asks about it. They counter this by touring the land playing Asian opponents in basketball with the hopes of drawing large crowds that will ask about their faith. During one of their trips, Tina and her teammates sat down with their Asian opponents after the game and began talking about the various struggles of life. As the discussion turned to relationships, one Asian player asked Tina what she does when she feels alone. Tina told her that she has a friend named Jesus who is always with her. The Asian woman silently looked around at all of the remaining people in the gym and then asked, "Which one is Jesus?" Throughout America and around the world people aren't sure who Jesus Christ is. We must make certain every person has an opportunity to meet him.[617]

Jesus When Warner Sallman painted his depiction of Christ, his intent was to draw people toward the Savior he loved. In May of 1995, the Supreme Court ruled that a reproduction of Sallman's painting was too offensive for the Bloomingdale High School to hang in their hallway. This Michigan school began taking the heat in 1992 when Eric Pensinger was a senior. He was an agnostic who found the painting offensive so he sought help from the American Civil Liberties Union. The Court upheld a lower court's decision that "the portrait advances religion." Sallman's goal was accomplished, but one kid found his goal offensive. The picture had been hanging in the same spot for thirty years with no complaints, but when one kid found it offensive, down it came. (See 1 Corinthians 1:23)[618]

Jesus Worldwide, over sixty-six thousand books have been written about Jesus.[619]

Jesus "You do well to learn, above all, the religion of Jesus Christ."
—*George Washington* [620]

Joy W. C. Fields said, "Start each day with a smile and get it over with." A lot of folks have adopted his tongue-in-cheek philosophy, but not Chelsey Thomas. In 1996 at the age of eight, Chelsey started beginning each day with a smile, but it wasn't so she could "get it over with." She began smiling because for the first time in her life she was able to do so. The little Californian is one of about one thousand Americans affected by a rare condition called Moebius syndrome. It impairs the use of facial muscles and renders the sufferer unable to smile. After three operations conducted by a team of surgeons at Kaiser Permanente Medical Center in Woodland Hills, California, Chelsey is all smiles. They grafted muscles and nerves from her leg to facial muscles used for chewing and biting. Now for the first time in her life she can smile. Although few Christians suffer from the physical condition that has plagued little Chelsey, far too many appear to be affected by spiritual Moebius syndrome. For such sufferers there is good news. The Great Physician can take a graft of joy from his crucified legs and put an eternal smile on your face. God created you to smile, how else can it be explained that it takes seventeen muscles to smile and forty to frown?[621]

Judgment "Before the Judgment Seat of Christ my service will be judged not by how much I have done, but by how much I could have done." —*A. W. Tozer* [622]

Judgment It is believed that Julius Caesar was the first notable person to decide an issue by flipping a coin. His methodology prevailed once again as recently as 1998. In a runoff election for the Chambers County commissioner's position in Southeast Texas, a coin toss was used to determine the winner. Judge Mark Davidson evaluated the evidence surrounding the tabulations of votes garnered on April 21, 1998, and saw no signs of fraud. David Abernathy and Judy Edmonds tied the race with 669 votes. So on May 21, 1998, Judge Davidson tossed a coin into the air and Edmonds became the new Precinct 2 commissioner. Aren't you glad our eternal destiny isn't decided like that? Thirty silver coins were tossed two millennia ago to secure the certainty of eternal life through Jesus Christ our Lord.[623]

Judgment Josh Hempel of Calgary, Alberta, engaged himself in an argument with a Christian about the existence of God. He stated his case against God, then closed the argument with an appeal for God to strike him with lightening if he was wrong. God obliged his request, but seasoned his judgment with grace as he allowed Hempel to recover after being hospitalized.[624]

Judgment "Only God is in a position to look down on anyone." — *Anonymous* [625]

Judgment The Pew Research Center for the *People and Press* compiled their results from a 1997 national survey. Under the heading of Judgment, 64 percent of the respondents completely agreed with the statement: "We all will be called before God at the Judgment Day to answer for our sins." Only 52 percent completely agreed a decade before. Regardless of how many people agree, the Bible clearly declares that such a day awaits every person (Hebrews 9:27).[626]

Judgmentalism Most everyone has heard of the dilemma concerning a glass of water with half its potential contents. We are left to decide if we are a pessimist because we view the glass as half-empty, or we say it's half-full and claim to be an optimist. In a recent article from *Parade Magazine*, an insightful writer brought out another option to the formula for determining one's view of life. This writer said, "All I see is a glass of water." Frequently we feel compelled to define and label not only ourselves but others as well. This forces us to judge people, when in reality we would do far better to simply see one another as people without prejudicial views. We don't have to see ourselves or anyone else as half-empty or half-full, we can just picture each other for what we are . . . people who are treasured by a loving and gracious Heavenly Father.[627]

Justice Research into the area of judicial sentencing revealed that prettier women receive less-severe sentences than their less-attractive counterparts. Our system of justice is skewed by human involvement but fortunately "righteousness and justice are the foundation of thy throne . . ." (Psalm 89:14)[628]

Kidnapping Worldwide, thirty thousand people are kidnapped each year.[629]

Kindness Dr. James DeLoach has related the incident of an unusually friendly and happy taxi driver. Unaccustomed to such a disposition, a curious passenger asked why he was so cheerful. The taxi driver's interesting response was: He said, "It all started when I heard about a taxi driver who was so kind to a passenger that the man remembered him in his will by leaving him $65,000. So, I thought I would try it and maybe, if I was polite and helpful, somebody might me leave me something. But after I tried it, I found it was so much fun being good that I decided that I would do it just for the fun of it, reward or no reward." Paul said, "Let us not become weary in doing good . . ." (Galatians 6:9) because he knew we actually become weary in our faith when we don't do good deeds. Acts of kindness give a boost of encouragement to those who give as well as those who receive.[630]

Laws We are frequently tempted to believe laws restrict us rather than protect us. Each year this erroneous philosophy inflicts great pain on thousands of innocent people. Every year in America, 260,000 accidents are caused by drivers who run red lights, and in the process, 850 people are killed. God has likewise provided red lights in his Word for the protection of all. Unfortunately, many see his stop signs as too restrictive so they ignore the mandate and plow through to inflict needless pain upon themselves and others.[631]

Lawsuits Litigation adds 2.5 percent to the average cost of a new product in America.[632]

Leadership Are you looking for a word that defines the governmental system of your church? Hopefully you won't need to use either of these words: mediocracy (government led by the mediocre), kakistocracy (government led by the least qualified).[633]

Leadership "At any moment in history the world is in the hands of 2 percent of the people: the excited and the committed." —*Winston Churchill*[634]

Leadership "Good leaders inspire people to have confidence in them, great leaders inspire people to have confidence in themselves." —*Sam Ewing*[635]

Leadership "I can get up at 9:00 A.M. and be rested, or I can get up at 6:00 A.M. and be President." —*Jimmy Carter*[636]

Leadership In frustration over a piano that was always out of tune, bandleader Count Basie told a club owner, "I'm not returning until you fix it!" A month later the club owner called Basie to let him know the piano had been fixed. Basie was irate when he sat down to play and discovered the instrument was still out of tune. He shouted at the owner, "You said you fixed it!" The musically inept owner replied, "I did. I had it painted." Effective leadership not only requires solving problems, but solving the right problems the right way.[637]

Leadership In May of 1996, one of the greatest tragedies in mountain-climbing history took place on the slopes of Mount Everest. In a quest to stand on the 29,028-foot summit, twelve climbers lost their lives and another required the amputation of an arm and the fingers on his opposite hand, and reconstructive surgery of his frostbitten face. Jon Krakauer was a part of this expedition and has written of the experience in his best-selling book, *Into Thin Air*. Krakauer describes how the imperiled group came to this dreadful fate. On their final ascent to the top, several climbers violated clear instructions not to be on the summit after 2:00 P.M. This delay caused the entire group to remain in a dangerous sector of the mountain far too long. A murderous storm blew in on the climbers and they found themselves in a fight for their lives. The full-blown blizzard sent the wind-chill factor plummeting one hundred degrees below zero. They were enveloped in darkness and blowing snow, and visibility dropped to less than twenty feet. Their oxygen was depleted and the batteries on their lights were fading. For two hours they simply staggered blindly through the snow hoping to stumble on the camp. Hypothermia and exhaustion were taking a terrible toll and their floundering steps nearly took them over the precipice of a seven-thousand-foot cliff. Nothing but chaos could describe their search for safety. The guide knew if they kept wandering in the storm they were going to lose somebody, so he huddled the group together and they waited for a break in the storm. With no protection from the teeth of this storm, they sat passively in the snow. Little did they know, they were less than fifteen minutes from the safety and shelter of their camp. Devastation occurred because leadership broke down within fifteen minutes of success and survival.[638]

Leadership Rick Koster came up with a great idea in the mid-1980s. The construction consultant from Oakville, Ontario, invented a flotation device designed to aid swimmers. It was unlike anything that had ever entered a pool. The long, slender floats looked more like spaghetti than human buoys. Today, it's hard to find a swimming pool that hasn't experienced the brightly colored noodles. Most stores have a hard time keeping adequate stock of the Funnoodles, which have sold millions nationwide since their massive release in 1994. Kidpower Inc.

of Brentwood, Tennessee, has made these stringy floats a national phenomenon and amassed a small fortune in the process. Koster, though, has not enjoyed the tremendous success of his creation. Unfortunately, he never pursued a patent for his invention and didn't seem interested in marketing his noodle-looking floats. He can only wish he had done more with the good idea he partially developed. All leaders know the agony of wishing they had given greater attention to a certain idea, project, or pursuit. Likewise, true leaders learn from such mistakes and move on to make sure all good ideas get the chance to reach their full potential. Demonstrate some of your leadership skills this month by developing one of those ideas you've been mulling over. Who knows, your idea may end up being even bigger than those crazy noodles.[639]

Leadership Several years ago, Robert Samuelson wrote an insightful editorial about government subsidies. His obvious point was to highlight the absurdity and waste that accompanies so many of these bureaucratic programs. In the midst of his article he posed a very significant question, "Would we create these programs today if they did not already exist?" Effective leaders must continually ask this very hard question because it forces us to objectively evaluate the value of all we do. Would we create this ministry if it didn't already exist? Would we create this type of budget planning process if it didn't already exist? Would we create this style of worship if it didn't already exist? This question can be applied to all we do, and it will assist us in determining what we actually need to be doing.[640]

Leadership "The number one characteristic of a leader is that they enjoy other people." —*Peter Drucker* [641]

Leadership "The secret of managing is to keep the guys who hate you away from the guys who are undecided." —*Casey Stengel* [642]

Leadership The White House serves as the official residence for each president of the United States. This majestic structure stands on eighteen acres along Pennsylvania Avenue in Washington, D.C. Its history is rich in that all but one U.S. president has lived there. Can you name the one president who lived elsewhere? It was none other than George Washington. Our nation's first president was never able to enjoy the fruits of his own vision. It was he who chose the site and the architect for the White House, but he was never able to live there. Washington's leadership played an important role in the birth and establishment of this country. His methods and demeanor made him a popular man because he consistently demonstrated servant leadership. His hand in the construction of the White House helps convey this truth. Although he knew he would never live in the White House, he took great pains to make certain it was a dwelling that befit the United States presidency. It is indeed a rare man who undertakes a project that will not bring benefit to himself. The historical fact that every president except Washington has enjoyed the elegance of this unique home is a tribute to servant leadership. All great leaders must look beyond personal benefit and gain to see the much larger picture: that of having concern for those who will walk into the future. Are you building great homes you will never own or occupy? A servant leader does just that! [643]

Leadership Twice a year, airline pilots are required to spend a week retraining and sharpening their skills. Regardless of how many years they have been flying, the same requirements apply. The demands for continual training are high because the airline industry realizes people's lives depend on their pilot's skills. Spiritual leaders need to embrace similar standards of excellence because far more than physical survival is at stake. May we all demonstrate wise leadership by continually submitting ourselves to the task of sharpening our skills. Our expertise, or lack thereof, holds eternal consequences.[644]

Legacy How will you be remembered? Clair Booth Luce once told Richard Nixon that the significance of any person in history, no matter how complex, can be summarized in just one sentence. Think about the following people and see if it's true: John F. Kennedy, Helen Keller, Jonas Salk, Jim Jones, Neil Armstrong, Babe Ruth, and Richard Nixon. Like these notable figures of history, the significance of your life will most likely take no more than one sentence to summarize. What will those brief words include? [645]

Legacy Tommy Lasorda is known for his tongue-in-cheek humor. When once asked about his future plans, the perennial Los Angeles Dodger said he plans to work for the Dodgers even after he's dead. "I told my wife to make sure the Dodger schedule is posted on my gravestone so that maybe someone comes by, sees it, and decides to go see a game." You can be sure the kidder in blue is joking, but his thought does have merit. We each have the capacity to leave a legacy that will continue to work for

Christ even after we're gone. The fact is, we should all be seeking to leave just such a legacy.[646]

Legalism Legalism insists that adherence to rules is the most important virtue. One bank teller learned a costly but valuable lesson about legalism. A distinguished-looking gentleman wearing blue jeans walked into a bank and sought to complete a transaction. The teller apologized that the man who handled such transactions was out for the day so he would need to come back tomorrow. Because that was the only business this gentleman needed, he prepared to leave by asking the teller to validate his parking receipt. The teller politely but firmly told him that their bank policy did not permit the validation of parking without the customer making a financial transaction. The man sought for an exception because he had come to do business but the appropriate personnel was not available. She didn't budge and said, "I'm sorry, but that's our policy." Disturbed by her relentless legalism, the man decided to make a transaction. John Akers, then chairman of IBM, withdrew all $1.5 million from his account. He left the bank with his validated parking ticket and, one teller was left with a resolve to not be so legalistic at her next place of employment.[647]

Lies David Lieberman is the author of a 1998 book titled *Never Be Lied to Again*. His research shows the average person lies three to four times a day. In marital relationships, lies enter the conversation about 10 percent of the time while communication between dating couples involves approximately 30 percent lies. Lieberman suggests making good eye contact when trying to determine whether or not someone is telling a lie. He notes if you ask a right-handed person where he's been and he's telling the truth, he'll look up and left because that's the side of the brain that's used for recalling visual information. If he's manufacturing a lie, you'll see him look up and to the right. Of course it would be a whole lot easier, and far better, if we would all just look down at God's Word and apply his straightforward command: "Don't lie to each other . . ." (Colossians 3:9).[648]

Life "It's not how long a man lives, but how well he uses the time allotted him." —*Martin Luther King*[649]

Life "O God, don't let me die until I'm dead. I've witnessed people who seem to die long before they're buried." — *Tom Haggai*[650]

Life "Whether or not you realize it, you are in an important time of your Christian life right now." —*Barbara Peil*[651]

Listening "Silent and listen are spelled with the same letters." — *Anonymous*[652]

Logic Pilots call it a "grease job" and all of their passengers call it a great landing. It's that experience of a plane gently landing on the runway. Conversely, when pilots do what they call a "firm" landing, most passengers feel like their captain needs a little more practice. Ironically, safety dictates the exact opposite of what we assume is logical. The task of landing sixty tons of plane within the three-thousand-foot "touchdown zone" is far safer when everyone feels a good thump. Although it seems to defy common sense and logic, a hard landing is the better option of these two landing styles. The firm landing forces the wheels to gain immediate and solid traction, thus giving the pilot greater control of his plane. If we are so easily confused about the common experience of landing a plane, how much more should we expect to find our logical expectations at odds with God's will and ways (Isaiah 55:8-9). Following the leadings of God may not always seem logical, so when you're in a dilemma about obeying God, just drive out to the airport and think about all of those passengers who have the whole landing thing totally backwards.[653]

Loneliness According to a Gallup poll, four in ten Americans admit to frequent feelings of intense loneliness.[654]

Longevity Does life ever seem unfair? Only an unusual optimist would answer No. When such times occur it can be helpful to remember one of the unique advantages we have over our American ancestors. In 1900, the life expectancy was age forty-six for men and age forty-eight for women. Presently, men can expect to live seventy-two years and women can hope for seven-nine. So the next time you get discouraged with life, you might get a boost by simply thanking God for the extra two or three decades he has provided.[655]

Longevity What does it take to increase the longevity of your life? A study of people who exceeded the century mark was completed to gain some insights for living longer. The study leaned heavily on centenarians in the Soviet Union. Here is the consensus of that research. Be married. Stay in one geographic location. Do some physical activity every day. Go to bed no later than 8:00 or 9:00 P.M. and sleep up to ten hours per day. Take long walks. Eat in moderation. Eat three to four times a day at specific times and always slightly undereat. Drink a bit of homemade wine before meals. Avoid smoking. Limit sexual activity. Of course there is one resource that was overlooked in this study. According to the Population Research Center at the University of Texas, "people who attend church weekly live an average of seven years longer than people who never attend worship services." The researchers noted this trend was true in both sexes and in various races. Regular church attendance literally can add years to your life.[656]

Lord's Supper Recent research has revealed additional benefits to drinking purple grape juice. A compound in purple grapes called quercetin has been found to have preventive agents against cataracts. Quercetin enhances the body's ability to keep the lenses of an eye clear. This physical benefit of an element used to observe the Lord's Supper reminds us of the spiritual value attached to the regular remembrance of Christ's sacrificial love. When we consistently take the Lord's Supper in a "worthy manner" (1 Corinthians 11:23–30) our spiritual sight is enhanced and the things of God are prevented from becoming a blur.[657]

Lottery In 1988, William "Bud" Post won the Pennsylvania lottery jackpot of $16.2 million. On September 26, 1996, he auctioned off the remaining $4.9 million of his winnings to get out of debt and kiss his bad luck good-bye. Post told Bankruptcy Judge Judith Fitzgerald, "I want to get rid of the lottery, believe me, Your Honor. It's really been a pain." Since the day Post hit it big, his brother has been convicted of trying to kill him so he could gain access to the money, his sixth wife moved out, his former landlady, won a lawsuit for one-third of his winnings, he lost his bar and used-car business, and the gas at his mansion was turned off (he said he felt lucky to still have electricity and a phone). To cover his debts, the court agreed to auction off the $4.9 million worth of payments he was to receive over the next seventeen years. Prosperity Partners bought the seventeen-year payout for $2.65 million and Post left the courtroom saying, "I'm happier today than the day I won the lottery." This fifty-eight-year-old former carnival worker discovered the truth of Paul's words to Timothy, "For the love of money is a root of all sorts of evil, and some by longing for it have wandered away from the faith, and pierced themselves with many a pang" (1 Timothy 6:10).[658]

Love At 5:54 P.M., Lieutenant John Blandford stood in Grand Central Station with his heart racing. In just six brief minutes he would meet the woman who had captured his heart. He had never seen her with his eyes, but his heart knew her through the words she had written. It all started when he picked up a book in the Army library. *Of Human Bondage* was littered with personal notes in the margins. He had always hated the practice of writing in books, but these remarks seemed to seize his heart. He found the name of Hollis Meynell on the bookplate and began his search for the woman to whom he was so attracted. When he secured her address, he wrote her and she responded. For the next thirteen months they corresponded, but she refused his every request to send a photograph. She explained, "If your feeling for me has any reality, any honest basis, what I look like won't matter. When you come to New York, you shall see me and make your decision. Remember, both of us are free to stop or to go after that—whichever we choose." They had agreed she would wear a red rose on her lapel to identify her among the sea of travelers. At one minute to six, he spotted a beautiful woman moving toward him. His heart leaped. She was young, slender, and blond. He started moving toward her without noticing she was not wearing a red rose. She gave him a provocative smile and asked, "Going my way, soldier?" He took one step closer then noticed Hollis Meynell. She was just a few feet behind the beautiful young lady. A red rose was on the lapel of a woman clearly past her forties, with graying hair tucked under a worn hat, and thick ankles thrust into low-heeled shoes. As the attractive young lady strolled away, Blandford felt as though he were being torn in two. He wanted to follow the beauty he had seen, yet it was the words of this unattractive woman that had so completely captured his heart. He responded as he felt he should and gripped the worn, blue copy of the book *Of Human Bondage* that would identify him to her. He realized what he would share with this woman would not be love, but it would be something special. They had established a friendship for which he was most grateful. With a twinge of disappointment, he squared his shoulders, saluted, held out the book and said, "I'm Lieutenant John Blandford, and you are Miss Meynell. I'm so glad to meet you. May I take you to dinner?" The woman extended a tolerant smile and remarked, "I don't know what this is all about, son. The young lady, who just went by, she begged me to wear this rose on my coat. She said that if you asked me to go out with you, I should tell you that she's waiting for you in that big restaurant across the street. She said it was some kind of test."[659]

Love Bruce Reynolds died quietly in a small, New York town. At his memorial service, people became aware of an incredible secret. Twenty-five years before his death, Bruce's first wife left him for another man and took his only child, a girl named Ivah. Bruce financially supported his daughter with monthly checks even though that expense prevented him from visiting her in Florida. His inability to see her did not keep him from telling her about his love. Every week for twenty-five years Bruce wrote his daughter. Ivah seldom wrote back but it didn't stop Bruce from communicating his love. Even after a series of strokes that made it impossible for him to write, Bruce dictated the weekly letter to his second wife, Belle. He did that until the day he died. Some thirteen hundred times, from 1964 to 1989, Bruce Reynolds used the modest resources of pen and paper to relay a message of unfailing love for his only child.[660]

Love During the reign of Cyrus, King of Persia, there was a rebel chieftain who constantly harassed the Persian armies. Exasperated by the havoc Cagular created, Cyrus dispatched his forces to capture this autonomous warrior so he could eliminate the problem. Not only would he kill Cagular, but his family as well. Yet, when the mighty Cagular arrived, Cyrus rethought his plans. While standing face to face in the throne room, the powerful king asked, "Cagular, if I were to save your life, what would you do?" He replied, "King, I would serve you the rest of my days." Cyrus pondered this response then asked, "What would you do if I spared the life of your wife?" Cagular declared, "Your Majesty, if you spared my wife, I would die for you." Upon further reflection, Cyrus not only decided to pardon this condemned soldier, but he made an alliance with Cagular and put him in charge of his troops along the southern border. As Cagular returned home with his family, he began to talk of the amazing wealth in Cyrus's court. He turned to his wife and asked, "Did you see all of the marble? The soldiers' armor of silver was magnificent, and what about the solid gold throne that Cyrus sat on?" His wife replied, "I didn't see any of that?" In dumbfounded surprise Cagular asked, "What did you see?" She said, "I saw only the face of the man who said he would die for me." Love of that nature and magnitude will transform any marriage.[661]

Love "Human love says, 'I will love you if . . .' God says, 'I will love you even . . .'" —*Stuart Briscoe* [662]

Love In 1991, Dr. Robertson McQuilkin made a courageous decision that has impacted the understanding of love in many people's heart.

McQuilkin had been the president of Columbia Bible College for twenty-two years when he walked away from that position to care for his ailing wife, Muriel McQuilkin who had Alzheimer's disease. Ten years before, she repeated a story to some friends while vacationing in Florida. That began a process of medical attention that ultimately proved she had the disease. McQuilkin suggested the board begin searching for a successor, yet everyone hoped he could continue until retirement. Some wise and godly friends encouraged him to consider institutional care. They too loved Muriel, but they also saw God's hand and calling on his leadership at the school. For several years he tried to juggle the challenge by using a caregiver during the day while he went to the college. With amazing love, Muriel would try to follow him to school. The walk was one-half mile and she would make that trip as many as ten times a day. Sometimes while preparing her for bed, he would find blood on her feet from the incessant walks. He knew a decision had to be made, yet in his mind the decision was resolved forty-two years prior when he vowed "in sickness and in health, till death do us part." He walked away from a thriving ministry and many unfulfilled dreams, but there was no regret. McQuilkin said, "I don't have to care for her, I get to. If I took care of her for forty years, I would never be out of her debt." Those who have heard this story have been deeply touched, yet McQuilkin didn't at first understand why. It became less of a mystery when a distinguished oncologist told him, "Almost all women stand by their men; very few men stand by their women." Maybe this unfailing love explains the uniqueness of Mrs. McQuilkin's communication. After losing the ability to speak in intelligible sentences, she retained the capacity to regularly tell her husband, "I love you." This is indeed the love that never fails![663]

Love In 1994, a young boy was dropped from a high-rise project building in Chicago (see *McHenry's Quips, Quotes & Other Notes* p.246). After the boy's death, a counselor began working with his younger brother. It was learned that the little boy raced down the stairs immediately after his brother was dropped. The counselor asked him what he was thinking while descending the stairs. The loving little brother said he hoped to catch his brother before he hit the ground. An impossible task, yet a beautiful expression of love. Irrational love does not first determine whether or not a particular expression of love is practical, logical, or possible, . . . it simply conveys its affection wholeheartedly.[664]

Love Joan Mills enjoyed a bedtime ritual with her little boy. They each compared how much they loved each other. She said, "I wouldn't trade you for all the boys in the world." Then he creatively compared his love for her by saying, "I wouldn't trade you for forty motorcycles," or, "I wouldn't trade you for Aunt Judi's pool if it were filled with cash and I was swimming in it." Joan says one comparison has stood out above all others. One time little Andy said, "I love you with all the pieces of my heart." Does your heart ever feel like it's in pieces? Maybe it has been broken by disappointment, or torn by decisions, priorities, and tasks. Andy is right, our hearts are made of many different pieces. The question is, how many of those pieces will be devoted to loving God and others? "You shall love the Lord your God with all the pieces of your heart . . ."[665]

Love Marilyn vos Savant has a weekly column called "Ask Marilyn." She is listed in the *Guiness Book of World Records* Hall of Fame for having the highest IQ. In a recent article one reader wrote, "What do you consider to be the ultimate compliment anyone could pay you?" Ms. vos Savant wisely replied, "To me, the ultimate compliment consists of only three words: 'I love you.'" Based on this brilliant woman's insight, God has given each of us the ultimate compliment and has asked all of us to give the same to others.[666]

Love On November 12, 1996, Alvin Straight died of a heart ailment, but his legacy of love will be remembered for generations to come. During the summer of 1994, Alvin was age seventy-four and unable to drive because of his poor eyesight. His brother, Henry, had suffered a stroke and Alvin desperately wanted to see him. As Alvin sized up his options, he decided his only mode of transportation was his riding lawn mower. So he set off in early July from his home in Iowa. He attached a trailer to his lawn mower to carry gasoline, clothes, food, and camping gear. In mid-August he reached his brother's house in Blue River, Wisconsin. This seventy-four-year-old man traveled 240 miles on a lawn mower to affirm the love and concern he had for his brother. Such love will not be forgotten. Maybe that's why his funeral procession included family members pulling a trailer with a lawn mower on top.[667]

Love Robert Hasty was devastated by the death of his wife, Frances, in 1995. The couple had been married fifty-two years. Because his home and her burial place were 240 miles apart, Hasty would make the drive about four times a year, usually in conjunction with a holiday or Frances's birthday. During the week before Easter in 1998, the seventy-five-year-old widower traveled from his residence in Spring, Texas, to his wife's grave in Fort Worth, Texas. He came with Easter lilies to decorate her place in the cemetery. After neatly securing them to her burial plot, he apparently knelt down to pray. At dusk, the maintenance workers of Laurel Land Memorial Park found his lifeless body still kneeling at his beloved wife's grave. Robert Hasty, Jr. said, "He loved my mother deeply, and missed her very, very much." Such endearing love is worth remembering.[668]

Love "There are many in the world who are dying for a piece of bread, but there are many more dying for a little love." —*Mother Teresa* [669]

Love The rebellion of a teenage daughter was breaking her mother's heart. Their struggle reached its zenith when the young girl was arrested for driving under the influence of alcohol. After posting bail for her daughter, the two did not speak until the next afternoon. When they came together, the woman handed her daughter a small wrapped gift. The girl flippantly opened it and was exasperated by what she saw. The box contained a small rock. She rolled her eyes and asked, "What's this for?" Her mother simply replied, "Read the card." She did and was overcome by the words inside. Tears began streaming down her cheeks as she reached out to embrace her mom. The card said, "This rock is more than a million years old. That's how long it will take before I give up on you." God broke through to us with his unrelenting and enduring love. We would do well to use that same strategy to break through to one another.[670]

Love The van Trujls are a Dutch family who began leisurely sailing around the world in 1995. Life was quite pleasant until they were attacked in March of 2000 about fifty miles from Honduras. They had anchored their steel, forty-four-foot yacht near Half Moon Reef in the Atlantic Ocean. Jacco van Trujl launched an inflatable dinghy with his son Willem to fish a few hundred yards from their boat. While they were gone, modern-day pirates pulled alongside their yacht and boarded. Sensing something was not right, the two headed back toward the yacht. The pirates opened fire on them and young Willem was instantly paralyzed from the waist down. Jacco desperately swam to the ship with his wounded son and the attackers quickly departed without hurting his wife, Jannie. She sent out a distress signal, but five hours would pass before any help arrived. She held her son and kept assuring him that he would be all right. While keeping continual pressure on her son's bleeding wound, Willem said, "I'm so happy they shot me, Mom." She quickly asked, "How can you say that?" He replied, "Because if they had shot one of you, I would have died from sadness." Twenty hours would elapse before Willem received medical attention at a hospital in Honduras, but he survived the experience. He will never walk or stand again, but his parents will always remember the words that made him stand taller than he ever would with healthy legs.[671]

Loyalty Sculptors in ancient Rome were wise to the disloyalty of their citizenry. Because heroes were so frequently discarded, they put detachable heads on their heroic statues so heads could be easily replaced when heroes were replaced.[672]

Luck In 1999, the sheriff's department of Bernalillo, New Mexico, reported a most unusual single-vehicle accident. The motorist veered off the road and rolled his car onto its side while trying to attach a lucky shamrock emblem to his key ring. So much for finding prosperity with a four-leaf clover.[673]

Luck Todd Obuchowski understands the true meaning of luck. In May of 1998, the thirty-four-year-old sheet metal worker was playing golf at the Beaver Brook Golf Course in Haydenville, Massachusetts. On the fourth hole, Obuchowski hit his tee shot well over the par three green just 116 yards away. The ball landed on the road adjacent to the green, bounced off Nancy Bachand's Toyota (which was passing by at thirty miles per hour) skipped back over to the green, and rolled into the cup for a hole in one. Eight witnesses attested to what one seasoned golfer called, "the most bizarre thing I've seen somebody do on a golf course in thirty years of playing." Bachand was less enthusiastic as she wanted to know who was going to pay for the $150 damage to her car. Obuchowski carded a single digit on that hole, but he realized it had nothing to do with his golfing skills. Luck is an unpredictable and fickle variable of life. None of us should plan on it to improve our lives.[674]

Luck What do most people call someone who wins the top prize in a lottery? Lucky! Buddy Post would care to differ. The fifty-eight-year-old former carnival worker and cook won $16.2 million in the 1988 Pennsylvania lottery. Since that "lucky" day, Post's wife left him, his brother is in jail for trying to kill him, and his landlady successfully sued him for one-third of the jackpot. Post said, "Money didn't change me, it changed people around me . . ." Lady luck looked much different than he imagined. Because of her arrival, Buddy is now trying to auction off the future lottery payments, valued at $5 million, to pay off taxes, legal fees, and a number of failed business ventures. Money acquired through luck isn't as sweet as we might think, that's why Post's story should be told to the five million Americans who are pathological or problem gamblers, and the fifteen million more who are at risk of becoming just like them.[675]

Lying While at summer camp, Charlie Brown reminded Linus they were supposed to write their parents and tell them they were having a great time. Linus asked his friend, "Even if we're not? Isn't that a lie?" Charlie Brown then explained, "Well . . . it's sort of a white lie." Linus then wondered out loud, "Lies come in colors?"[676]

Mail The U.S. Postal Service employs 225 employees in San Francisco, St. Paul (MN), and Atlanta to handle the annual accumulation of over one hundred million dead letters.[677]

Margins In the fall of 1999, Rush Limbaugh started getting some unusual email. Listeners by the thousands were wondering why there were more commercials on his three-hour talk show. He was confused because nothing about his format had changed. Then he discovered the culprit: technology. The millennium closed out with radio stations embracing a new piece of equipment called CASH. It certainly lives up to its name because this one product is adding millions of dollars to the radio industry. CASH works like a giant digital vacuum. It takes in every piece of a radio program then digitally removes the dead spaces of silence. Delays between a question and an answer are reduced, as are pauses in speech. CASH begins recording a live broadcast at real time for the first few minutes, then after the first commercial it becomes a delayed relay. Voices are not altered and the process is so smooth listeners can't even detect it. Yet, within the course of just one hour, radio stations can wedge in an additional four minutes of commercials. For a program like Limbaugh's, that means twelve extra minutes of revenue without losing a single word of his show. Such technology isn't surprising. It's a sign of the times in which we live. Every spare second must be converted into "productive" activity. But as we all know, the loss of such margins in our lives usually has the reverse effect and actually reduces the extra efficiency we're trying to create.[678]

Marital Test In 1998, *Boating* magazine asked their readers a very straightforward question, but received a rather unexpected response. Their survey included questions about retrieving objects that fall overboard. Of their respondents, 25 percent said they would jump in to save a hat, but 13 percent said they would *not* go overboard to save their spouse. Falling over the side of a boat apparently offers a unique way for testing the strength of your marriage.[679]

Marriage "Business is simple. This [marriage] is very complex."
—*Donald Trump* [680]

Marriage Elisabeth Elliot is the widow of missionary and martyr, Jim Elliot. Elliot and four other young missionaries were killed by the Auca Indians in Ecuador on January 8, 1956. She and Elliot had known each other five years before finally marrying. When he died, they had only been married 27 months. Thirteen years later she remarried, but her husband died of cancer within four and one-half years of their honeymoon. She married for a third time and understands well the dynamics of not only marriage, but suffering and loss as well. Ms. Elliot brings a unique perspective to marriage that is very profound. In a recent interview she noted marriage is both a birth and a death. Many ministers have talked about the turmoil of conducting a funeral and a wedding on the same day, but Ms. Elliot claims this reality occurs at every wedding. There is the birth of a new relationship and most all of the focus is on that truth, but the wedding ceremony also marks the death of independent thinking, selfish pursuits, and unilateral decisions. The birth of a marriage must be accompanied by the death of such thinking and behavior or it will bring certain death to the newborn relationship. Few newlyweds want to be reminded of death on their wedding day, but it is less than truthful if they are not called to bury self on the same day they commit themselves to one another.[681]

Marriage Even though the concept of marriage seems to take a lot of abuse in America, it is still the favored option for Americans. As of 1998, 110.6 million Americans aged eighteen and older were married and living with their spouse. That's 56 percent of the adult population. About 9.8 percent of the populace is divorced (19.4 million adults), and the remaining American adults are classified as single. For all the bad press marriage gets these days, it's refreshing to remember that the majority of Americans still believe in God's divine institution.[682]

Marriage Far too often couples rationalize their choice to remain unmarried with that little fictitious axiom, "It's just a piece of paper!" Unfortunately, the hypocrisy of such thinking is frequently overlooked. If you are pulled over by a law enforcement officer and he asks to see your driver's license, can you remain in good standing with the law and say, "I don't need one of those, it's just a piece of paper." If a potential employer asks for a resume to learn of your experience and needed references, is it likely you will be hired by simply replying, "I don't need one of those, it's just a piece of paper." Would a game warden be satisfied if you refused to present a fishing license because you told him, "I don't need one of those, it's just a piece of paper." A marriage license may be written on paper but it is far more than "just a piece of paper."[683]

Marriage Few people know family life better than the folks at Focus on the Family. In an article printed in 1995, they made the following statement: "One of the most respected studies in the field of psychiatry said, 'those in married relationships experienced a lower rate of severe depression than people in any other category.'" God was serious when he said, "It's not good for the man to be alone" (Genesis 2:18).[684]

Marriage Half of all marriages annually are remarriages.[685]

Marriage How would you describe your marriage? Billy Graham has a very insightful way of describing his marriage. He says, "we are happily incompatible." Dr. and Mrs. Graham are very different in many ways, but they have learned to see and use these differences to their advantage. Countless divorces are finalized under the pretense of "irreconcilable differences." It's refreshing to see an "incompatible" couple who has thrived for over five decades because they chose to be happy with their differences.[686]

Marriage "I'm old-fashioned, I'm trying to make one wife last me a lifetime." —*Zig Ziglar*[687]

Marriage "If there is any secret to our marriage, it's Ruth." —*Billy Graham*[688]

Marriage In America, 90 percent of married men call their wife their best friend.[689]

Marriage In America, the average cost of a wedding is $19,104, not including the honeymoon or engagement ring. The nation's wedding industry takes in $32 billion per year.[690]

Marriage In the midst of marital disagreement it is not uncommon for a spouse to wonder if there isn't somebody with whom they would be more compatible. Suleyman Guresci, of Izmir, Turkey, divorced his wife of twenty-one years after a bitter six-year court battle. In an effort to find the ideal woman, Guresci turned to a computer dating service. Ironically, from a list of two thousand prospective brides, the computer selected his former wife (his wife opted to use the same company in her search for a new husband). He responded to this information by deciding to remarry his wife just nine months after their divorce. He said, "I did not know that my ex-wife had been the ideal counterpart for a marriage. I decided to give it another try by being more tolerant toward her." The ideal mate might just be the one you've already married.[691]

Marriage Jake and Blanche Passa said they're happier than ever before with their marriage, they just don't want to live with each other. This couple from Grand Forks, North Dakota, had been married nearly fifty years when a special news report came out in 1995. From their wedding day in 1946 until 1991, theirs was a typical story. In 1991, however, things changed. After forty-five years of living together as husband and wife, they decided to live as spouses in separate houses. Blanche explained their logic for different dwellings and said, "Actually, we just existed together in the other house. We never enjoyed the same things." Now they reside next door to each other on Fourth Avenue in his and hers houses with the same basic floor plan. They each do their own cooking, housecleaning, and laundry. Divorce has never been a consideration for either spouse. Blanche told a curious reporter, "I don't believe in divorce, and there was no reason to get a divorce." She went on to say, "We had our good years and worked well together, but as far as living together, that was a horse of a different color. I guess I changed and he didn't." Defining their unique setup, Mrs. Passa said, "We sort of look after each other in an impersonal way." When asked about the success of their arrangement, they are both very affirming. She says, "It sure works good for us." He says, "I'm happy. We'll probably be the envy of everybody." It's an unusual setup that probably is enviable to some, but it's a far cry from God's Biblical plan for marriage. Isn't it strange that our society has experienced opposite extremes about marriage—couples who live together but won't get married, and now, a couple who won't live together but choose to remain married.[692]

Marriage Married people live longer (men eight to ten years and women three to four years) than nonmarried people. Divorced men have the highest death rates.[693]

Marriage "One of the hardest things for a man to survive is when he comes home and his wife says, 'Notice anything different?' —*Chuck Snyder*[694]

Marriage People who attend church at least once a month are more than twice as likely to stay married than those who attend church once a year or less.[695]

Marriage Research demonstrates the futility of unfaithfulness in marriage. Of those who destroy their marriage because of someone else, 80 percent ultimately regret their decision. Of the 10 percent who actually do marry the person with whom they had an affair, 70 percent of them get another divorce. Simple math reveals the chances of staying married to the person for whom you left your spouse are three in one hundred. Nobody in their right mind would board a plane with just a 3 percent chance of arriving safely, yet many choose to gamble with those same odds in marriage.[696]

Marriage Statistics show first marriages offer the greatest hope for preventing divorce. First marriages end in divorce 40 percent of the time. Second marriages have a divorce rate of 60 percent. And, third marriages succumb to divorce 75 percent of the time. Although divorce cannot always be prevented, there is great merit in trying to make that first marriage work.[697]

Marriage "The best way to remember your wife's birthday is to forget it once." —*Anonymous*[698]

Marriage "The making of a marriage is a lot like making a stew; it will only be as good as the ingredients you put into it." —*Chris Kelly*[699]

Marriage "This marriage was made in heaven, but so is lightning and thunder." —*Humorous Plaque*[700]

Marriage While serving as a Massachusetts legislator, Barbara Gray suggested marriage licenses should come with a warning. She filed a bill that would require each Massachusetts marriage license to have a warning printed on it stating that abusing one's spouse is a crime. Gray says the warning is a way to tell "couples with stars in their eyes and bliss in their hearts that too many relationships are doomed to become abusive and violent." Gray's concern mirrors the tragic epidemic of domestic violence in America. It also suggests that marriage should be taken more seriously. Whether or not violence ever enters the picture, each prospective bride and groom needs adequate warning that this new relationship is capable of fulfilling dreams, or inciting nightmares.[701]

Martyrdom David Barrett is a mission researcher who collects information on Christian martyrs. His thorough investigations have led him to estimate that an average of 160,000 Christians are killed for their faith every year. In 1995, 150 foreign missionaries were murdered. Barrett says, "For every killing of a Western missionary or a high-profile Christian leader that captures international attention, there are 1,000 anonymous Christians who die virtually unnoticed, except by God." Barrett likewise estimates that 50 million believers have died for their faith since the first Christmas. Of such martyrdom Barrett notes, "The evidence of the centuries is that evangelization proceeds very fast when there are Christians prepared to die for their faith."[702]

Materialism A very wealthy man was determined to beat the system and "take it all with him." He unrelentingly prayed for God to grant him this one request and eventually the Lord gave in. The billionaire knew his life was waning so he liquidated all of his assets and had it converted to gold bullion. After his death, he was greeted by a very confused St. Peter. The man was ecstatic about carrying all of his wealth into heaven and couldn't contain himself. He opened his large bag of gold and showed it to Peter. The heavenly gatekeeper wasn't at all impressed. With a puzzled look the apostle asked, "Why are you carrying all of that pavement with you?" How ironic that so many of us sell our souls to obtain nothing more than heavenly pavement.[703]

Materialism Charles Swindoll shared a most unusual occurrence that happened to one of his close friends, Ray Stedman. Stedman had traveled across the country for a series of meetings, but his luggage did not arrive at the same place. Knowing he needed some suits quickly and economically, he went to a local thrift shop. He was pleased to find exactly what he wanted. The salesman informed him these particular suits had been cleaned and pressed, but some people didn't want them because they came from the funeral home. That wasn't a problem for this minister, so he bought a couple of suits for just $25 each. When he returned to his hotel room and started dressing for the meeting, he discovered there were no pockets in these suits. It then dawned on him that dead men don't need any pockets because they can't carry a single thing with them. Life is indeed much richer if we live with the realization that the only thing we can take from this life is that which won't fit in a pocket.[704]

Materialism Larry Burkett is a well-known and well-respected financial advisor. In a recent interview, Burkett shared some significant concerns about materialism in America, especially in the American church. In pointing to Matthew 6:24 he said, "Christians are trying to serve God and mammon." Burkett noted "80 percent of Americans owe more than they own." He said this trend is prevalent in churches as well: "Christians pay more in interest (9.8 percent of their income) than they give to the church" (Southern Baptists give 2.3 percent of their income). He noted in a typical congregation of one hundred families, thirty-seven families give nothing to the church. In summary of his concerns, Burkett mused, "Christ said the greatest threat to Christianity is not drugs, sex, murder, rape, or even politicians. The greatest threat is materialism."[705]

Materialism The eye of an ostrich is bigger than its brain. When we are overcome by materialism we are not unlike the ostrich—our eyes become bigger than our brains. The next time you walk through a mall, take a few ostrich struts just to remind yourself that materialistic desires can cause us to look as ridiculous as a bug-eyed, flightless bird.[706]

Materialism When materialism starts clutching our heart, it serves us well to remember that one-fifth of the world's population lives on less than $1 a day. According to a report released by the World Bank on June 23, 1996, 1.31 billion people subsist on "less than a dollar a day." Instead of spending some more money on yourself, you might want to consider a few ways you could invest your resources in a ministry that seeks to touch these impoverished lives. It's a sure cure for materialism.[707]

Maturity Sometimes educational requirements seem downright insane. A classic example comes from the Seattle Police Department. During the spring of 1999, department heads required the twenty-six employees in its fingerprint and photo unit to attend a mandatory half-hour safety class devoted entirely to the subject of sitting in a chair. The workers were given instruction on the proper technique for sitting in a chair with rollers. Three of the unit's employees had filed worker compensation claims for injuries sustained while trying to sit in chairs with rollers. Consequently, educators were brought in and employees were told, "Take hold of the arms and get control of the chair before sitting down." It sounds ridiculous, but if we will allow ourselves to learn from this experience in the state of Washington, we might see areas in our own life that are equally absurd. The writer of Hebrews talked about people who should be engaged in spiritually mature pursuits but instead they were in need of "someone to teach the elementary principles of God . . ."(Hebrews 5:12). We may laugh at adults being taught how to sit in a chair, but are we struggling to grasp and practice equally elementary things of God?[708]

Maturity "The process of change is something like a walk across America. Every step is progress but there's such a long way to go." —*Larry Crabb*[709]

Maturity "Your mind is not a storehouse to be filled but a garden to be tilled." —*Anonymous*[710]

Medical Care In Kenya, there is one doctor per 6,552 patients. In the United States there is one doctor per 435 patients.[711]

Meditation Even though meditation is a viable spiritual discipline, many people feel uncomfortable with the concept. Images of weird religious antics generally surface when someone entertains the idea of meditating. John Ortberg has an idea that defuses some of the abstract mysticism that surrounds meditation. This teaching pastor from Willow Creek Community Church calls meditation "worry in the positive." Everyone knows how to worry and they have a clear picture as to what it looks like. When we worry, we stay focused on a certain concern and just keep mulling it over in our mind. Meditation can be that same process in reverse. It's simply focusing on God and his Word for an extended time . . . mulling over biblical truths and promptings of God's Holy Spirit. So for anyone who seems confused about meditation, encourage them with the realization that they have been practicing it for years, they were just doing it backwards and calling it worry.[712]

Memory Jokes about poor memory are prolific, but our collective lax memory skills are no laughing matter. Inefficient memory has become a deadly byproduct of our informationally inundated society. A recent study by the Mayo Clinic discovered that more than half of the patients they surveyed could not remember the most important health problem their doctors had diagnosed for them. Even more disheartening statistics could be gleaned from an exit poll at church on any given Sunday. Overloaded minds are dropping valuable information so now, more than ever, we need to pray for the Holy Spirit to help us remember what God wants us to know (John 14:26).[713]

Memory "When I was younger, I could remember anything, whether it had happened or not." —*Mark Twain*[714]

Men's Ministry Nicollette and her mom went to an evening church service by themselves because her dad was attending a Promise Keepers conference. When the little five-year-old arrived at church, a friend asked, "Where's your daddy?" Nicollette proudly replied, "He's at Housekeepers!" All of the adults not only got a good laugh, but a good reminder as well. An effective men's ministry will help men "keep their house" in a Christlike manner.[715]

Mentoring "I want to prepare a person to become better than I am." —*Howard Hendricks*[716]

Ministry After World War II, some German students volunteered to help rebuild a cathedral that had been damaged by enemy bombs. The English church had a large statue of Jesus that was badly damaged. The students worked diligently to restore the entire statue, but had trouble deciding how they would handle the delicate restoration of the hands. After great deliberation, they agreed to make a statement by leaving the statue without hands. The statue's inscription stands to this day: "Christ has no hands but ours."[717]

Ministry Almost every day you can pick up a newspaper and read about some type of sports car racing event. These articles tell of drivers racing around a track at unbelievable and radically dangerous speeds. At times they are moving three times faster than a normal car on the highway. One errant move could not only cost them the race, but their life as well. Ironically, these daring drivers do not face their highest levels of stress on the racetrack. To the contrary, "race car drivers report more stress waiting in the pit than on the track." For these professional motorists, the anticipation is worse than the event itself. Ministry is no different. We usually face the greatest stress and fears while anticipating a future role of ministry. If we are willing to fight through the anxiety, we generally experience an assignment that is far easier than we imagined. Don't let the stress in the pit keep you from getting on the track.[718]

Ministry "A man should only enter the Christian ministry if he cannot stay out of it." —*D. Martyn Lloyd-Jones*[719]

Ministry A parabolic legend has been passed down through the centuries to teach an important truth. A band of nomads were preparing to retire for the evening when they were greeted by a heavenly being. Mixed with fear and excitement, they waited for the angelic figure to speak. This being gave them clear but surprising instructions. He said, "Gather as many pebbles as you can and put them in your saddle bags. Travel a day's journey, then this time tomorrow you will be both happy and sad." As soon as the message was delivered, the angel departed. The nomads began to express their anger and frustration over such an insignificant encounter. They each reluctantly grabbed a small handful of pebbles and stuffed them in their bags as they continued to voice their displeasure. When they stopped the next night, they made a startling discovery. The pebbles they had collected were now diamonds. They shouted with joy over their newfound wealth, but mourned the greater riches they could have enjoyed. Ministry can often look like simple pebbles on the ground, work that's not worthy of our time. But if we remain faithful and our motives stay pure, we will someday know the joy of finding diamonds where pebbles once lay. And like those nomads of old, we will also be both happy and sad.[720]

Ministry "A prayerless preacher is a misnomer." —*E.M. Bounds*[721]

Ministry Each year in American hospitals, two million patients become infected by germs. They come to the hospital for healing, but get an infection along the way. When people come to us for ministry, we must be cautious that we don't cause further infection by permitting spiritual germs to linger in our lives.[722]

Ministry John Maxwell is well known for his practical approach to ministry. One of his pragmatic ideas helps solve two problems at once. People can tend to feel as though they are not receiving adequate ministry, or they are not a significant part of providing ministry to others. Either problem can be frustrating for a Christian. Maxwell suggests both of these problems can be remedied by leaders knowing and caring for three primary factors—the person's *name*, *need*, and *niche*. When we know who people are, where they hurt, and what they do best, we can help them experience the joy of both receiving and giving ministry.[723]

Ministry On June 14, 1999, an unidentified man boarded a New York City subway at rush hour and died in his seat. In the midst of all the passengers who rode that subway, he simply died and nobody noticed. Investigators say there was no sign of struggle or foul play; he just died. His dead body rode the subway four to five hours while people got on and off the train that runs from the southern tip of Manhattan to the Bronx. It's hard to imagine somebody dying on a busy subway and nobody noticing for several hours, but authorities speculate that "no one noticed him because the train was so crowded and people were in too much of a hurry." Such a description of negligence could define any number of occurrences in ministry. Crowded places and crowded schedules can tragically crowd out compassion and concern. Whether it's in a crowded subway or a crowded church, we can all easily miss the hurts of those around us. By taking a few extra minutes each day to more seriously consider the needs of the people we encounter, we may be able to prevent one of the greatest tragedies of life . . . negligent oversight of another human being.[724]

Ministry Over 80 percent of people say they would get involved in a ministry if someone asked them.[725]

Ministry Patty Wooten is a registered nurse who has taken the time to write down some insightful lessons she has learned from her life's work. During the second year of nursing school, her professor gave the class a pop quiz. As a diligent student, Wooten didn't have any problems with the test questions until she read the last one. It simply asked, "What is the name of the woman who cleans the school?" She felt certain it was some kind of joke, but the professor assured the class this question would affect their grade. He said, "In your careers you will meet many people. All are significant. They deserve your attention and care, even if all you do is smile and say hello." Wooten had seen the woman many times and could describe her features, but did not know her name. Since that day she has forgotten the other questions on that little exam, but she has never forgotten the lesson she learned about Dorothy. An important aspect of any ministry equation is that of knowing people by name, regardless of their status or position.[726]

Ministry "Prayer, meditation, and temptation make a minister." — *Martin Luther*[727]

Ministry "Service that is rendered without joy helps neither the servant nor the served." —*Mahatma Gandhi*[728]

Ministry "The Christian ministry is the worst of all trades, but the best of all professions." —*John Newton*[729]

Ministry The late Colonel Sanders of Kentucky Fried Chicken is remembered by a small band of airline passengers more for his compassion than his secret recipe. During a flight, one young infant was screaming and crying. The feverish mother tried desperately to calm the child but to no avail. She was even assisted by the flight attendants but nothing seemed to work. Finally, the Colonel asked if he might hold the baby. He gently cradled the child and rocked her to sleep. The plane's cabin became still and quiet. When Sanders returned to his seat a passenger said, "We all appreciate what you did for us." The stately old man replied, "I didn't do it for us. I did it for the baby." Ministry may provide benefits for those who engage in it, but the motive for such service must be others, not self.[730]

Ministry When Anthony Demello saw a starving child shivering in the cold, he became angry with God. He turned to heaven and said, "God, how could you allow such suffering? Why don't you do something?" After a long silence, Demello sensed God's answer. He said, "I have done something . . . I made you." When we pray for God to do something, we must be willing to become the agent of ministry through which he answers our prayers and "does something."[731]

Miracles *Newsweek* magazine released a report on miracles during April of 2000. The results showed 84 percent of Americans believe God performs miracles. Forty-eight percent have experienced a miracle in their own life, and 63 percent said they know people who have been part of a miracle.[732]

Miracles Unusual special effects came to Israel in August of 1999. In preparation for the anticipated four million visitors arriving for the millennium celebration, a private contractor built a submerged bridge on the Sea of Galilee so people could "walk on water." The crescent-shaped floating bridge is thirteen feet wide, twenty-eight feet long, and strong enough to hold fifty people at a time. This new attraction for Capernaum rests two inches below the water and doesn't have any railings so tourists can capture the full effect. It's a tragic irony that the city that would not embrace the true miracles of Christ (Matthew 11:20–24) is now marketing a cheap imitation of his miraculous work.[733]

Missions A different twist on John 3:16 forces us to reevaluate our true commitment to international missions. "For God so loved the *United States* that he gave his only begotten Son . . ." The same effect can be felt by doing this substitution with the Great Commission in Matthew 28:19.[734]

Missions David Livingston was a pioneer missionary to Africa (1813–1873). A native chief named Sachele once asked the missionary a piercing question: "Because it is true that all who die unforgiven are lost forever, why did your nation not come to tell us before now?" It's still a good question![735]

Missions One of the strongest advocates for mission work was Annie Walker Armstrong. She was impassioned by our Lord's command to be his witnesses throughout the world. As she sought to carry out this responsibility, she felt called to the role of raising missions awareness and support for missionaries. Her level of commitment to this calling is reflected in her zealous correspondence. Without the luxury of computers or telephones, she used a simple pen to revolutionize mission involvement. Each year she wrote thousands of letters, and in 1893 alone, Annie Armstrong wrote 17,718 letters as an advocate of missions. That's nearly 50 letters a day, seven days a week. When we think of missions and our commitment to reaching the world for Christ, may each of us pray for a passion equal to that of Annie Armstrong.[736]

Missions While serving as a missionary in Ivory Coast, Africa, George Stadsklev was working hard to complete a building before the rainy season arrived. During the construction, a woman from a distant village approached him and said, "I am told you are a man of God." She then insisted that the missionary return with her to the village. She declared, "We've been waiting for you for many years." Stadsklev informed her that he would be delighted to come once they had finished the building. She then replied, "All right, I will wait for you." In that culture this meant she would stay at their home until the missionary was ready. He promised he would come and encouraged her to go back home. She replied, "I can't go without you now that I have found you. The others will not forgive me if, after finding you, I fail to bring you back with me." Realizing the urgency of her request, the construction was postponed and he traveled the thirty miles to her village. Stadsklev was introduced to an elderly man who asked, "Where have you been for these many years?" The old man then explained that many years ago one of their villagers had gone to a distant town and heard about Christ. He became a Christian and the man told him to return to his people, burn all their fetishes, and build a house of God. He was then promised that someone would come to their village and tell them more about God's love. The elderly man then related how they had burned their fetishes and built a house of God. He said, "We waited and waited, but no man came." The house of God became old and fell down. They built another one and waited again, but it also deteriorated. A third and fourth house of God suffered the same fate. He pointed and said, "Now this is the fifth house of God that we have built." Stadsklev, knowing the materials and construction process used by these people, realized that each building would have lasted about five years. This meant they had been waiting for more than twenty years. The missionary spent the next two days telling the people about God and his amazing love. He then prepared to return home with the promise of returning to tell them more. Before departing, the old man insisted that this missionary accompany him to the cemetery. He was so feeble that he had to be carried. In the cemetery, he pointed to one grave after another and explained how they had waited to hear the gospel but no one came to tell them. The old man repeatedly asked, "Where have you been for these many years? So many waited. So many have died. Where have you been?" Those simple words have both haunted and transformed the ministry of George and Mable Stadsklev. May it likewise do the same for each of us.[737]

Mistakes "A winner is big enough to admit his mistakes, smart enough to profit from them, and strong enough to correct them." —*John Maxwell*[738]

Mistakes During a presidential debate in January of 2000, George W. Bush was asked to identify his biggest mistake as an adult. The then governor of Texas opted for a lighthearted response and said, "As you may remember, I was in the business world at one time. I was the managing general partner of the mighty Texas Rangers. I signed off on that wonderful transaction: Sammy Sosa for Harold Baines." Those present for this Republican Party debate in South Carolina roared with laughter and cheered his wry response. In a follow-up interview, Baines said, "I can see why he got out of the business." So the next time you blow a call, just think of President Bush's decision to trade Sammy Sosa for Harold Baines.[739]

Mistakes If you've made a seemingly big mistake lately, you might find consolation in knowing about the blunder of a French bond futures trader who worked in London. On July 23, 1998, this trader executed an $887 million sell order in a rising market, and he didn't even know it. The trader, whose name was not disclosed by his employer, Salomon Smith Barney, single-handedly processed 10 percent of the average daily volume on the Matif futures exchange in Paris with one inadvertent mistake. He simply leaned against one of the keyboards in their London office long enough to accidentally create 145 repetitious orders. These sales were worth nearly $1 billion in actual dollars and worth millions more in lost profits. Whether he was a little too relaxed during a coffee break or just plain careless on the job, he made a mistake big enough to probably make your little error seem less traumatic.[740]

Mistakes "Some people learn from the mistakes of others, but most of us are the others." —*Ivern Ball*[741]

Mistakes Tom Watson, Sr., founded IBM and guided "Big Blue" for over forty years. One of his most impressive moments in leadership occurred when a junior executive lost an enormous amount of money for the company. The promising young man had been involved in a risky venture for IBM and ended up losing over $10 million in the gamble. Watson called the man into his office and the nervous executive blurted out, "I guess you want my resignation?" Watson replied, "You can't be serious. We've just spent $10 million educating you!" As Watson so clearly demonstrated, mistakes should be teachers that provide us with invaluable lessons.[742]

Money "A lot of take-home pay is spent as foolishly as that which is withheld for taxes." —*Anonymous*[743]

Money Americans, on average, give just under 2 percent of their annual income to charity.[744]

Money Annually, Americans spend $26.6 billion on lottery tickets, and give $19.6 billion to churches.[745]

Money Bill Clinton successfully won the United States presidency in 1992 under the banner motto: "It's the economy, Stupid." Ironically, we as Americans are literally quite stupid in the area of economics. The National Council on Economic Education discovered the average American adult is economically illiterate. Forty-nine percent of those studied in this 1998–99 national research project received a failing grade for their knowledge of basic economic principles. Only 16 percent knew enough about the basics to earn a B grade or better. These are the guiding principles for managing personal finances, yet only a limited few have a satisfactory grasp of this important information. To be the best possible stewards of the resources with which God has blessed us, we need to understand the principles of money management as well as the Biblical mandates concerning material possessions.[746]

Money Could your wallet literally hurt you? Physicians now know of a malady called "walleta sciatica" from which a patient (generally a male) can suffer severe lower back pain because of their wallet. In such cases, a wallet in the back pocket is putting pressure on the sciatic nerve and causing intense discomfort. The remedy for most is to simply trim down the excess in their wallet, or move their wallet to another location. Whether or not your wallet is causing physical pain, it can still hurt you spiritually. The solution for either type of pain seems to be the same . . . reduce the size of your wallet (move from hoarding to giving), or switch locations for carrying it (move it from your pocket to the Lord's pocket). Such remedies will most certainly improve your spiritual health.[747]

Money Dean Hogue is the coauthor of *Money Matters: Personal Giving in American Churches*. The study evaluated the giving of five denominations: Baptist, Assemblies of God, Catholic, Lutheran, and Presbyterian. Uncovered in this massive assessment was the fact that "regularity of church attendance remains the number one predictor of an individual's contributions to the church." Additionally, researchers learned the largest givers are those who plan to give. A breakdown of giving reveals that those who plan and commit to tithe give an average of $4,042 per year, those who give a percentage below the tithe average annual contributions of $3,120, the people who give an annual dollar amount average $2,778, those who set a weekly dollar amount give an annual average of $1,882, and the ones who gave "what I can afford each week" averaged $869 in a year's worth of offerings. Also, those who sign a pledge card give more than those who don't. Hogue said the numbers confirmed "75 percent of the money comes from 25 percent of the people." It was likewise noted that Mormons lead all other denominations in per capita giving. They average slightly more than 7 percent of annual income given to the church. Southern Baptists are giving just over 3 percent of their incomes.[748]

Money "Have you ever noticed that when you bounce a check the bank charges you more of what they already know you don't have?" — *Anonymous*[749]

Money In Larry Burkett's book, *How Much Is Enough?*, several statistics are cited that should be noted by all Christians. Americans spend $1.17 for every $1 earned. The current rate of savings and giving is less than that which existed during the Great Depression. Individuals pay four times as much in interest as they give to the church (10.2 percent versus 2.3 percent). Fifty percent of those in the church give nothing at all. Of every $1 given to the church, eighty cents comes from those fifty-five years of age and older. As Burkett says, "Money is never a problem. It's a symptom." The above information should help us address the symptoms of spiritual concern in our churches today.[750]

Money In the United States, there are approximately 165,000 automated teller machines. The average machine handles 182 transactions per day with a withdrawal rate of $10,920 every twenty-four hours. That means Americans are running a daily tab of $1,801,800,000 at ATMs.[751]

Money More than half of all charitable giving comes from Americans earning less than $50,000 per year.[752]

Money "Most of us live on fixed incomes . . . fix the car, fix the VCR, fix the faucet." —*Sam Ewing*[753]

Money Seventy-one percent of Americans say they are not setting aside enough for retirement.[754]

Morality According to a 1997 survey by Public Opinion Strategies, 71 percent of Americans say the United States is "facing more of a moral crisis than an economic crisis." Ironically, this information was collected

just five years after President Clinton ran his campaign under the flag-
ship motto, "It's the economy, stupid." Equally ironic is the fact that this
research was completed before he confessed to adultery, and before his
historic speech at the Human Rights Campaign dinner on November 8,
1997. That night, Clinton became the first sitting president to publicly
address a gay rights organization. The Human Rights Campaign is a gay
lobby group of 200,000 people. At this particular dinner, 1,500 homosexuals came to hear the President and see Ellen DeGeneres receive a civil
rights award. Clinton spoke for twenty-three minutes and was interrupted twenty-five times by applause (seven of those were standing ova-
tions). In the course of his talk, the President declared, "We have to
broaden the imagination of America." That one statement speaks volumes about the moral crisis of our country. Our expanded imaginations
have led to unimaginable immorality. What we need far more than
"broadened imagination" is "focused imitation" of the Savior Jesus
Christ. Imitation of our Lord will lead to life. Immoral imagination will
lead to death. Incidentally, this moral crisis is being championed by a
much smaller group than we are being led to believe. We were told that
Hawaii's move to become the first state offering broad rights to domestic partners in July of 1997 would usher an onslaught of couples applying for these rights. Estimates were given that twenty to thirty thousand
people would immediately sign up. By December 1997, five months after
the law took effect, just 296 couples had signed up as "reciprocal bene-
ficiaries."755

Morality David Crenshaw made an interesting stand against
immorality. He operated a seven-screen movie theater outside of
Spartanburg, South Carolina. In August of 1998, he vowed to no longer
show R-rated movies even if he went bankrupt doing so. There was
strong community support of his position, but after the first month's ban,
his attendance dropped from two thousand customers per week to just
twelve hundred. To his surprise and disgust, the community was not as
supportive as he first believed. He called off the ban five months later
after an estimated loss of $20,000 in ticket sales. Crenshaw said, "I
thought people cared more. Apparently they don't care much." He went
on to say, "You can't make people want something they don't want. This
whole thing has left me really cynical." A disappointed local pastor, Troy
Gregg, wisely summarized the situation: "It does not surprise me that he
did not get support. Basically, people say they want morals, but they want

it for everybody but themselves." Are we bemoaning the state of our nation's moral decline while simultaneously supporting the production of immoral entertainment? We may not want morality as much as we think.[756]

Morality In 1996, Danny Wuerffel was a champion before the college football season even began. This senior quarterback at the University of Florida was chosen as a 1996 preseason all-American by *Playboy* magazine. He turned down the Scholar Athlete Award and said, "It's just not something I want to be associated with, and there's a whole lot of bad connotations that go along with that magazine." Wuerffel attended the First Baptist Church of High Springs, Florida, while in college and was a regular speaker at True Love Waits rallies and youth conferences. Wuerffel's Christian commitment to morality is a refreshing contrast to the cultural norm of blatant immorality.[757]

Morality "In America, our children are born swimming in polluted waters." —*Peggy Noonan*[758]

Morality In March of 1998, a Gallup poll revealed some opinions on morality in America. Based on the sexual scandals surrounding the White House during Bill Clinton's tenure, Americans were asked to compare their morals to that of the President. 69 percent said their morals were higher than Clinton's, 22 percent agreed their moral standards were about the same, 3 percent admitted they had lower standards, and 6 percent voiced no opinion.[759]

Moral Standards Larry Peterman found himself in hot water during 1999. He owned a video-store chain in Utah that rented everything from family classics to soft-core pornography. His thriving business came under attack when he was charged with selling obscene material. He faced the prospects of bankruptcy and jail. Before his trial came to court, Peterman's lawyer did some hard-core research. He sent an investigator to the nearby Provo Marriott to make a record of all the sex films that a guest could obtain through the hotel's pay-per-view channels. He also obtained records on how much sexual content was being purchased from cable and satellite television providers. As it turned out, people in Utah County were disproportionately large consumers of pornographic videos, they were just getting it from satellite dishes and cable TV in addition to Larry Peterman's video stores. The jury consequently found him not guilty in October 2000. The $10 billion per year industry of pornography in America has leaped from the adult book stores to corporate boardrooms. Guys like Flint and Hefner are no longer the major suppliers. General Motors, through their subsidiary of DirecTV, sells more graphic sex films each year than Larry Flint, owner of *Hustler*. EchoStar Communications, the number two satellite provider, makes more money selling pornographic films each year than Playboy does with its magazine, cable, and Internet business combined. Obviously, none of these big corporations (AT&T, Time-Warner, Marriott, Hilton, News Corp., and so on) wants to talk about their stakes in the sexually oriented economy. An official of AT&T said, "How can we? It's like the crazy aunt in the attic. Everyone knows she's there, but you can't say anything about it." Tragically, commerce supercedes morals in America.[760]

Motherhood At the age of thirty-two, Rebekah began chemotherapy for breast cancer. She gave the cancer a gallant fight for eighteen months, but it became obvious the cancer could not be conquered. Upon realizing she would not see her three young daughters grow up, Rebekah embarked on a challenge to make tape recordings that could be played on special occasions. She made a tape for their first day of school, sixteenth birthday, first date, baptism, wedding, etc. Each recording was filled with encouragement, motherly advice, and love. In typical fashion, Rebekah organized the whole project and explained the tapes to her girls. She told them she was going to live with God so she was giving Daddy some tapes they could listen to when they got older. Rebekah seemed satisfied with what she had done until it became clear that the end was very near. She began to panic and pleaded for the nurse to call her friend. She begged her to come quickly and bring a blank tape. When the friend arrived, Rebekah had her set up the recorder and explained, "This is my most important tape." With the microphone close to her lips, Rebekah said, "Ruthie, Hannah, and Molly, some day your daddy will bring a new mommy home. I want you to make her feel very special, and how proud you will make me feel if you are kind, patient, and encouraging to her as she learns to take care of each of you. Please bring her dandelions to put in the special vase, and most important, hug her often. Please don't be sad for long. Jesus cried. . . . He knows how sad you are and he knows you will be happy again. I love you so much, Hannah, Ruthie, and Molly. Big hugs, your first mommy." Rebekah was exhausted, but at peace after she finished the tape. She rested from her work, and then died two days later. Four years after Rebekah's death, Warren remarried and those three girls listened to a tape that defines the depths of a mother's love.[761]

Motherhood Some would say, "Being a housewife and mother is boring and monotonous!" Dr. James Dobson agrees, but he is quick to point out that practically every other occupation is also boring. A press operator can get bored with the monotonous hum of the presses. Bricklaying is rather predictable every day. The continuous visitation of sick patients seldom energizes a doctor. Airline pilots talk of the monotony that bridges the brief exhilaration of taking off and landing. Writers get tired of filling up blank pages. And what about the judge who spends his days holding court? The fact is, "few of us enjoy heart-thumping excitement each moment of our professional lives." Dobson went on to note a time in which he was staying in a Washington, D.C. hotel room adjacent to a famous cellist. Throughout the day he heard this man practice continuously yet he did not play beautiful scores. What filled the bulk of this musician's day were repeated scales, runs, and exercises. From early morning until the time of his departure for the concert, this celebrated musician isolated himself with an inanimate object and spent his day doing monotonous practice. No doubt, plenty of people left the concert hall thinking, "What a glamorous life." Motherhood does indeed contain large doses of boredom, but it is for a brief season of life and who can argue with the significance that mothers play in developing their children. No job can compete with the importance of motherhood.[762]

Motherhood When an L1011 left Orlando for its early flight to Atlanta, everything seemed normal. The flight was primarily carrying professionals who were traveling for business. These seasoned travelers were accustomed to occasional tense moments when malfunctions or excessive turbulence occurred. None of them was prepared for the fear that accompanied this flight. Just minutes after takeoff, the jet began to dip wildly. The pilot climbed higher to correct the problem, but it didn't help. He soon made an announcement that sent the entire galley into hysteria. Their hydraulic system had failed and they were returning to Orlando for what would most certainly be a crash landing. Fuel began rushing past the windows as the crew jettisoned all but the necessary fluids. The captain had the cabin readied for a crash landing, and everyone knew their lives might soon be over. Fear griped even the most stoic of travelers. Some were hysterical and all were scared. Amidst this chaos and fear, a lone calm voice stood out like a marker of hope. A mother was looking into the eyes of her four-year-old daughter and speaking words of assurance in a normal, conversational tone. With her daughter's rapt attention, she continually said, "I love you so much. Do you know for sure that I love you more than anything?" The little girl answered, "Yes, Mommy." It was a sobering picture as those travelers knew of a similar and recent situation in which a young girl survived a terrible plane crash. Experts speculated that the girl was alive because her mother had strapped her own body over her daughter to shield the impact. The mother did not survive the crash. Now these passengers couldn't help but wonder if that would happen again. Before strapping her body over her daughter, she told the little girl, "And remember, no matter what happens, I love you always. You are a good girl. Sometimes things happen that are not your fault. You are still a good girl and my love will always be with you." She then readied herself for the crash landing. Fortunately, her body was not needed as a shield. For unknown reasons, the landing gear locked, the hydraulics worked, and the jet landed safely. A planeload of thankful travelers walked away from the jetway knowing they had gazed into the face of death, and one little girl was carried off in the arms of woman who had demonstrated the incomparable love of a mother.[763]

Movies In 1998, The Dove Foundation released a comprehensive ten-year study that observed the ratio of profitability for movies rated G, PG, PG-13, and R. The study examined 2,380 films released between January 1, 1988 and December 31, 1997. This nonprofit organization discovered G-rated movies produce the highest level of return. Ironically, each level of increased intensity brought decreased profitability. PG movies averaged a 52 percent rate of return, PG-13 yielded a 50 percent return, and R-rated movies provided the lowest level of profit at 37 percent. Dick Rolfe, CEO of The Dove Foundation said, "Moviegoers are not crying out for endless sequels of Rugrats and Babe. What they want to see are more action/adventure films, comedies, dramas, and mysteries, but without naked bodies, exploding heads, and filthy language." In response to this study, Tom Sherak, chairman of 20th Century Fox, admitted that G, PG, and PG-13 movies make more money, but insisted there were considerations other than how much money a movie makes. In truth, few industries are not interested in making the most money. Hollywood has another agenda for which it is willing to make significant financial sacrifices. Beware![764]

Music As an eighteen-year-old, Isaac was tired of the music they sang at his church. He was so troubled by the predicament, he approached his father and voiced his complaint. The stern deacon scolded his son and said, "Those hymns were good enough for your grandfather and your father, so they will have to be good enough for you!" The young man boldly replied, "They will never do for me, regardless of what you and your father thought of them." In anger, Isaac's father shouted, "If you don't like the hymns we sing, then write better ones!" Isaac calmly answered, "I have written better ones, and if you will relax and listen, I will read one for you." The older man took the piece from his son and was amazed by what he saw. He was impressed enough to take the new hymn to church the following Sunday. The congregation sang this new song with delight and requested that Isaac prepare another hymn for the next Sunday. He obliged their request and this pattern continued for 222 consecutive Sundays. In so doing, Isaac Watts single-handedly revolutionized congregational singing three hundred years ago. Before the United States was born, he wrote great hymns like "Alas! and Did My Savior Bleed?", "When I Survey the Wondrous Cross, At the Cross", "O God Our Help in Ages Past", and "Joy to the World." When assessing the issues of church music today, it is wise to think about Isaac Watts and what happened three centuries ago.[765]

National Debt The cumulative debt of all government spending exceeds $8 trillion. Such debt is not surprising when you realize the government spends money at a rate of $7 billion per minute.[766]

Negativism She is no longer the reigning Miss America, but she will always be remembered as one of the most impressive winners of the coveted crown. Heather Whitestone overcame tremendous obstacles just to appear in Atlantic City, and then many more after walking down that historic runway. She was accused by some in the deaf community of giving the wrong impression about hearing loss. Because she is so adept at lipreading and speaking, some deaf leaders said the world would expect the same from all deaf people. She accepted the criticism with grace and continued to reflect the light of her Christian character. When she ended her reign, Heather knew she would be forever tagged as the "deaf Miss America." Although she does not resist this label, she reminded the world that there are disabilities far greater than physical impairment. She said, "Negative thinking is our country's greatest disability." She's an upbeat

Christian who understands adversity and insurmountable odds, yet in her mind there's no barrier greater than a negative outlook.[767]

Negligence "There is no such thing as "benign neglect" of either the body or the soul." —*Dr. Kenneth Cooper*[768]

New Age While serving as the associate director of the Southern Baptist's Home Mission Board's interfaith department, Bill Gordon attended the Life Enrichment Expo in Asheville, North Carolina. During the three-day gathering, Gordon helped distribute seven hundred Bibles to New Age perusers and shared the gospel with those who were willing to discuss it. One philosopher engaged in conversation with Gordon and put a new twist on the frequently used diagnostic questions presented by Evangelism Explosion. Gordon asked, "When you die, what will you say to God when he asks you, 'Why should I let you into my heaven?'" The New Age proponent responded, "I am God, and I would never ask myself that question." "Know that the Lord himself is God; It is he who made us, and not we ourselves . . ." (Psalm 100:3)[769]

Nike The popular Nike swoosh logo was created by a graduate design student for $35.[770]

Obedience In 1989, Marla Maples gained celebrity status through her relationship with Donald Trump. Of her affair she said, "I was never embarrassed because I never felt I did anything wrong." Such words are a far cry from the ones she used to read every night as a teenager. She called the Bible her favorite book and loved to read the Ten Commandments. Before Trump divorced Ivana to marry her, Maples told an interviewer, "As a girl I picked up the Bible and read 'Thou shalt not commit adultery, thou shalt not fornicate.' But after my parents' divorce, I learned you can't take the Bible literally and be happy." The former Mrs. Trump embraced a commonly held myth that denies any connection between Biblical obedience and true happiness. In John 15:11, Jesus denounced this myth by reminding his disciples that obedience to Scripture is what makes our joy "complete." Maybe that's why her marriage to Donald Trump didn't last.[771]

Obedience Translating God's Word into a tribal language is very challenging. One missionary was troubled by his inability to effectively communicate the idea of obedience. This was a concept that the natives seldom practiced or valued. His translation block was broken one day when he whistled for his dog and the animal came running at full speed. An old native was impressed by the dog's responsiveness and admiringly said in his native tongue, "Your dog is all ear." The missionary had his word for obedience and it's a pretty good translation for us as well. To paraphrase Samuel, "To be all ear, is better than sacrifice" (1 Samuel 15:22).[772]

Obstacles "Life is full of obstacle illusions." —*Grant Frazier*[773]

Obstacles On October 14, 1947, Chuck Yeager became the first human being to break the sound barrier. Aviation historians regard that accomplishment as the most significant flight between the Wright brothers' first flight in 1903 and the Apollo moon landing in 1969. On that historic day, Yeager climbed into the X-1 for the ninth time. This small rocket plane, known as the "orange beast," was carried into the sky by a B-29 bomber, then dropped like a bomb. Yeager wasn't supposed to break the sound barrier that day because the program was designed to gradually approach the perceived wall of sound. There were a dozen ways to die in the X-1, and many scientists believed the sound barrier would crumple a plane. Some pilots were inclined to agree because violent vibrations accompanied their approach to Mach speed. When the X-1 was dropped, Yeager spent the first few seconds fighting for control. After a five hundred-foot freefall, he got the nose down and fired the rockets. On his way to leveling off at forty-two thousand feet he had to change the setting and engage the stabilizer. Then, with just 30 percent of his fuel left, Yeager shot for his goal of 0.97 Mach. He then experienced the same frightening vibrations that caused many to believe death and disaster lurked on the other side. But on this day, something unusual began to happen. The Mach needle fluctuated, then tipped off the scale. The vibrations stopped and Yeager was flying supersonic. For a brief 20 seconds, he was racing through the sky at seven hundred miles per hour and it felt like gliding on glass. He noted, "Grandma could be sitting up there sipping lemonade. After all the anxiety, breaking the sound barrier turned out to be a perfectly paved speedway." Five decades later, obstacles are still as plentiful as they were back then. Fears of what lies on the other side prevents many people from trying to overcome them. But as Chuck Yeager's experience demonstrates, when we challenge those obstacles we might just run into the serenity that has eluded us.[774]

Olympics When the 1996 Olympic Games opened in Atlanta, Georgia, it marked the hundreth anniversary of the modern day Olympics. The ancient games began in Greece during the year of 776 B.C. At that time it involved just one event, a two hundred-yard race. A century ago, Baron Pierre de Coubertin had a vision to reactivate the games. This French educator saw the Olympics as a way to "foster better international understanding." So with the help of countless others, the Olympic Games were rebirthed in 1896 with nine nations coming together in Athens, Greece. In essence, Coubertin wanted to engage the world in international *fellowship*. May the Church seek this same goal by propagating the gospel of Jesus Christ.[775]

Opinions A young playwright was ecstatic when he learned that Carl Sandburg was going to attend the rehearsal of his play. The young writer had deep respect for Sandburg and cherished the opportunity to have this seasoned veteran critique his work. During the dress rehearsal, Sandburg fell asleep, which obviously crushed the hopeful young man. After the play, when this playwright caught up with his mentor, he asked, "How could you sleep when you knew I wanted your opinion?" Sandburg replied, "Young man, sleep is an opinion."[776]

Opinions Sometimes the majority only means all the fools are on the same side. —*Anonymous* [777]

Opportunity Did you know it's easier to become a millionaire in America if you were born in a country other than the United States? Statistics reveal that legal immigrants are four times more likely to become millionaires than those of us who have lived here all along. Why? The American-born citizen is raised around relatively vast affluence compared to most of the world. He tends to take for granted what is here and does not necessarily seize the opportunities that are readily available to all. The immigrant, on the other hand, has most likely been exposed to adversity that is unparalleled in America. He sees a country fraught with incredible opportunities and tries to seize every conceivable possibility. Opportunities surround all of us, but they only offer personal advantage to those who reach out and seize them.[778]

Opportunity "Opportunity is missed by most people because it is dressed in overalls and looks like work." —*Thomas Edison* [779]

Organization Can you name the main reason students fail in high school? It's probably not what you think. According to Cheri Fuller, a well-respected educational consultant, organization is the key to success for students. If a student is disorganized it will be reflected in his grades. "Show me a student's notebook and I'll tell you whether that individual is a B student or a D student," says Fuller. She stressed the chief problem is not laziness or poor study skills. The main reason for poor school performance is disorganization. Some children are naturally sloppy, but most of them can learn to be better organized. This is why Fuller advocates the teaching of organizational skills in elementary school. If we want our children to succeed, we must give them the tools that are critical to success. It's easy to see how relevant this information can be for churches as well. Too often ministries flounder or fail simply because there is a lack of organization. Likewise, many of us may be struggling with personal spiritual disciplines for no other reason than basic disorganization.[780]

Outreach The pastor of Ridglea West Baptist Church in Fort Worth, Texas, made a personal visit to follow-up on two boys who had visited their church. Unfortunately, he was met by a very domineering mother who denied him access to their house. She made it crystal clear neither he or anyone else from the church was welcome on their property. Sadly, the pastor was forced to retreat from an opportunity to reach those two young boys. The history of the older boy is not well known, but the younger boy died at the hands of Jack Ruby after he had been arrested for the assassination of President John Kennedy. As the church reaches out to those who are not in the community of faith, it is helpful to remember this story of Lee Harvey Oswald and realize the potential for changing world history with seemingly insignificant contact.[781]

Pain Congenital analgia is a very rare malady that leaves children with no sensitivity for pain. Bob and Christine Waters, a British couple who live outside of London, have three children who suffer from this pain-free phenomenon. They continually injure themselves even though they don't feel any pain. It is not uncommon for them to bite off the tips of their fingers, burn their hands severely, or break bones. Their youngest child, Victoria, has broken her right leg five times. One doctor, who was aware of the little girl's insensitivity to pain, reset her broken leg without the use of an anesthetic. Many times we cry out for the pain to be removed from our lives, but this family understands the enormous value of pain.

Whether your pain is physical or otherwise, remember these kids and be assured that pain is not just an unfortunate mistake.[782]

Paradigms Everyone has been affected by changes they wish had never occurred. Paradigm shifts have forced all of us to do and see things in a different light. Fortunately, we have the advantage of history to see that some of these frustrating changes can ultimately bring about positive reform once we learn to accept them. A case in point comes from the era of Queen Elizabeth. This popular queen ruled England for nearly fifty years (1558–1603) and because of her significant influence it is hailed as the Elizabethan Age. She and Shakespeare both lived during a time when most people bathed only once a year. Queen Elizabeth had an altered paradigm though. She bathed once a month. This radical departure from the norm worried the physicians of her day. They thought such excessive bathing habits would harm the queen's health. The clever, diplomatic, and never-married monarch disagreed with their convictions and continued to bathe once a month throughout England's Golden Age. Ironically, this world leader would be shunned in today's society for such poor hygienic practices, which only goes to show, sometimes change isn't as bad as we first think![783]

Parenting A cartoon pictured a little boy asking his father a very important question: "Daddy, what is a Christian?" The father thought for a moment and then replied, "A Christian is a person who loves and obeys God. He loves his friends, his neighbors, and even his enemies. He is kind and gentle and prays a lot. He looks forward to going to heaven and thinks that knowing God is better than anything on this earth. That, son, is a Christian!" The little boy took a couple of moments to contemplate what his father had said, and then asked, "Daddy, have I ever seen a Christian?" Parenting involves modeling Christlike behaviors, disciplines, and attitudes for our children because they need far more than a Christian's description, they need an example of one.[784]

Parenting A four-year study at Shands Hospital in Gainesville, Florida, revealed that newborn babies who are cared for in the maternity nursery cry more and secrete more stress hormones than those who stay with their mothers.[785]

Parenting A ten-year study by Harvard University runs contrary to many contemporaries who admonish lax parental discipline. This study revealed the best parents are "firm disciplinarians who simultaneously show great affection for their children." Effective parenting requires the healthy balance of displayed affection *and* firm discipline. Ephesian 6:4 concurs! This study also concluded, "the nuclear family is the most important educational delivery system."[786]

Parenting Attention deficit disorder is a serious problem that affects many families. In recent years, the disorder has become more readily recognized and diagnosed so that numerous children have gained needed medical help. Unfortunately, though, some children who don't have the disorder have been diagnosed with it because their behavior is contrary to the norm. A word of caution about this abuse appeared in the *Kudzu* comic strip. As a child sought counsel from her minister, she told of her brother's nonexistent attention span, his propensity to be easily distracted, his disruptive behavior, and his inability to complete his schoolwork. She then asked, "Is this what they call attention deficit disorder?" The pastor said, "Yes. He doesn't get enough attention from his parents!" Some children are simply suffering from a deficit of parental attention and medicine cannot cure that problem.[787]

Parenting Dr. Benjamin Spock penned *Baby and Child Care* in 1946. It was used in some forty million homes by parents who wanted to raise their children "right." Spock has changed his philosophy since writing those words fifty years ago. At age ninety-two, Spock said, "I used to think that all you had to do was be a decent person, and you didn't need to harp on morality or spirituality as my mother did with her six children. Now I believe you've got to." Spock mourns the condition of today's society and commented, "I think that there's been a real shift away from thinking of life as contributions by a person, or contributions to a family or contributions of a family to the rest of society to 'What's in it for me?'" To help turn the tide, parents should take heed to Spock's more contemporary view of parenting and "harp" on morality and spirituality.[788]

Parenting Dr. Nicholi, a psychiatrist from Harvard, noted current studies reveal American parents spend less time with their children than do parents in almost any other country. Nothing can replace the precious commodity of time spent with your children.[789]

Parenting From 1999 Barna Research shows parents are still the single greatest influence on their teenage children. Seventy-eight percent of teens from around the country identified their parents as the ones who most influence their thinking and behavior. Friends placed a distant second with 51 percent. Christian faith (48 percent), the Bible (40 percent), and siblings (40 percent) rounded out the top five influencers of teens.[790]

Parenting "Golf is secondary. The most important thing is to make the kid a better person, the parent a better person, the parent a better parent and the relationship between them better." —*Earl Woods, father of Tiger Woods*[791]

Parenting "Have you ever wondered why so many parents tie up their dog, but let their children run loose?" —*Anonymous*[792]

Parenting In a survey of American teenagers, 75 percent said they would welcome more discipline and need it. They noted more discipline would cause them to have greater respect for their parents.[793]

Parenting "Insanity is hereditary. You can get it from your children." —*Sam Levenson*[794]

Parenting "Life affords no greater responsibility, no greater privilege, than the raising of the next generation." —*C. Everett Koop*[795]

Parenting Mart De Haan helps lead the outstanding ministry of Radio Bible Class Ministries. He is a third-generation Christian who knows the value of Christian parenting. Of his formation in the faith he notes, "We heard right answers before we knew what the questions were." Advocates of value-free education would frown on such indoctrination, but the Bible supports such directive parenting. Life will provide plenty of opportunities to test the right answers. The tragedy comes when children are thrust into life with nothing more than questions.[796]

Parenting "One of the hardest jobs for a parent is making a child realize that "no" is a complete sentence." —*Anonymous*[797]

Parenting On May 3, 1999, the most deadly of all tornadoes, a category five, ripped through the Oklahoma town of Bridge Creek. Kara Wiese, age twenty-six, had just wrapped her six-year-old son, Jordan, in a heavy coat and was headed for the door of their mobile home when the whole house started rocking. She quickly shoved her only child into the bathroom and they held hands as the house started coming apart. Both Wiese and her son were sucked out of the trailer while holding hands.

Their grip broke and Jordan never saw his mother again. He was found along a creek bank across the street from his home. The little guy had three broken ribs, a swollen leg, and a bruised back. By the next day, he was released from the hospital and went out with his grandmother to look for his mom. Rescue teams searched with them when Jordan said, "I'm looking for my mom. You wanna help me?" The little boy found belongings from their home and located his mother's car, but he couldn't find her. The hard news of her death arrived two days later when the coroner was able to identify her fingerprints. As the broken-hearted boy tried to comprehend it all, he said, "I should have held on tighter." Somehow this little boy, who had not yet graduated from kindergarten, felt responsible for his mother's death. From this great tragedy may we be reminded of the tenderness in a child's heart, and determine to parent them in such a way that they will not feel undue burdens or responsibility for things they cannot control.[798]

Parenting Our society has definitely suffered from parental irresponsibility. Too often children are not adequately directed and turmoil results. On May 9, 1996, the community of St. Claire Shores, a suburb of Detroit, sent out a strong message to parents: "Pay attention and control your kids." A jury deliberated just fifteen minutes before convicting Anthony and Susan Provenzino of failing to control their sixteen-year-old son. Alex Provenzino committed a string of seven burglaries while living in his parents' home. The parents were the first to be convicted under a two-year-old ordinance that requires parents to "exercise reasonable control" in preventing their children from committing delinquent acts. District Judge William Crouchman fined each parent the maximum penalty of $100 and made them each pay $1,000 in court costs. The City Attorney, Robert Ihrie, issued a statement after the three-day trial: "This isn't about what the child did. We charged the parents for their own conduct. For what they failed to do." Mr. Provenzino seemed to have learned something from the ordeal that he called "terribly painful." He urged other parents "to do the best they can in raising their children." As L. M. Boyd has noted, "Pedarchy is a government run by children. Rare is the nation, but not so rare is the home that can be identified as such."[799]

Parenting Phil Downer has an interesting comparison that can help each of us reevaluate our parenting strategies. He noted that if we aren't careful, we can end up treating our children like fish in an aquarium.

Downer said, "You fill a big aquarium with water, dump in some fish, put fish food on top, and watch them eat. Most fish owners sort of sit back and watch the critters move around, and that's the way most folks raise kids." His challenge is well taken. Parenting involves much more than providing food and shelter.[800]

Parenting Social scientists, John DeFrain and Nick Stinnett, asked fifteen hundred schoolchildren, "What do you think makes a happy family?" The most frequently offered answer was "doing things together." Children still spell love t-i-m-e.[801]

Parenting "There are three ways to get something done: do it yourself, employ someone, or forbid your children to do it." —*Monta Crane*[802]

Parenting "Train up a child in the way he should go . . . and go there yourself once in a while." —*Anonymous*[803]

Partnership A little boy was selling pencils door-to-door for a nickel each. He greeted a woman at the door and began his sales pitch. He said, "Ma'am, would you like to buy one or two pencils from me? I'm selling these pencils at five cents a piece to help build a $30 million hospital for our community." She smiled and replied, "That's a mighty big job for just one boy selling pencils for a nickel." He then piped out with enthusiasm, "Oh, Ma'am, I'm not doing it all by myself. You see that boy across the street? He's my partner. We're doing this together!" Kingdom work can seem as impossible as constructing million-dollar buildings with nickel fund-raisers. But fortunately, we aren't doing it all alone. There are others to help and the collective energy of every believer is empowered by God himself.[804]

Pascal's Proposition Blaise Pascal was a scientist and philosopher of the seventeenth century. In seeking to disarm religious skeptics, he penned the logic that if God does not exist, one loses nothing by believing in him; but if God does exist, one can gain eternal life by believing in him. He then argued that belief in God is the only logical response. Although countless people have taken issue with Pascal's logic, it is nonetheless very logical.[805]

Passion Michael Jordan is now retired, but his method of basketball will not be forgotten any time soon. Another element of his game will also be well remembered—his passion for the sport. Until Jordan came around, the standard NBA contract included a clause that prevented any off-season games without approval from the team owner. Jordan's contract had to be written differently because he would not concede that part of his life. He became the first player to have what he called, "the love of the game clause." It gave him the freedom to play basketball whenever he wanted during the off-season. Of course such a request was befitting for a man who played just as hard in practice and he did in games. By his own admission, Jordan said, "I never stopped trying to get better." It's little wonder such raw passion for the game of basketball led to 29,277 points, five MVP awards, and six NBA championships. It also explains his unforgettable performance in the 1997 playoff game with the Utah Jazz. He was ravaged by the flu but still had 38 points and hit the game-winning 3-pointer even though the pain, fever, and severe dehydration caused him to collapse several times when leaving the game. If such intense passion can revolutionize the game of basketball, imagine what it could do in the church.[806]

Passion "The core problem is not that we are too passionate about bad things, but that we are not passionate enough about good things." —*Larry Crabb* [807]

Passion "The tragedy of today is that the situation is desperate, but the saints are not." —*Vance Havner* [808]

Passivity "All that is necessary for evil to triumph is for good men to do nothing." —*Edmund Burke* [809]

Passivity On May 27, 1998, Michael Fortier was sentenced to twelve years in prison for being passive. Fortier was the key witness whose testimony helped convict Timothy McVeigh and Terry Nichols in the Oklahoma City bombing. Fortier knew about the extensive plans of his two former Army buddies, but failed to warn the authorities. In a courtroom adjacent to where the Alfred P. Murrah Federal Building once stood, Fortier begged for the forgiveness of those who had lost loved ones. The worst episode of American terrorism claimed 168 lives, including nineteen children, and five hundred others were injured on that morning of April 19, 1995. Upon reflection, Fortier said, "I thought his (McVeigh) plan would never bear fruit. I was terribly wrong." He went on to describe his desire for things to be different: "I sometimes daydream that I told the police and I became a hero. But in reality I'm not." The courtroom's judgment on Fortier's passivity should speak to our tendencies toward spiritual passivity. Jesus condemned the servant who passively buried his talent. Spiritual passivity denies the importance and urgency of man's greatest need—salvation through Jesus Christ. Michael Fortier failed to speak up and thousands of lives were shattered. If Christians remain silent, far greater destruction will occur, and our passivity will not go unpunished. We can speak up and become a hero, or face the consequences of opting for silence.[810]

Patience Jell-O turned one hundred years old in 1997 and the story surrounding its inventor is truly ironic. In 1897, Pearl Wait wore several hats. He was a construction worker who dabbled in patent medicines and sold his ailment remedies door-to-door. In the midst of his tinkering, he hit on the idea of mixing fruit flavoring with granulated gelatin. His wife named it Jell-O and Wait had one more product to peddle. Unfortunately, sales weren't as strong as he'd hoped, so in 1899, Pearl Wait sold his Jell-O rights to Orator Woodward for $450. Woodward knew the value of marketing so within just eight brief years, Wait's neighbor turned a $450 investment into a $1 million business. Today, not a single relative of Pearl Wait receives royalties from the 1.1 million boxes of Jell-O that are sold each day. Why? Because Wait just couldn't wait.[811]

Patience Phillips Brooks was a pastor in New England during the late 1800s. He was known as a very calm and relaxed man, but like all of us, he had his moments of struggling with patience. A close friend recounted one such occasion when he found Brooks pacing the floor like a caged lion. He asked Brooks about the source of his troubles. The pastor replied, "The trouble is I'm in a hurry, but God isn't." When we are in a hurry it can be frustrating to realize God may not be moving as fast as we would desire. Fortunately, we can use those times to water the fruit of patience so we are able to more faithfully bear the entire fruit of God's Spirit (Galatians 5:22).[812]

Patriotic Spirit During a week at Vacation Bible School, a preschooler missed the correct words for the Pledge of Allegiance but he caught the right spirit. In explaining the pledge to his mother, the little guy said, "I pledge allegiance to the flag of the United States of a miracle" Our country is truly a miracle from God that has been bestowed on the entirety of mankind. May we cherish it as such and give gratitude to the One who has made it all possible.[813]

Peace A visual reminder for the source of true peace is on regular display along New York City's Fifth Avenue. At the entrance of the RCA building is a large statue of Atlas struggling to keep the world on his shoulders. On the other side of Fifth Avenue is Saint Patrick's Cathedral. Behind the high altar of this church is a small statue of Jesus effortlessly holding the whole world in one hand. Peace is hard to come by when we strive to balance the world on our own back, but when we heed God's invitation to give him our concerns (1 Peter 5:7), the weight of our world becomes an effortless lift for the Prince of Peace.[814]

Peace During the Korean War, Billy Graham had the opportunity of ministering to American soldiers. While there, he learned of an incident that stirred his heart. On Christmas Eve, a young Marine lay dying on Heartbreak Ridge. One of the chaplains climbed up to the young man and whispered, "May I help you, son?" The Marine replied, "No, it's all right." The chaplain was amazed at the soldier's tranquillity. When he glanced down at the man's side he understood the source. He was clutching a small New Testament in his bloody hand and his finger was placed on the calm assurance of John 14:27, "My peace I give to you . . ."[815]

Peer Pressure It's hard to find a Christian bookstore where Max Lucado's books aren't displayed on the best-seller's rack. This brilliant author and pastor stumbled into a situation where he was reminded how dangerous it can be to follow the crowd. He arrived at the airport for an early morning flight and made his way to the gate. The hour was early and he was extremely tired, so he soon found himself dozing off while waiting to board the plane. He was roused from his sleep by the noise of a crowd moving toward the jet ramp. Lucado gathered his belongings and found his seat on the aircraft. He again found his eyes heavy and slipped off into another nap. When he awakened to the bright morning sun gleaming through the window, he heard a peculiar message. He was headed to Denver, but the flight attendant was announcing their estimated time of arrival in Houston. Upon further clarification he discovered he had boarded the wrong plane. His slumber at the gate caused him to join the wrong crowd of passengers, and his inattentiveness aboard the plane sent him in the wrong direction. He's obviously much more cautious these days, but he learned an unforgettable lesson at thirty thousand feet. Simply following a crowd that seems to be going in the right direction might take you to the wrong place. In air travel it's a correctable situation, but in spiritual matters it could be an irreversible mistake.[816]

Perfection During the spring of 2000, Robbie Smart had the best day of his baseball career. The catcher for Newport, Arkansas High School, had a perfect day at the plate against Bald Knob High. He hit a solo home run, a two-run homer, a three-run homer, and a grand slam. In fact, it was such a perfect day that there isn't even a category in the record books for such a feat. Unfortunately, not every day is that perfect for Robbie or anyone else. Even when things go extremely well we are a far cry from true perfection. If hospitals handle newborns with 99.9 percent accuracy (near perfection) they will give twelve babies to the wrong parents every day. The same standard (99.9 percent) would leave the U.S. Postal Service mishandling 18,322 pieces of mail each hour . . . nearly half a million per day. At 99.9 percent efficiency the IRS would annually lose two million documents and incorrectly process 103,260 tax returns. Near perfection would mean 2.5 million books would be shipped out with wrong covers. It would result in twenty thousand drug prescriptions being incorrectly filled this year. The standard of 99.9 percent allows for 880,000 credit cards to have the wrong information on the magnetic tape, and makes certain that 315 entries in Webster's dictionary will be misspelled. We could also plan on missing one hundred heartbeats a day if 99.9 percent is the bench mark for perfection. Thankfully, God is 100 percent perfect 100 percent of the time and he expects us to make that our standard as well (Matt. 5:48).[817]

Perfection On May 17, 1998, David Wells pitched a perfect baseball game. The New York Yankees' left-hander became only the fifteenth pitcher in major league history to accomplish this feat, and just the thirteenth pitcher to do so in this century. To the unfortunate Minnesota Twins, Wells was the man who did not allow a single player to reach first base. According to the rules, a perfect game takes place when a pitcher retires every single batter in the game. That means in a normal nine-inning game, every one of the opposing twenty-seven batters makes an out. This requires the pitcher not to walk a single batter. That's exactly what happened when David Wells took the mound on that historic day. The term "perfect game" is somewhat deceiving though. You would think it might mean that the pitcher strikes out all of the batters, but that's not the case. Wells struck out just eleven of the twenty-seven batters . . . less than half. Another assumption one might make when using the definitive "perfect" would be that the pitcher threw nothing but strikes. Wells didn't even come close on this standard. Nearly half of his 120 pitches weren't in the strike zone. In short, to the nonenthusiast of baseball, it doesn't really sound much like a "perfect" game. This whole situation gives us an excellent opportunity to see the vast difference between ourselves and God. Were God defining the standards for pitching a perfect game in baseball, he would settle for nothing less than eighty-one consecutive strikes. But because professional ballplayers have determined that such a feat is impossible, their standard has been reduced to something more feasible. And even then, only fifteen pitchers have ever been able to do it. This same type of reductionary adjustment has occurred within the spiritual realm as well. God's idea of a perfect life is far different than what most people think. In Matthew 5:48, Jesus said we are to be perfect like God. People have been trying to tone down that statement ever since. "Did he really mean 'perfect' or just be as close to perfect as possible?" He literally meant perfect . . . flawless . . . sinless. And just to illustrate what God meant, Jesus achieved God's standard of perfection by never succumbing to the temptations of sin, not even once! The truth is, none of us will ever match such perfection on our own. Redefining "perfect" will never get us any closer to God's supreme standard. So rather than trying to find some illusive loophole, or doing tricky stuff with a dictionary, we would do far better to embrace the perfection that Jesus accomplished on the cross and thank him for providing a way to be perfectly forgiven of all our sins.[818]

Performance The U.S. Department of Transportation estimates that 80 percent of the nation's vehicles have underinflated tires.[819]

Persecution An estimated one hundred million Christians have been martyred in this century. That's more than the previous nineteen centuries combined.[820]

Persecution It's regular fodder for Sunday morning prayers, "Lord, thank you that we can come together today and worship without the threat of persecution." Fear of persecution is normal and none of us hunger for the pain and sorrow it brings. Paradoxically, though, persecution leads to church growth more than anything else. The World Evangelism Research Center has concluded from their studies that of the two thousand or so plans for global evangelization, "martyrdom is probably the most potent and significant factor of all." This would explain the unusual story of the Vins family. Peter and Lydia Vins were missionaries to the former Soviet Union. Peter was imprisoned and never seen again. Lydia was later imprisoned. Such persecution did not lead to their son rejecting Christianity, it simply lead to a similar passion for Christ. Like his parents, Georgi ended up in prison for his proclamation of the gospel. Two generations of persecution would understandably cause a young man to consider different pursuits, but Georgi's son, Peter, Jr., dedicated his life to Christ and was likewise imprisoned. In 1979, President Carter was able to secure the release of surviving family members and the Vins have continued to faithfully spread the gospel in the United States and abroad.[821]

Persecution Lai Man Peng was a twenty-two-year-old Chinese Christian evangelist who was martyred in 1994. (Many of China's estimated forty million Christians rise on Sunday at 3:00 A.M. to secretly worship in the homes of evangelists). While leading one such worship service, agents from the Public Security Bureau took hold of Man Peng and four other evangelists. In front of the congregation, these agents severely beat them. They then handed clubs to congregants and ordered them to beat their own ministers. Under the threat of torture themselves, these church members beat their leaders. Man Pengwas badly injured and the agents feared he would die in their presence, which would leave too much to explain, so they released him. He crawled and hobbled for several miles as he tried to reach his home, but he died alongside the road. Please remember to pray regularly and fervently for the estimated 200–250 million fellow Christians who face life-threatening persecution every day.[822]

Persecution Worldwide, an average of four hundred Christians are killed each day simply because of their faith in Christ. That's one murdered Christian every four minutes.[823]

Perseverance Even if you don't play golf, you've heard about Tiger Woods. His name is an international icon for youthful and unprecedented success on the links. His name is always in the golfing news whether he wins, loses, plays, or doesn't play in a tournament. Unlike the young sensation, two lesser-known guys from the world of golf had their names listed in the headlines of golf during the last week of February 2000. Kirk Triplett won his very first tournament by capturing the Nissan Open title. It was his first win since beginning the PGA Tour eleven years earlier. In real numbers, he competed in 266 tournaments before finally winning. Jim Carter also had a very special week, he won the Tucson Open. Carter's previous greatest accomplishment in golf occurred in 1983 when he won the NCAA championship. Since then, he labored in virtual obscurity before capturing his first victory in the 292nd event of his professional career. After nearly three hundred attempts, he finally won. Most people would like to take on the world like Tiger Woods and be a winner from the very beginning, but reality reminds us there are very few success stories like that of Woods. Jim Carter and Kirk Triplett represent a component of success that must never be forgotten. They stayed the course, practiced hard, and persevered until the prize was theirs to keep. There will always be those for whom success seems easy, but chances are you and I aren't part of that crowd. For most of us, perseverance is the trait that will carry us down the narrow path to which God has called us (Matthew 7:13–14). So hang in there and "don't get tired of doing what is good" (Galatians 6:9).[824]

Perseverance Gail Borden was the journalist in Texas who coined the phrase "remember the Alamo," but he is remembered for a far more significant piece of work. While on board a ship returning home from England, Borden saw children die as a result of drinking contaminated milk. Because of that experience he dedicated the remainder of his life to finding a way for humans to safely drink milk. His experiments with condensed milk failed until he saw how the Shakers in New York condensed their maple sugar in a vacuum-sealed pan. His success, which led to the safety of milk in a nonrefrigerated world, began the modern dairy industry, and launched a multibillion-dollar company. On Borden's tombstone are encouraging words of perseverance. It reads, "I tried and failed. I tried again and succeeded."[825]

Perseverance It took twenty years for the *Wizard of Oz* to financially break even.[826]

Perseverance "It was perseverance that got the snails to the ark." —*Charles Spurgeon* [827]

Perseverance July 4, 1998, marked the 150th birthday of the Washington Monument. Congressman Abraham Lincoln was among the guests who attended the laying of the cornerstone in 1848. By the time of completion, President Lincoln had been dead for twenty-three years. Money problems, followed by the Civil War, resulted in the project stalling out at just 150 feet. For nearly twenty-five years not a single stone was laid. In 1878, the effort was resumed and it reached its completed height of 555 feet in 1888. The world's largest freestanding stone building now reaches into the sky because of perseverance. When life expectancies were much shorter than today, these diligent people stayed the course even though it took the majority of their lifetime (forty years) to finish. When you're tempted to quit, take a minute to remember God's perspective in Zechariah 8:6: "If it's too difficult in your sight, will it also be too difficult in my sight?"[828]

Perseverance On February 6, 2000, both Charles Schulz and his comic strip, *Peanuts*, died. At the time of his death, Schulz's work appeared in twenty-six hundred newspapers worldwide, and was the basis of a franchise earning $1 billion a year. Since its modest debut in just seven papers on October 2, 1950, Charlie Brown and his gang became a constant feature of daily life for nearly fifty years. Ironically, the work of Charles Schulz should have never been noticed. He learned his trade through a correspondence school and earned a C in "the drawing of children." The tall, skinny outsider at St. Paul High School was a lousy student who hoped his gangly cartoons would be accepted for print in his 1940 senior yearbook. The annuals went to press without the drawings. Though discouraged, the fledgling artist was undaunted in the pursuit of his dream. Through determination and perseverance, Charles Schulz fulfilled his childhood goal and became the most widely syndicated cartoonist in the world.[829]

Perseverance On September 8, 1998, Mark McGwire broke the single-season home run record (61) that was set by Roger Maris exactly two years, to the day, before McGwire was born. In the 144th game of the St. Louis Cardinal's 1998 season, the burly first baseman hit his shortest home run of the season (342 feet) over the left-field fence and secured his place in baseball history. It was one of the biggest accomplishments to ever occur on a baseball diamond, but ironically, it was an event that nearly didn't occur. After a frustrating season in 1991, when he only hit for an average of .201 and was hampered by foot and back injuries, McGwire seriously considered retiring. He classified himself as an emotional wreck and thought about giving up. Before quitting, though, he remembered his dad's lifelong battle with polio. John McGwire contracted polio at age seven and must walk with a cane because one leg is shorter than the other. Nonetheless, McGwire's father fought through his disability to become a successful dentist, an avid golfer, and a cyclist at sixty-one years of age. McGwire decided he couldn't quit even if the future didn't look very bright in baseball. For the next four years he sought out therapy to deal with his depression, and persevered with his career even though he missed virtually all of the 1993 and 1994 seasons because of injuries. Then it happened, seven years after thinking it was time to retire, Mark McGwire became the new "Sultan of Swat." Incidentally, McGwire went to Southern California on a scholarship to pitch. It wasn't until his sophomore year that he made the transformation from a flame-throwing pitcher to a ball-crunching slugger.[830]

Perseverance When the United States Women's Softball team won the gold medal in Atlanta's 1996 Olympic games, they lost only one game, but from that loss came a remarkable story about perseverance. In the fifth inning against Australia, Danielle Tyler hit a home run over the center-field fence. The American third baseman floated around the bases with a rush of adrenaline. When she was greeted by a swarm of well-wishing teammates at home plate she let the excitement distract her focus and she did not touch the base. When all of the yelling subsided, the Australian team quietly appealed to the umpire who dramatically called Tyler out. Rather than scoring a run, Tyler's blast over the fence netted her team an out. As it ended up, had the lady slugger stepped on home plate, her team would have won 1-0. Instead, after seven innings of regulation play the game was tied at 0-0. In extra innings, Australia emerged with a 2-1 win and the U.S. team took their only loss of the Olympics. That disaster on the diamond reminds us of an important lesson in life— it's important that we finish well. It's not enough to hit a ball into the seats; you have to touch all of the bases as well. Whether you're talking about a day, a project, a church year, or a life, it's important that we finish well. To excel for a while is no guarantee of success. In Matthew 24:13, Jesus said, "But the one who endures to the end, he shall be saved." Likewise, Paul told of his strong finish when he wrote, "I have fought the good fight, I have finished the course . . ." (2 Timothy 4:7). We are not athletes competing for gold, but believers living for God. So whether at home or work, church or school, let's use the opportunities of every day, big or small, to finish well the tasks that have been bestowed on us.[831]

Persistence In 1997, Sue Evan-Jones of Yate, England, received her driver's license. This forty-five-year-old woman is obviously very persistent because that single accomplishment took her twenty-seven years, ten instructors, eighteen hundred driving lessons, and about $30,000 in fees. When the examiner said she passed, Jones asked, "Are you sure?"[832]

Persistence John Stockton has played the position of guard for the Utah Jazz in the NBA. In 1996, he joined an elite group when he scored his 13,000[th] career point. Of the experience Stockton said, "I've been around a long time. It's like my dad always says, 'You put a monkey at a typewriter long enough, and he'll come up with something good.'" Stockton's modest response does hold a kernel of truth. It's not always the most talented who get the job done. Oftentimes it is simply the most persistent who end up with the prize.[833]

Personality Multiple research studies have revealed approximately 45 percent of Americans are shy.[834]

Perspective During the fiftieth anniversary of D-Day in 1994, one documentary featured a very unique sequence of interviews. The commentators spoke with two men who were a part of the Normandy invasion in 1944. One was a soldier who fought on the ground. Reflecting back on that time he said, "I was convinced there was no way we could possibly win." The other interview involved a pilot who saw things much differently from his vantage point in the air. He said, "I was convinced there was no way we could possibly lose." From our limited view on earth we are often tempted to become discouraged and defeated, but God's omniscient take on life reminds us the victory is sure (Revelation 21–21).[835]

Perspective "In order to maintain a well-balanced perspective, the person who has a dog to worship him should have a cat to ignore him." —*Anonymous* [836]

Perspective Robert Louis Stevenson, the great Scottish author who wrote *Treasure Island,* was accustomed to bedridden illnesses. Although frequently ill, he remained eternally optimistic. One day his wife approached him after a terrible coughing spell and remarked, "I expect you still believe it's a wonderful day." Stevenson confidently replied, "I do. I will never permit a row of medicine bottles to block my horizon." We can focus on the medicine bottles (or debts, disappointments, conflicts, etc.,) or we can keep our sights set on the horizon of God's hope.[837]

Perspective "There are only two ways to live your life. One is as though nothing is a miracle. The other is as though everything is a miracle." —*Albert Einstein* [838]

Perspective "We don't see things as they are, we see them as we are." —*Ansais Nin* [839]

Perspective When things get a bit too stressful and frustration starts to set in, just contemplate the following realities and you might find some level of encouragement during your struggles. 40 percent of the world's population does not have electrical service. 60 percent does not have simple phone service, and half of those live more than two hours from the nearest telephone. One-third of the people on this planet have never made a phone call. Now that probably won't solve your problem, but it does remind us that things might not be as difficult as we first imagined. [840]

Perspective While addressing a graduating class at Southern University in Baton Rouge, Louisiana, Bill Cosby told about a lesson he learned in perspective while studying philosophy at college. The class was debating the age-old question of whether the glass is half empty or half full. Cosby took the issue home to run it by his father. Without hesitation the elder Cosby said, "It depends on whether you're pouring or drinking." That response helped Cosby earn an A while impressing both his professor and his peers. This simple thought reminds us that things seem worse when we're taking (drinking) and better when we're giving (pouring). [841]

Planning The Y2K computer problem had the attention of everyone regardless of whether or not you operated a computer. It involved the complications that could have occurred when computer clocks rolled over to the year 2000. Many computers couldn't process information correctly when this happened, so enormous amounts of money were spent solving this critical issue. Corporate computer budgets averaged 24 percent toward the Y2K problem in 1997, 29 percent in 1998, and in 1999 this problem consumed 44 percent of information technology budgets. Specialists estimated the total worldwide cost of preventing potential computer failures was $300–$600 billion. U.S. companies alone spent $150–$225 billion. Lack of adequate planning for the future in computer technology created an astronomical bill. Inadequate planning for one's eternal future will prove to be even more costly. [842]

Politically Incorrect According to *Free Inquiry*, a secular humanist magazine, anyone who says, "God bless you," after you sneeze is trying to deprive you of your constitutional rights. The magazine also condemned such activities as 1) asking someone, "Did you have a merry Christmas?" 2) inviting people to a wedding that includes a religious ceremony, and 3) saying grace at a dinner party in your own home. A heterosexual couple was thrown out of a San Francisco gay bar for kissing. Morgan Gorrono, manager of The Cafe, said he doesn't really mind heterosexual behavior among his customers as long as they don't openly flaunt it. Alvaro Cardona was rejected for a job tutoring needy students in English at UCLA because he was not politically correct. Cardona is a Latino honor student and an experienced tutor. During his interview, English and tutoring never came up. Instead, he was questioned about affirmative action and institutional racism. Cardona was rejected for the tutoring position because "he would have been the kind of person who stressed learning, which is only 50 percent of the job. The missing 50 percent was validating the feelings of students."[843]

Politics John Adams was the second president of the United States and the first chief executive to live in the White House. He moved in to the new home on November 1, 1800. The next day, President Adams wrote these words, "I pray heaven to bestow the best of blessings on this house and all that shall hereafter inhabit it. May none but honest and wise men ever rule under this roof." May we as citizens of this great land turn to heaven, as did he, and pray for the same.[844]

Pornography A sad irony has transpired in our country's military. Sexual scandals have become routine, and military careers are being destroyed by immoral improprieties. Tragically, our military leaders are refusing to make the connection between such misconduct and pornography. The Pentagon supports the sale of pornography to troops and deemed the January 22, 1997, ruling of Judge Shira Scheindlin a success. That ruling declared the 1996 defense authorization bill unconstitutional. This bill forbade the sale of sexually explicit magazines at U.S. military bases. So, the military is back in the pornography business (the Pentagon earns $4 million in annual sales of pornography), and Bob Guccione is thrilled because he sells nineteen thousand copies of his magazine, *Penthouse*, to the military every month.[845]

Pornography In the United States alone, there are nearly thirty thousand pornography sites on the Internet. Their collective gross income is almost $1 billion a year (1998). Since the beginning of Internet access, the percentage of people using this pornography has remained constant with about 32 percent of Internet users visiting a pornographic site. Additionally alarming is the reality that employees spend work time accessing pornography. Statistics reveal that employees spend 24 percent of their Internet time at work doing nonwork-related tasks. The number one type of site visited by employees is general news. The second most frequently visited sites are those offering sexually explicit content. In real numbers, roughly one-third of those on the Internet are accessing pornography, and one-fourth of the time that employees are on the Internet at work there is a strong likelihood they are accessing sexually explicit Web sites.[846]

Pornography The cover story for the February 10, 1997, issue of *U.S. News & World Report* addressed the issue of pornography in America. The feature story revealed these facts: In 1962, hard-core pornography had a total retail value of "no more than $10 million." In 1996, Americans spent $8 billion on hard-core videos, peep shows, live sex acts, adult cable programming, sexual devices, computer porn, and sex magazines. This figure ($8 billion) is an amount much larger than Hollywood's domestic box office receipts and larger than all the revenue generated by rock and country music recordings. Americans now spend more money at strip clubs than the combined intake of all performances at Broadway, off-Broadway, regional and nonprofit theaters, the opera, the ballet, and jazz and classical music concerts. The United States is now "by far" the world's leading producer of pornography with hard-core videos being produced at the rate of 150 new titles per week. Playboy's Web site, which offers free glimpses of its Playmates, now averages about five million hits a day. Every night, between the peak hours of 9:00 P.M. and 1:00 A.M., an estimated one-quarter million Americans call for commercial phone sex. The number of hard-core video rentals has risen from 75 million in 1985 to 665 million in 1996. In the face of all these alarming statistics, Larry Flynt said he believes that adults can safely read any book or see any movie without the risk of being corrupted. For this reason he thinks the obscenity laws are an insult to the intelligence of the American people. Pornography is eroding the morality of America![847]

Possessions "I have held many things in my hands, and I have lost them all; but whatever I have placed in God's hands, that I still possess." —*Martin Luther*[848]

Potential In 1988, Jack Canfield visited the most famous Buddhist temples in Bangkok, Thailand. One such holy place is called the Temple of the Golden Buddha. Inside this very small building is a solid gold statue of Buddha. It stands 10.5 feet tall, weighs over 2.5 tons, and is worth nearly $200 million. The history of this statue is fascinating. In 1957, a highway was slated to be built over the grounds of a monastery so the monks made preparations for their clay Buddha to be relocated. A crane was employed, but when the statue was being lifted it began to crack. The head monk was concerned about the damage and had the statue lowered back to the ground. When it rained they covered it with a tarp. That evening the monk took a flashlight to make certain the statue was staying dry under the tarp. When he shined his flashlight on the crack, it began to glisten. He took a closer look and then went for a hammer and chisel. He knocked off pieces of clay only to find a statue of solid gold. Historians believe the statue was covered with clay several centuries before when the Burmese army was about to invade Thailand. The monks were trying to protect their treasure but when the Burmese army attacked, all of those who knew the secret were killed. A similar secret exists today. Inside each of us is a largely unknown, yet valuable potential just waiting to be released. Don't keep it covered with shards of clay.[849]

Potential "Man was designed for accomplishment, engineered for success and endowed with the seeds of greatness." —*Zig Ziglar*[850]

Potential On average, people use only 13 percent of the features and programs on their computers.[851]

Potential What do you figure you're worth? According to an estimate by scientists from the American Chemical Society, the total value of all the elements in an average adult body would be $25. But before you settle on such a nominal fee, be sure to read what else these chemists had to say during National Chemistry Week in November of 1996. When you start combining the chemical properties of a human body to make complex biochemicals such as DNA, proteins, enzymes, and hormones, the market value increases to $6 million. The key for determining the value of a human body is dictated by what you examine. If you simply look at what is, rather than what could be, you'll end up with a blue-light special. If you take the time to research all of the inherent potential, you end up with an astronomical price tag. Most every situation is like the human body—the potential is determined by what you see. And with Christ, we all have exponential potential (Ephesians 3:20–21; Philippians 4:13).[852]

Potential "What if at this very moment you *are* living up to your potential?" *—Anonymous*[853]

Poverty Every day in the world, 9,500 children die from lack of water or from diseases caused by polluted water.[854]

Poverty Every fifty-three minutes an American child dies in poverty.[855]

Poverty Every minute of every day, more than 25 children worldwide die from preventable illnesses such as diarrhea, tetanus, and pneumonia.[856]

Poverty More than one billion people live right at the subsistence level in regards to food, shelter, and clothing.[857]

Poverty Of the world's population, 3 billion live on less than $2 a day and 1.3 billion live on less than $1 a day.[858]

Poverty The average North American consumes five times more than a Mexican, ten times more than a Chinese, and thirty times more than a person from India.[859]

Poverty Tim Cline has served as a Southern Baptist Missionary in Senegal, West Africa. In 1999, he was overwhelmed by something he saw. While driving, he noticed a large number of people running down the road. At first, it looked as though they were running from something. He followed after them and then discovered they were actually running to something: the city dump. A garbage truck had just arrived and they were running to find food, clothing, or anything of remote value. They were racing against each other and the dogs to cull through the refuse of their city. One hundred million children live on the streets of our world's largest cities. One million young girls become prostitutes each year. Over seventeen million children die each year of starvation. Two hundred million children throughout the world (under age 15) are exploited for their labor. Twenty-five thousand people die each day from drinking dirty water. May such information challenge us to more compassionately share the resource with which we have been so richly blessed.[860]

Practicality G. K. Chesterton, one of the great Christian authors of the twentieth century, was once asked what single book would he choose if he was stranded on an island. He answered, *Thomas's Guide to Practical Ship Building*. Commitment to God does at times require us to do the impractical, but there are also plenty of occasions where God expects us to use practical wisdom.[861]

Prayer A young lieutenant was hosting a four-star general. While they were in the subordinate's office, the phone rang and he instinctively reached over to answer it. The general intercepted the young man's hand and said, "You don't need to answer it. Whoever it is, they can't be more important than me." God far outranks everyone else and is therefore worthy of our undivided attention.[862]

Prayer "God will either give you what you ask, or something far better." —*Robert McCheyne* [863]

Prayer If you want to make certain your prayers get to God, visit www.newprayer.com. At least that's what the creators of this Web site are claiming. Crandall Stone, at the age of forty-nine, set up the Web site in 1999 after a night of sipping brandy and philosophizing with some friends in Vermont. The engineer and freelance consultant from Cambridge, Massachusetts, chipped in with his friends to build a $20,000 radio-wave-transmitting Web site. Believing that God was out there somewhere, they consulted with NASA scientists to determine where the Big Bang originated. Upon their discovery that a star cluster called M13 was the oldest known part of the universe, they aimed the Web site antennas to that location. Now, they transmit about fifty thousand prayers a week from people all around the world. Of the free service, Stone says, "It appears that most people take our service seriously and that a large number are gratified by the results." No doubt, the omnipresence of God exists in M13, but he's also available to receive prayers in the convenience of a contrite heart.[864]

Prayer In 1987, Vera Reeder of Fort Worth, Texas, received an amazing get-well card from her six-year-old granddaughter, Melissa, who also lived in Fort Worth at the time. Reeder was under the weather so little

Melissa made her a card that read, "Dear Nana, I hope you fel beter." Once she completed the card, Melissa asked her mother how to spell "Watson" and then later asked for a stamp. Carrie Reeder was busy doing housework and figured her daughter was just doing one of her little projects. When she asked for a stamp, Melissa's mom directed her to some S&H green stamps. The next day, Melissa's Nana found an envelope in her mailbox that was simply addressed, "Nana, 1712 Watson" (the 7 was printed backwards). The only return address was "Melissa." Her green stamp had been postmarked by the post office and it was delivered like a regular piece of mail. The anonymous heroine at the post office has remained a mystery, but the Postal Service officials were very proud of their employee's extra effort with Melissa's letter. Prayer can be a lot like Melissa's letter. It doesn't have to be letter perfect for God to receive it, it just needs to be delivered from the heart.[865]

Prayer In 1996, a group of Baptist women in Kigali, Rwanda, decided their three-hour prayer meetings weren't long enough. They doubled their efforts and started devoting six hours to pray for their war-torn country, which has seen the massive slaughter of its people. Prayer offers a clear reflection of our dependence on God. Humble dependency on God is more than evident in the lives of these women. What level of dependency does my prayer life reflect?[866]

Prayer In October of 1996, Yankelovich Partners surveyed 269 doctors at a meeting of the American Academy of Family Physicians. The results showed that 99 percent were convinced religious belief can heal. That's 20 percent higher than the figure gleaned from the general public. In response to the question, "Why do doctors feel this way?" Dr. Herbert Benson said, "Because we've seen the power of belief. We see it all the time, and we can't deny it." He went on to note, "The real breakthrough is the acceptance of these approaches by modern medicine."[867]

Prayer It doesn't always happen like this, and it shouldn't be the motive for praying, but sometimes prayer provides rather unique surprises. During the fall of 1996, Eduardo Sierra took a trip to Stockholm, Sweden. The thirty-five-year-old Spanish businessman sought out a church where he could spend some time in prayer. The only church he found to be open was an old Catholic church where a coffin was lying in state. The casket was unattended with a simple condolence book to the side. Noting there weren't any other signatures in the book, Sierra spent several minutes praying for the deceased and his family. When he was finished, he wrote his name and address like the registry instructed for all entries. He then left the church. Several weeks later in his hometown of Hamburg, Germany, Sierra received a call from officials in the Swedish capital. They informed him that he was now a millionaire. The man in the casket was Jens Svenson, a seventy-three-year-old real estate dealer who had died without any close relatives. He had specified in his will that whoever prayed for him would get all of his belongings. Eduardo Sierra, a complete stranger, was the only one whose name appeared in the condolence book so he became the heir. His simple prayer of compassion yielded a very surprising windfall. If we could only see as does God, we would realize that every prayer provides enormous benefits even though they seldom deliver a million-dollar inheritance.[868]

Prayer Just a year before her death, Princess Diana was taken off the prayer list of her former church. On November 24, 1996, the words "Charles, Prince of Wales" replaced the words "Prince and Princess of Wales" in the Church of England's prayer for the royal family. The move was ordered by Queen Elizabeth II as "a necessary matter of form" after the divorce of Charles and Diana. The princess probably didn't lose much sleep over the matter, yet such actions can't help but leave one feeling somewhat abandoned. Christians never have to worry about getting removed from the Lord's prayer list. Romans 8:26, 27, 34 and Hebrews 7:25 all remind us that Jesus and the Holy Spirit are continually interceding for us.[869]

Prayer Kenneth Bruner, the stepson of a Pentecostal minister, led his seven accomplices in prayer before they held up a jewelry store. Bruner asked God for his divine protection in preparation for the heist of Herman's Fine Jewelry store in Des Moines, Iowa. God answered his prayer for "divine protection" in that the robbery was foiled and nobody got hurt. The small congregation of thieves ended up with a federal indictment instead of fine jewels.[870]

Prayer Max Lucado has shared the story of a dying man who knew the vitality of prayer. A few days before his death, a minister visited with him in the hospital. Next to the man's bed was an empty chair so the minister asked if somebody had recently been by to visit. The old man smiled and gave this answer, "I place Jesus on that chair and I talk to him." He went on to explain, "Years ago a friend told me that prayer was as simple as talking to a good friend. So every day I pull up a chair, invite Jesus to sit, and we have a good talk." Several days later the man died. His daughter had been sitting with him but slipped out for a few hours because he seemed to be resting so peacefully. When she returned to the room, she found him dead. Strangely, though, his head was not resting on the pillow, but on an empty chair beside his bed. When she related this unusual scene to the minister he not only understood its meaning, but also gained a greater understanding of prayer.[871]

Prayer "May we never experience success without prayer." — *Raymond McHenry* [872]

Prayer Names such as Martin Luther, John Wesley, David Brainerd, George Fox, Adoniram Judson, and John Hyde are well known to those who have studied church history. The impact of these men has been very significant and can be traced to their practice of prayer. Martin Luther said, "I have so much business I cannot get on without spending three hours daily in prayer." Wesley declared, "God does nothing but in answer to prayer." His daily devotion of two hours in prayer demonstrated the depth of this conviction. David Brainerd wrote in his journal, "I love to be alone in my cottage, where I can spend much time in prayer." William Penn said of George Fox, "Above all he excelled in prayer. The most awful, living, reverent frame I ever felt or beheld, I must say was his in prayer." Adoniram Judson withdrew from business and company seven times a day for the purpose of prayer. He began at dawn, then continued again at nine o'clock, twelve o'clock, three o'clock, six o'clock, nine o'clock, and midnight. John Hyde was so characterized by prayer that he was nicknamed, "Praying Hyde." It is no small wonder that these prayer warriors wielded such powerful influence for the Kingdom of God.[873]

Prayer One moment of the 1996 Olympic games that will never miss a highlight reel is that of Kerri Strug vaulting to gold on a badly injured ankle. That one event changed her life. She became an American heroine. Such heroines catch the attention of people in high places and she was no exception. President Clinton called to congratulate her and when he did, Kerri was on another line with some friends. Her coach, Bela Karoli, told her the President was waiting on the other line. She thought he was kidding and continued the conversation with her friends. Karoli soon returned to the room and she still thought he was kidding until he got in her face and said, "Kerri, the President of the United States has called you and is waiting on the line." She quickly got off the other line and spoke with the President. Although you have not vaulted into the pages of sport's history, and even though you probably won't be hearing from any presidents, you have consistently been receiving calls from One that knows no equal. God's love for you leads him to call you regularly. Humbly accept this honor, get off the other line, and take his call.[874]

Prayer Pastor John Ramsey had grown accustomed to someone providing him with a rose boutonniere every Sunday. That routine took on dramatic new meaning when a young boy approached him after the service and politely asked if he could have the little rose. Ramsey knew the flower was destined for the trash so he offered it to the boy and asked what he planned to do with the used rose. The little guy replied, "Sir, I'm going to give it to my granny. My parents got divorced last year. I was living with my mother, but when she got married again she wanted me to live with my father. I lived with him for a while, but he said I couldn't stay so he sent me to live with my grandmother. She is so good to me. She cooks for me and takes care of me. She has been so good to me that I want to give that pretty flower to her for loving me." Ramsey said tears filled his eyes as he listened to the little boy. He then told the compassionate boy, "You can't have this flower because it's not enough." He pointed to the large spray of fresh flowers at the altar and said, "Please take those flowers to your granny because she deserves the very best." The little boy lit up with excitement and said, "What a wonderful day! I asked for one flower but got a beautiful bouquet." Our approach to God is not unlike what took place that day with this child and Pastor Ramsey. We come in our pain seeking a small response to our situation, but God points to a greater answer and invites us to take that instead.[875]

Prayer "Pray as you can, not as you can't." —*Don Chapman* [876]

Prayer "Prayer does not equip us for greater works...prayer is the greater work." —*Oswald Chambers* [877]

Prayer "Prayer is the lifelong chance of a lifetime." —*Max Lucado* [878]

Prayer Richard Swenson has identified a significant problem among Christians in America, and has written a very insightful book that addresses this threatening practice. He refers to this problem simply as "margin." We tend to operate without this necessary element in our lives. We allot forty-five minutes for a project that requires an hour, spend more money than we earn, and run out of time to do the important things of life. This is very evident in the area of prayer. Swenson noted that 85 percent of Christians admit the only praying they do is on the run. Although God hears such prayers, He deserves far more than a prayer-life confined to the shower, car, subway, or grocery line.[879]

Prayer Some creative minds around the University of Southern Mississippi came up with a catchy slogan for their football team: "Let Us Prey." Naturally, plenty of people have taken great offense since it was first introduced in 1998, but they may have reminded us of a very important truth. When we fail to pray, we avail ourselves to become prey. Peter couldn't watch and pray one hour in the Garden of Gethsemane, so he became prey for the Adversary. He later wrote, "the Devil prowls around like a roaring lion, looking for someone to 'prey' upon" (1 Peter 5:8). The locker room language is indeed a bit sacrilegious, but it does point to a key concern—we become prey when we don't pray.[880]

Prayer The Bible repeatedly refers to God's followers as sheep. With this metaphor in mind, nature paints a beautiful picture through the experience of a lamb nursing. The little sheep often gets down on its knees to nurse. Although it can walk forthrightly on all four legs, when it comes time for nourishment, the lamb kneels. As the sheep of God's pasture, we find strength and sustenance just like the little lambs—down on our knees.[881]

Prayer "The highest calling of Christians is the ministry of prayer." —*Max Lucado* [882]

Prayer Tony Campolo is a well-known Christian communicator who teaches sociology at Eastern College in St. Davids, Pennsylvania. One day he was invited to speak at a Pentecostal College near his home campus. When he arrived for the chapel service, he was escorted to a back room where eight men laid their hands on him and began to pray. Campolo said he was very appreciative of the heartfelt prayers, but one guy spent a long time praying about something that had nothing to do with the chapel service. The longer he prayed the more the others grew weary and leaned more heavily on Campolo. He prayed on and on about a friend of his named Charlie. He said, "God, you know Charlie. He lives in that silver trailer down the road about a mile. You know the trailer, Lord, just down the road on the right-hand side." Campolo was thinking, "Knock it off, fella. What do you think God's doing, saying, 'What's that address again?'" He went on, "Lord, Charlie told me this morning he's decided to leave his wife and three kids. He's going to walk out on his family. Lord, step in, do something, bring that family together again." Campolo said the guy just kept praying earnestly for his friend Charlie, and kept reiterating the fact that he was leaving his wife and three kids and that he lived in a silver trailer, just down the road on the right-hand side. Meanwhile, the others kept leaning more heavily on Campolo's head and he was just waiting for the lengthy prayer to end. Finally it was over and he went in to preach for the chapel service. Afterwards, he got into his car and started heading home. Soon thereafter, he saw a hitchhiker and pulled over to give him a ride. As they pulled back onto the road, Campolo introduced himself and the hitchhiker said his name was Charlie. Campolo's heart began to race and he took the next exit off the turnpike. The passenger asked him why he was exiting and Campolo said, "Because you just left your wife and three children, right?" Charlie's eyes got real big and he said, "R-r-r-ight." He leaned closer to the door and never took his eyes off Campolo. Then things got real strange when Campolo drove him right to his silver trailer. In complete amazement Charlie asked, "How'd you know I live here?" Campolo replied, "God told me." He then ordered Charlie to get in the trailer and Charlie hurried to the door. His wife greeted him at the doorway and shouted, "You're back, you're back!" Charlie then began whispering in her ear and her eyes got bigger and bigger. Campolo came up to the porch and said, "Sit down. I'm going to talk and the two of you are going to listen." It was the most captive audience he had ever addressed. That afternoon, those two people were led to Jesus Christ and today Charlie is a preacher of the gospel. Prayers aren't always answered that dramatically, but then again, they aren't always prayed that fervently.[883]

Prayer While pastoring the Guttenburg United Methodist Church in Guttenburg, Iowa, Karl Goodfellow conducted a prayer experiment with the children in his church. He planted soybean seeds in two pie tins, and then made certain one group of seeds received prayer while the others were left to Mother Nature. After a season, the congregation was amazed to see how the seeds that received prayer came out with a superior crop. This was the beginning of a special ministry to pray for farmers by name. The Safety Net Prayer chain now has over five thousand people praying for fifty thousand farmers by name. Although crops are part of their prayers, these prayer warriors are praying for more than the development of seeds. They have seen miraculous protection take place when farm accidents occurred. Frank Livingood initially laughed at the idea of people praying for him, but after his son was divinely spared from suffocating in a grain elevator he said, "I'm not laughing about it anymore. I think the prayers are great." Pastor Goodfellow has helped many of us see the vast expanse of things for which we can and should pray.[884]

Preaching "I go out to preach with two propositions in mind. First, every person ought to give his life to Christ. Second, whether or not anyone else gives him his life, I will give him mine." —*Jonathan Edwards* [885]

Preaching Preaching is a difficult task. The pastor must compete with a multitude of distractions and plenty of negative opinions. R. E. White described preaching as "a monstrous monologue by a moron to mutes." Some critics' words are even less flattering. Likewise, there are more than a few jokes about people falling asleep during the preacher's message. How about the guy who described preaching as "the art of talking in someone else's sleep." Of course there is a positive way of viewing this phenomenon. One pastor said, "When my deacons fall asleep while I'm preaching, I just see it as their vote of confidence that I won't say anything heretical." The next time you see somebody's eyes glazing over during a sermon, just remember what happened in 1974 during a slow sermon at the North Presbyterian Church in North Saint Paul, Minnesota. Art Fry was having trouble focusing on the sermon so he began to daydream. This 3M scientist was frustrated by the inability to mark hymnbooks without making a big mess. He used the sermon time to figure out a solution and that was the day Post-it notes were invented.[886]

Preaching Since 1991, Dr. Jimmy Draper has served as the president of LifeWay Christian Resources of the Southern Baptist Convention. This one organization provides discipleship materials for 600,000 churches throughout the world. As a young man, Draper felt the call of God on his life. He became a third-generation minister as his father and grandfather were both Southern Baptist pastors. At the age of nineteen, Jimmy Draper was a college student who loved to preach. During a summer visit to see his elderly grandfather, the old preacher asked his grandson, "Jimmy, would you like to know where you can find a good sermon?" Any young preacher knows the challenge of putting together a sermon, so a question like that always perks great interest. The teenage evangelist readily replied, "Yes, I sure would!" With a twinkle in his eye, L. M. Keeling picked up his Bible and said, "From Genesis to Revelation." May all who have been called to preach and teach God's Word be reminded that great sermons are not built around inspiring stories. No, the true greatness of a message is dependent on the foundation of God's Word. Plumb the depths of that which is found in those sixty-six books and you will never lack for a good sermon.[887]

Preaching The ferry that crosses the Berbice River in Guyana is always well supplied with vendors selling cold drinks. Warren Rice has been a missionary who frequently traveled on this ferry and has known most of the vendors. One day he was surprised to see a cold drink vendor turned preacher. He was holding a Bible and announced he was going to preach a sermon on tithing. He delivered his message and then walked through the crowd collecting an offering. The man made no pretense about his objective, he was collecting the money for himself. A few weeks later, Rice saw the same vendor but now he had returned to selling cold drinks. He asked the man, "What happened to preaching?" The vendor replied, "Preaching don't pay."[888]

Predictions "Baseball will never make it. It's too slow." —*Chad Bigelow, sports reporter, 1902*[889]

Prejudices During the years of Archie Bunker running the world from his recliner, he once engaged in a debate with his neighbor about the color of Jesus' skin. Bunker's neighbor was none other than the equally opinionated but racially different George Jefferson. As they debated the issue of Jesus' color, Bunker referred to Warner Sallman's picture of Christ. He told Jefferson, "Jesus is white." Jefferson countered, "How do you know?" Bunker declared, "I saw the picture." Jefferson then diffused Archie's logic with a little twisted rationale of his own. He told his neighbor, "Maybe you saw the negative." Whenever we look with eyes of prejudice we would do well to remember this televised debate and recognize we don't always see as clearly as we sometimes think we do.[890]

Prevention "What we prevent needs no cure." —*Frances Murphy*[891]

Pride An ancient Indonesian parable tells of a turtle who flew through the air by biting hard on a stick that was carried by two geese. The turtle was thrilled to take flight, but became increasingly troubled by comments from onlookers. Those who viewed the spectacle praised the geese for being so clever. The turtle felt he was the one who deserved attention and praise so he opened his mouth and shouted, "This was my idea." Pride is a destructive force that robs us of life.[892]

Pride "Anyone who thinks he knows all the answers just isn't up to date on the questions." —*Thomas LaMance* [893]

Pride "A wise man is never as sure of anything as a fool is of everything." —*Anonymous* [894]

Pride "God is dead." —*Friedrich Nietzsche (1882)* "Nietzsche is dead." —*God (1900)* [895]

Pride In a German monastery hangs a very unusual trophy of antlers. The mount includes not one, but two sets of antlers. Although the monks don't normally display such things, the history of these racks reveals why they have been placed on the wall. Two bucks got into a brawl and could not untangle their antlers. In the fury of trying to gain their freedom, both deer died. They both entered that battle with the intent of establishing their superiority, but they died in humiliating disgrace. This entanglement of interlocking antlers provides these monks with a daily reminder of pride's deadly results.[896]

Pride The immortal golfer, Arnold Palmer, learned a hard but valuable lesson about pride in the 1961 Masters tournament. He had a one-stroke lead going into the final hole and hit a great tee shot to start the eighteenth hole. He was walking with great confidence to hit his second shot when he spotted an old friend standing at the edge of the gallery. He walked over to the friend who extended his hand and said, "Congratulations." As soon as he heard those words and shook that hand, Palmer knew he had lost his focus. He was right. He hit into a sand trap, then knocked it over the green, missed a putt, and lost the Masters. Of that experience this legendary golfer said, "You don't forget a mistake like that. You just learn from it and become determined that you will never do that again. I haven't in all the years since." Palmer's strategy for overcoming pride is one that we can all practice: see it for what it is, learn from it, determine to never do it again, and stay faithful to that commitment.[897]

Pride "The sun will set without thy assistance." —*The Talmud* [898]

Pride "The trouble with self-made men is they worship their creator." —*Anonymous* [899]

Pride While playing in the NFL, Marcus Allen was reluctant to talk about his accomplishments on the football field. The well-known running back has a philosophy about bragging. He said, "I'm really not comfortable talking about myself. You know, it's a little bit like a whale. He doesn't get harpooned until he comes up to blow."[900]

Priorities Had Payne Stewart died five years earlier, he would have been remembered in an entirely different manner. But because of the rearrangement of his priorities just a few years before his death, he has been memorialized as a family man who loved God. His relationship with Jesus Christ was the most important aspect of his life but it hadn't always been that way. Throughout most of his career, this celebrity golfer was known more for his competitive spirit, unusual clothes, and cocky attitude. When he reevaluated his life as a man approaching forty, he discovered the need to abandon his self-serving priorities and embrace Jesus Christ as his Lord. Ironically, his golf game dramatically improved once he put his priorities in proper order. When his jet went down on October 25, 1999, grief surrounded those closest to him because of the wonderful man he had become. Some of those most deeply affected by Stewart's death were his numerous friends on the Professional Golf Association Tour. Many of these were making preparations for the Tour Championship in Houston, Texas, when they learned of their friend's death. All of them wrestled with ways to appropriately remember him. One of the most unique memorials was provided by Bob Estes, a fellow golfer and Christian who was deeply affected by Stewart's faith. On the first hole of his first round, Estes took his putter to the tee box. He stood over the ball for a few moments then putted it about fifteen feet. He then quietly said, "That's for Payne." In a game where each stroke can be worth hundreds of thousands of dollars, Bob Estes voluntarily gave up a stroke to make an important point. He later said, "It was symbolic of the last putt he (Stewart) made to win the U.S. Open. But maybe more importantly, it also had to do with the way Payne had changed. The way faith and family and friends were his top priorities. It meant I wasn't worried about the first hole or the score I shot. All of us need to remember what's most important."[901]

Priorities Lora Patterson's family is now rich, but she won't be able to enjoy their wealth. On the Thursday before the 1997 Super Bowl, Lora was killed in a rehearsal for the $1.2 million halftime show. She was one of eight performers slated to bungee jump from the top of the New Orleans Superdome. During the practice session her assistants let out too much line and she crashed to the artificial turf. Tragically, her death could have easily been prevented. Branam Enterprises, the company in charge of this act, did not secure experienced workers for the job of handling these bungee lines. On the morning of the rehearsal, inexperienced people were invited to help out. These crew members were only given a two-minute course on managing the cords. Shortly thereafter, they were hoisted to the top of the dome, placed on a narrow walkway, and given charge of the jumpers. In preparation for a show that would be seen by 750 million people worldwide, and with a million-dollar budget, only two minutes were invested in a potentially life-threatening stunt. Thousands of hours went into the setting of lights, music rehearsals, and choreography. But only two minutes were spent on making sure eight performers were adequately protected. The spiritual correlation is easy to see. How often do we take just a two-minute glance at spiritual matters but spend countless hours on less significant endeavors? If we aren't spiritually attentive, we can find ourselves giving greater concern to changing the oil in our cars, vacuuming our carpet, or reading the newspaper. Like bungee jumping, life can be very dangerous. That's why we need more than just an occasional two-minute briefing with God.[902]

Priorities One hundred people nearly lost their lives because of spilled coffee. On April 3, 1998, an air traffic control supervisor spilled his coffee in the control tower of New York City's LaGuardia Airport. Another controller turned to help clean up the mess but the supervisor said, "Don't worry, I'll get it." By the time the controller got his bearings back on the planes, two jets came within twenty feet of colliding with each other about two hundred feet above the runway intersection. The coffee spill caused the controller to miss a needed call for one jet to abort its landing. Consequently, a US Airways plane passed beneath the tail of an Air Canada jet at 130 mph. Fortunately, nobody was injured, but the potential for disaster was enormous. Misplaced priorities frequently don't seem real significant, but they are laden with potentially disastrous results.[903]

Priorities Patrick Morley is a well-known author and leader of Christian businessmen. His impact today can be largely credited to a decision he made years ago. His business was finally starting to take off. For the first time he was getting offers and invitations to be a part of the business community's in-crowd. He said yes to about everything that came his way. Time with his young children was going into remission as he gave more and more attention to shallow relationships that were established for the sole purpose of financial gain. Although he was oblivious to what was happening, his wife, Patsy, had a clear understanding. When he told her, "We've arrived!" she added, "Yes, but at the wrong place." Morley then began to realize the folly of his pursuits. One night as he was reviewing his bulging calendar, he thought of a way to prioritize his days. He pondered to his wife, "Why not prioritize everything we do on the basis of who's going to be crying at our funeral?" Morley says, "This simple question saved our family." Ask who's going to cry at my funeral, and you'll be using an excellent tool for the prioritization of your time.[904]

Priorities Stephen Covey shared a visual illustration that powerfully demonstrates the urgent need for priorities. A seminar leader introduced the audience to a wide-mouthed gallon jar. He then showed them some fist-sized rocks and asked them to guess how many rocks would fit in the jar. The audience made their guesses as he filled up the jar with those large rocks. He then asked, "Is the container full?" They looked at the jar full of rocks and replied, "Yes." He smiled, then pulled out some gravel and began pouring it into the jar until it reached the rim. He then asked, "Is it full?" This time the listeners were thinking differently. They replied, "Probably not." He affirmed their response while reaching for some sand. Once the sand came to the top, his question returned, "Is it full?" By now the audience was in tune with the ploy. They shouted, "No." He smiled and began pouring water until the jar was filled to the brim. Then he asked, "What's the point?" Someone instantly said, "Well, there are gaps, and if you really work at it, you can always fit more into your life." The reply was rather stern. "No, that's not the point! The point is this: If you hadn't put these big rocks in first, would you ever have gotten any of them in?" If we fail to give our highest priorities our greatest attention, something of lesser significance will quickly take their place and fill up our time.[905]

Prison America incarcerates 1.7 million people (one in every 160 U.S. residents). This is the highest rate of any nation in the world.

According to a recent study by Columbia University's National Center on Addiction and Substance Abuse, drug and alcohol abuse played a part in the crimes committed by 80 percent of these prisoners. Approximately 94 percent of these inmates are men.[906]

Problems At the age of thirty-eight, Bonnie Booth may have taken extreme measures to solve one of her problems. In February of 1996, the Muncie, Indiana, resident had unsuccessfully tried to remove a callous from her foot with a razor so she resorted to more drastic measures. She drank a bottle of vodka and had two or three beers before doing "surgery" in her backyard with a .410 shotgun. She was afraid the callous was getting infected because of some severe pain so she opted to try shooting it off with a shotgun. Needless to say, she not only ended up in the medical hospital, but in the psychiatric center as well. Booth's attempt at a solution is no doubt strange, but it might not be that very different from our own approach to problems. How many times have we exaggerated our troubles and sought to solve them through extreme measures? Regardless of the size or complexity of our problems, we can remember God's request for us to give them to him (1 Peter 5:7).[907]

Problems "Everyone is a problem, has a problem, or lives with one." —*Anonymous* [908]

Problems Isn't it amazing how many times we struggle to decide whether or not we want to pay the price to solve a problem. It may be a cracked glass that needs replacing, an apology that should be given, or an employee who needs to be confronted. The Ritz-Carlton hotels are synonymous with wealth and extravagance and it may have been their philosophy about problems that has put them at the top. They believe the immediate resolution of a problem is a wise investment. That's why their housekeepers are authorized to spend up to $2,000 to solve a problem for any guest in their hotel. They don't need any additional authorization to invest $2,000 in the resolving of a problem because customer service is their top priority. Few of us have the financial means to duplicate this policy, but we all have the capacity to completely give of ourselves to solve the problems we encounter. You don't have to work at the Ritz-Carlton to be an extravagant resolver of problems. Just remember the resources you do have to draw from (Philippians 4:19) and you will realize how well you're prepared to invest in solutions.[909]

Problems On May 11, 1996, Domingo Pacheco had a major problem. He was on a tight schedule to catch his plane out of Miami when the left rear tire of his 1985 Cadillac blew out on the Palmetto Expressway. For nearly an hour he sweated under the hot Florida sun as he struggled to change that tire. With the soot from the tire still clinging to his hands, he answered a call on his cellular phone. It was his mother and she was overjoyed to hear his voice. He explained how the flat tire caused him to miss his flight. She shouted, "Turn on your radio. The plane you were going to be on just crashed in the Everglades. I'm glad you got a flat." Domingo Pacheco should have been aboard ValuJet flight 592, but a flat tire saved his life. Problems always seem to complicate our lives, but we should be mindful that some problems are actually saving us from graver consequences.[910]

Problems Solutions for problems are frequently presented by those who have little contact with the issue at hand. An exception to this thought was played out in China. Leadership in Beijing was concerned about the potential problems that could have developed in air travel due to the millennium computer virus threat. To make certain a safe resolution was provided in a timely fashion, the Chinese government issued a decree that "all the heads of airlines have got to be in the air on January 1, 2000." Zhao Bo, who was in charge of dealing with the problem at the Chinese Ministry of Information Industries, said, "We have to make sure there are no problems in aviation." The Chinese implemented a proven strategy for solving problems—be sure the people giving out solutions are affected by their own decisions.[911]

Problems "The next best thing to solving a problem is finding some humor in it." —*Frank Clark* [912]

Problems "The only guy whose troubles are all behind him is a school bus driver." —*Yvonne Woods* [913]

Profanity Ron Howard has again captured the attention of movie goers with his epic film, *Apollo 13*. The blockbuster movie drew millions of people to the theater with a very realistic dramatization of the ill-fated voyage of Apollo 13. The mission was NASA's third attempt to land men on the moon. Due to a major explosion on the spaceship en route to the moon, the lunar landing was aborted and the sole mission was to save the three astronauts, James Lovell, Fred Haise, and Jack Swigert. These men cheated death under incredible odds and splashed down to worldwide attention and jubilation. Their mission became known as a "successful failure." With such adversity, pressure, and life-threatening uncertainty, the movie's use of profanity doesn't seem unrealistic. Yet, in an interview with Fred Haise, he noted, "I went over all the air-to-ground transcripts. We never said a curse word for the entire flight." Haise went on to admit, "None of us were so pure that we wouldn't have cursed. We just didn't." Few people will ever engage in a project more dangerous, complicated, or frightening as that of Apollo 13. If they could survive their difficult mission without profanity so can everyone else. It's still true, real men don't cuss![914]

Prosperity John Steinbeck, the famed author who wrote *The Grapes of Wrath*, once penned his concerns about the dangers of prosperity. In a personal letter he noted, "If I wanted to destroy a nation, I would give it too much. I would have it on its knees . . . miserable, greedy and sick." Today we are seeing the validity of Steinbeck's concerns.[915]

Providence In 1996, contemporary Christian singer/songwriter Cindy Morgan arrived for a series of concerts in Los Angeles. As she unpacked her clothes for that evening's concert, she discovered her dress was terribly wrinkled. A woman helping with the concert set out to find an iron. She was sent to a church staff member's house with a key and instructions as to where she would find the ironing board. To her horror, she entered the house only to find the teenage daughter was home with a loaded gun. She was about to commit suicide when the woman arrived. Through quick thinking, a cool head, and the presence of God, she was able to talk the troubled teen into dropping the gun and returning with her for help. In response to God's miraculous intervention, Cindy Morgan said, "to rescue a life, he wrinkled a dress."[916]

Psychics In December of 1995, news broke that the U.S. military and the CIA ran Operation Stargate. It was a two-decade project in which our government hired psychics to give them intelligence information. At the program's peak in the late 1970s and early 1980s, American tax dollars paid for salaries and perks to six psychics who were referred to as "The Naturals." Since the project began in the 1970s, the CIA and Defense Department spent $20 million employing at least sixteen psychics. Americans got an early Christmas present in December of 1995 when a recommendation was made to kill the project. This whole thing started "when the CIA concluded that the Soviets were dangerously far ahead of the United States in the use of the paranormal." (That's one race we should have let them win). Supporters of this program acknowledged the quality of psychics degenerated over the years. Joe McMoneagle was one of the initial psychics who later noted that by the mid-1980s the military started letting any old "kook" into Stargate. This is confirmed by the fact that one of these government employees left the project when he became convinced there was a Martian colony hidden beneath the New Mexico desert. Defenders of the program admitted that psychics are wrong about 80 percent of the time, but they say the other 20 percent can be really helpful.[917]

Purpose A soldier stood at attention in an isolated corner of the Russian palace. When questioned about his purpose, the soldier could only say he was following his captain's orders. The captain was summoned and he too did not know the purpose for this guard, but just knew regulations required it. Upon investigation, it was discovered that a century earlier, Catherine the Great (Empress from 1762 to 1796) had established the post to protect a newly planted rose bush. One hundred years later, guards were still being posted to keep watch over a barren spot of turf. Occasionally, it's wise to ask, "Why are we doing this?"[918]

Purpose During World War II, concentration camps were filled with Jews who suffered unspeakable horror. One such camp in Hungary was used to employ the labor of Jews for the creation of a special fuel additive that helped run the Nazi war machine. The prisoners were forced to distill tons of human waste and garbage into alcohol for fuel enhancement. The stench was as foul as the reality they were aiding the enemy's cause. Yet month after month they endured the inhumane conditions and work. In 1944, this factory was gutted by Allied bombs. The prisoners were ordered to move the debris over to the other end of the compound. They despised the Germans' plan to rebuild. After the task was complete, these prisoners were forced to move the carnage back to its original site. Anger over the Germans' stupidity escalated. Yet when the pile was reconstructed, the Nazis had them move the remains back to the other end of the compound. Their evil plan was now coming to light. Rather than reemploy the prisoners in the hideous work they had once done, they were now simply being beaten down with senseless work. Amazingly, these prisoners who had survived previous atrocities, started falling apart once their work became meaningless. Men broke rank and ran into the electric fence. Others were shot while trying to flee. Some were beaten into silence when they screamed relentlessly. The vile but purposeful work had sustained them for the better part of three years, but within just a matter of days the futility was killing them. Noticing these results, the commandant applauded himself for this "experiment in mental health." He smugly noted there soon would be "no more need to use the crematoria." Senseless repetition can destroy life.[919]

Purpose Given the opportunity to get a direct and clear response from God, what one question would you ask him? A survey in *USA Today* posed that thought to Americans and the top five questions were posted in their paper on May 28, 1999. The clear winner was that which addressed the issue of purpose where 34 percent said they would ask God, "Why am I here on earth?" The second-leading question was, "Is there life after death (19 percent)." Sixteen percent wanted to know, "Why bad things happen." The fourth and fifth questions were almost an even split with 7 percent wondering if there is intelligent life elsewhere, and 6 percent being curious about the length of their life. Such snapshots of American culture affirm people's need to have and understand the true purpose of life. May the Church be motivated by such information to help people discover real meaning and purpose through Jesus Christ.[920]

Purpose His name was David Dugan. He was a construction contractor who lived life straight up and straight ahead. Dugan's contact with Robert Fulghum eventually led to active involvement in the church. He was invited to serve on the church board, but his business travel prevented him from making the commitment. Nonetheless, when he was available, he would sit in on the meetings as a nonvoting spectator. Unbeknownst to the board, Dugan was bonded to carry up to $500,000 as certain jobs required easy access to large amounts of cash. In addition, he was registered to carry a gun to protect his money. He carried both the large sums of money and his gun in a briefcase. Dugan sat through long meetings where the board debated prices on paper towels and toilet paper. During this particular meeting, the church board was wrestling a more arduous problem concerning the front driveway. Smooth paving on one side allowed people to drive dangerously fast so they needed speed bumps and signs. The other side of the drive had large potholes and needed paving. After three hours they were nowhere closer to a resolution. From outside the main circle Dugan raised his hand with a suggestion. He counseled the board to leave the potholes on one side, dig potholes on the other side, spray the holes with tar and call them "speed-holes." He also offered to do the job for free. The board then spent the next hour hankering over the proposal. Dugan's fuse finally lit and he stood up. He threw his briefcase on the table and asked how much the church was worth, buildings, land, and everything. The treasurer said about $300,000. Dugan replied, "Great, I'm gonna buy it!" He took his gun out of the briefcase and then started throwing out bundles of $100 bills until the price was reached. He said, "Gimme the deed and it's done." From the stunned silence one of the board members asked, "What are you going to do with it?" Dugan explained how he would have his crew come over, level the place and haul it all to the dump before sundown. "And I'll use the land for the cemetery you guys are headed toward in these meetings of the living dead." Dugan continued to chew out the board for spending so much time on trivial business because he came to church for religion, not discounted paper plates. One anxious board member asked about Dugan's gun. He answered, "I was thinking about putting every last one of you out of your misery. Too bad it's against the law." Dugan then packed up all of his money and told the board to let him know when they wanted to start getting serious about all the things the church ought to be doing in the world. As he walked out of that meeting he repeatedly said, "The offer still stands." Dugan's approach might lack a bit of tact but it's filled with truth. People are literally dying while the church is gridlocked with trivial pursuits. Jesus has promised to make good on Dugan's offer and turn churches into cemeteries if they don't revive their passion for spiritual matters. (See Revelation 2–3.)[921]

Purpose "I want to take our entire culture and push it closer to God." —*Phil Vischer, creator of "VeggieTales®"*[922]

Purpose Most every garage has a role of duct tape because it can be used to repair just about anything. It's purposes seem almost endless but a new study recently showed that duct tape doesn't succeed well at the purpose for which it was created. Scientists at Lawrence Berkeley National Laboratory in California found that duct tape is not a good product for sealing duct work. Max Sherman, a physicist who conducted these experiments to monitor the effectiveness of different air-conditioning and heating sealants, said, "What we found was that duct tape almost always failed." This failure rate has resulted in approximately 30 percent of the heat or cool air generated in an average home to be lost in the attic or wall space because of poorly sealed ducts. Although you can tape up a bicycle seat, seal off a leaky radiator hose, secure a broken window, or keep an alligator's mouth shut with it, you can't depend on duct tape to fulfill its primary purpose. Duct tape isn't alone in accomplishing some great things while simultaneously failing at the purpose for which it was created. Churches and their members can be guilty of doing this, parents are often in this boat, employees frequently get the "duct tape syndrome," and human beings who fail to surrender their lives to the Lordship of Jesus Christ are not fulfilling their created purpose either. To avoid this pitfall, we might do well to tear off some duct tape and put it on the binding of our Bible as a reminder of our central purpose in life (Psalm 34:3).[923]

Racism South African Archbishop, Desmond Tutu, was walking by a construction site when he came upon a temporary sidewalk with room enough for only one person to pass. At the other end of the narrow passageway was a white man filled with prejudicial venom. He shouted, "I don't make way for gorillas." Tutu wittingly stepped aside, made a large sweeping gesture with his hand and replied, "Ah, yes, but I do."[924]

Reality An old saying quipped, "Reality is for those who can't handle drugs." Even without drugs reality can be confusing. It can be difficult to comprehend what is blurred between the lines of truth and fiction, the real and the surreal. Many people remember the popular 1970s TV series, *Marcus Welby, M.D.,* starring Robert Young. In the first five years of that show, more than 250,000 people wrote letters to Young asking for medical advice.[925]

Reality If you were to name the top three places you would like to go on your next vacation, would Haiti, Vietnam, or the slums of Mexico top your list? Global Exchange is a San Francisco-based nonprofit organization that plans vacations to some of the world's most woeful places. People pay good money to be depressed by the harsh realities of life. That's why these packages are called Reality Tours. Participants aren't invited to do much hands-on work to remedy problems. The objective is to get people inspired about making lasting changes and investments once they return home. This $1-million-a-year business is attracting people of all ages and backgrounds. They are coming in increasing numbers to see women working for $4 a day assembling typewriters, people living in subhuman conditions, and to learn of the heartbreaks these people face. From early in the morning until late at night, they are exposed to the reality that much of the world endures. Most of us would greatly benefit from such an experience, but even if we don't sign up for one of these twenty annual trips, we can make a point to take daily reality tours right where we live. When we struggle with frustrations about mechanical problems in a car, we can embrace the reality that most of the world's citizens don't even own a car. When we grumble about an office that is too cold or too hot, we can remember that the majority of the world doesn't have the luxury of air-conditioning or heat. When finances seemed too cramped, we can think about the billions of people who will never own a home, wear more than one set of clothes, and seldom eat to their heart's content. Regular reality tours like this will certainly cause us to be more thankful for the reality that is ours, and will inspire compassion that can easily be translated into effective help for those who are less fortunate than ourselves.[926]

Reconciliation "The best way to destroy an enemy is to change him into a friend." —*Anonymous* [927]

Relationships According to *Psychology Today,* 90percent of those who go for counseling don't really want answers, they just want someone to hear them out and listen. People of our society hunger for relationships that will provide concern and understanding. As Dr. R. B. Robins told a large group of physicians, "The psychiatrist's couch cannot take the place of the church in solving the problems of a frustrated society."[928]

Relationships "I will pay more for the ability to deal with people than any other ability under the sun." —*John D. Rockefeller* [929]

Relationships "The most important single ingredient to the formula of success is knowing how to get along with people." — *Teddy Roosevelt* [930]

Relevance Sometimes the message of Christ is not seen as relevant because the bearer of that message is oblivious to a person's needs. One of the most dramatic pictures of this occurred while President Lincoln was visiting wounded soldiers during the Civil War. Prior to his visit, a woman had come through the infirmary distributing religious tracts. When Lincoln arrived, one soldier was holding up a leaflet and laughing. He said, "Mr. President, she has given me a tract on the 'Sin of Dancing' and both of my legs are shot off." The gospel is universally relevant. Let's not tarnish its relevance with thoughtless behavior.[931]

Religion "Stripping religion, life's supernatural dimension, from education, public or private, secondary or university, is a disservice to the mind." —*William F. Buckley*[932]

Religion There are more than fifteen hundred religious groups in the United States, at least six hundred of which are non-Christian.[933]

Religious Liberty Alabama Circuit Court Judge Roy Moore stirred quite a controversy with his insistence on keeping a copy of the Ten Commandments in his courtroom. Of course, the American Civil Liberties Union (ACLU) made sure he was taken to court. A peer of Judge Moore, Montgomery County Circuit Judge, Charles Price, ruled on separate occasions that Moore must cease courtroom prayers and remove the plaque of the Ten Commandments, or surround it with other historical documents. Ironically, few people noticed that Judge Moore already had other historical documents in his courtroom. The Mayflower Compact of 1620 and the Declaration of Independence hang on separate walls, but were deemed too far away from the Ten Commandments. Even more ironic is the fact that Judge Price was named winner of the John F. Kennedy Profile in Courage Award on April 24, 1997. His position against Judge Moore's Ten Commandments was lauded in a statement by the late president's daughter, Caroline Kennedy. She said, "Though he may have been vilified by many of his constituents as being antireligion, Judge Price has in fact made a heroic stance to defend our country's proud history of religious tolerance and diversity." Tragically, religious tolerance in America has come to mean little more than intolerance of Christianity.[934]

Renewal One of the commencement addresses given to Columbine High School seniors, just one month after its tragic carnage on April 20, 1999, provided a beautiful picture of renewal. Sara Martin talked about the experience of people in Cambridge, England, during World War II. To save the stained-glass windows of King's College Chapel, the residents broke out each little section of glass and safely stored them. After the war, they reassembled all of the little pieces and brought them back to their original beauty. Pain, suffering, and disappointment will certainly fragment all of our lives, but God can certainly take the broken pieces and turn them into a supernatural work of art.[935]

Renewal Regardless of when scholars say Jesus was born, A.D. 2000 was the year that his birth received extra attention. In preparation for the two thousandth anniversary of our Savior's birth, the United Nations allotted $2.26 million for a Bethlehem facelift. The City of David had become a run-down town so a four-year project was initiated to renovate it. The objective of this endeavor was to "restore its religious and historical monuments and highlight its contributions to civilization." The U.N. thought Bethlehem needed to be cleaned up and rejuvenated for this important date. Their concern for the physical can be easily translated to the spiritual. How many of us need a spiritual facelift? Haven't some of us become a run-down place for the Holy Spirit to indwell? Maybe we should likewise make a greater investment and give the Bethlehem of our hearts a sprucing up.[936]

Repentance Billy Graham's son, Franklin, led a crusade in Australia during the spring of 1996. At one of the invitations, a fifteen-year-old boy told a counselor he came forward because, as he said, "I haven't been decent to Jesus." Repentance starts with a confession that we "haven't been decent to Jesus."[937]

Repentance "Everyone thinks of changing humanity and nobody thinks of changing himself." —*Leo Tolstoy*[938]

Repentance Gary Richmond gained an interesting perspective on snakes while working with a snake handler at a zoo. The curator was joined by Richmond and three other professionals as they milked the venom of a king cobra. The tension was high because of the deadly potential. The man noted that in Africa, several elephants die every year as a result of the king cobra. While clenching the snake's neck, the curator explained the need for milking the cobra as quickly as possible because "no man could ever survive a bite from a full load of venom." The snake's venom glands contain enough poison to kill one thousand adults. Once the rags were saturated with the lethal venom and they were ready to release the snake, this skilled curator gave a profound warning. He cautioned the others and said, "More people are bitten trying to let go of snakes than when they grab them." When it comes to repenting of our sins, we frequently find the greatest struggle occurs after the repentance instead of before. This lesson about snakes helps us understand why. When we try to turn loose of Satan he will quickly lunge at us with a full load of venom. Like the wise snake handler, be cautious and aware.[939]

Repentance While traveling on business, an executive had a very bad experience at one particular hotel. When he climbed into bed, a bug started racing up his leg. He jumped from the bed, turned on the lights, and threw back the covers. The bug wasn't alone; there were numerous other critters between the sheets. Although the man was granted another room, he was not satisfied with the situation. Upon returning home, he wrote a letter to the hotel's corporate office. Within a few weeks he received a letter directly from the company's president. With flattering remarks and penitent words, the president made it quite clear the problem should have never occurred and that he would make sure it wouldn't happen again. The businessman felt somewhat vindicated by the letter until a small Post-it note fell from the envelope. The secretary had inadvertently left her boss's directives on the reply. The little note simply said, "Send this man the bug letter." It's not repentance when we just try to cover our tracks after getting caught. Repentance involves a commitment to correct our ways.[940]

Respect Years ago, Woody Hayes and Paul "Bear" Bryant were both speaking at the same clinic. At the time, these two men represented some of the greatest expertise in the arena of collegiate football. Woody Hayes was the successful head coach at Ohio State and Bear Bryant led Alabama's Crimson Tide. After these living legends had addressed the gathering, the floor was opened for questions. A high school coach asked, "What is the highest priority for recruiting young men to come play at your university?" The inquisitive coach speculated it must be speed, strength, size, or intelligence, but all of his answers were wrong. Hayes and Bryant had already proven themselves with multiple national titles so their answer to this one question was worth the whole clinic. The two looked at each other as though they knew the question was coming. Bear Bryant then gave an answer that surprised everyone. He said, "What I want to know is how does that young man feel about his momma and his daddy. Because if he respects and honors his momma and daddy, then he will respect others and will become an effective part of a winning team." Respect is an attribute that must always supersede talent and ability.[941]

Response On October 8, 1871, the Great Chicago Fire charred four square miles of the Windy City. Three hundred people were killed, 100,000 people were left homeless, 18,000 buildings were destroyed, and the cumulative damage was assessed at $200 million. Although everyone has heard it was Mrs. O'Leary's cow named Daisy who started it all by kicking over a lantern in her barn, O'Leary insisted there was no lantern in the barn. Regardless of the fire's true origin, its destruction cannot be questioned. Nonetheless, rather than harp on the past, Chicago responded with two positive results. First, National Fire Prevention Week was created, and second, on what was once Mrs. O'Leary's barn, there now stands the Chicago Fire Department Training Academy. In similar fashion, we can respond to each tragedy of our lives by seeking to bring about positive results. As believers, we have a God who specializes in such challenges (Romans 8:28).[942]

Responsibility During the summer of 2000, Torrence Johnson filed an interesting lawsuit in Spartanburg, South Carolina. In 1998, Johnson was serving time in the Spartanburg County Jail. Due to his "constant behavioral problems," Jail Director Larry Powers said Johnson was placed in maximum security. While there, Johnson stood on a desk in his cell and started doing back flips. He missed one flip and ended up paralyzed. Two years later, he convinced an attorney, Joseph Mooneyham, to represent him with the notion that the jail is liable because the guards should have stopped him from doing flips off of a desk. He crushed a vertebra while choosing to act irresponsibly, but thinks it's someone else's fault.[943]

Responsibility The bloodbath at Columbine High School on April 20, 1999, took a unique twist during October of that same year. As would be expected, multiple lawsuits were filed, but one of those seemed to defy any logic or reason. Thomas and Susan Klebold, parents of one of the killers, Dylan, filed a notice of intent to sue Sheriff John Stone. They say Sheriff Stone failed to inform them about the violent tendencies of the other gunman. The Klebolds claim they would have made sure their son stayed away from Eric Harris if they had known he was such a dangerous young man. If the tragedy of Columbine was a telling sign of our society's decay, surely this legal denial of responsibility is an indicator of things being even worse than we may have thought. It's reminiscent of another shift in blame that took place in a garden called Eden.[944]

Responsibility The epidemic of shirking responsibility was tragically highlighted in the pastor's office of an inner-city church. A stranger to the church requested an audience with the pastor. He told of a terrible situation facing a poverty-stricken family. The single mom was in failing health and unable to work or properly care for her four children. Their financial situation prevented her from seeing a doctor, they were behind on the rent, and there wasn't enough food to go around. He explained to the pastor that they would be evicted from their apartment if they could not make a payment in the next twenty-four hours. He then asked if there was anything the pastor could do to help. Moved by this very bleak situation, the minister commended the man for his concern and then asked if he was a close friend or neighbor to the indigent family. The man said, "No, I'm just their landlord." James 4:17 reminds us of our ongoing personal responsibility, "to one who knows the right thing to do, and does not do it, to him it is sin."[945]

Resurrection Eva Peron was one of Argentina's most celebrated first ladies. Although her husband, Juan Peron, reigned as president of Argentina, Eva far exceeded him in popularity. In fact, her influence was so formidable that in 1955, three years after her premature death from cancer at age thirty-three, Peron's enemies moved her body to Italy because they feared her corpse would incite a revolution. (Twenty years later her body was returned to Argentina). The enemies of Jesus had the same fears so they posted guards at his tomb. Taxpayers didn't lose much money on that assignment though, the guards only worked from Friday to Sunday. His corpse didn't incite a revolution, but his resurrected body started a revolt that has permanently altered the spiritual destiny of mankind.[946]

Retirement "When the devil retires, we'll retire." —*Gary and Evelyn Harthcock (seventy-nine and seventy-eight-year-old missionaries)*[947]

Retreat The Australian national coat of arms features the ostrichlike emu and a kangaroo. The presence of these two creatures from Australia's wildlife communicates a strong message. Neither the emu nor the kangaroo are able to move backwards. Their physical makeup prevents any reverse movement. Australia has inscribed their likeness on the coat of arms to define themselves as a people who are unable to retreat. Christians would do well to emulate Australia's philosophy and refuse to retreat from the spiritual battles we encounter.[948]

Revenge Linda Stewart was infuriated by her husband's carelessness with cigarettes. On February 13, 1999, Tim Stewart fell asleep with a cigarette and burned a small area on their bed. This was the last straw for Mrs. Stewart. She decided she would teach her husband an important lesson. On the following day, Valentines Day, she lit a cigarette and laid it on their bed. She then left their house in Columbia, Tennessee. When her husband returned home, he found their house completely destroyed by fire. Detective Mickey Jones arrested Mrs. Stewart for arson and told reporters, "She admitted to intentionally starting the fire. She said she was going to show him what could happen if she didn't catch it." In the process of revenge we seldom realize how destructive our actions will be not only to others, but to ourselves as well.[949]

Revenge On Father's Day, 1999, one of the most chilling accounts of revenge began to unfold in Franklin, Indiana. Amy Shanabarger found her seven-month-old son, Tyler, facedown and dead in his crib. The coroner ruled it sudden infant death syndrome, but just hours after the little boy's funeral, Ronald Shanabarger told his wife he had killed their son as revenge. Before the couple was married, Amy refused to cut short a vacation cruise to comfort Ronald when his father died in October of 1996. Shanabarger concocted a plan to make Amy feel the way he did when his father died. In his confession to authorities, Shanabarger said he married her, got her pregnant, allowed her time to bond with the child, then killed their son. While Amy was at her night job of checking groceries, Shanabarger wrapped Tyler's head in plastic then ate a snack and brushed his teeth. Twenty minutes later, he removed the plastic, put the baby's face down in the crib, and then went to bed. When Amy got home she assumed Tyler was asleep so she went straight to bed. She discovered his death when she went to his crib the next morning. Shanabarger said he confessed his crime because he was haunted by the guilt of what he had done. The thirty-year-old man begged officers to shoot him after making his confession. His three separate confessions have all been consistent and detectives said relatives confirmed Shanabarger's long-standing resentment of his wife's refusal to return early from a cruise in 1996. No event or story could more clearly communicate the destructive nature of revenge.[950]

Reverence In 1999, pastor Jim Holmes was part of an evangelism team that went to Kenya. During their trip three thousand people embraced Christ as their Lord and Savior. One of the most moving conversions occurred with a woman who was dying. Her declining condition left her unable to get off of her primitive mat. When the team shared the gospel with her, they asked if she wanted to pray and receive Christ. She said, "No, no, no." Then with great effort, she crawled off her simple bed and pulled herself across the dirt floor of her hut to those who had told her about Christ. She reached out and grabbed one of their pant legs and painstakingly lifted herself up on her knees. In utter exhaustion, she then said, "Now I am ready to pray for Jesus to come into my heart."[951]

Reverse Offering The people at Sweet Haven Holy Church of God in Wight County, Virginia, have found new motivation to be in church on Sunday mornings. Each Sunday after the morning worship service, Bishop Nathaniel Johnson does a "reverse offering." He passes out green play money and everybody grabs a bill. On the back of four imitation greenbacks are the bishop's initials. Those four special bills are worth anywhere between $10 and $100. Because there are four winners each Sunday, people have started climbing out of bed to find their place in the pew. In fact, attendance has doubled to about one hundred people since Bishop Johnson hit on the idea in 1993. Of course there is one small catch—you must be at church for the entire two-hour service to participate in the sanctimonious offertory. Admittedly, Johnson realizes greed may be the driving force for some attenders, but he's glad they're bringing their greed to the church rather than to the racetrack or some other less spiritual setting. A gimmick like this might indeed increase church attendance, but it also raises a serious question about motive. What's our motive for attending church? Would our attendance improve if we had the chance of gaining $10 to $100 each week? Would the prospect of fattening our wallets cause us to prioritize our calendars around worship? Would a one in twenty-five chance for extra cash reduce our list of excuses for not attending church? On Sunday, your church probably won't be handing out money, but it will be seeking to draw you and others closer to God. May that be motive enough for each of us to find our way to Sunday school and worship.[952]

Revival During his famous crusade in Los Angeles, Billy Graham demonstrated some of his keen wisdom at a press conference. A young reporter said, "Mr. Graham, one minister told me that he thinks you have set the Church back fifty years, maybe one hundred years. What do you have to say about that?" Dr. Graham paused to contemplate the question, then replied, "Well, I would ask the Lord to forgive me. When I came here, my prayer was that He would set the Church back two thousand years." True church growth occurs when we return to the passion and power of Pentecost.[953]

Revival During the Welsh Revival of 1904–1905, two children were overheard giving their understanding of revival. One child asked the other, "Do you know what happened at Rhos? The second child answered, "No, I don't, except that Sunday comes every day now." The first child asked again, "Don't you know?" The second child replied, "No, I don't." So the first said, "Why, Jesus Christ has come to live in Rhos now." Revival has occurred when Jesus takes up residency in our community and every day feels like Sunday.[954]

Revival Harley Sheffield gained celebrity status through an unusual mishap. He was part of the fifteen thousand-mile relay that carried the Olympic torch to the one hundreth gathering of the games in Atlanta. His section of the relay went over the Tacoma Narrows Bridge in Washington on May 7, 1996. While carrying the flame in a special stand on his bicycle, the rear tire blew out, Sheffield lost control of his bike, and the Olympic flame went out. People gasped in disbelief, but the attenders of the torch knew exactly what to do. They simply reached into the van that accompanied the traveling torch, pulled out a new torch and lighted it from the "mother flame" which always stays in the van. The procession continued and Sheffield earned a spot on *The Tonight Show* with Jay Leno. What happened on that Washington bridge happens all of the time in our Christian pilgrimage. We stumble and the flame of spiritual zeal is dowsed. We stare at the extinguished torch and wonder if we can ever again burn with spiritual passion. When we turn in repentance we find that the Holy Spirit has been with us all of the time and he carries the "mother flame" that can never go out. Our zeal can be reignited and the standard of Christ can once again burn brightly in our lives.[955]

Revival The last time revival swept the United States, leaders were talking about connecting the country through railroads. The invention of air travel was a half-century away, electrical lightbulbs were just a fantasy in the mind of a ten-year-old boy named Thomas Edison, and the Civil War hadn't yet been fought. Our last national revival occurred in 1857. Since then, people have not only prayed for revival, but occasionally tried to manufacture it. In 1996, Eric Harris was pastoring the Kentucky Missionary Baptist Church in Saline County, Arkansas. There were divisions in the church so Pastor Harris came up with a plan for revival. He set the church on fire. Instead of reviving the church, Harris ended up pleading guilty to arson charges for burning down the building. In his testimony, the former pastor said, "They needed a project to unify them." We have too often been guilty of trying to light the fires of revival with a project rather than letting God do it through prayer.[956]

Righteousness "Are the things you're living for, worth Christ dying for?" —*Leonard Ravenhill*[957]

Righteousness "In this life you sometimes have to choose between pleasing God and pleasing man. In the long run it's better to please God. . . . He's more apt to remember." —*Harry Kemelman*[958]

Righteousness "The only contribution you make to your righteousness is your own confession and admission of sin." —*Max Lucado*[959]

Righteousness "We can easily forgive a child who is afraid of the dark; the real tragedy of life is when men are afraid of the light." —*Plato*[960]

Risks "Bite off more than you can chew—then chew it." —*Mary Kay Ash*[961]

Risks "If no one ever took risks, Michelangelo would have painted the Sistine floor." —*Neil Simon*[962]

Risks "Statistically, 100 percent of the shots you don't take don't go in." —*Wayne Gretzky*[963]

Road Rage Road rage is a relatively new term that seeks to define the uncontrollable anger that occurs on the roadways of America. The destructive nature of such behavior was recently demonstrated on the Golden State Freeway in Sylmar, California. Delfina Morales, forty-two, and her twenty-six-year-old daughter were irritated by an unnamed driver. Other motorists saw the two women tailgate the van and make angry gestures at the driver. When the van exited from the freeway, Morales followed closely then got into a position to spin her tires and splash the van with mud. She quickly spun around slinging mud, and then drove up the ramp from which both vehicles had just exited. In her state of intense anger, she lost her bearings and treated the off-ramp like an on-ramp. She drove straight into oncoming freeway traffic. She an her daughter were instantly killed when they crashed into a Federal Express truck. The driver of the truck suffered minor injuries. Whether you call it road rage or inappropriate anger, it's a dangerous emotion that can literally destroy lives.[964]

Road Signs *Parade* magazine hosted an interesting photo contest. The contest was restricted to pictures of actual road signs in America. Among the top ten winners were these: In the Mojave Desert there is a sign that reads, "Absolutely Nothing—Next 22 Miles". . . near Tallahassee, Florida, you can find a sign that states, "Water on Road When Raining". . . in Shreveport, Louisiana, there really is a stop sign with an official subtitle "And Smell The Roses". . . central Oregon boasts a sign that says, "Soft Shoulder— Blind Curves—Steep Grade—Big Trucks—Good Luck!". . . And my personal favorite can be found hanging next to a traffic light in Fort Walton Beach, Florida. The sign declares, "This Light Never Turns Green." Along the road of life we encounter a variety of messages and experiences, but wherever we go and whatever we encounter, we can journey with the confidence that Jesus Christ not only goes before us, but he goes with us.[965]

Romance According to a recent *Psychology Today* poll, 96 percent of men and women feel romance is important, but less than half believe they have experienced much of it.[966]

Sacrifice Commenting on his rigorous presidential schedule, Jimmy Carter once said, "I can get up at 9:00 A.M. and be rested, or I can get up at 6:00A.M. and be President." As Christians we must guard against the martyr complex, but we must likewise realize that Kingdom work does require sacrifices. We cannot always be perfectly rested and actively engaged in ministry too. (See Mark 1:29–37)[967]

Sacrifice Tom Elliff, a past president of the Southern Baptist Convention, recently spoke on the need for sacrificial commitment to Christ. His words are convicting: "If we continue to buy what we want, drive what we want, eat what we want, and live where we want, then we have not submitted to the lordship of Jesus Christ and God can't do with us and through us what he wants to do." Too often we want convenience and commitment to be synonymous.[968]

Salvation Lon Grammer was just a month away from his graduation at Yale University when his deceptive scheme was discovered. The twenty-six-year-old resident of California had gained entrance into Yale by altering his transcripts and producing recommendation letters from nonexistent teachers. Through deceptive artwork, he converted his C average at Cuesta Community College in San Luis Obispo, California, into nearly straight As. The Ivy League school expelled Grammer in

1995, just four weeks before he would have received, of all things, a political science degree. The aspiring politician bragged to his roommate who then blew the whistle on his plan. Grammer's exploits are not that different from many applicants for heaven. With gallons of correction fluid they are attempting to make themselves look better than they are with the hopes that some absent-minded admissions clerk will assign them a dorm room on the celestial campus. To such applicants there is great news. They needn't worry about covering up their failures, just ask the Perennial Valedictorian to cover them with his blood.[969]

Salvation Mickey Mantle was a hero even if he never pictured himself as a role model. His death on August 13, 1995, was a sorrowful experience for the world of sports. When Mickey Mantle gave a press conference following his liver transplant just two months before his death, he said, "You talk about a role model, this is a role model: Don't be like me." Mantle was obviously reflecting on his abuse of alcohol and the way he neglected his family. Given the chance to do it over again Mantle seemed to truly believe he would live much differently. In the closing days of the Hall of Famer's life, former Yankee teammate Bobby Richardson said Mantle had a deathbed conversion to Christ. Richardson, who officiated the funeral, noted that the slugger had resisted Christ all of his life but finally came to embrace the Savior as his Lord. Mantle's words about not following his example have a twofold meaning. First, as he said in July, don't abuse alcohol or neglect your family. Second, don't wait until you're dying to receive Christ. His greatest hit came long after the cheers had died at Yankee Stadium.[970]

Salvation Most people who were alive during the assassination of President Kennedy can remember where they were when that great tragedy occurred. Now another generation will have that same kind of experience as they remember the day Kennedy's son crashed his plane in the Atlantic ocean. That perilous flight came to an end because young Kennedy's single-engine airplane went into what aviators call a "graveyard spiral." According to radar tracking, the aircraft was in a virtual free fall at a rate of speed exceeding four thousand feet per minute. In this particular predicament, the pilot has usually become disoriented and lost his horizon. The G-force causes you to lose your orientation so you cannot tell if you're flying upside down, level, or at an angle. When you realize what is happening, your natural tendency is to do the exact opposite of what you need to do. You're diving rapidly so you automatically think the solution is to accelerate and pull up out of the dive. That has the reverse effect though, it simply makes you spiral down faster. The real solution feels very unnatural—let off the accelerator and straighten your wings. Experts agree, John Kennedy Jr., who was not yet trained to use airplane instruments, simply did what seemed right at the time. He tried to give his plane more power so he could pull up out of the dive. The end result was death. In Proverbs 14:12, we are reminded that each of us is born into a spiritual graveyard spiral and our natural tendency is to handle it dangerously wrong. What seems right only leads to death. Many try to save their soul by doing what seems natural, but there is only One solution for pulling out of a spiritual dive: Jesus Christ (Acts 4:12).[971]

Salvation Nothing exceeds the importance of a person's relationship with Christ. E. Stanley Jones (1884–1973) illustrated this truth by telling of an African who changed his name to "After" once he became a Christian. The new believer explained that everything important in his life happened after he met Jesus Christ. Salvation ushers in the most important happenings of our lives.[972]

Salvation On April 18, 2000, ten-year-old Candace Newmaker tragically died in a counselor's office. Her adoptive mother, Jeane Newmaker, took Candace to Connell Watkins' home-based therapy center in Evergreen, Colorado, to help her overcome reactive attachment disorder. As part of the therapy, Candace was wrapped in a blanket, then four people pushed against the blanket with pillows. The little girl was told to fight her way out of it to become "reborn." A video tape reveals Candace repeatedly saying she couldn't breathe, but the session continued. After seventy minutes of this exercise, Candace died of asphyxiation. This little girl's horrific death is but one more grim reminder that our culture is spiritually confused. Salvation through Christ is the only avenue through which we can find new birth and new life.[973]

Salvation On October 4, 1997, over a million men gathered in Washington, D.C. for Promise Keeper's Stand in the Gap. The day-long event featured many different speakers. One of those worship leaders was Max Lucado. In typical fashion, he creatively illustrated a significant point about salvation. He called for the massive crowd to shout the names of their individual denominations. Denominational names were lost in the verbalization of church affiliations and created nothing more than a loud rumble. He then called on the assembly to shout the name of their Savior. From a pathway of men over one mile in length reverberated the same name and message: Jesus Christ. It was clear, obvious, and strong. If we look to salvation in the church of our choice we will find a confusing and contradictory message. Yet when we look to Christ for the security of our hope and salvation we will find consistency, clarity, and truth. "There is salvation in no one else . . ." (Acts 4:12).[974]

Salvation On the night of May 26, 1996, a great tragedy occurred in Houston, Texas. Cora Lee Taylor, her husband, and their two grandchildren were awakened by fire. In panic, they fled the burning house. All four of them escaped safely, but the fifty-eight-year-old grandmother didn't see that her husband had rescued both grandchildren. Without thought or inquiry, Mrs. Taylor ran back into the flames to rescue the grandchild she believed was still in the house. Tragically, Cora Lee Taylor died searching for the child that had already been rescued. A similar tragedy happens repeatedly every day. People try to do what Jesus has already done. Our rescue from hell's flames was accomplished on a cross two thousand years ago, we must simply realize it and accept it.[975]

Salvation The Gold Rush of 1849 had people from all over the world heading to California with dollar signs in their eyes. Each person came with visions of finding a fortune and many miners did indeed strike it rich. This phenomenon was all started by James Marshall who discovered gold in Sutter's Creek. You would think the man responsible for starting all of that gold craze would have died knee-deep in wealth. Ironically, Marshall died in the late 1880s as a penniless itinerant miner just a few hours from the place he first struck gold. His fortune was never realized because he failed to stake his own claim. An individual can know all about God and the abundant life he has to offer, but if you don't stake your claim through a life-long commitment to Christ, you will never experience the riches of eternal life.[976]

Salvation Watchman Nee wrote about the episode of a Chinese man who was drowning. Several men were watching their countryman struggle in the water but they themselves could not swim. They yelled for help and one man raced to the shoreline. He assured them he could swim and could indeed save the man, but he took no action toward staging a rescue. The others became agitated with his passivity and began to verbally question his character. The man stood unaffected until the drowning man seemed to exhaust himself of all his energy. He then dove into the water and pulled the man to safety. The other men demanded an explanation for his seeming reluctance to show compassion on a drowning man. He simply told them that he was unable to save the man as long as he was still trying to save himself. When his efforts to save himself were expended, then it became possible for him to supply a safe rescue. In similar fashion, our endeavors to save ourselves leave us flailing in an ocean of sin. Until we give up on the idea that we can save ourselves, we can't be saved. We must acknowledge our inability to bring about salvation and embrace the salvation that only Jesus Christ can provide.[977]

Salvation While swimming at the beach, a boy got caught in the undertow and began crying out for help. With no lifeguard on duty, an avid swimmer quickly swam to his rescue. When they fell to the sand after surviving the pull of the current, the boy exclaimed, "Thank you, sir, for saving my life!" The man waited to catch his breath, then looked straight into the boys eyes. He gave a slight smile and then said, "Just do me one favor. Make sure your life was worth saving." The atoning death of Jesus Christ cries out with the same request—make sure your life was worth saving.[978]

Salvation "You have made us for Yourself, and the heart of man is restless until it finds its rest in Thee." —*Augustine*[979]

Sanctification "'Putting on Christ' is not one among many jobs a Christian has to do; and it is not a sort of special exercise for the top class. It is the whole of Christianity. —*C.S. Lewis*[980]

Satan "If you're sinking in quicksand, Satan will gladly pat you on the head." —*Adrian Rodgers*[981]

Satan 1999, the *New England Journal of Medicine* published a study concerning people who had been bitten by dead snakes. The research was conducted by Dr. Jeffrey Suchard and Dr. Frank LoVecchio. Both men are toxicologists at Good Samaritan Regional Medical Center in Phoenix, Arizona. Their interest in this study began several years earlier after admitting a patient who was bitten by a snake while gardening. The man had cut off a rattlesnake's head with his shovel. When he bent down to pick up the snake's head, it bit him. From June 1997 to April 1998, Suchard and LoVecchio focused their research on this phenomenon. They discovered 15 percent of those being admitted for a snakebite were bitten by a dead snake. Suchard said, "We were surprised the percentage was that high. We were also surprised most people didn't know dead snakes still bite." Snakes have a reflex action that continues even after being killed. For this reason, a decapitated rattlesnake can still bite up to an hour after death. Such information can not only protect us from venomous snakes, but can also provide spiritual safeguards as well. Satan's classification as a serpent reminds us that he is still dangerous even though Christ has delivered a fatal blow. We can celebrate his inevitable demise, but we should exercise wisdom by remaining spiritually armed until his funeral is complete.[982]

Satan On March 31, 1998, Daniel Remeta was executed in the Florida electric chair for killing five people in 1985. In an interview not long before his death, Remeta exclaimed, "I just like to kill people." That chilling declaration is reminiscent of another calculated killer who "prowls around like a roaring lion seeking someone to devour" (1 Peter 5:8). Stated succinctly, Satan just likes to kill.[983]

Satan On October 12, 1998, six men were killed in the predawn hours while sleeping inside the rails of a train track. The incident took place around 3:15 A.M. when a southbound Union Pacific train with 105 cars was about fifty miles north of Harlingen, Texas. The crew was unable to stop the forty-five-mile-per-hour train in time and none of the six men were adequately awakened by the horn. Tragically, this is not an uncommon occurrence among undocumented immigrants and other transients. There is a mistaken belief that snakes will not cross railroad tracks, therefore, it is believed one can sleep between the rails and be protected from snakes. This tragedy is only accentuated by the reality that this is erroneous information. Officials from Union Pacific Railroad have noted their tracks are littered with snakes that have been cut in half while crossing the rails. The warm rocks under an elevated rail bed actually attract snakes at night. These six men became victims of a lie, and countless others fall prey to a similar myth about a far more deadly snake. We can be duped into believing there are certain havens where Satan won't go, but his deceptive schemes will make sure we are never beyond his deadly desires. The peaceful sleep that he offers is always between the rails of death and destruction.[984]

Satan The masterful magician and escapologist, Harry Houdini (1874–1926), maintained a standing challenge that he could get out of any locked jail within one hour. The only stipulations were that he would be allowed to enter the cell in his street clothes, and nobody could watch him work. A small town in the British Isles accepted Houdini's challenge after they had constructed what many people thought was an escape-proof jail. Upon entering the cell, Houdini immediately went to work. He pulled out the instruments he had smuggled in and began trying to trip the lock. He worked feverishly for two hours, an hour past his allotted time, but still could not release the lock. In exhaustion, he withdrew his file from the lock and leaned against the door. To his amazement, the door swung open. The townspeople had tricked Houdini by closing the jail door but never bolting the lock. He thought he was locked in, but in reality he was free from the very beginning. Satan attacks us in much the same way. His schemes are designed to make us believe we're trapped and ensnared when in actuality Christ has freed us from Satan's deceptive locks.[985]

Satan Years ago, when Billy Graham's children were small, their family was enjoying a meal together when someone began singing the chorus, "I've got the joy, joy, joy, joy down in my heart." The rest of the family chimed in on the song. The young choir concluded their impromptu anthem with that famous verse, "And if the devil doesn't like it he can sit on a tack. (Ouch!)" When they finished, Graham sternly looked at his children and said, "I don't want you to sing that verse anymore." The children quickly asked, "Why?" The famous evangelist replied, "Because the devil is a good devil." They looked confused so he explained further. "The devil does a very good job being the devil. He is real and powerful, and he is no joking matter." That counsel from the 1950s is more relevant today than we can imagine, especially after reading the following information. When the Barna Research Group asked Americans about Satan, they discovered 62 percent of the adult population believe Satan "is not a living being but is a symbol of evil." The angel of light (2 Corinthians 11:14) has masterfully disguised himself among the American populace. As Graham's daughter, Gigi, has wisely said, "A sober warning at the dinner table so many years ago seems wiser than ever."[986]

Scandal On March 17, 1997, *U.S. News & World Report* introduced a new feature to their weekly periodical. The "Scandometer" was created to monitor all of the current scandals and rate their significance on a scale of one to ten. The "Scandometer" was a blatant reminder from the 1990s of what happens when a nation drifts without a moral compass.[987]

School Every school day in America, 13,076 public school students are suspended.[988]

Science "Science without religion is lame, religion without science is blind." —*Albert Einstein* [989]

Scripture Memory Bill Gates is the richest man in the world with a net worth of $12.9 billion. One irony of this man comes from an incident when he was just eleven years old. His pastor, Dale Turner, challenged his congregation to memorize the Sermon on the Mount. The pastor promised any successful parishioners to an all expenses paid dinner at the top of Seattle's Space Needle. Bill Gates's phenomenal mental capacity allowed him to memorize the entire sermon during a two and one-half hour drive with his parents. After reciting the lengthy passage to the pastor, Gates said, "I can do anything I put my mind to." Unfortunately, he hasn't put his mind to Christianity. When a reporter asked if he believes in God, Gates said, "Oh, I guess, agnostic, atheist, I must be one of those." He later said, "Well, it might sound better to call me a Protestant who hasn't gone to church in a while." Imagine that, this man who made a perfect score on his SAT, graduated from Harvard with disappointment because he was never intellectually challenged, and he hasn't even thought about God enough to determine whether he is an atheist, agnostic, or just a backsliden Protestant. Memorizing Scripture does precious little if we don't allow the Spirit of God to use those words for the transformation of our lives.[990]

Second Coming In May of 1999, a Christian organization from Hereford, England, announced they have an eye on Jerusalem's eastern gate. They set up a camera to monitor the gate twenty-four hours a day and are hoping to capture Jesus' return so they can broadcast it for the world to see. If it works, I hope I'm not around to see the telecast.[991]

Second Coming In northern Italy, a tourist found this beautiful picture of what it means to be expectant of Christ's return. At the Villa Asconati, along the shore of Lake Como, he was introduced to a friendly older man who cared for the castle's garden. The grounds were immaculate and the gardener was doing everything he could to further improve their beauty. To his surprise, the tourist discovered the owner of this castle had not been on the property in twelve years. He seemed confused by the man's compulsion for perfection when the owner had not appeared in over a decade. So he said, "You keep this garden in such fine condition, just as though you expected your master to come tomorrow." The gardener promptly replied, "Today, sir, today!" That groundskeeper had the expectancy that every believer should possess. Are you looking for his return tomorrow, or today?[992]

Security After World War II, the Allied armies provided food and shelter for many homeless children. They were put together in large camps where they received more than sufficient food and care. Surprisingly, these well-fed children did not sleep well at night. They appeared to be restless and afraid. To remedy the problem, a psychologist suggested that each child should be given a slice of bread to hold at night. If they were hungry, another piece of bread would be provided, but the single slice was to be held, not eaten. The results were astounding. The children began to rest peacefully. The sensation of holding the bread gave them a sense of security and hope. They began to experience the peace that David knew when he wrote, "The Lord is my Shepherd, I shall not want."[993]

Self-Esteem Johnny can't read or write, but we want to make sure he feels good about himself. That's what research says is best, right? Not according to a recent issue of *Psychological Review.* Three researchers thoroughly examined the literature and concluded there is a much stronger link between high self-esteem and violence. "It is difficult to maintain belief in the low self-esteem view after seeing that the more violent groups are generally the ones with higher self-esteem." This conclusion by Roy Baumeister of Case Western Reserve University, and Laura Smart and Joseph Boden of the University of Virginia flies in the face of conventional wisdom. A strongly held view is that people with low self-esteem try to gain it by hurting others. The researchers found that violence is more often the work of people with unrealistically high self-esteem attacking others who challenge their self-image. The study's conclusion was: "Certain forms of high self-esteem seem to increase one's proneness to violence. An uncritical endorsement of the cultural value of self-esteem may, therefore, be counterproductive and even dangerous. The societal pursuit of high self-esteem for everyone may literally end up doing considerable harm." In response to the prison programs that try to enhance inmates' self-esteem, these researchers wrote, "Perhaps it would be better to try instilling modesty and humility." In a separate interview with the *Boston Globe,* Baumeister said, "What would work better for the country is to forget about self-esteem and concentrate on self-control." There are many people who have a poor self-image and need assistance to find their worth in Christ, but we would do well to remember that the fruit of the Spirit includes self-control, not self-esteem.[994]

Self-Esteem "Self-esteem cannot be sought as an end in itself but must come as a byproduct of meeting standards of excellence." —*Aaron Wildavsky*[995]

Senior Adults A common misconception among the elderly is that their age prevents them from making a significant impact. May these seniors be encouraged by the following: Tennyson was eighty years old when he wrote "Crossing the Bar" and Robert Louis Stevenson left an unfinished novel, *Weir of Hermiston*, when he died. His death conceivably occurred while he was writing because the story stops in mid-sentence. One of Whittier's most beautiful poems, "To Oliver Wendell Holmes," was written just a few weeks before his death. Charles Dickens was working on what promised to be his best novel when he died. Few of us will die in the midst of producing our life's greatest work, but we can all strive to give our best until the moment of death arrives.[996]

Senior Adults Americans over the age of sixty have $10 trillion in financial resources.[997]

Senior Adults An African folk song declares, "when an old person dies, it's as if a library has been destroyed by fire." How true! Every senior adult represents a bridge to the past. That bridge can only be crossed if the younger generation takes time to draw out the history and heritage that is stored within the heart and mind. Picturing every senior adult as a walking library is a novel idea, so take some time and check out a more meaningful relationship with an older adult.[998]

Servanthood During a conference in 1999, Leith Anderson told about a friend of his who pastors a church in Cincinnati. This minister is serious about demonstrating servanthood to people outside the walls of his church. In the trunk of his car he carries rubber gloves and a bucket filled with toilet cleaning supplies. On a regular basis he stops at places of business and asks if he can clean their toilets as an expression of God's love for them. You can only imagine the strange but appreciative looks he receives. On one occasion he met a rather hardened manager of a truck stop. The pastor offered to clean toilets and the man matter-of-factly said they had twenty toilets. The minister was caught off guard and confessed he was thinking more like two toilets. The man said, "Nope, it's twenty." He hesitated then negotiated for four toilets. The man curtly replied, "It's twenty or none!" The pastor saw the height of these stakes and agreed to clean all twenty toilets. The man then said, "I only have two but I wanted to see what kind of Christian you are." People all around us are wanting to see what kind of Christian we are and the best way to demonstrate the authenticity of our faith is through acts of servanthood.[999]

Servanthood "God helps those who help others—not those who help themselves." —*Anonymous* [1000]

Servanthood "It is one of the most beautiful compensations of this life that no man can sincerely try to help another without helping himself." —*Ralph Waldo Emerson* [1001]

Servanthood "The best way to find out whether or not you really have a servant's heart is to see what your reaction is when somebody treats you like one." —*Elisabeth Elliot* [1002]

Service General William Booth founded the Salvation Army. At the age of eighty-three, he was told he would not regain his sight. Booth spoke to his son, Bramwell, and said, "You mean that I am blind?" Bramwell replied, "Well, General, I fear that we must contemplate that." After a pause the elder Booth asked, "I shall never see your face again?" "No, probably not in this world," said Bramwell. The senior's hand then extended to take hold of his son's hand and he then said, "God must know best!" After another pause he stated, "Bramwell, I have done what I could for God and for the people with my eyes. Now I shall do what I can for God and for the people without my eyes."[1003]

Service Napoleon once lost control of his horse and a young private grabbed the reins to pull the horse back under control. Napoleon turned to the private and said, "Thank you, Captain." When we come to the aide of others we not only help them, but oftentimes we help ourselves as well.[1004]

Service The world lost a true servant when Mother Teresa died in 1997. Her acts of service are beyond number, but one particular incident reflects the heart from which she served. She was working among the slums of Calcutta dressing the wounds of a leper. An American tourist observed her work and asked if he could take a picture. She granted permission and the tourist framed his shot. Through the camera's lens he could see this world-renowned nun tenderly replacing a bloody bandage that covered a gaping hole where the leper's nose used to exist. The photographer could also smell the stench of this wound as he moved in for a closer shot. After capturing several pictures, the American tourist said, "Sister, I wouldn't do what you're doing for $10 million!" Mother Teresa replied, "Neither would I, my friend. Neither would I!" True service can't be bought, and wouldn't want to be even if it could.[1005]

Service "We make a living by what we get; we make a life by what we give." —*Winston Churchill*[1006]

Service While shopping in New York, one woman noticed a young boy shivering in the cold November weather. He was pressed against a store window looking at a pair of shoes. She asked what he was doing out in the cold and he replied, "I was asking God to give me a pair of those shoes." A quick glance down at his feet revealed tattered shoes that barely covered his protruding bare feet. Her arm immediately wrapped around him and she whisped him into the store. She pulled several pairs of socks from the shelf and instructed the department employee to bring the pair of shoes her young friend wanted. He was soon walking around the shoe department with not only the shoes for which he had prayed, but socks to go with them. The woman paid for everything without asking for a cent. She then turned for the door and said, "You'll be a lot more comfortable now." The little boy looked up into her eyes with an inquisitive expression and asked, "Are you God's wife?" When the bride of Christ selflessly serves others, people will notice our relationship to God.[1007]

Sex Americans suffer ten to fifty times more sexually transmitted diseases than people in other developed countries. This translates to $10 billion a year for treatment, not counting the enormous and ever-growing amount of money spent on treating AIDS.[1008]

Sex A report from the Centers for Disease Control and Prevention reveals that states without sex education or those that stress sexual abstinence have fewer teen pregnancies than those that promote the use of condoms.[1009]

Sex Every day in America, eight thousand non-adults are infected with a Sexually Transmitted Disease.[1010]

Sex In 2000, a national survey by Reuters News discovered nearly two-thirds of American teenagers who have had sex regretted that decision to lose their virginity (boys 55 percent, girls 72 percent).[1011]

Sex The University of Chicago recently completed the first extensive study of sexual problems among American since the Kinsey reports of a half-century ago. Edward Laumann, a sociology professor at the university, was the lead author of this study featured in *JAMA* (Journal of American Medical Association). The research involved 3,159 men and women who represented 97 percent of the nation. From the data, Laumann noted the levels of dysfunction "are far higher than anyone had really anticipated." In reality, these findings actually help to confirm a frequently overlooked truth from Scripture. God has ordained sex to be experienced exclusively between a husband and wife. The American culture has invested enormous energy in trying to refute this Biblical truth. Repeatedly, our nation has been seduced by the lie that monogamy is monotonous. Ironically, Laumann's study reflects the exact opposite. It revealed that "married men and women appear to have fewer sexual problems than singles." The level of sexual enjoyment is one and one-half times greater for married women, and married men have twice as much interest in sex than unmarried men. If nothing else, this extensive research in the area of sex has affirmed what God has told us all along, the greatest sexual fulfillment can only be attained through marital love and commitment. What a contrast to the debacle our country has faced with the immoral behavior of President Clinton. Tragically, some people don't comprehend the damage and disgrace that accompany such actions. Bob Guccione, publisher of *Penthouse* magazine, said he would offer Monica Lewinsky a job in advertising sales any day. He said, "I was very impressed with her, and she is obviously liberated sexually." How sad that numerous key people, as well as an entire nation, can experience untold carnage from the immoral relationship between President Clinton and Lewinsky, and this is defined as "liberated." To the contrary, immorality creates the antithesis of liberation—slavery and death.[1012]

Sexual Fulfillment Several years ago a letter appeared in the "Dear Abby" column that addressed the subject of sexual dissatisfaction. The woman's letter noted that she was fifty years old and had been married thirty years. The letter said she had just about given up on sex and was tired of it because there was no satisfaction in it. This woman said she continues to have sex because of her love for her husband and his desire for sex. As for her, she has no desire for any more sex. She then signed her letter, "Tired in Lincoln, Nebraska." Within two weeks Abigail Van Buren received over 250,000 letters from women that voiced their agreement with this letter. Current statistics affirm this is a significant problem. In a recent report cited by *U.S. News & World Report*, only 26 percent of women in America said they experience mutually satisfying sex. The message to men is strong. Sex involves much more than just physical mechanics. Unfortunately, though, many men think they know everything about sex and refuse to seek more education on how they can make sexual intercourse mutually satisfying for their wife. A man who learns to truly satisfy his wife's emotional and sexual needs will quickly remove himself from the large ranks of men who complain they never get enough sex.[1013]

Sexual Purity The October 19, 1997 edition of *The Washington Times* clearly displayed the truth and the deception about sexual purity. The front page contained a picture of the Promise Keeper's Sacred Assembly in Washington, and an article about Jane Fonda condemning the government's new campaign for "sexual abstinence." A picture of history's largest gathering on the National Mall stood next to Fonda's comment that, "Abstinence until marriage is based on an unreal world that isn't out there." On October 1, 1997, Jane Fonda declared on *Good Morning America*, "Many Americans were stunned that the federal government, starting today, is giving $50 million a year for five years to states for abstinence-until-marriage programs." She went on to say, "Most Americans don't know their tax money is being used for that and most Americans don't want it." Ironically, just three days later on October 4, 1997, over one million men stood together under the autumn sun in Washington, D.C. The third of seven commitments made by these Promise Keepers is, "Practice spiritual, moral, ethical, and sexual purity." The deception: one celebrity using national television to declare abstinence is unreal. The truth: 1.3 million common men, traveling great distances at personal expense to prove abstinence is not only real, but it's right.[1014]

Sexual Purity There are still plenty of naysayers who buck the idea of sexual purity but they can't argue with the results of a 1996 event in Brazil. Brazil is a sensual society that is saturated with immorality. In the midst of this culture, Brazilian Baptist youths sponsored a community blood drive in Campinas. It was held in conjunction with their national congress and the True Love Waits Campaign. The blood drive broke two significant records. First, more people than ever before donated blood. Second, not one of the 472 pints of blood were contaminated. The largest-recorded donation produced a perfect score of purity. These Brazilian youths have dramatically demonstrated that there are not only spiritual benefits to sexual purity, but also physical benefits as well.[1015]

Shame In 1998, George Michael, a well-known pop singer, was arrested for lewd conduct in a Beverly Hills park area known as a meeting spot for homosexuals. The thirty-four-year-old British-born singer acknowledged his homosexuality during an interview with CNN, but then declared, "I don't feel any shame whatsoever." Jeremiah faced similar thinking when he penned God's warnings for those who "don't even know how to blush" (Jeremiah 6:15).[1016]

Sin Allen Adams had a bad day on September 8, 1996. On that particular Sunday, he was watching the Pittsburgh Steelers play the Baltimore Ravens in Three Rivers Stadium. At halftime, Adams was one of three fans chosen to come onto the field and attempt a field goal. The promotional contest let these lucky fans try to win either a free dinner at a very exclusive restaurant or round-trip airline tickets. During the contest, another fan took interest of Adams's trip to the playing field. When Sergeant John Kearney heard Adams's name announced over the loudspeakers, he called his office to confirm a warrant for the arrest of this "would-be kicking specialist." As Adams walked off the field, Sergeant Kearney arrested him for a previous assault charge. Some people just think they're getting away with sin, but soon enough "your sin will find you out."[1017]

Sin Can you name the creature that is most deadly to humans? You might immediately conjure up thoughts of sharks, cobras, or bears, but the biggest killer by far is the one we seem to fear the least. Throughout human history, mosquitoes have probably killed more people than the combined fatalities of all wars. Every year, this parasite-carrying insect leaves over three hundred million people sick, and in Africa alone, it kills nearly one million children annually. Mosquitoes, like sin, are generally seen as a nuisance, not a danger. May we draw a lesson from nature and realize sin is deadly.[1018]

Sin Hundreds of seagoing vessels have sunk in the depths of the seas, but few have captured attention like the *Titanic*. She sank on her maiden voyage in April of 1912 and the persistent theory was that an iceberg tore a three hundred-foot gash in the side of the nine hundred-foot ship. In 1985, the wreckage was discovered two and one-half miles beneath the sea near Newfoundland. Since that time, fascinating footage has displayed the mystique of this sunken ship. In August of 1995, an international team of scientists and engineers repeatedly dove to the remains for an exhaustive study of the ship's demise. The fateful damage is buried beneath the ocean floor so these experts peered through the mud with sound waves. Their findings were astonishing. Rather than a massive three hundred-foot gash, as previously theorized, the total area of damage was about twelve to thirteen square feet (less than the area of two sidewalk squares). Six punctures across six watertight holds was all it took to sink the ship that some said even God couldn't sink. Many times we tend to believe that avoidance of the "big" sins will keep us afloat, but in reality, sin of any size can sink us.[1019]

Sin 1847, women were dying at an alarming rate in the Vienna Lying-In Hospital. They arrived as healthy, pregnant women, but became deathly ill after giving birth. These new mothers contracted a bacterial infection known as childbed fever. This phenomenon piqued the curiosity and concern of Dr. Ignaz Semmelweis. He observed that the rates of infection were much higher in a maternity ward attended by medical students than in the ward that used midwives. Semmelweis deduced there must be some inherent problem related to the students' moving directly from the autopsy room, where they were dissecting cadavers, to the delivery room. Semmelweis experimented with this correlation by requiring students to wash their hands in chlorinated lime before delivering a baby. The rate of infection dropped from 18 percent to 1 percent. Unfortunately, Semmelweis's ideas about hand washing were not accepted in his time. He died at the age of forty-seven in an insane asylum. Sin operates much like these lethal germs. The sin on our hands may bring destruction to innocent people around us because we were too careless, or thoughtless, to apply God's cleansing. And just as people did not believe Semmelweis 150 years ago, there are many today who think their sin doesn't affect others.[1020]

Sin In September of 1999, Israel rolled back its clocks by one hour to support Orthodox Jewish prayer schedules. The Palestinian West Bank remained on the normal summer time. On September 5, three Palestinian terrorists loaded bombs into their car and took off for their targets in Haifa and Tiberius. They never reached their destinations though because at 5:00 P.M. the bombs detonated while they were in route. Security sources said the bomb makers in the West Bank had set the timers for 6:00 P.M. and the terrorists assumed the hour difference had been factored into their plan. Like those bombs, the fallout of sin can never be accurately calculated and it always explodes with deadly force.[1021]

Sin It's called "trimethylaminuria" but few doctors have heard about it. This rare disease also carries a name that approximates its effects on the body—"fish malodor syndrome." Patients with this disease emit a foul odor through their sweat, breath, and body fluids because digestive enzymes fail to break down trimethylamine. The problem, though rare, radically impacts those who have it. Many become reclusive, depressed, and feel like social outcasts. Regardless of how many times they bathe or immerse themselves in cologne, the odor remains. For this reason sufferers often lose or quit their jobs because of the social stigma. To address this problem, researchers from around the world convened in Bethesda, Maryland, during the spring of 1999. They heard from, and examined patients who, on average, wait twenty years for doctors to make a correct diagnosis. Some patients have amassed enormous medical bills in pursuit of a remedy or cure. Unfortunately, there is no known cure for this unusual disease. In reality, we all suffer from spiritual trimethylaminuria. Our soul reeks from the corruption of sin and no matter how hard we try to cover it up, the smell remains. Regardless of how many avenues for resolve we pursue, we must eventually realize there is but one cure, the cleansing blood of Jesus Christ. He will not only remove the stench of sin, but the power and penalty that accompany our defiant deeds.[1022]

Sin Need a few more examples of sin's folly? During the summer of 1998, a crook in Fullerton, California, accidentally, and fatally, shot himself while pistol whipping the manager of a computer store that he was robbing. In the same time period, a thirty-two-year-old man from Tahlequah, Oklahoma, lost his balance and fell to his death while painting graffiti on a sixty-four-foot water tower. Brandon Hughes, age eighteen, was in a Memphis, Tennessee, courtroom during 1997 to face charges against him for various traffic offenses. When he raised his hand to be sworn in, a packet of cocaine fell from his shirt. He went straight to jail. James Newsome tried to rob a convenience store in January of 1999. The Fort Smith, Arkansas, resident thought his robbery was successfully until the police arrested him just a few hours later. With the surveillance camera, detective Jeff Barrows could not only see Newsome hold up the clerk at gunpoint, but he could read his name boldly printed on the front of the hard hat he was wearing as a disguise. During 1997 in Wyoming, Charles Taylor went on trial for robbing a shoe store and stealing a pair of tan hiking boots. In the courtroom, Taylor propped his feet on the defense table, and to the amazement of everyone, he was wearing the pair of stolen hiking boots. The judge sent him to jail in his socks.[1023]

Sin On February 2, 1997, two French soldiers died when a shell from World War I exploded on what was once the 1916 battlefield of Verdun. The two noncommissioned officers lost their lives while walking in the countryside eighty-one years after the war. Sin is just like that. It can have far-reaching consequences that might lay dormant for years, and tragically, it is often the innocent who experience some of sin's most devastating results.[1024]

Sin "Sin is not hurtful because it is forbidden, but it is forbidden because it is hurtful." —*Benjamin Franklin* [1025]

Sin "Whatever else is or is not true, this one thing is certain—man is not what he was meant to be." —*G.K. Chesterton* [1026]

Sincerity "The most exhausting thing in life is being insincere." —*Anne Morrow Lindbergh* [1027]

Sin's Curse Paul wrote about the whole creation groaning over the curse of sin (Romans 8:22). Japanese researchers may have literally discovered what he meant. In the summer of 1999, Naoki Suda and Kaqunari Nawa revealed the results of their study concerning a mysterious hum emitted by the earth. They dredged through a mass of seismic data to discover our planet produces fifty notes that are about sixteen octaves below middle C. These notes are impossible to hear without the proper instruments and are so subtle that an earthquake anywhere on the planet will blot them out. The two researchers said the earth's hum is like "an endless banging on a trash can." Sin leaves us, and our world, with a song as unsettling as thugs beating on a garbage can.[1028]

Sleep According to a recent U.S. News/CNN poll, only 28 percent of American adults get eight hours of sleep. Half of all respondents said they would take a nap every afternoon if they could. Charles Spurgeon said, "Sometimes the most spiritual thing a person can do is sleep." Unfortunately, many people combine the two (spiritual and sleep) in the pew on Sunday mornings.[1029]

Sleep Fourteen million sleeping pill prescriptions are filled each year and Americans spend an additional $33 million (in grocery stores alone) on over-the-counter sleeping pills.[1030]

Smiling Frowning requires forty-three muscles but a smile only needs seventeen.[1031]

Smiling That little smiley face, which is known throughout the world, was created in 1965 by a graphic artist named Harvey Ball. He made just $45 off the yellow icon he designed for an insurance company.[1032]

Smoking Americans spend $45.7 billion a year on cigarettes.[1033]

Smoking Each year in the United States, three thousand nonsmokers die of lung cancer resulting from second-hand smoke.[1034]

Smoking Each year the tobacco industry sells $1.26 billion in tobacco products to children under the age of eighteen—over one billion packs of cigarettes and twenty-six million canisters of chewing tobacco.[1035]

Smoking Every day, three thousand American children start smoking.[1036]

Smoking More young children are killed by parental smoking than by all unintentional injuries combined.[1037]

Smoking Worldwide, three million people die each year from smoking-related illnesses and cigarette companies spend a combined arsenal of roughly $13 million per day to advertise and promote their products.[1038]

Sovereignty "It is certain that not one drop of rain falls without God's sure command." —*John Calvin* [1039]

Speech "Be careful of your thoughts; they may become words at any moment." —*Iara Gassen* [1040]

Speech "No one has a finer command of language than the person who keeps his mouth shut." —*Sam Rayburn* [1041]

Spiritual Activity Fifty-four percent of Americans live sedentary lives, and such a lifestyle is responsible for an estimated 250,000 deaths per year. According to the American Heart Association, "being sedentary has as negative an effect on your heart's health as high cholesterol, high blood pressure, or smoking." Many Christians are not physically sedentary, but have succumbed to spiritual lethargy. It is a ploy of the devil to keep us so busy with nonspiritually redeeming activities that we become spiritually sedentary. When we find ourselves in this position we need to remember that our spiritual health depends on Christlike activity. Spiritual inactivity is just as dangerous as active sin. [1042]

Spiritual Gifts Benjamin Franklin left behind a small poem about talents: "Hide not your talents, They for use were made. What's a sundial in the shade?" When it comes to the use of spiritual gifts many people are like a sundial in the shade. If they will but come out into the Light, the Son will make them useful. [1043]

Spiritual Gifts Bill Hybels once visited a hardware store that had been in operation for one hundred years. As the proud owner showed him around, he was intrigued by some old tools that had never been sold. There were shovels, sledge hammers, and axes made in the early 1900s. These eighty-year-old tools had never been used. They just collected decades of dust. Ephesians 2:10 reminds us that we were created for good works so don't just hang around. . . . Do the work God has assigned you. [1044]

Spiritual Gifts Donald Liddle died on June 5, 2000, at the age of seventy-five. His claim to fame is that he was a major league pitcher who threw the ball that Willie Mays ran down to make one of baseball's greatest catches. In the first game of the 1954 World Series at New York's Polo Grounds, Liddle was called in to relieve Sal Maglie. The New York Giants's manager, Leo Durocher, wanted Liddle to throw against Cleveland's Vic Wertz. Wertz hit a 460-foot fly ball that Mays raced after and caught over his shoulder. It is a piece of baseball history that will never be forgotten because it is often replayed on highlight clips. Immediately following Mays spectacular catch, Marv Grissom came to the mound as Liddle's replacement. Liddle smiled at his fellow reliever and said, "I got my man." Spiritual gifts are sometimes used in a similar way. Our role may be little more than setting the stage for another to excel, but in the end, we'll know it was a team effort regardless of how insignificant our part may have appeared. That's what leads to smiles and success.[1045]

Spiritual Gifts It's a true story that sounds like a remake of the *Beverly Hillbillies*. During the Great Depression, a man named Yates was operating a sheep ranch in the rolling hills of West Texas. His business wasn't generating enough money to pay the principal and interest on his mortgage so he ended up living on a government subsidy. His days were filled with stress over the financial concerns of his family. They lived, dressed, and ate in poverty. One day a seismographic crew asked if they might explore his land for oil. Yates agreed and signed a lease contract. At 1,115 feet they struck a huge reserve of oil. The first well produced 80,000 barrels a day while many subsequent wells generated more than twice that amount. Thirty years after the discovery, one well was estimated to still have a potential flow of 125,000 barrels a day. This vast sea of wealth, known as Yates Pool, had always belonged to Yates. He was a multimillionaire who had spent years in heart-wrenching poverty just because he didn't realize what he already possessed. When we don't explore and realize the tremendous resources God has provided for Christian service, we experience spiritual poverty and frustration. You may be dwelling on a huge reserve of talent and joy that God is ready to release if you will just let him.[1046]

Spiritual Gifts Jamie Scott had his heart set on being in the school play. Although his talent would probably prevent him from getting a part, he went to tryouts with great expectancy. On the day that parts were announced, Jamie came running home to tell his mom. He was beaming with pride when he shouted, "I've been chosen to clap and cheer." In 1 Corinthians 12:22, Paul wrote, "those parts of the body that seem to be weaker are indispensable . . ." Clapping and cheering may not seem very special to some, but little Jamie Scott understood that such roles are noble indeed.[1047]

Spiritual Gifts Moses initially had some big reservations about serving God. He ran an entire list of excuses by God. In response, God simply told Moses his name. Moses said, "I am not able to speak very well." God replied, "I know, but I AM." Moses worried, "I am not believable." God remarked, "I understand, but I AM." Moses suggested, "I am not capable." God declared, "You're right, but I AM." God's answer to our belief that we can't is his declaration of who he is. The answer to our worries is wrapped up in God's name. When we think, "I am not resourceful enough to serve God," just remember God's name and be reminded of his words to Moses, "I AM."[1048]

Spiritual Growth "God loves us just the way we are, but he wants us to be just the way Christ is." —*Max Lucado* [1049]

Spiritual Growth Most of the time we feel as though spiritual growth is an incremental occurrence that could be traced on a graph with a gradual, upward sloping line. Ironically, though, it probably looks more like a graph that has periodic upward bursts followed by lingering plateaus. This is understood more clearly when we think about the growth of trees. Trees grow rapidly during a four-to-six week period in the spring. During the balance of the year, this new growth solidifies and becomes sturdy. Many times we will grow and develop much like trees. Spurts of growth will be followed by times of strengthening the growth that has occurred. Most importantly, whether our growth comes incrementally or in spurts, we must remember that Jesus is the vine and we are the branches. Growth of any kind depends on us remaining in him (John 15:5).[1050]

Spiritual Healing Viktor Yazykov gained international fame when he operated on himself, without anesthetic, in the middle of the ocean. The fifty-year-old Russian was one thousand miles from shore in the South Atlantic when he realized there was something terribly wrong with his arm. Forty days earlier he joined a group of daring souls who set out from Charleston, South Carolina, on a twenty-seven-thousand-mile solo sailboat race around the world. This eight-month odyssey was called Around Alone. Each competitor must navigate around the globe by himself and that's where things got sticky for Yazykov. His elbow, which had ached since leaving Charleston six weeks before, was now five times its normal size and he had lost all feeling in that arm. This became a double threat in that Yazykov needed both arms to survive at sea and now the infection was itself posing a risk to his health. Without drastic measures he would certainly die before the closest boat could reach him. Through high-tech communication, Yazykov sent an email to Dr. Dan Carlin in Boston. Carlin runs a practice called World Clinic that provides emergency care through computer technology to people around the world.

Carlin walked Yazykov through the fourteen-step surgical procedure via email. With very deliberate instructions, Carlin told the seasoned sailor to "make your incision rapidly. It will hurt less if you do." He also typed, "It hurts a great deal when you insert the gauze, but you must get it down into the depths of the wound as much as possible." The former Soviet commando tolerated the pain but became very concerned about his inability to stop the excessive bleeding. Before Carlin could respond back, Yazykov lost consciousness. Although emails were repeatedly sent throughout the night, no response came from the forty-foot "Wind of Change" sailboat. Twelve hours later, Yazykov typed in a simple message, "I am OK." Within another five days he sailed into the port of Cape Town to the cheers of a crowd that had heard his story. After just three weeks of rest, Yazykov's arm was completely healed and he set off on the second leg of the race to Auckland, New Zealand. By the middle of May 1999, Viktor Yazykov sailed into Charleston, South Carolina, after an incredible boat ride around the world. The success of this man's amazing journey is due in part to his willingness to experience great pain for the sake of healing. His self-inflicted incision lanced a deadly wound and opened up a passageway for healing. Figuratively speaking, the same type of radical procedures are occasionally required for spiritual healing to begin (Matthew 18:8–9). And just as Carlin advised, it is far less painful if we "make the incision rapidly" rather than hesitating, procrastinating, or partially dressing the wound.[1051]

Spiritual Hunger Easter of 1998 reflected a shift in the thinking of Americans. The major greeting card companies unveiled the results of their trend analyses by producing a significantly enhanced number of spiritually related cards. Hallmark Cards, the nation's top seller, created a new line of cards called, Yours in Christ. Gibson Greetings launched their Share the Miracle cards, and American Greetings, the second-largest manufacturer of cards, boosted its offering of religious cards by 13 percent. American Greetings has a team of employees called Trend Central. They study the American culture and track changing trends. Among other things, they noticed the number of spiritually oriented television shows quadrupled in the last decade. American Greetings spokesperson, Laurie Heinrichsen, said, "There's no doubt there's a resurgence in spiritual faith. Our cards reflect that." Don French, general manager of seasonal products for Gibson Greetings, noted similar results from their studies of current trends. He said, "What came across was that very few of our cards focused on the Resurrection and people wanted that message. They wanted to focus on the spiritual aspect of Easter." The headlines to this article read, "People want religion, not bunnies and eggs." Research has confirmed the existence of America's spiritual hunger.[1052]

Spiritual Warfare Call it a bad day at the tattoo parlor. Dan O'Connor was an avid fan of Notre Dame. To further demonstrate his allegiance, he had the university's mascot, a boxing leprechaun, tattooed to his arm with the inscription, "Fighting Irish." When he removed the bandage from that $125 drawing, his girlfriend began laughing. The twenty-two-year-old's upper arm didn't reveal much fight because the tattoo artist left out the "t" in "fighting." O'Connor sued the Tattoo Shoppe in Carlstadt, New Jersey, for misspelling "Fighing Irish." Sometimes Christians appear more like O'Connor's tattoo than the spiritual warriors God has called us to be. We can lose the "t" in our fight and reap nothing more than laughter from Satan and his crew. As believers we've been "sealed" (tattooed) with the Holy Spirit. Let him put the "t" back in your spiritual fight against darkness.[1053]

Spiritual Warfare In Walter Lord's book, *Day of Infamy*, the reader is given a stirring account of the attack on Pearl Harbor. Not only does it describe the horror of that historic day, but it also spells out a tragedy that is equally disconcerting—the length of time it took people to realize they were under attack. Japanese Zeroes were screaming through the air and bombs were exploding everywhere, but most people just thought it was a drill. One seaman had the sentiments of many, "Somebody is going to catch it for putting live bombs on those planes." A quicker response to the attack would have prevented much of the destruction. What a picture of our situation today. Our culture is under a full-scale attack yet many view it as simply a drill. It is clearly time for us to hear and respond to the alarms that are sounding.[1054]

Spiritual Warfare Texans have always sought bragging rights whether or not they truly deserved them. Down in South Texas, though, there is one tough Texan who has quite a story about which to brag. At age forty, Valentin Grimaldo was bitten by a poisonous coral snake in May of 1996. He was walking with his brother along a highway near Encino when he reached into some tall grass and was bitten on the hand. He then grabbed the snake and bit the head off. He skinned it and used the snakeskin as a tourniquet to keep the venom from spreading.

Hospital officials said the bite left him in excruciating pain for several days, but his aggressive response to the snake saved his life. Grimaldo's brother, Fidel, kept the snake's head as a keepsake. Satan's attacks are painful and can be lethal, but if we will retaliate against him under the power and authority of Jesus Christ, God can sustain us with the very thing with which Satan intended to kill us.[1055]

Sportsmanship Had he thrown another club, Arnold Palmer may have never become a household name. While playing in the West Penn junior finals as a high school student, Palmer missed a short putt and reacted by throwing his putter over the gallery into a clump of trees. That frustration soon vanished when he won the tournament and received a trophy. His joy of winning was short-lived, however, when he was greeted by deafening silence when he got into the family car. His father sternly said, "If you ever throw a club again, you'll never play in another golf tournament." Palmer realized he had violated one of his father's fundamental rules of life: "learning to be a gracious loser is as important as being a gracious winner." Arnold Palmer learned a valuable lesson that day and it has stayed with him throughout his career. You can see footage of him winning and losing with grace, but you won't find any clips of him throwing a club.[1056]

Standards On October 1, 1996, Donald McDougall was bludgeoned to death by a fellow Florida prison inmate. A prison spokeswoman was not surprised by the killing because McDougall was serving time for torturing and killing a five-year-old girl. The prison authority said, "Inmates have a code of honor for certain crimes. Even hardened criminals hate a child killer." If imprisoned criminals have standards, it simply stands to reason that a holy God has standards by which he expects us to live.[1057]

Stealing Ahmed Awadh showed up at his own funeral . . . alive. In early October of 1997, Awadh's family was huddled together in a funeral tent paying their last respects to their beloved son and brother. The memorial was interrupted when Awadh, in his thirties, walked in as the picture of perfect health. The corpse they were preparing to bury had been washed up on the Mediterranean coast and was badly decomposed. Inside a pocket was Awadh's wallet so authorities contacted his family and a funeral was set. The resident of Egypt's northern port city, Alexandria, told his stunned family that a thief had stolen his wallet and identity card.

Although not all thieves suffer the same fate, stealing ultimately leads to self-destruction.[1058]

Stealing Basketball enthusiasts know the significance of March 2, 1962. On that day, Wilt Chamberlain set the National Basketball Association record for single-game scoring when he dropped in one hundred points. Kerry Ryman, a fourteen-year-old at the time, attended the famous game in Hershey, Pennsylvania. When the final buzzer sounded, Ryman hustled onto the court, shook Chamberlain's hand, grabbed the ball, and outran a security guard. The teenager successfully stole one of basketball's most prized trophies. The stress of his misdeed was greatly reduced in 1975 when the statute of limitations ran out and he could no longer be prosecuted for the crime. On April 28, 2000, Ryman's robbery took on new proportions when Leland's auction house sold the ball for $551,844. The the fifty-two-year-old crane operator in Annville, Pennsylvania, said, "It's not something I'm proud of. I was fourteen and I made a mistake." Rationalizing his actions, Ryman noted, "I would have given the ball to charity, but I would never have been able to make sure the money was actually put to good use. Now, I have direct control of the money." Kerry Ryman is now a half-million dollars richer and he has given Americans one more sad reason to believe that crime does indeed pay.[1059]

Stress According to the American Institute of Stress in Yonkers, New York, as many as 90 percent of visits to primary-care physicians are stress related. Eighty-four percent of baby boomers say they need to reduce their stress.[1060]

Stress According to the American Institute of Stress, stress-related illnesses cost the American economy $100 billion annually. It is no surprise that "four out of five Americans report a need to reduce stress in their lives, and that spending for mental health is escalating more rapidly than all other health categories." Stress is a relatively new term, which derived in the 1950s for a very old problem. Interestingly enough its remedy has never changed. "Come to Me, all who are weary and heavy laden, and I will give you rest" (Matthew 11:28–30).[1061]

Stress Experts in the area of stress remind us of the "FUD" factor. Stress is sure to follow any person involved with *F*ear, *U*ncertainty, or *D*oubt. Effective stress management requires an awareness of what these three bears can do, plus a strategy to minimize each one of them.[1062]

Stress Fifty-seven percent of men feel stressed out during a typical day.[1063]

Stress Not only is stress a problem with many Americans, it's now affecting animals as well. On January 5, 1999, the Food and Drug Administration approved the first antidepressant for dogs. The drug, Clomicalm, is designed specifically for dogs in helping them deal with separation anxiety. Of the fifty-five million dogs in the United States, about 10 percent of them have this problem to some degree. This drug is supposed to help calm dogs when they are left to themselves by eliminating symptoms such as excessive barking, destructive chewing, clawing, and uncontrollable urination. Specialists say dogs have a strong need to be around other animals or people and if they are left too long by themselves they begin to engage in destructive behavior. Clomicalm, at about $1 per pill, is being billed as a drug that will help dogs cope with the anxiety that can accompany aloneness. When they start approving antidepressants for dogs it's time to reevaluate the lifestyles of their masters.[1064]

Stress Stress has become one of the most frequently used words in America as problems are often described as "stress related." Ironically, those who understand the pressures of life have estimated that 80 percent of our stress is created solely by our minds. That means most of what we call "stress related" is really just "mind related." Set your mind on the things above (Colossians 3:2) and life will seem a lot less stressful.[1065]

Success "Always remember that the soundest way to progress in any organization is to help the person ahead of you get promoted." —*Richard Zera* [1066]

Success "Behind every successful man there is a loving wife and a surprised mother-in-law." —*Anonymous* [1067]

Success Charles Spurgeon appropriately said, "Success can go to my head and will unless I remember that it is God who accomplishes the work, that he can continue to do so without my help, and that he will be able to make out with other means whenever he wants to cut me out." A true leader of God will recognize the reality that he or she is simply an instrument in the hands of God, and any success belongs exclusively to the Lord.[1068]

Success "If a person wakes up and finds himself a success, rest assured, he hasn't been asleep." —*Anonymous* [1069]

Success Jeff Foxworthy has made millions of dollars off his "redneck" humor. In August of 1998, the comedian told an audience of high school students in Roswell, Georgia, that all of his apparent success has not made him happy. He explained that God was the source of true happiness. After his TV show was canceled, he started reevaluating his life and turned back to his Christian roots. He even considered becoming a preacher. Foxworthy said, "Because I have decided to walk with God, it has changed my entire life." Success apart from God is an impossible pursuit. [1070]

Success Robert Fulghum became an instant celebrity in 1986 with his best-selling book, *All I Really Need to Know I Learned in Kindergarten.* He has since written numerous books that reveal his unique and perceptive outlook on life. In one of his best-sellers he listed nine rules from the *Fulghum Guide to Being Handy around the House.* The eighth rule states, "If at first you don't succeed, redefine success." It's both humorous and Biblical. How many times have we worked toward what we define as success only to later see it didn't fit God's definition of success? Proverbs 14:12 reminds us of this problem. If we really want true success, we must define it in accordance with God's Word (See Joshua 1:8). [1071]

Success Several years ago, *Success* magazine reported on a Gallup poll that sought to define success. The people's responses fell into twelve categories. Topping the dozen definitions was "good health." of those surveyed 58 percent equated good health with success. Good health is to be valued and never taken for granted, but success is far more than dodging the doctor's office. The Bible doesn't speak of success in terms of health. Jesus said, "By this is my Father glorified, that you bear much fruit, and so prove to be my disciples" (John 15:8). [1072]

Success "Success is a terrible teacher." —*Bill Gates* [1073]

Success "Success is not the key to happiness. Happiness is the key to success." —*Herman Cain, CEO of Godfather's Pizza* [1074]

Success *The Executives' Digest* made an interesting observation concerning the potential price tag of success. The periodical reported, "The trouble with success is that the formula is the same as the one for a nervous breakdown." Sadly, many feet have headed up the corporate ladder without this warning. Success can be achieved without losing your mind if your focus stays on God (See Psalm 32:8).[1075]

Success To know that even one life has breathed easier because you lived. This is to have succeeded. —*Ralph Waldo Emerson*[1076]

Success "Wealth, like happiness, is never attained when sought after directly. It always comes as a byproduct of providing a useful service." —*Henry Ford*[1077]

Success Zoe Koplowitz participated in the 1998 Boston Marathon, but it took her twenty-five hours to finish. The fifty-year-old New York woman suffers from multiple sclerosis and with two walking canes she could only manage a pace of one mile per hour. Koplowitz, who has walked the route of the New York City Marathon each of the past ten years, began the race with all of the other runners and vowed not to stop until she had completed the twenty-six-mile course. She walked through the night and required assistance in clearing traffic from the roads that were a marathon track just one day prior. A day after the race had been run, Koplowitz crossed the finish line. To intrigued spectators and reporters she declared, "People need to know that success isn't always about winning." Nearly twelve thousand runners ran in the 102nd Boston Marathon, but none of them gave a more significant showing.[1078]

Suffering According to a recent Gallup poll, four out of ten Americans feel pain every day, and half of them don't seek medical help.[1079]

Suffering Experts estimate that persistent physical pain costs around $100 billion a year in lost productivity.[1080]

Suffering In a interview about his Parkinson's disease, Billy Graham said, "I think God sent it to me at this age to show me I am totally dependent on him." Suffering is a feared intruder to us all, but it can bring the benefit of greater dependence on God.[1081]

Suffering On July 17, 1996, TWA Flight 800 suddenly exploded just minutes after takeoff. Before the lengthy investigation determined the disaster was caused by a mechanical failure in the fuel tanks, there was strong belief that a terroristic act downed the large 747. During those first few days, William Kalaidjian tried to help the families deal with their intense grief. This senior chaplain for the New York police department told the heartbroken families, "This is not an act of God. This is what happens when people have no God." Reverend Kalaidjian's words are well stated and address the frequent blame that is leveled at God when tragedy occurs.[1082]

Suffering You may recall Ted Turner's comment in 1990 when he said, "Christianity is a religion for losers." He later made a public apology and the whole situation got a few researchers digging into Turner's past. Some speculated that his comment was rooted in an upbringing that did not include religion. To the contrary, Turner grew up in a Christian home and once planned to be a missionary. He later distanced himself from the faith because he "couldn't reconcile the concept of an all-powerful God with so much suffering on earth." Suffering is truly a difficult aspect of life, but it need not be a point of eternal stumbling—at least that's what Paul said in Romans 8:18 (See 2 Corinthians 11:24–28).[1083]

Suicide Every day in America, 84 people take their own life. Suicide is the eighth largest killer in the United States with an estimated 765,000 Americans attempting to kill themselves each year and 30,500 actually succeeding. This tragedy has an expanding impact as each suicide is known to closely affect at least 6 people. Of unique interest is the reality that divorced men and women attempt suicide at a rate 2.5 times higher than those who are married. Singles have a 50 percent higher likelihood of contemplating suicide than people in a marriage.[1084]

Suicide The suicide rate in America is 12 per 100,000. In Japan it's 17.2 per 100,000 and Finland's rate is 27.3.[1085]

Sunday Church leaders hear this all the time: "It's just so hard to get the kids up and dressed in time for Sunday school." The next time that sad excuse floats your way, take a minute to tell those struggling parents about Kenny and Bobbi McCaughey. Most people will remember they are the couple who made medical history on November 19, 1997, by giving birth to the world's first surviving septuplets. Imagine what it must be like to get seven babies ready for church. Most of us would probably just settle for a good TV preacher until the kids were old enough to dress themselves. Yet because of the commitment the McCaugheys made on their wedding day, church is an integral part of their lives. Seven newborns did not change that conviction. Every Sunday morning and evening they load up the family and head to the Missionary Baptist Church in their town of Carlisle, Iowa. And to top it off, it's a well-known fact in their church that the McCaugheys are often the first family to arrive for Sunday School at 9:30 A.M. But enough about them, tell me again about the problems your having getting your three kids ready for Sunday school.[1086]

Sunday For some folks it's just another day of the week, but to Truett Cathy, Sunday is very special. In May, 1996, Cathy celebrated his fiftieth anniversary in the restaurant business. The seventy-five-year-old entrepreneur made up his mind at age eight that he was going to have his own business. In between selling soft drinks and throwing newspapers, the young Cathy regularly attended Sunday school. At twelve, he made a profession of faith in Jesus Christ. To him it was just the natural thing to do. After a hitch in the military, Cathy and his brother pooled their resources to open the Dwarf House restaurant in Southwest Atlanta. He determined then that he would not work on Sunday. "Sunday had been a special day for me when I was a child and I didn't want to be robbed of that day." As a businessman, his logic is brilliant: "If it takes seven days to make a living, I ought to be doing something else." In the Dwarf House he developed the Chick-fil-A sandwich, and by 1967 he opened his first restaurant with this single big seller. Although the road has not always been easy, Chick-fil-A is a leader in the fast-food industry. In Cathy's book, *It's Easier to Succeed Than to Fail,* he intentionally communicated to the business world that religion and business not only mix, but are a good mix. "I believe that Sunday should be honored and set aside for employees to worship God, to rest and to spend time with their families. Our track record proves that in the vast majority of malls we are the food sales leader even though we are open only six days." On Sundays, Truett Cathy isn't at the shop, he's working at his church doing what he's done for over three decades—teaching a Sunday School class for thirteen-year-old boys. He shares with them that the three most important decisions they will make are: Who will be my Master? What will be my mission in life? Who will be my mate? As he says, "All of us were created in the image and the likeness of our Creator. It puts a responsibility on us to be our very best at all times." Making Sunday special is part of our responsibility "to be our very best."[1087]

Sunday He's rich and smart, but Bill Gates may not be very wise. The Bible tells us it is foolish to disobey the Lord's commands but that's what

Gates seems intent on doing when it comes to the Fourth Commandment. In an interview with *Time* magazine, Gates said, "Just in terms of allocation of time resources, religion is not very efficient. There's a lot more I could be doing on a Sunday morning." No doubt, we all could be doing other things on Sunday, but God has called all of humanity to set aside daily routines once a week and worship him.[1088]

Sunday If a person isn't in church, what are they doing? Leisure Trends research discovered the answer to that question and highlighted the top three events Americans pursue most on Sundays. Like any other day, TV topped the list, but interestingly enough, it consumes less leisure time on Sundays than other days of the week. Socializing ranks second on the list. Americans spend an average of three and one-half hours socializing on Sundays. Again, that's more than any other day of the week. Reading comes in third with an average of two hours spent on the newspaper or a good book. Sunday finds more people reading than any other day of the week. For the millions of Americans who don't attend church, Sunday is still a day that is uniquely different from all other days of the week.[1089]

Superstition Superstitious beliefs have made it impossible to get a hotel room on the thirteenth floor because that number is skipped when counting the floors of a high-rise building. Mild superstition may also cause you to think twice before leaving your car on space thirteen in a parking garage, but the powers of evil use superstition in mighty ways to imprison the beliefs and actions of many people. During July of 2000, this was made very evident through a most bizarre wedding ceremony in Mohanpur, India. In this village just thirty-five miles north of Calcutta, a four-year-old girl was married to a stray dog for the purpose of removing an evil influence on her life. Anju Karmakar had suffered fractured bones, several illnesses, a severe burn, and once fell into a pond. An astrologer advised her Hindu father, Subal Karmakar, that a wedding ceremony would transfer the evil effects of the planet Saturn from the girl to the dog. So with over 150 guests present, Hindu priests chanted hymns while the little girl and dog were married. One resident who attended the ceremony said, "He is superstitious, but why should I care if he wants to waste money and give us a feast." In response to such criticism, the young bride's father replied, "I did the right thing for my child. My grandfather had arranged a marriage of a relative with a dog forty years ago and the remedy worked." Experiences like this remind us why Jesus said he came to set the captives free.[1090]

Taxes Although Americans lead the world in tax compliance, dishonesty on tax returns robs the IRS of $80 billion a year—enough to fund the salaries and benefits of the entire U.S. military.[1091]

Taxes In 1913, the sixteenth Amendment brought federal income tax into existence. At that time one senator spoke these words in opposition to the new tax: "If we allow this 1 percent foot in the door, at some future date it might rise to 5 percent.[1092]

Taxes The botanical name for the yew that is used extensively for shrubbery around Washington government buildings is "Taxus."[1093]

Teachability Teachability isn't about a teacher's skills, it's about the student's skills. Nan-in was a Japanese master during the Meiji era (1868–1912). On one occasion he received a professor who had come under the pretense of wanting to learn about Zen. As they sat down for tea, Nan-in served his visitor tea. He began pouring from the teakettle, but did not stop after the man's cup was full. He just kept on pouring. Finally the professor yelled, "It's full! No more will go in!" Nan-in then carefully set down the tea and said, "Like this cup, you are full of your own opinions and speculations. How can I show you Zen unless you first empty your cup?" To grow as Christians, we must empty our hearts and minds of our own opinions about God and let the Holy Spirit fulfill the prayer of Paul, "that you may be filled up to all the fullness of God" (Ephesians 3:19). By way of contrast, the goal of Zen is to become empty. The goal of Christianity is to become empty so you can be filled with the righteousness of God.[1094]

Technology One of those little greeting cards that plays "Happy Birthday," has more computer processing power than existed in the entire world before 1950.[1095]

Teenagers American teenagers had a combined income of $105 billion in 1996.[1096]

Teenagers In 1940, a national survey done by Purdue University revealed that one-third of American teenagers agreed that the number one problem facing them was acne.[1097]

Teenagers Teenagers accounted for $109 billion in purchases in 1995.[1098]

Teenagers The Search Institute surveyed twenty-three hundred Christian teenagers and discovered that 74 percent want to learn friendship-making skills, 71 percent want to learn to know and love Jesus, 69 percent want to learn more about who God is, 68 percent want to learn to make decisions about right and wrong, 65 percent want to gain a sense of purpose in their lives, and 61 percent want to develop more compassion and concern for people.[1099]

Television A few years ago, one well-known minister called for a fast from television. Several reasons supported his stance. Americans spend 250 billion hours a year in front of the TV. If that same time was spent working for $5 an hour, U.S. wages would jump $1.25 trillion (if you counted one number per second, 24 hours a day, it would take you forty thousand years to reach 1.25 trillion). In a survey of four-to six-year-olds, 54 percent chose TV over spending time with their father. *TV Guide* surveyed American adults and discovered that 25 percent would not permanently give up TV even if they were given $1 million to do so.[1100]

Television Each night on prime-time television, about 350 characters are seen. On average, seven of these characters are murdered every night. If this same ratio was applied to reality, everyone in the United States would be killed in just fifty days.[1101]

Television Forty-three percent of Americans watch soap operas at least one day a week.[1102]

Television Groucho Marx was ahead of his time. He said, "I find television very educational. Every time someone switches it on I go into another room and read a good book." With the ongoing deterioration of morals in television, it is interesting to know that in America 98 percent of the homes have a TV but only 96 percent have an indoor toilet. As Bob DeMoss notes, "This is the first time in history we have more garbage coming into our homes than flowing out of them."[1103]

Television Jim Davis had an interesting thought about TV in his syndicated comic strip, *Garfield*. The lazy cat was watching TV when the news came on. The reporter opened the newscast with these words,

"There's no news today because everybody everywhere spent all day watching TV."[1104]

Television The average American will, in the course of a lifetime, spend thirteen years watching TV.[1105]

Temptation In 1 Peter 5:8, the apostle classified Satan as a "roaring lion looking for someone to devour." This verse took on new meaning after interviewing a man who had just returned from Africa. He noted lions are nocturnal animals and most of their hunting is done at night. A conversation with my friends at the Houston Public Library Research Center confirmed his insight. Lions do not hunt exclusively at night, but most of their hunting does occur under the cloak of darkness. Their eyesight is designed for preying on unsuspecting victims in the dark. No wonder Peter spoke of the deceiver as a lion. It was in the dark, away from Christ, that he fell prey to the temptation of denial. When we drift from the light and start loitering in the shadows we become easy prey for the lurking lion. Stay out of the dark and you will have a much greater chance of staying alive.[1106]

Temptation Research scientists have discovered an interesting truth about temptation through experimentation with laboratory rats and alcohol. Through lengthy tests, it has been proven that rats drink more alcohol when the lights are turned down. Like rats, we also succumb to temptation more easily when we allow the light of Christ's Lordship to grow dim in our lives.[1107]

Temptation Scripture reminds us of the danger in thinking something could never happen to us. On October 26, 2000, Destiny Lopez began the day as any other first-grader at Youens Elementary School in Alief, Texas. By 2:20 P.M. that afternoon, everything had changed. She was walking up to her teacher's desk to turn in an assignment when she tripped and fell on her pencil. The pencil pierced her abdomen and traveled into the right ventricle of her heart. The wound was bloodless as the pencil plugged the hole it created. Destiny's teacher, Terry Kirksey, reacted like a pro and used the classroom phone to call for help. She dismissed the other students to another class, then lay on the floor next to Destiny and kept her calm by talking about Barbie, Barney, and what they had done that day. Paramedics arrived quickly and took the little girl to Ben Taub Hospital where open heart surgery was performed to remove the pencil. Destiny has now recovered and is trying to once again be just a normal kid. Imagine a child nearly stabbing herself to death by simply tripping on her way to the teacher's desk. It just doesn't seem possible, but it happened. Temptation can approach us in the same way. What seems like an impossible trap can quickly become a potentially lethal snare (1 Corinthians 10:12).[1108]

Temptation "The devil will always have a ship ready when a man wants to sail away from God." —*Billy Graham* [1109]

Ten Commandments Everyone is familiar with the Ten Commandments, but most of us don't know much about the Ted commandments. In response to his frustrations about religion, Ted Turner compiled what he calls ten "voluntary initiatives." He said, "I'm just sick of all-isms, whether it's Catholicism, Protestantism, communism, or capitalism, because everybody always thinks their-ism is better than everybody else's-ism." Consequently, he penned his own values after noting, "There is no amendment procedure to the Ten Commandments." He said he believes some of those commands are "obsolete." So, in 1989, he wrote his own and now carries them in his wallet. His list begins with "love and respect the planet Earth and all living things thereon, especially my fellow species, mankind." Number three is a "promise to have no more than one child." The final directive calls for allegiance and loyalty not to a god or government, but to "the United Nations and its efforts to collectively improve the conditions of the planet." Like so many, Turner has failed to hear and believe Jesus' declaration that God's law remains unchanged until the end of time (Matthew 5:18).[1110]

Ten Commandments Several years ago, Chuck Colson, founder of Prison Fellowship, was speaking before a board of newspaper editors. During the question and answer time, one man boasted of his success in leading a campaign to remove the Ten Commandments from his city's schoolroom walls. Yet within fifteen minutes this same man was bemoaning the high rate of violence and theft that has infected our schools. Colson seized the moment with Columbolike inquisition. He replied, "Hmmm, maybe you should put a sign on the wall: 'You shall not steal.'" The newspaper editor became embarrassed when he finally made the connection. Our society has come to what Attorney Phillip Johnson calls the modernist impasse. We want freedom from all restraints, but we want protection from the violence and injustice created by the absence of these restraints. The two ideals are not only incompatible, but illogical as well. It is just as Augustine wrote, "The consequences of sin are sin."[1111]

Testimony The ceiling of New York's Grand Central Terminal received a $4.4 million cleaning. In October of 1995, Marina Yashina and Mary Flinn started cleaning the 1945 mural under which half a million people walk, or run, to catch trains each day. They removed fifty-two years of residue from diesel fumes, cigarette smoke, steel dust, and floating dirt. In one spot they found a half-inch-thick layer of grime. To make certain their work doesn't go unnoticed, they left a spot. They purposefully did not clean an eight-by-three-foot section of the mural. Marina Yashina, a Moscow native who helped restore the Kremlin, said, "If we don't leave something dirty, people will forget how it looked before." Our testimony should be something like that old train station's cleaned mural. We need to remember just enough of our life without Christ so we won't be tempted to return to the filth of our sin.[1112]

Testimony Tony Campolo has recalled an experience of being a counselor for a junior high camp. He noted, "Everybody should do it . . . just once." At this awkward age kids can be extremely cruel and this camp was no exception. A boy named Billy was one of the campers and he had cerebral palsy. He instantly became the target of nearly every joke. They mocked the way he walked and the labored manner in which he spoke. Maybe the cruelest trick occurred when it was time for Billy's cabin to give camp devotions. The kids elected Billy to be the speaker. Campolo said he raged with anger because they only did this so they could make fun of him. At the appointed time, Billy lumbered forward with his unusual gait. Snickers could be heard all across the crowd. Once he made it to the front, it literally took him several minutes just to say seven words. With all of his energy and heart he stammered out, "Jesus . . . loves . . . me . . . and . . . I . . . love . . . Jesus." By the time he finished that one sentence, kids were bawling and revival broke out. Campolo remembers how they brought in celebrity speakers to impact those kids for Christ, but it was the powerful testimony of Billy that connected them to God. Since that time, he recalls the different times throughout his travels that he has met a missionary or pastor who asks, "Do you remember me? I was converted at that junior high camp." The power of a Christlike life is limitless.[1113]

Thankfulness Margaret Craven wrote a novel titled *I Heard the Owl Call My Name*. In this book she tells of a young minister who was sent to the Kwakiutl Indians in a remote part of British Columbia. Through the course of his ministry, he learned these people do not have a word for "thank you." It was confusing to the young man because these tribesmen were extremely generous. He later discovered why the important word was absent from their vocabulary. It was their custom to return every favor with a favor of their own, and every kindness with an equal or superior gesture of love. Mark Brian, the young minister, realized they don't say "thank you," because they *do* their thanks. Advocating the dismissal of an indispensable phrase wouldn't be prudent, but the addition of such a custom would truly give new meaning to our expressions of gratitude.[1114]

Thanksgiving During his years in the White House, President Harry Truman began an unusual Thanksgiving tradition. Every year since, United States presidents have used the Wednesday before Thanksgiving to pardon a turkey. A preselected bird is brought into the Rose Garden and the Commander in Chief grants that big bird a pardon. The saved turkey is then ushered to a Virginia farm where he is granted immunity from the carving knife. This crazy ritual always provides levity for those who watch, but it also gives each of us a great reminder at Thanksgiving. But for the grace of God, we are all turkeys headed to slaughter. Our merits haven't gained his favor. It is simply by his pardon alone that we are saved. It's a Thanksgiving reminder we can't afford to forget.[1115]

Thanksgiving In August of 1620, Puritans from England left their homes and comforts to begin a new life in the New World. They boarded two small ships, the Speedwell and the Mayflower, to pursue religious freedom in America. Not long after leaving, the Speedwell developed leaks. Most of her passengers and crew transferred over to the Mayflower before the Speedwell turned back. A total of 102 Pilgrims suffered through sixty-seven days of rough sailing before they arrived at Plymouth Bay in November. There was nobody to greet them, no stores for supplies, nor homes to buy. They endured the hardship of a very cold winter and the perils of sickness. At one point, only 6 people were well enough to care for the sick and dying. By March of the following year, only 51 of the original 102 Pilgrims were still alive and it would be another two years before a ship arrived with more supplies. Nonetheless, these brave pioneers celebrated their newfound freedom to worship as they desired. This may have been a difficult year for you, but the fact remains, we still have much for which we can be thankful. Even in hardship we can rest on the promise of God's presence and plan as defined in Philippians 1:6.[1116]

Thanksgiving Too often our gratitude is dependent on the circumstances of life. A beautiful hymn to counteract such thinking was written by Martin Rinkart during the Thirty Year's War (1618–48). Rinkart was a pastor in Saxony, Germany, as these turbulent years unfurled, and for a season he was the only pastor in Eilenburg. His pastoral duties caused him to preside at nearly forty-five hundred burials in 1637 alone. In the context of this calamitous era, Rinkart penned the words to "Now Thank We All Our God." It is a hymn of unconditional gratitude to God. Whether or not you know this hymn, the background of its authorship provides a good motive for learning it during the Thanksgiving season.[1117]

Theft Burglars hit more than five million U.S. homes per year and steal more than $4 billion in property.[1118]

Theft In 1995, retailers lost an estimated $30 billion to theft by employees and customers. Such shoplifting increases the cost of goods by as much as 15 percent.[1119]

Thinking "A great many people think they are thinking when they are merely rearranging their prejudices." —*William James*[1120]

Thinking As a Congressman, Gary Franks represented the people of Connecticut. His experience on Capitol Hill was enhanced by a lesson he learned in college. While studying for his first test at Yale, he reviewed his very meticulous notes. He had written down virtually everything the teacher had said. For the exam he reiterated what he had written down in class. He left that examination confident he had secured an A, and thought college was going to be a breeze. To his chagrin, he received a C. The teacher used big, red letters to write, "I know what I said. What do you think?" Sometimes our opinions and convictions are little more than the recitation of what someone else believes. Convictions are formed through careful thought, not rote memorization.[1121]

Thoughts The average human being has around fifty thousand thoughts per day.[1122]

Time During the Civil Rights Movement, Martin Luther King spent time behind bars. During his incarceration in a Birmingham jail, the wise leader lamented, "I am coming to feel that the people of ill will have used time much more effectively than the people of good will." God's people are called to use time more wisely than those who wield a worldly agenda.[1123]

Time During the first weekend of April, people "spring ahead" to set their timepieces for daylight savings time. Two children were huddled around a watch as they worked to make the time change. The older brother instructed his sister that not everyone has to adjust their watch. He said, "Granddad doesn't have to set his watch because he's on eternal standard time." Successfully moving through a time change is important, but of far greater concern is the task of making sure our soul is ready for the shift to eternal standard time.[1124]

Time Management A seminary-preaching professor once conducted a secret experiment with his students. The entire class was to preach on the Good Samaritan. On the day that the sermons were to begin, the professor planted an indigent man in the corridor leading from their classroom to the preaching room. The teacher then scheduled students to preach at certain times. After they were assigned their time slot, they were to walk over to the preaching room. Each student had to file pass this indigent man who was in obvious need. As part of the experiment, the professor gave some students more time than others to get from one room to the other. Some had ample time to complete their task while others were pressed for time. The end results showed that the tighter the schedule the less likely people were to stop and help. Even with good intentions in our hearts, if our schedules are too full we will crowd out opportunities for ministry.[1125]

Time Management Have you ever sounded like Joshua asking for a little extra time (Joshua 10:12–13)? If you follow the advice of some experts, you will need to pray that the sun will stand still every day. *USA Today* asked experts from various fields to chart how much time was needed for accomplishing the necessities of daily life. These experts noted how much time was needed for such activities as exercise, hygiene, work and commuting, domestic chores and maintenance, eating, entertainment, spiritual development, sleep, family time, and so on. When these figures were all added together, the experts' suggested times for a normal day equaled forty-two hours. No wonder we're always exhausted and behind, we're trying to do more than is physically possible.[1126]

Tithing "A lot of people are willing to give God credit, but so few ever give him cash." —*Anonymous* [1127]

Tithing Protestants now bring less than 2.5 percent of their household income to church. In the Great Depression they gave 3.3 percent.[1128]

Tithing The average Evangelical Protestant church member gives 4 percent of his income to the church.[1129]

Titles "A judge is merely a lawyer who has been benched." —*Judge Charles Clark* [1130]

Tolerance Alan Wolfe is a leading sociologist from Boston University who spent two years in suburban America engaging people in lengthy dialogue about their beliefs, fears, and dreams. The end result was his book, *One Nation, After All.* Wolfe said most Americans are embracing three central values: God, family, and country. But he also notes we seem to have created an "Eleventh Commandment: 'Thou shalt not judge.'" Wolfe has confirmed what Josh McDowell has been heralding for several years—our country has embraced a new value called tolerance. Wolfe helps us to see that philosophers have long recognized tolerance is an important virtue, but it should not always have precedence over values. As David Gergen, editor at large for *U.S. News & World Report*, notes, "Some things are just plain wrong, and we should condemn them." Wolfe concurs by writing, "Morality is not meant to please [intellectual critics]. It is instead meant to work." Gergen insightfully declares, "There may indeed be too much pluribus and not enough unum in our public discourse . . ." Tolerance of truth must be defended, tolerance of sin must not![1131]

Tradition An interesting experiment with monkeys communicates volumes about tradition. Four monkeys were placed in a confine with one pole in the center. At the top of the pole was a bunch of bananas. One monkey soon scampered up that pole for the bananas, but just before reaching the prize, he received a blast of cold water from a showerhead over the bananas. He quickly retreated down the pole and abandoned his quest for the food. In turn, each of the remaining three monkeys climbed the pole and got the same result. After repeated attempts, the four monkeys quit trying to retrieve the bananas. The scientists then replaced one of the monkeys with a new recruit. When he started for the pole, the other three original monkeys quickly prevented his attempted climb. He soon got the message that the pole was prohibited. One by one, each of the original three monkeys were replaced by new ones. Every time the new monkey went for the pole, the others stopped him. Eventually, the room contained four monkeys who had never experienced the cold blast of water, but they wouldn't venture up the pole for those bananas. Tradition had been established and they wouldn't break it. Rich tradition should never be discarded just because it's no longer new, but it should not be maintained just because it's comfortable and familiar. This little experiment reminds us we can be like primates when we simply dismiss an idea with that old cliché, "We've always done it like this."[1132]

Transformation Antonio Stradivarius was an Italian violin maker who lived from 1644–1737. His violins are now the most prized violins ever made because of the rich and resonating sound they produce. The unique sound of a Stradivarius violin cannot be duplicated. Surprisingly, these precious instruments were not made from treasured pieces of wood, but instead were carved from discarded lumber. Stradivarius, who was very poor and could not afford fine materials like his contemporaries, got most of his wood from the dirty harbors where he lived. He would take those waterlogged pieces of wood to his shop, clean them up, and from those pieces of trashed lumber, he would create instruments of rare beauty. It has since been discovered that while the wood floated in those dirty harbors, microbes went into the wood and ate out the center of those cells. This left just the fibrous infrastructure of the wood that created resonating chambers for the music. From wood that nobody wanted, Stradivarius produced violins that everybody wants. Just as this poor violin maker transformed trash into treasures, God can and wants to transform every one of us into the treasured image of his Son, Jesus Christ. He can rescue us from the sludge of our sin and transform us into instruments of beauty and grace.[1133]

Transformation Cassie Bernall was the seventeen-year-old student who died for her faith in Columbine High School on April 20, 1999. Fellow students, Eric Harris and Dylan Klebold, stormed the school and gunned down twelve students and one teacher before taking their own lives. Cassie was the brave young lady who took a bullet because of her faith in Christ. One of the gunman had yelled, "Anybody in here believe in God?" With all of the students lying on the floor, Cassie stood up and replied, "Yes, I believe in God. I belong to the Lord Jesus." The young killer then asked, "Why?" but shot her before she could answer. This radiant teenager died a martyr, but just a few years prior she might have been an accomplice to such a massacre. When Cassie was in the ninth grade, her parents, Brad and Misty Bernall, became very concerned about their daughter's behavior. They discovered she was interested in witchcraft and involved with alcohol and drugs. When they searched her room they found letters that talked about harming parents and other people. The Bernalls immediately intervened. Cassie was enrolled in another school and cut off from friends who had exerted evil influence. They regularly searched her belongings and monitored her activities. Apart from school, she could only attend their church, West Bowles Community Church in Littleton, Colorado. Cassie reluctantly went on a weekend youth retreat that changed her life. Her dad said she went away as a gloomy, troubled teen and came back transformed by the power of Jesus Christ. She discovered the joy of salvation that she carried to her early grave. Her transformation can be summarized by the words she shared on a video just two days before her death. She said, "You really can't live without Christ. It's like, impossible to really have a really true life without him." Just two years earlier, Cassie Bernall was very similar to Eric Harris and Dylan Klebold, but Jesus Christ changed all of that. We can't help but ask the same question posed by Baptist Standard editor, Marv Knox who wrote, "One wonders how thousands of lives might be different today if the parents of Harris and Klebold had intervened in their lives, if those boys had been exposed to the sweet gospel of Jesus in a loving church youth group."[1134]

Transformation In 1989, Phil Brewster was standing in front of a chipped, scratched chalkboard nailed to a post in a barrio. This missionary was teaching a seminary extension course when he was handed a new piece of chalk from a student. Brewster noted the chalk was different from what he usually used so he asked the student where he obtained the chalk. The pastor smiled and explained, "When we gave up our idols, we broke them up. Now we use them for chalk." What a statement of God's transforming power. Broken idols are now being used as chalk to teach about the one true God.[1135]

Transformation Most people know the Wesley brothers transformed some barroom melodies into beautiful hymns. Another unusual twist to their transformations is the unique desk that John Wesley used to accomplish such tasks. The desk in his study, which is on display at his old home in London, once belonged to a bookie. The desk was originally designed for taking bets, but it was transformed into a place of holy words. The same wood that handled the bets of men was used to pen some of the greatest sermons about God's wager against sin. What is true of Wesley's desk can be true of anyone who allows the Carpenter of Nazareth to refinish their life with the cleansing power of his sacrificial blood.[1136]

Transformation Tony Campolo has told a stirring story about a drunk who was miraculously converted at a Bowery mission. Prior to Joe's conversion, he was viewed as a hopeless, dirty wino. It seemed as though his existence in the ghetto would fade away one night in a drunken stupor. But God had a different plan for Joe. He made a life-changing commitment to Christ and was supernaturally transformed. He became a compassionate and caring person who spent his days helping in the mission. No task was too lowly for Joe. He cleaned up the vomit of alcoholics, scrubbed down the restrooms of careless drunks, assisted men into bed when they were too drunk to find their bunk, and always maintained a smile that communicated his gratitude for being able to help. One night when the mission's director was giving an evangelistic appeal, a repentant drunk came to the altar and began to pray. He prayed, "Oh God, make me like Joe. Please make me like Joe!" He shouted this prayer over and over. Finally, the director stepped down and said, "I think it would be better if you prayed, 'Make me like Jesus!'" The man looked up and asked, "Is he like Joe?" If a person didn't know about Jesus, would he want to be like you?[1137]

Trust What's the best way to increase the financial resources of your church? Trust! A recent study examined the Assemblies of God, the Southern Baptist Convention, The Evangelical Lutheran Church in America, the Presbyterian Church (U.S.A.), and the Roman Catholic Church. Researchers discovered that the church's size, style of government, or denominational positions have little impact on giving. Initially, they thought democratic procedures encouraged giving but found it to be secondary. "What is crucial is trust in leadership, in whoever has the power in the congregation, whether clergy or lay leaders. If trust is missing, giving will be low." Members give freely to their churches when they trust the leadership and have feelings of community and ownership.[1138]

Trust While serving as a missionary for the Southern Baptist International Mission Board, Lanette Thompson provided an insightful truth about trust. Because Africa is not a safe environment, she was regularly approached by people who said, "In order for you to go to West Africa, I guess you just have to trust in God's protection." Her response is shocking but true. She has answered this question by stating, "I can show you the grave of a fifteen-year-old missionary's child who died of hepatitis and a four-year-old who died of malaria. If my trust were in God's protection, my trust would crumble under such circumstances. My trust is in God, in the belief that he is in control and that whatever happens will happen for his glory." We can mistakenly place our trust in God's protection rather than God himself. The results of such misplaced trust will ultimately lead to spiritual disillusionment.[1139]

Truth Abraham Lincoln once used a very clever ploy to teach some people about truth. They had come to him with a decision that was based on suppositions rather than truth. After hearing their logic, Lincoln asked, "How many legs would a sheep have if you called its tail a leg?" They quickly answered, "Five!" The President then said, "No, it would only have four legs. Calling a tail a leg doesn't make it one." The doctrine of salvation has been given many tails by those who think they are creating new legs. In truth, salvation has but one leg and that is a large, wooden beam upon which the Savior of the world was slain. Call the truth what you wish, but the fact remains, "There is salvation in no one else!" (Acts 4:12)[1140]

Truth "If you tell the truth, you don't have to remember anything." —*Mark Twain*[1141]

Truth "It is always the best policy to speak the truth, unless of course you are an exceptionally good liar." —*Jerome K. Jerome*[1142]

Truth There is a vast difference between truth, and the perception of truth. In a survey of American health, it was learned that 40 percent of overweight men thought they looked fine and "felt they were at about the right weight." In contrast, 29 percent of women who were not overweight "felt they needed to lose pounds to achieve a healthy body weight." Both groups were operating under the perception of truth rather than truth itself. Such thinking leads to erroneous behavior.[1143]

Truth Two college students learned a hard lesson about telling the truth while attending Duke University. They were both A students but got carried away at an out-of-town party the night before their final chemistry exam. They missed the exam and started scrambling for a "justifiable" excuse. After collaborating on their story, they went to see the professor. They explained how they were out of town and could not return in time because they had a flat tire. With this logic, they asked for a chance to take a make-up test. The professor agreed and prepared a special test. He assigned them to different rooms and unveiled their personalized final exams. On the front page was a simple chemistry question worth five points. On the back page was the second and final question. It was worth ninety-five points. The question simply asked, "Which tire was flat?" Those two students may not remember much about chemistry, but they sure won't forget their education in honesty.[1144]

Understanding Isn't it amazing how easily criticism can roll from our lips when we see the unusual behavior of another person? Mary Lou Lacy has presented an insightful illustration that helps us realize there may be a good reason for the behavior we don't condone. Imagine a group of fish swimming together in a school. All of them are moving in the same direction with comparable style when suddenly one of them starts destroying the unity. He begins to twist and swerve from side to side with precarious moves. The older fish are annoyed with the nonconformity of this immature adolescent. They show their disapproval while voicing disgust, "We don't swim like that around here." Turning to their offspring, they declare, "That type of behavior is totally unacceptable." Before they can take action against the renegade fish, his thrashing tail disappears at the surface of the lake. A hook in his mouth rather than rebellion in his heart was the cause of all his distasteful activity. How many times have we been equally guilty of displaying our displeasure when someone wrestling with a hook needed a friend to understand their painful predicament? There may be a much deeper explanation for the behavior that we quickly dismiss as "wrong."[1145]

Urgency Secured to most cars is a vivid reminder that life is much briefer than we expect. When you change lanes to the right, a convex mirror on the passenger's side reminds you that "objects are closer than they appear." Not only is that true on the road, but it's equally true in life. We frequently live with the erroneous belief that there will be plenty of time to encourage a friend, communicate our love to a spouse or child, share the gospel with a lost world, or develop Godly traits. The truth is, the window of opportunity through which we must accomplish these tasks is far closer than it appears. As Amy Carmichael, the stalwart Christian saint, has said, "We will have all of eternity to celebrate victories, but only a few hours before sunset in which to win them." Life's opportunities are closer than they appear so live each day with Christlike urgency.[1146]

Value The pastor held up a brand new $50 bill and asked if anyone in the congregation would like to have it. Every hand went up. He then wadded the bill into a grumbled mess. The new bill now looked old and worn. "Does anybody want it now?" he asked. The same number of hands rose with the offer. He then said, "But wait." He dropped the $50 and ground it into the floor with his shoe. The money was now dirty, wrinkled, and slightly frayed. "Surely nobody wants this thing now," he suggested. But every person raised their hand because they saw the truth of his point. The money was not devalued because of dirt or condition. It was still worth the same as a brand new bill. When we likewise make poor decisions or stumble with mistakes, we don't lose our value to God.[1147]

Values Janice Hume, an assistant journalism professor at Kansas State University, did some very interesting research for her doctoral dissertation. She spent more than a year studying over eight thousand obituaries from various periods of U.S. history. Concerning her work she said, "I'm using obituaries as a little window to look at cultural values." That tiny window ultimately startled Hume. She discovered that the obituaries of the nineteenth century focused on the deceased's character, while the twentieth century notices detailed the dead person's work and wealth. She noted, "It was such a stark contrast between remembering someone for their strong character and remembering someone for the size of his bank account." From a very unlikely source we can gaze into a mirror that reveals our cultural values and see the need for significant change.[1148]

Vanity In December of 1999, Jennifer Lopez insured her body for $1 billion. It is believed to be the biggest such policy ever taken out by a celebrity. A publicist for the movie star said, "Her looks are her fortune and she wants reassurance that, if something goes wrong, she will be well covered." Ms. Lopez's insurance policy is a reflection of our cultural values and priorities.[1149]

Victorious Living Most people recall the infamous "seven last words" of the church, "We've never done it this way before!" Leonard Sweet placed an interesting twist on this phrase and called it the "first seven words" of victorious living. This septet of words is taken from Philippians 4:13, "I can do all things through Christ." Victorious living declares, "We've never done it this way before, but through Christ, we can do all things . . . even this."[1150]

Violence Gunshot violence in the United States costs $20 billion a year. That's $200 per household.[1151]

Violence In America, forty-six hundred children die as a result of guns each year. That translates to one American child being killed by gunfire every two hours. Placed within a different perspective, this means the fourteen students who died at Columbine High School in Littleton, Colorado, on April 20, 1999, represent the daily average of nonadults killed by guns every day of the year in America. Apparently we have not yet realized that the equivalent carnage of Columbine occurs each and every day within the United States's borders.[1152]

Violence In a recent study of gun-related deaths in thirty-six of the world's richest countries, the United States had the highest fatality rate with 14.2 gun-related deaths per one hundred thousand people. The U.S. accounted for 45 percent of the *total* gun-related deaths in *all* thirty-six countries.[1153]

Violence The genocide of over five hundred thousand people in Rwanda during 1994 left over three hundred thousand children orphaned. In 1999, there were 65,000 children as the heads of households in Rwanda.[1154]

Vision "A man is what he thinks about all day long." —*Ralph Waldo Emerson* [1155]

Vision "If your vision is for a year . . . plant wheat. If your vision is for ten years . . . plant trees. If your vision is for a lifetime . . . plant people." —*Chinese Proverb* [1156]

Vision In 1999, Apple stock was one of the hottest in the computer industry. Buried in the past of this unique company is an interesting story about vision, or more appropriately, the lack thereof. Ronald Wayne is an unknown name to most people even though he was in the original group who helped launch the novel Apple computer. During those early days, Wayne got cold feet and sold his 10 percent interest in Apple for $800. With a little more vision and foresight he might have seen the wisdom in taking a greater risk with that $800 investment because he could have sold it in 1999 for more than $300 million. Vision, in any field, looks beyond the initial investment and focuses on the long-term dividends.[1157]

Vision "More people are humbugged by believing nothing, than by believing too much." —*P.T. Barnum*[1158]

Vision Stewart Babbage was a great Australian churchman. In his office there were four pictures that looked remarkably the same. Their similarity told a sticking story. When he visited the ancient site of Ur, he climbed on the ruins and pointed his camera to the North, East, South, and West. These four pictures were enlarged and symbolically placed on the walls of his study. Within the frame of each picture there is little to behold. In every direction from Ur there is apparent nothingness. These snapshots were not prized for their aesthetic value, but they were daily reminders of what Abraham saw when God called him to leave. The vision wasn't found on the horizon, but in the patriarch's soul. Godly vision isn't cast on the landscape of certainty. It's forged in the fire of faith.[1159]

Vision "Whatever you can do or dream you can do, begin it. Boldness has genius, power and magic in it." —*Johann Wolfgang von Goethe*[1160]

Vision While serving as the CEO of Pepsi, Wayne Calloway said, "You should have more dreams than memories. If you don't, you're in trouble." Whether casting a vision for your church, business, family, or personal life, keep looking to make more memories rather than just reminiscing over the ones you've already made.[1161]

Visitation Research demonstrates that if lay people will make a fifteen-minute visit in the homes of church guests within thirty-six hours of their first visit, 85 percent of them will return the following week. If the lag time is seventy-two hours, the return rate drops to 60 percent and after one week it slips to 15 percent. If the pastor makes the visit instead of lay people, the percentage that return is about half compared to when the visit is made by a lay person. Herb Miller, the specialist who did this research, said, "No other single factor makes a greater difference in improving annual membership additions than an immediate visit to the homes of first-time worshipers."[1162]

Volunteerism The ratio of people who volunteer for church work is one out of four.[1163]

Volunteerism The Search Institute, based in Minneapolis, recently reported their findings on a study of 625 congregations. The research revealed Southern Baptist church members volunteer an average of 3.4 hours per month for church activities, Assembly of God members volunteer 3.2 hours, Presbyterians (U.S.) and Evangelical Lutherans both average 2.7 hours per month, and Catholics volunteer 1.6 hours of service per month. Researchers estimated the value of church-related volunteerism at $9.60 per hour.[1164]

Walking The average person walks about 115,000 miles in a lifetime.[1165]

War As the millennium came to an end, the combined military expenditures of all the countries in the world was $701 billion. Such spending has not only killed countless people, (over five hundred thousand children are killed or maimed each year in war), but has also resulted in sixty to one hundred million land mines littering the planet. The cost of clearing all these explosives, which kill and maim thousands each year, is estimated to be $33 billion.[1166]

Warnings The blockbuster movie, *Titanic*, certainly didn't sink at the box office. It's mixture of fiction and facts brought the infamous ship back into contemporary conversation. This great tragedy has been used to communicate many lessons. One such lesson involves that of heeding warnings. It is a well-known fact that the huge ship was mortally wounded by an iceberg and that this fate could have easily been prevented if the captain had taken heed to the six separate warnings he received about icebergs. The ship had been counseled to change course and take the southern route, but instead chose to ignore this advice. As Gary Smalley noted, "If you change course when warned, you can avoid disaster, and then celebrate the voyage." Ironically, fourteen years before the Titanic set sail, an amateur writer named Morgan Robertson wrote a novel that closely paralleled the fateful voyage. In *Futility*, the fictitious boat was named *Titan*, it carried about the same number of people as the *Titanic*, it didn't have enough lifeboats, and it sank after hitting an iceberg.[1167]

Warnings There is a constant temptation to soften and dilute warnings in hopes of not sounding to harsh or alarming. The danger of such soft-peddling can be seen in the tobacco industry. In a test of nearly twenty-five hundred children in the United States and Canada, 83 percent could remember the warning on Canadian cigarettes, but only 6 percent were able to recall what was printed on U.S. cigarette packs. The reason is simple, in Canada the warning is clear and direct. On the front of the packet in bold letters read the words, "Smoking can kill you." Softening a deadly message doesn't reduce the danger, it simply increases the risk of people not taking it seriously. That may explain why Edward DeHart died of lung cancer on September 24, 1997. DeHart was a tobacco industry consultant credited with developing the warning labels printed on all cigarette packs sold in the United States. He helped craft the first surgeon general's warning in 1962 while working with the Tobacco Institute. He created a warning that wasn't even convincing enough to make himself stop smoking.[1168]

Water The human body consists of more than 70 percent water. It takes just a 1 percent deficiency to make us thirsty. A 5 percent deficit will bring on a slight fever. At the 8 percent deficiency mark your glands will stop producing saliva and your skin will turn blue. With a 10 percent loss of water a person can no longer walk, and death will occur with just a 12 percent deficiency of water. It's rather remarkable to realize how significantly our bodies are impacted by the smallest reductions of water. Interestingly, Jesus identified himself as the provider of "living water" (John 4:10; 7:38). If we take what we know about the physical property of water along with the impact deficits can have on our bodies, and relate that to the living water that Jesus offers, we suddenly realize how quickly we can become spiritually depleted. Just the slightest deficits of living water can leave us spiritually dehydrated, spiritually debilitated, or spiritually destroyed. "If any man is thirsty, let him come to me and drink" (John 7:37).[1169]

Wealth Andrea Scancarella, age twenty-nine, wasn't going to take any chances on the Y2K problem. The resident of Florence, Italy, went to his bank just three days before the turn of the millennium and withdrew all of his savings. Within a few minutes of making the withdrawal, robbers ripped the bag from his hand as he stood on the sidewalk looking into a shop window. The $5,730 he was preserving from a computer virus was taken by a couple of thieves (Matthew 6:19).[1170]

Weapons of War On November 29, 1947, the United Nations voted to partition Palestine into separate Jewish and Palestinian states. The following day, Swissair flight 442 left Lydda Airport in Tel Aviv for Paris. On board that airplane were two unsuspecting men who were oblivious to the other's presence. Captain Abdul-Aziz Kerine was on a mission for the Syrian government to purchase weapons for an anticipated war with the Jews. Just a few rows away, Ehud Avriel was contemplating a similar mission as David Ben-Gurion had sent him to buy weapons for an expected conflict with the Arabs. After landing in Paris, both men took different routes but ended up at the same place, the Zbrojovka Brno company in Prague, Czechoslovakia. In an irony of ironies, these two men, representing opposing people, flew on the same plane to buy weapons from the same company. Weapons of death and destruction are always purchased from the same vendor, and lasting peace can only be found through the entrance of a single door (John 10:9-10).[1171]

Wedding Vows Fred Smith has been a mentor for many Christian leaders. His success in the business world has added immeasurably to his influence on laymen as well as vocational ministers. When asked about one of his most treasured memories, Smith told of an experience that took place in a doughnut shop in Grand Saline, Texas. A young, farming couple was seated next to his booth. When it came time for them to leave, the woman couldn't get up by herself. This, of course, was no surprise to her husband. He gently picked her up and she placed her arms around his neck. As they moved away from the booth it became evident that she was wearing a full-body brace. The farmer carefully backed his way through the front door of the doughnut shop, then gracefully placed his wife in the passenger seat of their truck. Smith said everyone in the shop was captivated by this beautiful demonstration of love. No one said anything until the waitress remarked, almost reverently, "He took his vows seriously."[1172]

Weirdness Index According to the *Fortean Times*, the world isn't as weird as it used to be. The newspaper's annual weirdness index reported that in 1995, the "strange phenomena" declined 2 percent worldwide. You may have thought the opposite but who can argue with the official "weirdness index?"[1173]

White-Collar Crime *Time* magazine reported that American workers steal $40 billion per year by doing such things as lying about their hours, making personal long-distance calls, and taking office supplies home. That sum is ten times the cost of street crime. In addition, companies lose up to $350 billion annually from employees taking dishonest sick days. Sadly, Christians are included among those that partake in these crimes. Doug Sherman and William Hendricks wrote *Keeping Your Ethical Edge Sharp*. In this book they note, "A growing body of research suggests that religious beliefs and convictions make little difference in the behavior of people on the job." For example, a little boy got caught stealing pencils from school and when his father found out he was enraged. He said, "Why'd you go and do something like that? If you need pencils just tell me . . . I can bring some home from work."[1174]

Wisdom Attorneys are the primary professionals who draft wills. Ironically, though, 80 percent of the lawyers who die in America haven't taken heed to the wisdom of their own field and die without a valid will. Recent studies have also revealed that those who fight germs the most, doctors, often fail to observe the wisdom of the American Medical Association. Doctors wash their hands less than 50 percent of the time before seeing a patient. Ministers are likewise suspect of neglecting the wisdom of their field. Research on the clergy unearthed the fact that 27 percent of pastors don't tithe. Wisdom involves doing what you know to be right.[1175]

Wisdom It has been cleverly noted that when it comes to thinking, there are two kinds of people: those who stop to think, and those who stop thinking. Wisdom comes from the former, never the latter.[1176]

Women "Women are not the opposite sex, they're a whole other species." — *Tim Allen* [1177]

Words Most Americans don't know it, but while serving as president, Bill Clinton carried the results of nuclear disarmament in his golf bag. When the United States signed a treaty in 1986 with the former Soviet Union to begin destroying nuclear weapons, Cary Schuman started thinking about the possibility of getting some missile parts. In 1995, his dream came true and he obtained surplus Russian SS-23 and American

Polaris A-3 missiles. He melted down the parts and used the material to make golf clubs. The end result was his Peace Missile Driver, which our president used from the tee box. Schuman's entrepreneurial spirit reminds us of what can happen when we decide to take destructive elements and recreate them into things of greater peace. By simply taking the everyday weapons of words and converting them to statements of encouragement and affirmation, we can begin to realize a small portion of what Micah saw in the future, "Then they will hammer their swords into plowshares and their spears into pruning hooks . . ." (Micah 4:3).[1178]

Work Although God has ordained work to be a good and productive part of our lives, vocational employment is too frequently interpreted as a necessary evil. In *The One-Minute Manager To Work*, Ken Blanchard highlighted a study which revealed 80 percent of the employees in America are dissatisfied with their work. This may explain why more heart attacks occur on Monday than any other day of the week.[1179]

Work Bill McCartney, former coach of the Colorado Buffaloes, has been used by God to launch the Promise Keeper movement. When he was initially interviewed for the head coaching job at Colorado, he told the search committee that they needed to understand "I am not a coach who happens to be a Christian. I'm a Christian who happens to be a coach." All Christians needs a similar view of their vocation and calling.[1180]

Work In America, the average desk worker has thirty-six hours worth of work on his or her desk and wastes three hours a week just searching for things in the maze of clutter.[1181]

Work On one occasion, Thomas Edison came home very exhausted from an extended season of work. His wife insisted that he needed some rest so she suggested a vacation. Edison mulled it over but wasn't sure where he should go. His wife said, "Just decide where you would rather be more than anywhere else on earth." The great inventor thought about it for a while then replied, "Very well, I'll go there tomorrow." The next morning he set off for . . . his laboratory. Though very exhausting at times, work was a joy and a place of revitalization for Thomas Edison. Vacations are a necessary ingredient for maintaining a balanced perspective on work, especially in our era of rampant workaholism, but it is also healthy to remember work was ordained before the fall of Adam and was intended to give us a level of satisfaction and purpose. So the next time someone near you starts moaning about Mondays, take a minute to tell them about Edison's favorite vacation spot.[1182]

Work The average American work week has increased from 43.6 hours in 1977 to 47.1 hours in 1997.[1183]

Work "The days of maintenance far outnumber the days of magnificence." —*David Davis* [1184]

Work The United Nations's World Employment Report for 1998 states that one billion (one-third or the world's workforce) are either out of work or underemployed. In addition, 150 million workers are unemployed and additional 850 million are underemployed.[1185]

Work "What you're doing is only work if you'd rather be doing something else." —*Thomas Jefferson* [1186]

Work Ethic On March 8, 1999, one of baseball's greatest legends died. At the age of eighty-four, Joe DiMaggio passed away in his Florida home. DiMaggio made a tremendous impact on the game of baseball as his play was nearly flawless and his attitude was impeccable. This popular Hall of Famer may never lose his record for hitting safely in fifty-six consecutive games during 1941, but his work ethic may be what true fans appreciate most about him. Two examples of this were highlighted after his death. One occurred when Chuck Dressen was a New York Yankee coach. Dressen protested an umpire's call by angrily throwing towels from the dugout. DiMaggio quickly reprimanded his coach by saying, "Go out and pick up that stuff now. On this ball club, when we don't like decisions, we don't throw things. We hit home runs." The second event took place during Yogi Berra's rookie year. Berra didn't run full speed to first base after popping up. DiMaggio pulled him aside and said, "You're a Yankee now. You give 100 percent all the time. You run out every popup." Imagine the change in complexion each church would have if every member chose to "hit home runs" instead of complaining about decisions they don't like, and gave 100 percent all the time. With that kind of work ethic we would see far more wins for the cause of Christ.[1187]

Work Ethic The Pennsylvania Department of Transportation had some explaining to do during the summer of 1996. Walter Bortree admitted to the media that there was some sloppy work performed by one of their road crews. Bortree told the press, "Yes, the operator should have seen the deer, and yes, it should have been removed." He was referring to the incident where one of his repair crews paved over a dead deer. In practice, Bortree's experience was quite uncommon, but in principle it wasn't that unusual. Apathetic work ethic will cause any of us to just "pave over the deer" rather than exerting the extra effort to make sure the job is done right. If you're tempted to start creating unplanned speed bumps, fight off the temptation by remembering for whom you really work (Colossians 3:23).[1188]

Works It is not surprising that 55 percent of Americans believe "a good person can earn his way to heaven," but an alarmingly high percentage of professing Christians believe the same thing. Recent studies by George Barna show 40 percent of those in America who say they have committed their life to Jesus Christ agree with the statement, "If you are a good person or do enough good things for others, you can earn a place in heaven." Such thinking runs contrary to the clear teaching of Scripture (Ephesians 2:8–9), dilutes evangelistic fervor, and gives scores of people fictitious hope.[1189]

Works Rick Chollet was a financially successful entrepreneur until March 18, 1991. That's the day that Chollet locked the garage door of his New Hampshire house, climbed into his BMW, and turned on the engine. He left behind a note that read, "Please forgive me, but the thought of going through the torture of living is just too much to bear." Steven Berglas has addressed such tragedy in his book, *The Success Syndrome: Hitting Bottom When You Reach The Top.* Berglas suggests one of the major causes of emotional collapse among successful workers is "encore anxiety." He describes this as the ongoing fear that you won't be able to repeat or sustain earlier achievements. Gerald Kraines, a psychiatrist who treated Chollet, added, "They're on a treadmill where they can never savor their success, because they have to keep working harder." The same thing happens among many Christians. In our quest to be a devoted follower of Christ we can fall prey to encore anxiety and start believing we must do more and more for God to find favor with us. Although we are saved for good works (Ephesians 2:10), we must not allow encore anxiety to victimize our spiritual progress and stability.[1190]

Worry A psychiatrist has this sign in his office, "In two days, tomorrow (with all of it's worries) will be yesterday." Maybe that's why today is called the "present"—it's a gift! [1191]

Worry "I have been through some terrible things in my life, some of which actually happened." —*Mark Twain* [1192]

Worry "Never bear more than one kind of trouble at a time. Some people bear three kinds: all they have had, all they have now, and all they expect to have. —*Edward Hale* [1193]

Worry "Worry gives small things a big shadow." —*Swedish Proverb* [1194]

Worship Bonnie Hanson had a problem. Her three-year-old grandson begged her to take him with her to "big church." Little Daniel asked, "Can we just go into God's house and see God?" She consented to take him but worried about his expectations. Her fears were dispelled when they entered the sanctuary and Daniel pointed to a large cross. He grinned and said, "See, Grandma Bonnie, Jesus is already here waiting for us!" Worship might take on new meaning if we entered the sanctuary like little Daniel. [1195]

Worship Here are some numbers that cannot be ignored. If your parents worshipped with you regularly while you were growing up, you have an 80 percent chance of worshipping regularly as an adult. If only your mother worshipped regularly with you, your chances of regular worship as an adult are only 30 percent. If only your dad worshipped regularly with you, there's a 70 percent chance that you will worship God on a regular basis as an adult. Regular family worship is a priority that cannot be compromised. [1196]

Worship The French have a proverb that provides insight for worship that states, "A good meal ought to begin with hunger." It is hard to enjoy a meal when you are not yet hungry, but when you are starving, anything tastes good. As we approach worship with a hunger to meet God we will be filled and satiated. And when we come to worship filled up with our own self-sufficiency or full of preoccupied thoughts, we probably won't experience meaningful worship. It's true . . . good worship begins with a hunger for God. [1197]

Worship "There are two times to sing: when you feel like it, and when you don't feel like it." —*B. B. McKinney* [1198]

Worship Wellington Boone gained a new perspective on worship after traveling to Africa. He learned about the unique prelude that takes place before a group of Ugandans begin their worship. These people walk long distances to hear the Word of God and often do so with great personal discomfort. As they sit in anticipation of worship, these believers chant, "Boga, boga." That translates to, "Serious, serious." They believe worship and the study of God's Word is serious business. Does "boga, boga" describe your approach to worship?[1199]

Worship What does it take to keep you from attending a worship service? Bad weather? Good fishing? A runny nose? How about a plane crash? Three Texas men were flying a private plane from Houston to worship at the Promise Keeper's 1997 Stand in the Gap prayer rally in Washington, D.C. when their plane lost power and they had to crash land in Mississippi. Just after leaving the Jackson International airport where they had stopped to refuel, the engine started sputtering. At about 9:45 A.M. on October 3, 1997, the Cessna 182 lost power and pilot Ed Moer made an emergency landing on a public road. The plane was heavily damaged with parts littering a one hundred yard stretch of property. Pilot Moer, and his two passengers, Phil Skrabanek and Lester Neidigk, miraculously escaped injury. These three men didn't let that plane crash stop them from joining the worship at our nation's capitol. They promptly rented a car and drove to Washington. May their determination to worship be a new standard for us all.[1200]

WWBD Since November of 1999, people have been forced to look a little more closely at those colored, cloth bracelets. Just before 2000, California-based Ulysses Press started selling books and wristbands labeled "WWBD." Jesus' name was substituted by Buddha so wearers are encouraged to think through their daily actions and reactions in respect to Buddha rather than Christ. For ten years Jesus was alone in the WWD equation, but now it seems he will be just one among many more imminent options for guidance. Maybe it's time Christians came up with a new calling card suggested by Steve Saubert: WDJD (What Did Jesus Do?) Buddha may be able to compete with the Lord when you ask, "What would Jesus (or Buddha) do about discourteous drivers," but nobody can come close to the incomparable Christ who conquered both sin and death. What did Buddha do? He died! What did Jesus do? He died and rose again![1201]

Youth "Our youth love luxury. They have bad manners, contempt for authority; they show disrespect for their elders, and love to chatter in place of exercise. Children are now tyrants, not the servants of their households. They no longer rise when their elders enter the room. They contradict their parents, chatter before company, gobble up their food, and tyrannize their teachers." —*Socrates*, 400 B.C.[1202]

Youth Picture a high school student and what do you see? Possibly a cluster of teenagers hanging around the mall, maybe students filling the bleachers for a football game, or a kid sprawled out on the couch talking endlessly on the phone. John Ralph saw a completely different picture while serving as a missionary in Nigeria several years ago. He told of a student at Baptist High School who spent his free time on Saturday hiking five hours into the bush to reach a village without a Christian witness. When he arrived, the young man began telling people about Christ. He was met with strong opposition from idol-worshipping leaders, but the student persisted in sharing the gospel. As a result, several villagers accepted Christ and started a small Baptist church. Within just two months, more than one hundred people were meeting each week for worship in a mud-brick church they had built. Included in the congregation was the tribal chief who had received Christ and become a part of the church. An entire village was eternally changed because one high school student hiked five hours to share the good news of Jesus Christ. Teenagers will rise to the occasion of what we believe they can do for God if we will light a fire of evangelistic encouragement under them and provide a model to follow. It just may be the purpose for which they are so often searching.[1203]

Youth Ministry Dr. Robert Laurent asked teens from across America why they lost interest in God and the church. Three primary reasons surfaced. The church did not take them seriously—they didn't feel needed . . . The disproportionate amount of time spent with secular entertainment (TV, movies, music, and so on) made Christian values seem archaic and irrelevant . . . A poor relationship with parents caused teens to reject their parents' faith. The current generation of youth is the most aborted generation in American history, has been struck harder with parental divorce than any other American generation, is the most incarcerated generation of American history, and their rate of teen suicide is the highest of any generation in this country. A generation that inherited such adverse circumstances needs ministry in an unprecedented manner with an unparalleled intensity.[1204]

Uplifting Humor

Academic A history teacher helped his students understand the importance of his class. He regularly told them, "You can take this class one of two ways. You can take it seriously, or you can take it over."[1205]

Academics A college professor overheard the following exchange in the student snackbar. One coed asked, "Have you read any good mysteries lately?" The other replied, "I'm reading one right now." The snacking partner inquisitively asked, "What's the title?" "Advanced Algebra," was the answer.[1206]

Advent When asked to explain what the four candles of an Advent wreath represent, seven-year-old Luke began to explain, "There's love, joy, peace, and . . ." His six-year-old sister piped up, "I know!" She then finished her brother's sentence by proclaiming, "Peace and quiet!"[1207]

Advice A first-grade teacher told her class, "If you need to go to the bathroom, I want you to raise your hand." A little boy then asked, "How will that help?"[1208]

Affection Did you hear about the unemotional Baptist minister who was married for nearly fifty years? He loved his wife so much that he almost told her.[1209]

Age Calculator When Elizabeth Sphar's grandson asked her how old she was, she teasingly replied, "I'm not sure." Undaunted by his grandmother's ignorance, the little boy gave her some advice. He said, "Look in your underwear, Grandma. Mine says I'm four."[1210]

Aging A little boy was vigorously playing with his friends in the yard. His grandmother watched with enthusiasm as the little guys burned off so much energy. After a while her grandson came over and asked her to join his team. As a woman in her late sixties she automatically said, "I'm too old to play those games now." Two-year-old Alan looked up at her and asked, "Grandma, when were you ever new?"[1211]

Aging One woman who was struggling with the reality of her age asked a friend, "I don't think I look forty-years-old, do you?" Her friend answered, "No, but you used to!"[1212]

Aging During a TV commercial break, an eighty-five-year-old man climbed out of his recliner and said, "Honey, I'm going into the kitchen to get some ice cream, would you like some?" The elderly woman was pleased with her husband's willingness to serve a bowl of ice cream but she wanted to make sure he brought her the right kind. She said, "I want vanilla with chocolate sauce on top. Write it down so you won't forget." He just shook his head and walked into the kitchen. Fifteen minutes later he returned carrying a plateful of scrambled eggs. When he handed it to his wife she grumbled, "I told you to write it down so you wouldn't forget. But instead of making a note, you show up with eggs and forgot my bacon!"[1213]

Aging It was quite a shock when Slim, a ninety-year-old man, married a woman of just fifty-five years. People were talking and one of them decided to get some answers. He asked Slim a series of probing questions. Rufus asked, "Did you marry her because she's pretty?" Slim said, "No, truth is she's not that pretty." Rufus persisted, "Did you marry her 'cause she's rich?" Slim denied she had any money to speak of. Rufus speculated, "You must have married her because she's a good cook." Slim admitted she really couldn't cook very well. Rufus was dumbfounded so he asked straight out, "Why in the world did you marry her then?" Slim answered, "Because she can drive after dark."[1214]

Aging One senior adult recently made the following comment: "If you're over sixty-five and wake up without something hurting—you're dead."[1215]

Air Travel While taxiing toward the runway, a jetliner suddenly stopped and returned to the gate. The passengers became visibly concerned when the wait continued for almost an hour. Finally, as the plane started pushing away from the gate, a flight attendant calmly explained the situation. She said, "Ladies and gentlemen we apologize for this unexpected delay. Earlier, our pilot was bothered by a noise he heard in the engine so we aborted our takeoff. Unfortunately it took nearly an hour to find another pilot, but now that we have a new pilot, we will be taking off momentarily."[1216]

Amateur Engineering Two little boys ransacked their father's toolbench to build a fort in their backyard. The preschool-aged brothers went to opposite sides of a big oak tree and started banging nails into plywood. They bent most of the nails so the youngest brother went back in for more nails. When he didn't return for a long time, his older brother headed to the garage. He found his sibling on the floor sorting nails. He had one small pile in front of him and was throwing away all of the others. Sensing his brother's disapproval, the younger guy said, "I'm throwing these away because the top of the nail is on the wrong end." The older brother quickly replied, "You dummy, we can use those nails on the *other* side of the fort!"[1217]

Angels As a little first grader Jenny loved to sing. One day while driving in the car, she sang along with a tape by Michael W. Smith. The song was "Angels Unaware." When it got to the line, "Maybe we are entertaining angels unaware," she sang a different version. Little Jenny belted out, "Maybe we are irritating angels unaware." Her rendition may be more truthful than Mr. Smith's.[1218]

Anniversary Anxiety A jeweler was taken aback by a man who stormed into his shop looking for diamonds. He spoke fast, moved fast, and seemed content to pay almost anything for a diamond bracelet as long as the jeweler could wrap it immediately. The diamond curator promised a rapid response but couldn't help but ask the man why he was in such a big rush. The frantic shopper replied, "I forgot our anniversary and my wife thinks I'm taking out the trash."[1219]

Anniversary Shopping Clarence wanted to buy a nice anniversary gift for his wife, but in typical fashion, he did not want to spend much on the purchase. Calculating that perfume would be his best choice for pleasing his wife while also saving himself some money, Clarence headed straight to the perfume counter. He told the saleswoman that he wanted to buy his wife a nice bottle of perfume for their anniversary. She pulled out a container of their best perfume and told him it was on sale for just $50. Clarence noted $50 was more than he wanted to spend so she pulled out a smaller bottle for $30. He told her the price was still too high so she reached for their most economically brand of perfume. The clerk showed him a small bottle that cost just $15. Clarence still wasn't satisfied with the price so he specifically stated, "I want to see something that is real cheap." The frustrated clerk reached across the counter and handed him a mirror.[1220]

Answered Prayer Two hunters were out tracking a bear. They finally found their prey but this grizzly was far more than what they had bargained. Both hunters unloaded their complete supply of ammunition but it only served to anger the bear. With all of their cartridges spent, they began running from the pursuing bear. The mammoth beast was rapidly closing in on the poorly conditioned men. Thinking it prudent to climb a tree for safety, the two men scampered up a tall pine. The bear quickly found them and it became very evident the tree-climbing idea wasn't so smart. One of the desperate hunters began to loudly pray, "Oh Lord, please let this be a Christian bear!" They then noticed the bear kneel down at the base of the tree and say, "Lord, we give thanks for the food we're about to receive."[1221]

Assumptions A very tall man was tired of people assuming he played basketball. His resentment finally hit the boiling point when a rather short man said, "Because you're so tall I bet you play basketball." The unimpressed giant shot back, "And because you're so short I bet you play miniature golf!"[1222]

Atheistic Dilemma After a very severe ice storm, an atheist called his insurance agent about a fallen tree. The ice-laden tree toppled over onto his neighbor's house and he wanted to make sure he was covered. The insurance agent thrust the hardened atheist on the sharp horns of a dilemma and said, "If the tree was dead prior to the storm, we cannot cover the damages and you will have to pay for the repairs. If the tree fell due to 'an act of God' then your policy will take care of all expenses." On that cold day the old atheist embraced temporal faith.[1223]

Atheist's Nightmare An atheist was enjoying a relaxing day of fishing when, all of a sudden, the Loch Ness monster surfaced and attacked his boat. He was thrown from the boat and landed helplessly in the water. As the large behemoth swam toward him, the atheist screamed, "God, help me!" Instantly, everything froze in time and a booming voice descended from the sky, "I thought you didn't believe in me." The atheist hollered back, "Come on, God, you've gotta give me a break. I didn't believe in the Loch Ness monster either."[1224]

Baby Pictures Three-year-old Jared was looking through an album of his baby pictures. After viewing several shots of himself without hair, he explained, "That's me before my hair was born."[1225]

Baby-Sitting Fees Everyone knows how unruly pastor's kids can be, right? One minister, oblivious to the rambunctious reputation of his three young boys, invited one of the teenagers from the youth group to baby-sit. As the pastor and his wife were going over the final details before leaving on their date, the baby-sitter reminded them of her fees.

She said, "Pastor, I need to warn you, I don't charge by the hour. I charge by how long it SEEMS you've been gone."[1226]

Bad News A friend found his buddy sobbing on a park bench. He tried to console the old man by asking what was troubling him. The weeping man explained, "I just went to the doctor and she told me I would have to take these pills for the rest of my life." His friend replied, "Hey, that's not so bad. Lots of people take pills." The upset man said, "I know, but she only gave me ten pills."[1227]

Baggage Claim A mild-mannered man stepped to the airline ticket counter with three pieces of luggage. He told the attendant that he wanted his first suitcase sent to Phoenix, his smaller suitcase sent to Seattle, and his biggest case sent to New York. The dumbfounded clerk said, "I'm sorry, sir, but we can't do that." The man replied, "Why not? You did it last week."[1228]

Balanced Meal The new kindergarten teacher was visibly shaken when she learned one of her students had just eaten a worm. She tried logic and compassion to teach him that eating worms was inappropriate and said, "You shouldn't have eaten that worm because now that baby worm's mother will be very sad." The little guy broadcast a beaming smile and replied, "No she won't, because I ate her too."[1229]

Bald Spots As the middle-aged man sat down in the barber's chair, he pointed to the triangular shape of his receding hairline and said, "My wife calls this 'The Bermuda Triangle' because my hair keeps mysteriously disappearing."[1230]

Beliefs A pollster got an earful of confusing rhetoric when he stopped a woman in the mall to survey her religious beliefs. He said, "Ma'am, I'm taking a survey on religious beliefs in America. Would you tell me what you believe about God?" The woman emphatically stated, "I believe what my church believes!" He then asked, "What does your church believe?" She firmly replied, "My church believes what I believe." He then took another angle and inquired, "What do you and your church believe about God?" She assertively said, "My church and I believe the same thing!"[1231]

Bird's Legs A college student felt he was very prepared for the final exam in ornithology (the study of birds). He had studied each bird in great detail and felt as though he had positioned himself for a very strong showing on the final. To his chagrin, the test was far different than he had expected. The professor placed twenty-five pictures on the front board and each picture contained one set of bird's-legs—nothing else. The professor explained that each student was to identify all twenty-five birds by examining the picture of their legs. The student was enraged, he bolted to the front of the large classroom, and contested the legitimacy of such a test. The professor held his ground and told the young man he could either take the test like everyone else, or fail the class. The student loudly declared, "I'd rather take an F than take this ridiculous test!" The professor then said, "Very well, I'll be glad to give you an F. What's your name?" The young man gleefully pulled up his pant leg and said, "Figure it out for yourself."[1232]

Birthdays A man made two flagrant mistakes in one day. He forgot his wife's birthday, then tried to cover the oversight without thoroughly thinking through the consequences of his words. He said, "I didn't forget your birthday. I just didn't get you anything." Even if she doesn't exactly have "birthdays" anymore, just anniversaries of her twenty-ninth birthday, it's not wise to forget.[1233]

Birthdays Anita Milner fared well on her fiftieth birthday. Colleagues bestowed compliments on her all day. She heard them use multiple variations of, "You don't look old enough to be fiftieth!" By the time she left work, Anita didn't feel or act anything like a fifty-year-old woman. That changed rather abruptly, however, when she answered the doorbell after arriving at home. A delivery truck was bringing by some flowers from a friend. The card simply read, "Congratulations on your fiftieth!" The carrier also conveyed her congratulations and then asked, "Is it your fiftieth birthday or fiftieth anniversary?"[1234]

Birthright Sue Mosher read the story of Jacob and Esau to her five-year-old daughter, Sarah. After they read how Esau had given up his birthright for one paltry meal, Mosher said, "Esau traded the right to lead his family, and all he got for it was a bowl of stew." Little Sarah piped up and replied, "Yeah, and he didn't even get dessert!"[1235]

Black Widow Mrs. Mohler was on trial for the murder of her third husband. As the court proceedings transpired, Mohler was called to the witness stand. The prosecuting attorney asked, "What happened to your first husband?" She answered, "He died of mushroom poisoning." The prosecutor then asked about her second husband. She told the courtroom that he also died from mushroom poisoning. The attorney then queried, "And what happened to your third husband?" Mohler replied, "He died of a brain concussion." The lawyer asked, "And how did that happen?" The widow confessed, "I hit him with an iron skillet because he wouldn't eat the mushrooms."[1236]

Body Piercing A young newlywed took the advice of his father and set out to purchase some life insurance for the protection of his bride. Like most policies, a general exam was required. After a routine examination, the attending physician was humored by the young man's unexpected fears. The prospective policy holder had his body pierced over an eyebrow, through his nose, on his lip, multiple times in his ears, and in his belly button. Yet when the doctor said a nurse would be in to draw some blood, the frequently pierced young man nervously replied, "You mean they're going to stick me with a needle?"[1237]

Book of Life On the way home from Vacation Bible School, Melissa asked her mother if they could stop by the library. The question seemed peculiar so Nora Newport asked her daughter why she was suddenly so interested in visiting the library. The little girl explained, "This morning my teacher told me that the only way we get to heaven is if our name is written in the Lamb's Book of Life. I just want to make sure my name is in there!"[1238]

Bragging Three ladies were exercising pride in their grown sons. The first lady told of the extravagant birthday parties her son provided her. "Why he even hired a full band for my last birthday." The second lady bragged about how her son gave such lavish vacations. "Just last month he sent me to Hawaii for the *fourth* time." The third woman was not to be outdone and she piped up, "That's nothing. My son has been paying a psychiatrist $150 a week for the last three years just so he can talk about me."[1239]

Bulletins After a lot of prodding, a wife finally talked her husband into visiting a church. She reminded him that, although the two of them had been raised in church, they weren't providing their children with a religious upbringing. He wasn't convinced of her argument until they entered the church lobby and were greeted by an usher. The church host handed the adults a bulletin but didn't give one to the kids. The oldest daughter convinced her dad they needed more church when she turned to the usher and said, "Hey, we want a menu too!"[1240]

Bumper Sticker One teenager decorated his truck with an edi-torialized version of the parentally oriented bumper sticker, "Have you hugged your child today?" His decal asked, "Have you bugged your parents today?"[1241]

Career Change Norman Hardy might need to consider making a career change. When this Brattleboro, Vermont, resident appeared in court on December 28, 1999, he pleaded innocent to drug charges. The twenty-two-year-old had been arrested three days before when police officers saw a small pipe in the front seat of his car. When confronted about the pipe, Hardy confessed to having two rocks of cocaine. His innocent plea was invalidated when the court asked Hardy to list his occupation. He replied, "Selling drugs."[1242]

Cheating Until the final exam, Fred had not excelled on any of the tests or assignments. He was simply known as a football player who did not fare well in the classroom. The professor realized this and accepted Fred's poor academic record without comment until he ended up acing the final. The professor knew Fred sat beside an excellent student during the test and clearly suspected foul play. His hunch was well founded when he compared their exams. Fred only missed one question but it was the same question missed by the A student. The professor called Fred into his office and confronted him about the scores. Fred defended his test results until he was shown the two exams. Both students missed question number thirty-five. The A student answered it, "I don't know." Fred's answer was, "I don't know either."[1243]

Children A little preschooler pulled out an old family album and saw some pictures that didn't include her. She asked her mom, "Why aren't I in this picture?" The mother hugged her little girl and said, "Because you weren't born yet." The answer didn't satisfy this demanding young-ster so she repeated the question. Once again the mother told her that was what the family looked like before she was born. Satisfaction was no closer so she ran the question by again. When her mother's answer didn't change, the child became agitated. She again inquired why she wasn't in the family picture then added, "And don't tell me I wasn't born yet." The mother assured her this was the correct answer. The child then took a dif-ferent tack. "If I wasn't born yet, where was I?" The lady replied, "You were in heaven." That quieted the child for a few minutes and she then put the album back in its place. Upon returning, she looked at her mom and shouted, "Well, I'm sure not there now!"[1244]

Children Henry Leabo spoke with his grandson a few days after the boy's fifth birthday. He asked, "Mark, how old are you?" The little guy held up five fingers and declared, "I'm a handful!"[1245]

Children Lynne Allen found herself face to face with one of those tough kid's questions. Her son was intrigued with the moon still high in the sky when he got up one morning. After bringing the phenomenon to his mom's full attention, he asked, "Why is the moon so high?" Lynne suggested God put it up there for many reasons then tried to note a few. Almost oblivious to his mother's reply, he turned to her and asked, "Did God put it that high so little kids can't touch it?"[1246]

Child Strategist Two kids were overheard discussing their survival strategies at home. One child had an interesting plan. He said, "I try to mess up the rest of our house so my mom won't notice my room."[1247]

Christmas It was clearly a perfect Christmas for little Jessica. She got all of the presents she wanted, her cousins were with her to share the holiday, and she had eaten great food all day long. As her mother tucked her into bed, Jessica smiled and sighed, "I sure hope Mary and Joseph have another baby next year."[1248]

Christmas Card Each year a few Christmas cards arrive after the season has passed. One card, which arrived late and smacked of irony, was from my mortgage company. The greeting simply said, "From *our* house, to *our* house. Merry Christmas."[1249]

Christmas Caroling The church group made the rounds to serenade all their homebound members with a strain of Christmas carols. On their return trip to the fellowship hall for hot chocolate and cookies, one little girl was touched by what she had heard in one of the carols. Although the carolers had sung, ". . . while shepherds watched their flocks by night," this sensitive young child heard something entirely different. While reflecting on that carol she turned to her mother and said, "Mommy, wasn't it nice of those shepherds to wash those sheep before taking them to Jesus?"[1250]

Christmas Gifts A rather aloof woman kept a very tight lid on the amount of money she spent on Christmas gifts. Each year when her family gathered with other relatives she always made sure the purchasing cost remained a big secret. This worked fine until her daughter was old enough to start talking. On this particular Christmas the little girl's uncle started prying for the price. The young niece told her uncle, "I'm not allowed to tell you how much we paid, but I can tell you we got it at the dollar store."[1251]

Christmas Pageantry Commotion erupted backstage when a five-year-old girl, who was slated to play Mary, refused to wear anything but her new red dress. The adults backstage pleaded with her, the director spoke to her, and finally her parents talked to her about the need to wear the costume for Mary instead of her new red dress. The little girl would not be moved and insisted on wearing the dress or she would not go onstage. The play was already late in starting so the director stepped onstage and announced, "Due to circumstances beyond our control, Mary, the mother of Jesus, will appear tonight in a new red dress." The congregation erupted in laughter when a voice from behind the curtain could be heard shouting, "If Mary had had a new red dress, she would have worn it."[1252]

Christmas Shopping After several hours of shopping at the mall, a woman rewarded her grandson's good behavior with a trip to see Santa Claus. The boy spit out his entire wish list for Santa, then hopped off his lap. Santa handed him a candy cane and the boy turned away without saying a word. His grandmother prompted him with, "What do you say to Santa?" The little boy shouted, "Charge it!"[1253]

Christmas Shopping After turning ninety, Marie decided she could no longer shop for Christmas gifts so she planned to send checks instead. Because she wanted all of her friends and family to purchase their gifts before Christmas, she feverishly worked to get everything in the mail early. At the bottom of each card she simply wrote, "Buy your own present." Because she finished everything early, Marie was able to really enjoy the Christmas season. After the holidays, she began to clean off her cluttered desk. To her chagrin she discovered, under a pile of papers, all of the checks she had forgotten to enclose with the Christmas cards.[1254]

Christmas Shopping Two young boys were discussing the upcoming Christmas season and all of the toys they hoped to receive.

One kid explained to the other, "Money can't buy happiness, you know. To be happy, you have to convert the money into toys."[1255]

Christmas Stress On Christmas Eve, Jarod's parents became concerned because they could not find their young son. Finally, they checked his room and found the five-year-old sitting quietly on his bed. His mom said, "Jarod, we've been looking everywhere for you. What are you doing in your room?" Jarod replied, "Nothing! With you and God and Santa Claus watching me all the time, I can't do anything!"[1256]

Church Attendance Comedian Alan King, talked about his poor attendance record in church. His rabbi confronted him about the frequent absences and challenged King to make more concerted efforts to be in worship. King gave a long list of excuses that contained very little merit. He then became a bit defensive and said, "Every time I come, people make a big deal about me being there. That makes me feel very uncomfortable." The wise rabbi replied, "If you came more often they wouldn't be that excited to see you!"[1257]

Church Discipline A little boy was creating quite a disruption in his Sunday school class. In exasperation, the teacher finally grabbed him by the shoulders and shook the fear of God into him while exclaiming, "Young man, I think the Devil's got hold of you." The little rebel rouser shook his head in agreement and replied, "I think so too!"[1258]

Church Membership During the course of his sermon, an evangelist wanted to emphasize the brevity of life. He took a long pause, then said, "Every member of this church is going to die." To his ultimate surprise, a man in the back row responded to this statement with a big smile. The evangelist was taken aback so he repeated the phrase with greater volume. This time he noticed the man cross his arms and look even happier than before. This rattled the preacher so much that he literally shouted the words a third time, "Every member of this church is going to die." In the midst of a loud but somber cry of "Amen" from the congregation, that guy in the back seat just kept beaming from ear to ear. Immediately after the service, the evangelist tracked down the man and asked, "Why did you smile so big when I said 'Every member of this church is going to die?'" The man erupted with a huge smile and said, "Because I'm not a member of this church."[1259]

Church Workday Reverend Milborn was excited to see so many members of the congregation show up for a church workday. He had pages of jobs that needed to be done because the church had fallen into disrepair. He began reading off the various jobs for which people could volunteer. Everything went rather smoothly until all but one man had taken an assignment. The pastor continued to read off tasks but the man didn't seem interested in any of them. The pastor finally asked, "Jim, what job would you like to work on?" Jim answered, "Pastor, I just came up here to try and fix last week's sermon."[1260]

Classified Dating A single woman was shocked by the response she received from a personal ad she had placed in the local newspaper. Her ad simply defined who she was and then ended with a straightforward appeal: "I'm actively looking for a husband." Several ladies responded to this woman's ad by writing, "You can have mine!"[1261]

Class Reunion Bubba was elated about going to his tenth reunion so he could see all of his buddies from high school. At the reunion, his old friends pulled out a copy of their yearbook and began to laugh at Bubba's senior picture. He better understood their laughter when he read what they had written under his name ten years before. Someone had neatly printed: "Most likely to have his senior picture in the yearbook again next year."[1262]

College Concerns A college freshman wrote home to his parents. In the letter he expressed great concern for their well-being because they had not recently written. He wrote, "Dear Mom and Dad, I haven't heard from you in nearly a month. Please send a check so I will know you are all right."[1263]

College Rivalry A college athlete from had struggled with his classes and spent nine years pursuing a degree. He was now just one class shy of graduation but his grades in his basic math class were terrible. Out of compassion, the professor agreed to give him a one-question oral exam for his final grade. If he passed this one test he would be able to graduate. His tenure at the school was legendary and the entire student body was deeply interested in the outcome of the test. To accommodate this schoolwide support, the administrators arranged for the final test to be held in the basketball arena. On that big day the arena was packed to overflowing with supportive fellow students and faculty. With the microphone booming, the professor asked Bubba, "What is three times three?"

The crowd roared and Bubba beamed with a smile of confidence. He quickly answered, "Nine!" The crowd groaned, fell silent, then started chanting, "One more chance! Give him one more chance!"[1264]

College Rivalry One day Albert Einstein was serving on the welcoming committee to heaven. As he greeted heavenly newcomers, he asked each one of them about their IQ. The first person he greeted posted an IQ of 190. Einstein was thrilled and said, "Excellent. We can spend countless hours through eternity discussing theories on relativity, black holes, and quantum electrodynamics." The next newcomer told of his 160 IQ and his expertise as a neurosurgeon. Einstein explained how interesting it would be to discuss the limitless facets of a human brain and the various principles of neurological functions. Einstein's third guest was proud to announce his IQ of 65. Einstein looked him in the eye and said, "How 'bout them Aggies?!"[1265]

Communication A couple had been married forty-two years and had become quite blunt with each other. During the course of one particular evening, Alice bluntly yelled, "Edward, you're not listening to me!" He quietly put down his newspaper and replied, "Of course I'm listening to you . . . can't you see me yawning?"[1266]

Communication During a marriage retreat, the speaker devoted an entire session to discussing the differences between men and women. When it came to communication, the lecturer gave statistical data that suggested women speak about twice as much as men. He noted that the average man churns out roughly two thousand words a day and the average woman doubles that with four thousand words. Upon hearing this information, a smug husband turned to his wife with a smirky smile and asked, "I wonder why it takes you twice as many words to communicate?" She replied, "Because I have to repeat everything twice before you hear it!"[1267]

Communication The team was down by three points with just under five minutes left in the fourth quarter. Because the first two quarterbacks had been taken out of the game with injuries, the coach turned to his third-string player. He was certain the inexperienced player would choke under the pressure of his team being pinned down inside the ten yard line. The coach wanted just to survive the poor field position and hoped for a better position after they punted. To make sure his young quarterback would understand what he expected, the coach called for a time-out and repeatedly said, "Just hand off to Jeffries three times then punt." He screamed the commands a half-dozen times to make sure his plan would be carried out. The quarterback ran the plays his coach had called. On the first play, Jeffries broke free for a twenty-five yard gain. He got the handoff on their second play and scampered for forty-five more yards. The crowd went crazy when he broke free on the third carry and went all the way down to the five-yard line. On the fourth play the quarterback dropped back and punted the ball out of the end zone. The coach went berserk and ran onto the field screaming at his quarterback, "You idiot! What were you thinking?" The player replied, "I was thinking we have a pretty dumb coach!"[1268]

Communication Three Lutheran ministers were invited to attend a special ecumenical service at a neighboring Catholic church. The ministers arrived a few minutes late and discovered all of the seats were taken. The priest noticed his friends standing in the back so he whispered to the altar boy, "Please get three chairs for our Lutheran brethren." The boy couldn't hear these instructions so the priest spoke a little louder and motioned to the three ministers standing in the back. He said, "Three chairs for the Lutheran." The boy thought it strange but he went ahead and followed the priest's instructions. He stepped up to the altar and yelled, "Three cheers for the Lutheran!"[1269]

Communication Two older men were commiserating on a bench in the mall while their wives were shopping. One guy sarcastically noted, "With my wife I always get the last word's . . . 'yes, dear.'"[1270]

Communication While two American tourists were sitting on a park bench in Sweden, a car pulled up to the adjacent curb. The driver rolled down his window and began asking for directions in Swedish. Neither of the two men could understand him so the driver made his request in French. They shook their head in confusion so the driver tried his plea in German. The message still didn't come through so the frustrated man drove off to find help elsewhere. One of the Americans sympathetically said, "I wish I could speak a second language." His buddy asked, "What for? That guy spoke three languages and it didn't help him!"[1271]

Compatibility A group of businessmen were marveling at an unusual zoo exhibition. In the same cage were a monkey and a lion. Seeing some possible lessons that might be translated to the business world, one supervisor asked, "How do they get along?" The zookeeper said, "Usually, okay." Sometimes they have a disagreement, though, and we have to get a new monkey."[1272]

Competition While two guys are on a walking tour in an African jungle, a lion steps onto their path. They both stop in their tracks but one of the guys sits down, opens his backpack, pulls out a pair of running shoes, and takes off his hiking boots. The other guy nervously laughs in the stressful moment and remarks, "Running shoes aren't going to do you any good. There's no way you can outrun that lion." As the fellow hiker laced up his Nikes he replied, "Who said anything about outrunning the lion? All I have to do is outrun you."[1273]

Complaining A young girl surprised her mother with a beautiful and unexpected gift that she had purchased with her allowance. The little girl said, "Mom, this is for you because you work so hard and nobody seems to appreciate it around here." The mother tried to be modest by saying, "Well, your father works hard too." The astute girl replied, "I know, but he doesn't complain about it."[1274]

Complimentary Sermon One Sunday a woman thanked the pastor for his sermon. The pastor tried to be humble and replied, "Don't thank me, thank the Lord." She said, "Well, I thought about that but it wasn't that good."[1275]

Conditional Confession Long after bedtime, Arthur turned to his wife and quietly whispered, "Are you asleep?" There was no response so he waited a few minutes and repeated the question. He did this two more times without getting an answer. Feeling confident that she was sound asleep, Arthur said, "OK, I admit it, I was wrong."[1276]

Contemporary Time-Out After several players knelt down around the pitcher's mound, the home plate umpire called time-out and walked over to investigate. They were diligently searching for something as each man was scouring the infield on his hands and knees. It was a familiar scene so the umpire asked the obvious, "Lose a contact?" The players all responded in unison, "No, an earring."[1277]

Convenient Robbery Two masked gunmen stormed a bank and ordered all of the employees into the vault. They covered everyone's mouth with duct tape and tied their hands before proceeding to clean out all of the cash drawers. As they prepared to leave the bank, they rechecked the employees to make certain everyone was securely tied. When they reentered the vault, one lady was frantically trying to say something through the duct tape that covered her mouth. The curiosity of one robber got the best of him and he removed the tape. She quickly yelled, "Please take the books, I'm $10,000 short."[1278]

Cosmetic Surgery Carol was struggling with a decision about cosmetic surgery. The procedure to have a face-lift was very expensive so she wrestled back and forth over whether or not she should do it. During a discussion with her husband, she blurted out, "But what if I drop dead three months later? Then what would you do?" He thought for a moment then said, "I guess we'd have an open casket."[1279]

Counseling Nightmare Pastor Evans had been unsuccessfully counseling with a very disturbed church member for several weeks. He was getting more and more agitated with the man's crazy and bizarre stories. The guy was always claiming to be a different, famous person and would share the resulting problems that this famed persona had brought him. On one particular day, he was complaining about all of the problems he was facing as the Invisible Man. As he rambled nonstop for several minutes, Pastor Evans began to gloat. He had the perfect response to shut down this lunatic's ridiculous story. When the man stopped long enough for the pastor to speak, Reverend Evans quickly shouted, "If you're the Invisible Man, how come I can see you?" The wild-eyed man calmly replied, "Because it's my day off."[1280]

Court Reporting The following questions were actually rendered by attorneys in a court of law. Now doctor, isn't it true that when a person dies in his sleep, he doesn't know about it until the next morning? — The youngest son, the twenty-year-old, how old is he?—Were you alone or by yourself?—Was it you or your younger brother who was killed in the war?—How far apart were the vehicles at the time of the collision? — You were there until the time you left, is that true?—You say these stairs went down to the basement. Did these stairs go up also?—Doctor, how many autopsies have you performed on dead people?[1281]

Creation Dr. John Ortberg is a teaching pastor at Willow Creek Community Church. He has told the true story that occurred in a church where he formerly pastored. A Sunday school teacher was letting the children act out the story of creation. Five-year-old Matthew got the role of God and was given a flashlight to turn on when the teacher read, "Let there be light!" Matthew did OK at first, but as the creation story continued he lost his focus and the beam of light started wiggling all over the room. The teacher tried to regain his attention several times but he soon had the beam darting around the room again. Finally, in the middle of her story, Matthew tugged on his teacher's dress and handed her the flashlight. He said, "Please take the flashlight back, Mrs. Berg. I'm just feeling too goofy to be God today."[1282]

Credit Card A businessman was explaining an unusual situation that took place with his credit card. His wife's card was stolen but he decided against reporting it to the bank because the thief was charging less than his wife.[1283]

Criticism A pastor had been facing repeated attacks from a very negative and critical woman. Her mouth was making his job almost unbearable so he sought some counsel from his dad. His father's remedy to the problem was simple. He said, "Son, the next time that lady starts making your life miserable, you just get down on your knees and thank God she's not your wife."[1284]

Criticism A sea captain and his chief engineer got into an argument over which one was more important. Unable to resolve the debate, they agreed to swap places for a day. The captain descended into the bowels of the ship to run the engine room while the engineer ascended to the bridge to guide the large boat. After about an hour, the oil-covered captain came up to the bridge and yelled, "Chief, you'll have to come down here and give me a hand. I can't get her going." The chief shot back, "Well of course you can't. We've run aground!"[1285]

Dating One college coed was overheard explaining her recent breakup. She said, "Yeah, I thought he was going to be my knight in shining armor, but he turned out to be just an idiot in a metal suit."[1286]

Dating Diet Ellen hit Larry with a tough line: "Larry, you're the salt of the earth, but unfortunately, I need to cut the sodium out of my diet."[1287]

Deadly Jackpot It happened. They won the lottery. The wife discovered their newfound wealth but was afraid to tell her husband due to his heart condition. After considerable thought, she called on the pastor to assist her in sharing the good news. She said, "Pastor, you must be very careful to not get him overly excited or he might have a heart attack." The minister understood the magnitude of his assignment so he started off with a different approach. He asked, "Jim, what would you do if you won the lottery?" Jim quickly exclaimed, "Oh, pastor, I'd give half of it to the church!" Upon hearing Jim's response, the minister died of a heart attack.[1288]

Debt After paying the bills, Leroy turned to his wife and sighed, "I wouldn't say we're broke . . . but any decent CPA would."[1289]

Decisions As the retired man sat in his recliner trying to make an important decision, his wife stormed into the room and shouted, "Why can't you just do what I tell you and think for yourself?!" Needless to say, it made his decision much more difficult.[1290]

Delusional Driver Sometimes it's hard to accept the reality that we're wrong and everyone else is right. This seemed most evident when a man picked up his ringing car phone while driving down the freeway. The caller was his wife and she urged him to be careful because the news had just reported a car going the wrong way on Central Expressway. The husband frantically replied, "It's not just one car, Honey, it's hundreds of them!"[1291]

Dental Nightmare Fred's fingernails dug into the dental chair when he heard his dentist's instructions for the assistant: "Elaine, would you please take the batteries out of the smoke detector. I'm going to do some serious drilling here."[1292]

Dieting Jeanne wanted to get serious about losing some weight so she joined a club to help monitor her weight. Each Tuesday evening the club members would step on the scales and record their losses or gains. After a while, Jeanne realized she wasn't really dieting at all. She was simply eating like normal throughout the week then fasting all day on Tuesday to get ready for the weigh in. One day she vented some of her frustrations by blurting out, "I wish I could lose some of this weight!" Her ten-year-old daughter heard this remark so she offered some unsolicited advice. She said, "I know how you can lose some weight. Just pretend like every day is Tuesday."[1293]

Dieting "The longer I keep putting off my diet . . . the more I keep putting on!" — *Ziggy, comic strip* [1294]

Dining Out Anita got out of the cooking habit after her children left home. Her infrequent jaunts to the kitchen became rather obvious one evening. Her two children were home for the weekend so she prepared a large meal for dinner. When the meal was complete, she phoned her husband and said, "Come home, Honey. Dinner is ready." He then asked, "Who is this?"[1295]

Dining Out Lorene Workman thought she had presented some rather convincing logic to her five-year-old grandson. When she asked him why he had not yet picked up his toys, he told her he didn't feel like it. With the cleverness of a district attorney she asked, "And where would you be if I didn't feel like making dinner?" He thought for a moment then said, "In a restaurant."[1296]

Dining Out Max Lucado noted an interesting peculiarity of our culture. He recalled eating most every meal at home when he was growing up. It's now the opposite with many families. He said, "When we tell our kids it's time for dinner, they go to the garage instead of the kitchen."[1297]

Dinner Blessing Four-year-old Robbie wanted to say the blessing for dinner. He carefully folded his hands and rattled off his usual prayer, "God is great, God is good..." Once he came to the normal conclusion of his "kid's prayer," he tried to throw in a little "adult prayer." He prayed, "And thank you, God, for the hands that repaired it."[1298]

Diplomacy A military captain was being interviewed by a group of high-ranking officers for a position with their department. He successfully answered all of the technical questions, but the officers wanted to know if his outside interests would mesh with their recreational pursuits. For this reason one of the colonels asked, "Do you golf?" This wise captain secured the new job with his brilliant answer, "No, sir, but I caddie!"[1299]

Directions In frustration, a businessman pulled into a convenience store for directions. He was already late for the appointment and could not locate the correct street. The hired hand listened as this lost bundle of nerves tried to explain the destination for which he was searching. After a few seconds of thought, the clerk began to describe a travel plan. Halfway through his mental map, however, he stopped and shook his head. He then started to explain another possible route, but likewise aborted the plan and tried to think of another way. Finally, after several minutes of unsuccessfully providing directions, the clerk looked at the distraught salesman and sighed, "Mister, I'm afraid you can't get there from here!"[1300]

Directions While driving in a remote camping area, the father of a vacationing family came across a large sign that read, "Road Closed. Do Not Enter." The man proceeded around the sign because he was confident it would save them time on their journey. His wife was resistant to the adventure but there was no turning back for this persistent road warrior. After a few miles of successful navigation, he began to boast about his gift of discernment. His proud smile was quickly replaced with humble sweat when the road led to a washed-out bridge. He turned the car around and retraced his tracks to the main road. When they arrived at the original warning sign he was greeted by large block letters on the back side of the sign. His wife and three children all read the hand-painted message out loud, "Welcome back, stupid!"[1301]

Disagreements A man told his buddies about a disagreement he had with his wife. He summed up the whole experience by saying, "My wife and I had words, but I never got a chance to use mine."[1302]

Disciplinary Protocol Seven-years-old, Myles exceeded his father's threshold of tolerance. He had carried an attitude most of the day and now he was at it again. While in the car and just a few miles from home, the father gave him one of those rear-view mirror rebukes. At the close of the high-octane speech, he guaranteed Myles a spanking when they got home. When his wife saw that he was finished, she explained how much they love him and why they needed to discipline him. A few silent moments followed her caring comments and then Myles very seriously replied, "Mom, you're not supposed to tell me that until after you spank me." Isn't it amazing how early we learn to say, "we've never done it that way before?"[1303]

Dispensable Dads A little girl posed a curious question to her mom. She asked, "If the stork brings babies, and if Santa Claus brings presents, and if the Lord gives us our daily bread, then why do we keep Daddy around?"[1304]

Divine Access Three-year-old Cari was so excited to get a beautiful *What Would Jesus Do* bracelet. Cari's mom had purchased two matching bracelets for herself and her little girl. She also explained the significance of the letters. When Cari's father got home, she ran to show off her new treasure. He admired his daughter's beautiful purple bracelet then asked, "What are the letters?" Cari got real excited and said, "W . . . W . . ." before she got stuck. She paused in forgetful frustration, then lit up with a triumphant smile and shouted, "w.w. dot com."[1305]

Divine Collection Alaina Dewing was deeply impressed with all the trappings that accompanied a morning worship service. The little two-year-old was most impressed with the usher who took up the offering. Her mother provided some coins for the offering plate and explained that they were giving their money to God. As the usher neared their aisle, Alaina watched him intently. She then turned to her mom and asked, "Mommy, is that God?"[1306]

Dog Wash A little boy felt the need to wash his dog so he went to the store for some soap. Because he was alone, a store clerk asked if he needed some help. The little guy pointed to a big box of laundry detergent and requested assistance in getting it down from the shelf. The clerk remarked, "You must have a bunch of clothes to wash." The boy said, "No, I'm gonna use this soap to wash my dog." The man told him such a strong detergent would be dangerous to a dog and added, "In fact, this soap could kill your dog." The boy was confident of his purchase and insisted on buying it. A week later the little boy was back in the store. The clerk asked how the dog was doing and the boy sadly replied, "My dog died." The storekeeper reiterated his warning; "I told you that kind of soap might kill him." The boy said, "Oh, it wasn't the soap. It was the rinse cycle that did him in."[1307]

Driver's Education A daughter wrote her father a note not long after she received her driver's license. The note said, "Dad, you taught me a lot of things over the years. But one thing I learned all by myself . . . your car won't go over one hundred miles per hour."[1308]

Easter Confusion Bill Cosby and Art Linkletter have built a humorous legacy from their interviews with children. Their combined efforts have created some interesting dialogues. One such conversation with a five-year-old girl produced the following thoughts on Easter. Cosby asked, "Do you know what Easter is?" She replied, "Oh yes. Easter is when Jesus died and they put him in a tomb with a big rock and then three days later they rolled back the rock and Jesus walked out and he didn't see his shadow."[1309]

Egomaniac How many egomaniacs does it take to screw in a light bulb? Just one. He simply holds the light bulb in the socket and lets the world revolve around him.[1310]

Elvis Update In 1973, America had 457 impersonators of Elvis Presley. By 1993, that number had grown to 2,736. If this trend continues, one out of ten Americans will be an Elvis impersonator in 2075.[1311]

Email An overzealous and concerned mom struggled with her son's departure for college. After several days of worry, she resolved to use the Internet as a means to help him stay focused on proper priorities. She began sending daily doses of email filled with advice and counsel. After a week of receiving reminders to eat right, study hard, dress nice, and keep his room clean, the young freshman called home. After assuring his mother that all was going well, he said, "By the way, Mom, I think you've invented cybernagging."[1312]

Email A little girl's confusion with the Lord's model prayer may have contained more truth than error. She prayed, "And do not lead us into temptation, but deliver us from email."[1313]

Encouragement A boxer was sprawled out on the trainer's table after getting knocked out in the twelfth round. His trainer was an eternal optimist who excelled in finding ways to encourage this young contender. When the boxer regained consciousness, his trainer smiled and said, "Hey kid, you came in second!"[1314]

Encouragement Little Shane was ecstatic when he came home from preschool. He shouted, "Mom! Vance said I'm the best basketball player in the class!" His mom could see him just bursting with pride so she affirmed the young playmate's assessment of Shane's skills. After a moment of quiet thought, Shane turned back to his mom and said, "Vance is my new best friend."[1315]

Estate Planning An elderly woman was discussing her estate with two of her children. She seemed worried that there wasn't more money in her accounts. The oldest son then tried to assure her that she had plenty of money and should quit living so frugally. He said, "Mom, you have enough money to last you until you're one hundred years old." The old woman then asked, "And then what will I do?"[1316]

Ethnicity Sandi Lewis teaches in a Texas elementary school that is racially diverse. One morning she overheard two kindergarten boys talking about a mutual friend who was absent from school. One child asked the other, "Do you think he's suspended?" The little boy quickly replied, "Oh no, he's Korean just like me!"[1317]

Excellence A little boy was playing baseball by himself in the backyard. He pretended he was one of the greatest players ever to participate in the game. He proclaimed, "I'm the greatest hitter of all time." He then threw the ball up, swung at it with his bat, and missed. He again recited his decree as the best hitter and tossed the ball in the air. He swung the bat and missed again. He then took careful inventory of his bat and the ball. Then with even greater enthusiasm he once again declared himself to be the greatest hitter of all time. He threw the ball higher and swung the bat harder but the two never met. He paused for a second then yelled, "I'm the greatest pitcher of all time."[1318]

Exercise A newspaper ad from Sonora, California, read: "Stationary bike. Lifestyle change. Fat guy wants money for a new sofa."[1319]

Exercise An Old Testament professor, who despised exercise, loved to quote Bernard Baruch: "I get my exercise being pall bearer for people who exercised." He would likewise say, "If you ever see me running, look to see what's chasing me." A fellow professor who consistently walked for exercise tried to convince his colleague of the need for fitness. Ironically, the walking professor ended up having open-heart surgery. Upon returning to the campus, he told his sedentary friend, "The doctor said that if I had not exercised, I would be dead right now." The professor remained unmoved. He simply replied, "Now that you have had surgery, you will probably live as long as I do."[1320]

Exercise One guy knew he was in bad shape when he took a physical and the doctor gave him an "incomplete."[1321]

Eye Trouble A guy went to the welfare office and applied for financial assistance. At the beginning of his interview an official asked, "Why do you need financial aid?" The man replied, "I'm having trouble with my eyes." The official inquired further about this "eye trouble." The applicant said, "I can't see myself going to work."[1322]

False Advertising Mrs. H. A. Renfroe was humored by her five-year-old great-grandson's reaction to his first Vacation Bible School. Kelly returned from his first day with a tinge of disappointment. When asked if he had a good time, the little prekindergartner replied, "Yes, but they never did take us on the vacation."[1323]

Fat-Free Diet   Counting all of the fat in your diet can be mind-boggling. One physician has made such dieting much easier. His formula is simple—if it tastes good, spit it out.[1324]

Fatherhood   It's been said a father is a man who carries pictures where he once carried money. A man sat quietly on a bench inside the mall. Periodically, one of his three daughters would momentarily appear and he would hand them some money. After patiently sitting on the bench for nearly an hour, the man stood up to go purchase a cold drink. Emblazoned on the back of his T-shirt were these words . . . "Human ATM."[1325]

Fatherly Advice   While a father and son were playing in the front yard, the son started asking questions about a flattened squirrel in the street. The boy's father recognized this as a good opportunity to teach his son about safety. He pointed at the dead squirrel and said, "That's what happens when you aren't careful and play in the street." A few days later the little boy was talking with one of his playmates and shared his new-found wisdom. He bragged to his buddy, "I know what happens to you when you die." His friend's eyes got real big and asked, "What?" The enlightened youngster replied, "You turn into a squirrel!"[1326]

Father's Day   A young boy was asked to explain Father's Day. He quietly contemplated his answer, then made the following observation: "Father's Day is just like Mother's Day except you don't have to spend as much money on the present."[1327]

Fatigue   In between the final rounds of a boxing match, the losing fighter was getting extensive attention by his team in the corner. They tried to spruce him up for the last round, but his manager was concerned about the boxer's condition. To get a feel for how the young man was doing after being pummeled for nine rounds, the manager asked, "Kid, do you think you can still get him?" The dazed fighter replied, "Yeah, but I should have got him in the first round when he was alone."[1328]

Fishing   As a little boy slipped in late to Sunday school, his teacher asked him why he was tardy. He hesitated in embarrassment then said, "I started to go fishing this morning but my dad wouldn't let me." The teacher raised his shoulders and prepared to expound on the wisdom of a father who would place greater emphasis on Sunday school than fishing. But before he delivered his linguistic pearls, the young boy gave a further explanation. He said, "Yeah, my dad told me there wasn't enough bait for both of us to go fishing."[1329]

Fishing One fishermen told his partner, "My wife gave me an ultimatum this morning. She said if I go fishing one more time she's gonna leave me." The fishing buddy asked, "So whata ya gonna do?" As he cast his line, the die-hard fisherman sighed, "I think I'm really gonna miss her."[1330]

Flexibility An eager college graduate was desperate for a teaching position in a small, rural community. During the interview he was asked if he thought the world was round or flat. He quickly replied, "Sir, I can teach it either way."[1331]

Flight Plans Buster wanted to take an earlier flight home but the plane appeared to be completely full. The gate agent confirmed his thoughts and placed his name on the standby list. Just moments before the plane was scheduled to depart, a large group of people disembarked. After some discussion with the agent, the group sat down in the lounge area. And then it happened, Buster heard his name called from the standby list. He rushed to the counter and paid for his ticket. Then with his boarding pass in hand, he asked about the sudden availability. The attendant replied, "That group that got off of the plane is headed to a psychics' convention and they felt directed to take the next flight."[1332]

Foot Care Terrence showed up late for a committee meeting and apologized to the rest of the group for being tardy. He explained that his visit with the podiatrist took longer than anticipated. A concerned committee member asked Terrence what type of foot problem was causing him to see a podiatrist. He replied, "My wife insisted that I see someone who could help me get my foot out of my mouth."[1333]

Foxholes During a training exercise in the field, a young recruit naively asked his commander, "Sir, where is my foxhole?" The officer barked back, "You're standing on it. Just throw out the dirt!"[1334]

Fund-Raising The chairman of a building committee was very nervous about having his pastor lead in their fund-raising endeavor rather than hiring a consulting firm to spearhead the campaign. His worries dissolved after reading a letter the pastor mailed to each church member. He was so impressed that he told his minister, "Dr. Richardson, with this letter you could get a pledge out of a tree stump. How'd you think of all this stuff?" The minister humbly confided, "I didn't. I just picked some of the best lines my son has sent home in his letters from college."[1335]

Generational Stuff A teenager and his preteen nephew were out riding bikes when the younger boy's cell phone started ringing. After he answered the call, the older teen started whining about how much better the "younger generation" had it with all of the latest technology. He said, "You just don't understand how lucky you are. When I was your age, we had to rely on pagers to keep in touch.". . . A young boy went with his father to his very first professional baseball game. On the way to their seats, they stopped to buy the little boy a baseball cap from the home team. He promptly turned the bill of the cap toward his back and put it on. When they got settled into their seats, the youngster asked his dad a very intriguing question. He pointed at the players down on the field and asked, "Daddy, why do all of those men have their hats on backwards?" . . . In hopes of building some bridges with their teenage son, the Emersons accompanied him to a concert featuring one of his favorite groups. After a few numbers, Mr. Emerson leaned over to his wife and yelled, "The music is way too loud!" Mrs. Emerson burst out laughing and simply pointed to the back of a fan in front of them. His T-shirt read, "If it's too loud—you're too old!"[1336]

Giving Bags of old, worn out currency were returned to the U.S. Treasury. In one bag, two tattered bills began to talk. The $20 bill boasted of all the wonderful places he had seen. He said, "I went to some of the nicest stores and restaurants in the world, had the distinction of being in numerous country clubs, and visited some very exotic places." The $1 bill humbly replied, "All I ever did was go to church, go to church, and go to church."[1337]

God's Will A Sunday school teacher of young boys was trying to explain the concept of God's will. He introduced the topic by declaring the importance of honoring God's will, the necessity of understanding God's will, and the significance of being in God's will. One little boy seemed confused so he raised his hand and asked, "If God is going to live forever, why does he need a will?"[1338]

God's Will One day while Bil Keane was sketching out his beloved comic strip, *Family Circus,* his little boy, Jeffy, asked, "Daddy, how do you know what to draw?" Keane told his son, "God tells me." Jeffy wondered, "Then why do you keep erasing parts of it."[1339]

Golden Anniversary A man was found crying on the front porch of his house after a quiet celebration of his fiftieth wedding anniversary. His wife saw the tears and asked him why he was crying. He said, "When we were dating, you threatened to have me thrown in jail for fifty years if I didn't ask you to marry me. I just realized that today I would have been free."[1340]

Golf A minister sat around the dinner table at one of the church fellowships. When the subject turned to golf, all of the men seemed to talk as though they were just a few strokes from touring with the PGA. After most of the guys had embellished their abilities and adjusted their handicaps to fit their great golfing tales, someone asked the pastor, "So preacher, what's your handicap?" The minister paused, gave a big smile, then said, "Honesty."[1341]

Golf A pastor went out for a round of golf with some more seasoned players in his church. He shot his usual game of military golf (left, right, left, right) and lost several sleeves of balls in the process. His previous loses were nothing in comparison to a short water hole where he baptized four new Titleist golf balls. One guy asked, "Pastor, why don't you use an old ball on these water holes?" The minister teed up another brand-new ball and said, "Believe me, the way I play I never have an old ball!" He could appreciate Hank Aaron's sentiments on the game of golf. The home run king said, "It took me seventeen years to get three thousand hits in baseball. In golf, it took just one afternoon."[1342]

Golf As two men approached the tee box, one asked the other for some advice. "It's 180 yards with a slight dog leg to the left. It's uphill with a five-mile-per-hour tailwind and water to the right. Would you suggest I use my orange ball or my yellow ball?"[1343]

Golf Fred was vying for a promotion at work so he thought he would help the process by treating his boss to a round of golf. He then went a step further by bringing his five-year-old son Ethan along in hopes of showing Mr. Hart that he was a real family man. Everything went smoothly for the first five holes, then Fred's little boy just about eliminated any hopes for a raise. Mr. Hart was not a very good golfer but Fred had been doing everything he could to butter him up. On the sixth hole, Mr. Hart missed four putts and was getting more agitated with every putt. When he finally sank a putt, little Ethan said, "Gee, Mr. Hart, you're really good at keeping the ball out of those holes."[1344]

Golf Grandpa thought it would be a great idea to expose his grandson to the game of golf. He planned for them to visit the course on a slow day so they could enjoy the time together. Grandpa drove the golf cart and little Garret mainly just asked a bunch of questions. He wanted to know about everything from why there are dimples on a golf ball to why there are ducks swimming at the golf course. One of his more intriguing questions concerned the terminology of golf clubs. Grandpa repeatedly explained the name of each club as they played the game. After Grandpa sliced his drive on the seventh hole, David matter-of-factly said, "Grandpa, I know why you call those clubs woods, because every time you swing one the ball goes in the woods."[1345]

Golf One creative golfer figured out a way to wed his golf game and taxes. Each year he deducts half of his greens fees as medical expenses on his income tax. His logic is simple: "The second nine holes are necessary to relieve the stress caused by the first nine holes."[1346]

Golfing Gaffe After serving a self-imposed, two-year, moratorium on golf, Pastor Nichols believed he could once again handle the sport without losing his temper. His judgment was proven wrong by the twelfth hole. The dogleg around a lake cost him five balls and a dozen strokes. In total frustration, he ripped the clubs off the cart and threw them in the lake. He started marching off to the clubhouse and shouted at his partner, "You'll have to finish without me!" Pastor Nichols's golfing buddy spun the cart around and pulled up beside him. He told the pastor, "I can't do that." The irritated minister barked, "Why not?" His friend said, "Because you just threw *my* clubs in the lake."[1347]

Government Spending If the government is going to keep arguing over our money, maybe we should just stop sending it to them.[1348]

Grades A college student went shopping for a fancy homecoming dress that her father had promised. When she returned from the store, she called her dad to confess that the one she had picked was more expensive than what he had allotted. She quickly offered to pay the difference but her father replied, "Don't worry about it. Just work hard and make good grades. That will be payment enough." There was a pause on the phone, then she asked, "Dad, couldn't I just pay you back instead?"[1349]

Grades After a boy came home with an atrocious report card, his father remarked, "Well, at least we know one good thing. With grades like this you couldn't possibly be cheating."[1350]

Graduation After graduation, a young man sought to find employment. During his first interview the personnel manager asked, "Did you graduate in the upper half of your class?" The recent graduate confidently replied, "Ma'am, I was in the portion of the class that makes the upper half of the class possible."[1351]

Grandparents After Sunday School one day, a little girl told her father, "My Sunday school teacher must be Jesus' grandmother because she talks about him all the time."[1352]

Grandparents Little Freddie crawled up in his grandfather's lap after hearing the story about Noah and the ark. He asked, "Were you in the ark, Grandpa?" His grandfather answered, "Why, no I wasn't." The little boy looked at him quizzically and asked, "Then why weren't you drowned?"[1353]

Grave Compliment A woman tentatively showed her driver's license to a store clerk and then said, "Try not to pay attention to the picture; it makes me look like I'm dead." The witty cashier replied, "Oh no, ma'am, the funeral home will make you look a lot better than that when you die."[1354]

Grief 101 A mother tried to soften the blow of their family cat's death by telling her young daughter, "Tabby is in heaven now." The little girl gave her mother a strange look then asked, "Why would God want a dead cat?"[1355]

Growing Up Little Jeremy was on a walk with his grandfather when a stranger smiled at him and asked, "How old are you?" Jeremy replied, "Three." The man then asked, "When will you be four?" Jeremy answered, "When I'm through being three."[1356]

Guarantees After a man had received his last issue from the one-year subscription he paid to a major publication, he wrote a letter that expressed his dissatisfaction with the periodical. He acknowledged the money-back guarantee and stated, "I want a complete refund." A customer service representative called him about the letter and asked the man if he would like the refund in the form of a check or would he prefer that they credit his Visa card. The man replied, "Just apply it toward another one-year subscription to your magazine."[1357]

Guesswork Art Holst was a referee in the National Football League. During a preseason game in Memphis, he made a call that didn't set well with one of the players. As he got up from the play, this football star yelled something at Holst. The referee turned around and shouted, "What did you call me?" The player replied, "Guess! You've guessed at everything else today."[1358]

Hair Problems Larry's wife was struggling to finish her hair before rushing off to church. When Larry reminded her they needed to go, she snapped at him and said, "Don't rush me! I'm having a bad hair day!" Larry, who had lost most of his hair before turning forty, coolly replied, "Count your blessings, Loretta. At least you're not having a bad hair *life* like me."[1359]

Headlines Here are some headlines that actually ran in American newspapers. "Something Went Wrong in Jet Crash, Expert Says," "Police Begin Campaign to Run Down Jaywalkers," "Plane Too Close to Ground, Crash Probe Told", "Miners Refuse to Work after Death," "If Strike Isn't Settled Quickly, It May Last a While," "Cold Wave Linked to Temperatures," "Couple Slain: Police Suspect Homicide'" "New Study of Obesity Looks for Larger Test Group," "Typhoon Rips Through Cemetery, Hundreds Dead."[1360]

Hearing Aids An older gentleman was so proud of his new hearing aid that he went over to a friend's house just to show it off. After telling his neighbor about all of the features contained in this little technological wonder, the friend asked, "What kind is it?" The old man looked at his watch and replied, "Six o'clock."[1361]

Hearing Check Everybody knows about that high-pitched shrill that hearing aids occasionally make. While a little girl was enjoying the opportunity of sitting in her grandfather's lap, his hearing aid made one of those beeps. She looked up at him and said, "Grandpa, you've got mail."[1362]

Heaven Janet Sketchely was trying to teach her children the truth of salvation while reading through their evening Bible story. To check their comprehension she asked, "What do you have to do to get into heaven?" Her six-year-old sat back to ponder the question, but their little four-year-old quickly replied, "Die!"[1363]

Heavenly Concern Maggie and Eleanor were sitting side by side in rockers at a nursing home while talking about their age. Maggie said, "I can't believe I'm almost one hundred years old." Eleanor replied, "I still can't believe I've already passed one hundred." They both pondered their age for a moment then Eleanor expressed a critical concern and said, "Maggie, we're getting so old our friends in heaven are going to start thinking we didn't make it."[1364]

Heavenly Healthcare By strange coincidence, three people affiliated with the medical field approached heaven's entrance at the same time. Peter greeted each one of them and they gave their corresponding reasons for admittance. The first one, a nurse, explained how she had spent her entire life caring for people so Peter allowed her to enter. The doctor confessed that he had not always done everything he could to save people, but he had genuinely tried to be a very thorough and honest physician. Peter felt good about the doctor's heart so he let him in. The third person was a CEO of a health maintenance organization. He told Peter he was forced to deal with a tremendous amount of bureaucracy and red tape, but through it all he sought to be a true humanitarian and did the best he could to help an enormous number of patients. Peter took a moment to ponder the CEO's comments then he said, "OK, you can come in, but you can only stay two days then you have to leave."[1365]

Heavenly Ride One of the central attractions in New York City is the Empire State Building. Although other buildings are taller, it still holds a unique mystique that attracts scores of tourists. Such was the case when a little boy boarded the observation elevator with his father. As they journeyed upwards, the boy noticed those little lights that indicate what floor the elevator has reached. He watched this happen repeatedly . . . 10 . . . 20 . . . 30 . . . 40 . . . 50 . . . 60 . . . so by the time they hit the 70th floor, he nervously reached over for his dad's hand and quietly asked, "Daddy, does God know we're coming?"[1366]

Hen-Pecked A department store adjusted their hours so senior citizens could do some Christmas shopping without having to fight the crowds. During one of these special shopping days, a large crowd of senior adults were milling around a rack of men's clothing marked "50 percent off." One of the attending clerks overheard a lady snap at her husband. The older woman barked, "Stop shuffling your feet!" Immediately, three men mumbled, "Yes, Dear."[1367]

Heroes A second-grader was given the assignment of writing about her personal hero. Her father was flattered that his little girl had chosen him. He pushed his luck though when he asked, "Why did you pick me?" She pulled the valve on his inflated chest when she replied, "Because I couldn't spell Arnold Schwarzenegger."[1368]

Homework The eight-year-old did a good job of setting up his dad. He asked, "Dad, you wouldn't punish me for something I didn't do, would you?" The father replied, "Of course not." The little diplomat then confidently stated, "Good, because I really didn't want to do my homework anyway."[1369]

Homework While correcting some class papers, a teacher was appalled at the disastrous results on one student's homework. In exasperation, she pulled the student aside and said, "I fail to understand how one person can make so many mistakes." The student then spoke as intelligently as he had handled the homework and said, "But it wasn't just one person . . . my dad helped me."[1370]

Honest Appreciation Letters from children always seem to provide fresh honesty and usually give a mix of humor as well. A recent thank you note from a child proved this point exactly. The little guy wrote, "Thank you for the fire engine. It's almost as good as the one I really wanted."[1371]

Honest Confession A young mother of two children was driving in the High Occupancy Vehicle lane when she noticed the flashing lights of a police car in her rearview mirror. She pulled over and nervously waited for the policeman to approach her car. When he got to the window he quickly apologized for the stop. He suspected she was violating the requirement for at least two passengers when traveling in the HOV lane. He confessed, "I couldn't see your kids in the backseat." The nervous mom blurted out, "Oh, thank goodness! I thought you pulled me over for driving eighty miles per hour."[1372]

Honest Diagnosis The anxious patient blurted out, "Doc, shoot it to me straight, what have I got?" The doctor very honestly told him, "You've basically got bad timing. I just bought a new house on the lake."[1373]

Honest Liar Two Hollywood executives were carrying on a very intense conversation while dining at a local restaurant. Suddenly, one film guru slammed his fist on the table and shouted, "You're lying to me!" The other executive calmly replied, "You're right, but hear me out."[1374]

Honest Prayer Little Aaron was envious of his older brother's new bike. Because he wanted a new bicycle as well, he asked his big brother how he went about getting one. The senior sibling explained that he had prayed a long time for this bike. He suggested Aaron start praying for a new bicycle. After giving it a little thought, Aaron realized his older brother was a lot better at prayer than he, so Aaron said, "Why don't you just give me your bike and you can ask God for another one."[1375]

Honey-Do Linda is an industrious housewife who has a list for everything. One day she had an exceptionally long list of chores she wanted to finish. Halfway through the day, she ran out for a few errands and left her list on the kitchen table. When she returned, she discovered her husband, Ed, had come home for lunch. He left a short note next to her list. "Dear Linda. I'm sorry I didn't have time to do all of these jobs. I only have an hour for lunch. Love, Ed."[1376]

Horse Sense While traveling through the countryside, a man's tire blew out. As he fumbled with the jack, he heard someone comment, "That trip to Japan was wonderful last spring." He stood up but didn't see anybody but a horse. Sensing the heat was causing him to hear things he bent down and started working with the lugnuts. The voice appeared again and he quickly turned around. As he did, the horse looked at him and said, "Yes, that trip to Japan was almost as good as the one to Paris and Rome the year before." The man became hysterical with excitement. He rapidly fixed his flat and drove up to the farmhouse. He pulled out his wallet and told the farmer, "I'll buy that old horse in the meadow for any price." The farmer calmly replied, "Awh, shucks, you don't want that horse. He hasn't been to half the places he talks about."[1377]

Horsing Around A little boy returned to school after his family had taken a vacation at a dude ranch in Arizona. The first-grader couldn't wait to tell his teacher what he saw. He told her, "Mrs. Jenkins, we went to a ranch where they make horses." The teacher assumed the little boy's family visited a breeding ranch for horses so she asked if he got to see some little ponies. He said, "No, ma'am. They made big horses and I got to see them nail on their feet."[1378]

Hospitals Mr. Stevens felt the enigma of hospitalization as he was totally uninformed about his physical status. One night the head nurse answered a phone call at the nurses' station on Mr. Stevens's floor. The caller authoritatively inquired, "How is Mr. Stevens doing this evening?" The nurse replied, "He's doing very well. In fact, he is scheduled to go home in the morning. May I ask who is calling?" The voice said, "This is Mr. Stevens—the doctors won't tell me a blasted thing."[1379]

Housekeeping During Homecoming Weekend, Matt's parents came to visit him at college. Although Matt and his roommates did a little pregame straightening up, the apartment was still in pretty bad shape. When his family arrived, Matt gave them a quick tour of the apartment. His mom had something to say about the clutter in every room. On the other hand, Matt's dad remained surprisingly quiet throughout the entire tour. When they returned to Matt's room, his dad looked all around the messy room, completely oblivious to his wife's nagging. He pulled his son aside and said, "I sure miss college life."[1380]

Housewife A man came home to find the house in shambles. The beds weren't made, the sink was full of dishes, clean clothes covered the couch, and dirty clothes lined the bathroom floor. Toys were scattered throughout the entire house and no dinner was waiting on the table. In amazement, he asked his wife, "What happened?" She simply replied, "Nothing. You're always wondering what I do all day so take a look. Today I didn't do it!"[1381]

Humorous Marriage Several guys were talking about why their wives chose to marry them. One guy said, "My wife married me because she thought I was funny. Now she just thinks I'm a big joke."[1382]

Hygiene Two young boys were arguing over who was the greatest when one of them suggested a challenge to determine superiority. He said, "Without any help, I bet I can tell you what you had for breakfast this morning." The other boy smiled and stuck out his hand to shake on the wager. The would-be prophet calmly said, "You had eggs for breakfast." The challenger shrieked in victory, "Nope! I had oatmeal." His friend scoffed at the response and replied, "Then why do you have yellow egg yolk around your lips?" "Because I had eggs for breakfast yesterday," was the rebuttal.[1383]

Hymnody The following edited hymn titles may reflect more accurately the beliefs, practices, and expectations of some church members. "There Shall Be Sprinkles of Blessings;" "I Love to Mumble the Story;" "Onward Christian Reserves;" "My Hope Is Built on Nothing Much;" "I'm Fairly Certain My Redeemer Lives;" "What an Acquaintance We Have in Jesus;" "Spirit of the Living God, Fall Somewhere Near Me;" "Blessed Hunch;" "My Faith Looks around for Thee;" "Blest Be the Tie That Doesn't Cramp My Style."[1384]

Hypochondriac After numerous visits to his office, a doctor asked a hypochondriac patient why he was always so concerned about his health. The patient curtly replied, "Because, death runs in my family!"[1385]

Hypocrisy It was one of those *big* oops. A man professed to be a Bible-believing, church-attending and totally abstaining Baptist. One evening he had the pleasure (misfortune) of dining with his pastor. He was excited about this particular restaurant. The place had some delicious guacamole dip and he couldn't brag about it enough. He had everyone at the table anxiously looking forward to this wonderful dip, but to his chagrin, the waitress did not bring any of the dip with the appetizers and neither did she bring it with the salad or the main course. The man saw other dinner guests enjoying the tasty green sauce but was quite irritated that none was sitting on his table. He finally confronted the waitress publicly about the apparent oversight. "Where's our guacamole dip? When I was here last week we had some of the best dip I've ever eaten. I see other tables have it so why don't we have any of your special dip on our table?" The waitress quickly changed the mood of the table by replying, "Sir, we only serve the guacamole dip to customers who have ordered drinks from the bar?"[1386]

Imagination Two-year-old Zachary approached his mom about a new helicopter that wouldn't fly. The simple toy had no electronic devices so she explained it was designed for him to use with his imagination. He looked somewhat confused so she asked, "Do you know what imagination is, Zachary?" He woefully replied, "Yes, Mommy. It means no batteries."[1387]

Improvement The coach told his ball club two buses would be taking their team from the hotel to the stadium. He further explained the use of these two buses: "The two o'clock bus will take all of the players who need extra batting practice. The empty bus will leave the hotel at five o'clock."[1388]

In-Laws Against his better judgment, Alfred allowed his wife to convince him that her mother should accompany them on a mission trip to Africa. Alfred spent a great deal of his time trying to keep his mother-in-law out of trouble and out of danger. One morning his wife woke him up screaming, "Mother's gone! They've taken mother!" Alfred quickly dressed and they went out looking for his mother-in-law. Within fifteen minutes they found her standing face to face with a lion. The wife yelled, "What should we do?" Alfred replied, "Nothing! The lion got himself into this, he'll have to get himself out of it."[1389]

Income Tax Arthur Godfrey once said, "I'm proud to be paying taxes in the United States. The only thing is, I could be just as proud for half the money."[1390]

Inevitability A funeral director in California signs all of his correspondence with, "Eventually Yours."[1391]

Innovation An aspiring young recruit was determined to bolster the morale of his large and impersonal company. Citing the trauma of layoffs as the single greatest threat to their employees' sense of worth, he took the initiative to change the color of termination slips from pink to blue. When the company president saw the bill for this young man's innovation, he handed him the very first blue slip.[1392]

Interim Pastor An interim pastor was trying to explain his role to a new convert in the church. He used an illustration to visualize his unique pastoral position. He said, "When a window pane gets broken, you put a piece of wood behind the hole until the new glass is installed. As an interim pastor I am like the board that protects the broken window pane until some new glass arrives." An older member who had overheard the explanation chimed in and said, "Dr. Bailey, you're not like that piece of wood. You're a *real* pain."[1393]

Investments Myles is a resident child accountant. He watches his money closely and has turned into a savings fanatic. Sensing he was old enough to begin investing his money, a couple helped him open a mutual fund. He was very excited to be making grownup investments at the young age of eight. Little did he realize how "adult" his understanding was when he kept calling his mutual fund a "neutral" fund. Ironically, his investment was made at the peak of the market before it stumbled back to reality. It really is a "neutral" fund.[1394]

Job Description Several years ago, Phil Reynolds was considering a new job opportunity. While operating his own consulting business, he was offered a position with a college. As his family was discussing the pros and cons, his six-year-old son, James, asked, "But Daddy, can you still do your insulting business?"[1395]

Job Performance Joey Adams noted a job benefit that most employees overlook. He said a lot of people complain about having to work for such a dumb boss. What they don't realize is, if their boss were any smarter they wouldn't have a job.[1396]

Juggling Men frequently hear their wife say, "These kids are driving me insane." Larry better understood his wife's frustrations when he took a day off to spend with his children. Upon entering the kitchen after taking a shower he saw his five-year-old son standing in the middle of a dozen broken eggs. The little boy scratched his head and said, "You know, Dad, juggling is a lot harder than it looks."[1397]

Justice Ellen sent her four children outside to play in the backyard while she finished cooking dinner. To tide them over, she gave them a small bag of potato chips to snack on. Within just a few minutes, her youngest daughter ran in sobbing. She cried, "Daniel, Ben, and Heather ate all the potato chips. That's not fair!" Ellen tried to console her little girl. She said, "Katy, life is not always fair." Katy abruptly replied, "I'm not talking about life. I'm talking about potato chips!"[1398]

Labor Day Will Rogers once said, "Tomorrow is Labor Day; I suppose set by an act of Congress. How Congress knew anything about labor is beyond me."[1399]

Last Words After the death of an older man, the family lawyer called on the widow to help resolve their estate. He told the elderly woman there was no will on file so they needed to know if he mentioned anything before he died. The widow stated she didn't want to share that information because it was private. The attorney expressed his empathy concerning her desires for privacy but reminded her of the need to determine what her husband said at the end of his life. She insisted, "It was something between just the two of us." Her lawyer said he understood but pressed her for a more detailed explanation. After a few minutes of resistance, the widow said, "Well, if you must know, I'll tell you. The last thing he ever said was, 'You don't scare me. You couldn't hit the broad side of a barn with that old gun.'"[1400]

Leadership A young Marine was reenlisting for another tour of duty. As he was doing so, a public affairs officer asked him why he was returning to the Marines. The young man explained, "Sir, there's no one in charge on the outside."[1401]

Legacy While eating dessert, nine-year-old Karen proclaimed, "Grandma makes the best apple pie in the whole world." She then realized her comment might have hurt her mother's feelings so she quickly added, "And Mommy makes really good pies too." Karen's dad chimed in, "Of course she does, because she's a chip off the old block." Karen then leaned over to her grandmother and whispered, "Grandma, you're the old block."[1402]

Legal Prayers A pastor was using a children's sermon to teach the little boys and girls about prayer. He focused their attention on Jesus in the Garden of Gethsemane and helped them see how he talked with God when he had a problem. The pastor then noted that when we have a problem we can talk with our parents, grandparents, friends, or the pastor. He sought to transition toward a more direct look at God's role in prayer by asking, "Is there someone I haven't named who will listen to our problems?" He got a surprising answer when a little boy shouted, "A lawyer?"[1403]

Listening Skills As the wife droned on with a lecture to her husband, she suddenly realized he had fallen asleep during her lengthy monologue. She roused him from his slumber and scolded him for not listening. The man retorted, "But I was listening . . . that's why I fell asleep."[1404]

Longevity Albert Amateau went in for a routine exam at the age of 105. His doctor was fifty years younger and amazed by Amateau's physical condition. The doctor was even more astonished when he learned the old man maintained a daily routine of walking four or five miles. This caused the physician to ask, "What do you do when it rains?" The centenarian's answer was priceless. He said, "I put on a raincoat."[1405]

Loose Soup While baby-sitting, a woman realized she did not have enough soup to feed the children in her house. Because she was unable to rush out to the store, she decided to stretch the tomato soup by adding extra milk. When she served the children, one boy inquisitively stirred his soup then remarked, "Boy, this sure is loose soup."[1406]

Lord's Supper During a game of Bible Trivia, Beverly Paul asked her eight-year-old daughter, "What is another name for the Lord's Supper?" She thought real hard then replied, "Pot luck!"[1407]

Lost Dog A little boy brought home a dog and asked his mom to let him keep it. The mother passed the decision to her husband and told her son he would have to wait until his father got home. The boy played with the dog all afternoon as he anticipated his dad's return. When the father finally arrived, the boy met him in the driveway. His enthusiasm erupted as he begged his dad to let him keep the dog. The father probed to find out more about the dog. The son assured his dad the dog was lost and he would now provide a wonderful home for the little pup. The father suggested the dog might not be lost but was just out of his yard playing so he asked, "How do you know the dog was lost?" The son answered, "Because I saw a man looking for him."[1408]

Love A Nashville bumper sticker shared this sentiment on love: "Do You Believe in Love at First Sight or Shall I Drive By Again?"[1409]

Love Letter Little Britney loves Jesus and wanted to make sure he knew it. To find the best way for communicating her love she sought her mom's counsel and asked, "Mom, I know that Jesus lives inside my heart but how do I tell him I love him? Do you think if I write 'I love you' on a piece of paper and eat it, he'll get the note?"[1410]

Lying In 1983, while serving as the Chicago White Sox board chairman, Jerry Reinsdorf was asked a very pointed question about the veracity of New York Yankees' controversial owner, George Steinbrenner. The interviewer asked, "How do you know when Mr. Steinbrenner is lying?" Reinsdorf's classic reply was, "When his lips are moving."[1411]

Lying While taking a late afternoon walk, a minister came upon a group of young neighborhood boys standing around a dog. He curiously asked them what they were doing. The oldest boy explained how the dog was a stray and they all wanted to take him home. So, to determine who got him they were seeing who could tell the best lie. The minister immediately reprimanded them for lying and then tagged on an impromptu ten-minute sermon. He finally concluded his remarks by stating, "When I was your age, I never even dreamed of telling a lie." After a few moments of silence, the youngest boy turned to his friends, gave a big sigh and said, "OK, give him the dog."[1412]

Male Shopping A husband and wife went shopping to find some new clothes for his outdated wardrobe. The salesman found great humor in the man's approach to finding clothes. The husband would take each clothing item off the rack, show it to his wife, and then ask, "Honey, do I like this?"[1413]

Marital Bliss Janice found herself "odd woman out" while dining with some of her old friends. Each lady had been married around fifty years and expressed concern over their husband's health. Several of them repeated the same phrase: "I don't know what I'd do without my husband." Janice took a different approach and said, "I don't know what I'd do *first* without Jerry."[1414]

Marital Conflict After a bitter argument with her husband, a young bride called her mother to gain a little sympathy. In the course of their conversation, the mother reminded her daughter of a happier moment when she declared her husband was, "Mr. Right." The bride said, "Yeah, but I had no idea his first name was Always."[1415]

Marital Conflict Conflicts within a marriage are a natural phenomenon, especially because a marriage is made up of two seasoned sinners. One lady was convinced her relationship would never encounter turbulent waters. In a premarital counseling session, the counselor addressed the issue of conflict resolution by asking, "How do you two handle disagreements?" The soon-to-be-married woman informed the counselor she and her fiancé never had conflicts. The counselor gently smiled and assured her that every couple has conflicts. She denied the reality in their relationship and insisted they were perfectly compatible. The wise counselor would not be moved and pressed the issue. The bride in waiting began arguing her position and suggested the counselor move on to another topic. He would not relent so she squared off for battle. The young man sensed the mounting tension and started to make a peace-keeping comment. He no sooner began to speak when his adamant fiance jumped down his throat and yelled, "*You stay out of this!*"[1416]

Marital Conflict While playing in the garage during the holidays, little Nathan heard his dad telling his uncle about a recent argument. Nathan's dad said, "I let her know exactly where I stood and told her how it was going to be around here. Then the next thing I know, she's crawling toward me on her hands and knees." Nathan then piped up and yelled out, "Is that when Mommy told you to get out from underneath the bed and fight like a man?"[1417]

Marital Decisions When asked to share the secret of their success in staying married for over fifty years, the wife provided some very interesting logic. She said, "On our wedding day, we decided my husband would make all of the major decisions and I would make all of the minor decisions. This has worked out especially well for us because in fifty-three years of marriage we've not yet had to make a single major decisions."[1418]

Marital Hierarchy Connie's husband was running for vice president at his local union. Due to her work schedule, Connie was unable to see him on the day of the election. Wanting to provide him with a pleasant greeting when he returned home, she called during the day and left a message on their answering machine. When he walked in, the machine was blinking so he pushed the button and heard his wife say, "Honey, don't worry. No matter how the election turns out, you'll always be vice president at our house."[1419]

Marital Sacrifice During a debate in college-level psychology, a male and a female spared over the question, "Who makes the larger sacrifice when a couple gets married?" After some rather intense discussion, the female slyly conceded that in a marital relationship men give up far more than women. Just as the male was about to congratulate himself for winning the debate, the female student added, "Men generally give up doing their cleaning, they give up doing their laundry, they give up doing their shopping, and they give up doing their cooking. You're right, men do give up a lot more than women!"[1420]

Marital Strife JoAnn Ridings's five-year-old grandson, John, was playing in the sandbox with his four-year-old neighbor, Emily. Suddenly John burst through the door in frustration. He was obviously upset. Through squinting and blinking eyes he groaned, "Emily threw sand in my eyes. If she does that again, I'm not going to marry her."[1421]

Marketing Summer is filled with merchants advertising their "special" sales. One store is hoping their integrity will turn out to be a marketing sensation. Their ad reads, "50 percent Off on Everything We Overpriced in the First Place."[1422]

Marriage A little girl was discussing her first experience of hearing *Snow White and the Seven Dwarfs*. Her mother listened intently as her daughter talked with such animated expressions. This classic took on new meaning when the little girl asked her mom if she knew how the story ended. The woman said, "Of course I know. Snow White and the Prince lived happily ever after." The youngster quickly corrected her mother. She said, "No they didn't. They got married![1423]

Marriage At a 45th wedding anniversary party, the men sat on the porch while the ladies stayed in the house. The men were giving the elder husband a hard time about the length of his marriage. They asked him how he was able to stay married to the same woman for forty-five years. The man revealed his secret for success by saying, "I know her like a book." Another guy quickly added, "Yeah, but I bet you never know what page she's on!"[1424]

Marriage Debra Johnson's seven-year-old daughter decided she would like to take violin lessons. Johnson wanted her daughter to understand the importance of practice so she told her violin lessons were expensive and would require a lot of hard work. After they rented an instrument from the music store, she gave a brief word of final exhortation. She said, "There may be times when you feel like giving up, but I want you to hang in there and keep on trying." The little girl nodded as though she understood, then said, "It will be just like marriage, right Mommy?"[1425]

Marriage During a rather small and informal evening worship service, the pastor decided to throw out a few questions for the congregation to ponder. He didn't expect anyone would attempt an answer but he got one anyway. After teaching on several of the Proverbs he asked, "Why do you think Solomon was so wise?" A lady quickly responded for everyone to hear, "Because he had so many wives to advise him!"[1426]

Marriage If it weren't for marriage, most men would go through life thinking they had no faults at all. . . . Married men live longer than single men, but married men are a lot more willing to die. . . . Any married man should forget his mistakes because there's no reason for two people to remember the same thing. . . . A woman always has the last word in any argument. Anything a man says after that is just the beginning of a new argument.[1427]

Marriage Counseling Pastor Clarence knew his success in counseling Mr. and Mrs. McIver was going to be highly improbable when she showed up for their appointment alone and stated, "I would have brought my husband, but we'd just end up arguing."[1428]

Marriage Counseling Pastor Harold knew he'd made a flagrant mistake by agreeing to counsel Mrs. Finwick when she opened their first session by saying, "I want to thank you for seeing me, especially because my husband said he'd kill anybody that I talked to about our problems."[1429]

Marriage Proposal A widower knelt down beside the woman he had been seeing and said, "I have two questions for you. The first is, 'Will you marry me?'" She quickly replied, "Yes!" She then asked, "And what is the second question?" He replied, "Will you help me up?"[1430]

Married Life A middle-aged husband was getting irritated with his wife's complimentary opinion of a young, Hollywood celebrity. He chided, "Yeah, but what do you have if you take away his money, good looks, and muscular body?" His wife wryly replied, "You!"[1431]

Married Millionaire One CEO told his assistant, "My wife made a millionaire out of me." The assistant was keenly interested in what appeared to be a rags-to-riches story so he asked, "What were you before?" The CEO stoically remarked, "A multimillionaire."[1432]

Maternal Chauffeur One young mother asked her husband a very legitimate question. She pondered, "If a woman's place is in the home, why am I always in the car?"[1433]

Maternity Luck A six-year-old girl was questioning her grandmother about the new baby her parents were expecting. The little girl wanted to know if it was going to be a girl. Grandma LaMance explained they wouldn't know until the baby was born. She then added, "We have to take what we get." Her granddaughter's eyes brightened with understanding as she exclaimed, "Oh, I know. It's just like gum-ball machines."[1434]

Mechanical Failure When Jerry came by the shop to pick up his car, he was surprised to hear the mechanic's assessment. He explained, "I couldn't fix your brakes so I installed a louder horn."[1435]

Medical Coverage After a very thorough examination, the doctor turned to his patient and said, "You have a very rare disease." The patient was obviously concerned so he asked, "What's so rare about it?" The doctor replied, "It's fully covered by your HMO!"[1436]

Medical Fears Going to see the doctor carries a certain level of built-in anxiety. One patient had heightened anxiety while awaiting extensive surgery. As he lay on the gurney, he heard his anesthesiologist softly whistling the *Wizard of Oz* tune, "If I Only Had a Brain."[1437]

Medical Protection During his days as a premedical student, Dr. Arumugam was required to take a difficult class in physics. One day the professor was losing most everyone as he lectured on a very complicated concept. In frustration, a student rudely interrupted the professor and asked, "Why do we have to learn this stuff?" "To save lives," was the professor's immediate response. He then resumed his lecture. Several minutes later the same student spoke up again and asked, "So how does physics save lives?" The professor coolly replied, "It keeps the ignoramuses out of medical school."[1438]

Medical Referral After years of being under his medical care, a doctor told his friend he needed to quit smoking and drinking or he would have to send him to a specialist. The friend asked, "What kind of specialist?" The doctor replied, "A mortician!"[1439]

Memory "I used to be terrible with names. I couldn't ever remember a name, but not anymore. Names are a breeze ever since I took that Fred Carnegie memory course." . . . "Memory is what tells a man his wedding anniversary was yesterday."[1440]

Memory While visiting his elderly parents, a middle-aged man was very impressed with the way his father spoke to his mother. Whenever she asked a question or made a comment, the older man responded with "Dear, Sweetheart, Darling, or Honey." It seemed so tender, especially because they had been married over fifty years. After an evening of observing this behavior, the son waited for his mother to leave the room so he could compliment his dad on the many terms of endearment. He said, "Dad, I think it's great the way you speak to Mom with so many tenderhearted pet names." The old man said, "I have to because for the last two months I haven't been able to remember her name."[1441]

Memory Loss A young man sat down next to a much older man and sighed in frustration, "If I only knew then what I know now!" The old-timer paused for a few moments, looked at the young man and then sighed, "It's just the opposite with me. I wish I knew now what I knew then."[1442]

Ministerial Vacation An inquisitive young boy was curious about their pastor taking off a whole month for vacation. He asked his mother why Pastor Stevens got to take such a long vacation. She replied, "Our church believes that if a pastor is a good preacher then he needs that much time off. If he's not a good preacher then we think the congregation needs for him to take that much time off."[1443]

Minister's Clothes A pastor was interrupted from his studies by a phone call from a charitable organization for the homeless. The caller said they would have a truck in the pastor's neighborhood next Friday and wanted to know if he had any old clothes he might wish to donate. The pastor acknowledged that he had plenty of old clothes but would not be able to give any of them to the organization. The caller was intrigued by the pastor's response and probed deeper. He asked, "Sir, if you have plenty of old clothes but don't care to donate any of them, may I ask what you plan to do with them?" The pastor replied, "I plan to keep wearing them!"[1444]

Momentary Pride Mrs. Thornton was feeling a wave of pride sweep over her when she learned of her daughter's conversation about God with a neighborhood child. She and her husband worked hard at communicating the importance of telling other people about Christ. On this particular day, her seven-year-old daughter, Brooke, ran into the house and yelled, "Mom, you're not going to believe this! The new girl across the street doesn't even know who God is!" Mrs. Thornton savored the moment of hearing about her child's effort to tell the new girl about God's love. Her proud moment was quickly interrupted by a shout from upstairs. It was her four-year-old daughter loudly asking, "God who?"[1445]

Mommy's Helper A little girl was trying very hard to take care of her sick mother. She did everything to make her mom feel more comfortable in bed, then quietly slipped into the kitchen. She had seen her mother make hot tea for her father when he was sick so she set out to do the same for her ailing mom. With cup and saucer in hand, she took the tea into the bedroom and her mother was touched by this sweet act of compassion. The mother showered her daughter with praise and then said, "I didn't know you could make tea." The little girl beamed with pride as she told her mom how she made it, "I boiled the water and tea leaves together just like you always do." The mother listened attentively while sipping the tea. The girl continued her story by stating, "But I couldn't find the little strainer thing so I used the flyswatter." Her mom nearly spit out the tea as she exclaimed, "You used the flyswatter?!" The little girl comforted her mother's concerns by explaining, "Oh, but don't worry, Mommy. I used the old flyswatter so I wouldn't mess up the new one."[1446]

Money Most Americans get depressed when they look at their savings account, and with good reason because the average savings balance is $83.42. Of course there is great consolation when you realize such a meager balance makes you $4.6 trillion richer than the U.S. government.[1447]

Money Matters After paying the bills, Larry turned to his wife and said, "I guess we can stop fighting about money, because we don't have any left to fight over."[1448]

Morning Devotions "Lord, I want to thank you that so far today I haven't been rude, obstinate, selfish, or grumpy. But in just a few minutes I'm going to get out of bed and from then on I'm probably going to need a lot more of your help!"[1449]

Motherhood A tired and frazzled mother of two toddlers attended a women's retreat at her church. The keynote speaker delivered a talk on "Women of Excellence" with Proverbs 31 as her text. She spoke eloquently and brought her message to a conclusion with the Biblical quote,

"Her children shall rise up and call her blessed." The worn-out mother turned to a friend and sighed, "So far my children just rise up and call me!"[1450]

Motorcycle Message Paul Harvey told of a biker who had the following message printed on the back of his leather jacket: "If you can read this, my girlfriend fell off."[1451]

Nepotism Mr. Davis called the new employee into his office and gave the following speech: "Young man, you have been selected for this job over hundreds of highly qualified applicants. You should regard our hiring of you as a strong vote of confidence in your skills and abilities. If you work hard, you will find yourself rapidly climbing the ladder of success and this will be the beginning of a very impressive career." The young man fidgeted in the chair, then replied, "Gee, thanks, Dad!"[1452]

New Age Commitment In our syncretistic culture it was just a matter of time before someone started a new sect for those who want a little religion without much commitment. This new faith for the fickle is called, "Jehovah's Bystanders." It's a "Witness" who doesn't want to get involved.[1453]

Offertory Blues A very skilled musician played an elaborate rendition of "Amazing Grace" for the morning's offertory. All of the additional chords gave the old hymn a new sound. After the service, an exuberant young man approached the gifted organist and complimented her on the beautiful song. He then asked, "Can you play 'Amazing Grace?'" The woman looked at him in disbelief then said, "Apparently not."[1454]

Omnipresence A missionary told her children to go wash their hands before dinner. She reminded her youngest son to use plenty of soap to get all the germs off. On his way to the restroom, the little boy was overheard saying, "Germs and Jesus, Germs and Jesus. That's all I hear and I haven't ever seen either one of them."[1455]

Opening Remarks A visiting pastor, who had a reputation for being long-winded, stood to address the congregation. In his opening remarks he mused, "Where do I begin?" A deacon, who had opposed the idea of inviting this speaker, muttered back, "As close to the end as possible!"[1456]

Opportunity Have you ever noticed how the "Window of Opportunity" is located right next to the "Trap Door of Disaster?"[1457]

Optimist It was recently observed that optimists and pessimists do indeed have some common ground. People of both persuasions say the same thing, "This too shall pass." The difference is, the optimist says it when times are tough, the pessimist says it when times are good. The difference between an optimist, a pessimist, and a cynic is that the optimist will lend his cousin money, the pessimist won't, and the cynic did.[1458]

Oxymoron Rob Sherman is a prominent anti-religion media activist based out of Chicago. He is known as "The Atheist Guy." In 1998, he was charged with misdemeanor domestic battery for punching his six-teen-year-old son. Sherman testified that he was simply disciplining the boy for refusing to do his chores. Sherman said he "merely wanted to put the fear of God into him."[1459]

Painful Offering The church was in the middle of a building program and behind on their budget. The pastor was feeling the heat of these financial obligations so he took a few minutes before the offering to challenge his congregation. He exhorted, "Give until it hurts!" When the offering plates were returned to the altar, he could tell it was a meager array of low-denomination bills. With a bit of disgust he said, "From the looks of these offering plates I can tell most of you have a very low threshold of pain."[1460]

Parental Blooper The pastor's family sat down to dinner with a host of guests they had invited to their home. The minister's wife had slaved all week to make sure the house was spotless and the food was perfect. By the time their guests arrived, she was exhausted and irritable. As they all held hands to pray before their meal, the hostess asked her six-year-old daughter if she would like to say the blessing. The little girl shyly explained she wouldn't know what to say. The woman then reassured her daughter and said, "Just say what you hear Mommy say." The girl then bowed her head and prayed, "Dear Lord, why on earth did I invite all of these people to dinner?"[1461]

Parental Boomerang Six-year-old David was very excited about his dad's boss coming over for dinner. When they finished the blessing, little David never even looked at his own food, he just kept looking at their guest of honor. After a few minutes of staring, David blurted out, "Wow, I didn't think you would ever need a fork or knife!" The humored boss asked, "What do you mean?" "Because," David replied, "my dad said you eat like a horse."[1462]

Parenting A distraught father was venting some of his frustrations about the conflicts which were occurring with his son over the use of their family car. He explained to his friend, "I'm sick and tired of arguing with my teenage son about borrowing the car. Next time, I'm just going to take it when I want it."[1463]

Parenting Dennis the Menace had a tough question for his scolding mother to answer. From his chair during his time-out he yelled, "If you're raisin' me right, how come I get into so much trouble?"[1464]

Parenting Dennis the Menace lay motionless in the arms of his mother. As he slept on her lap, Mrs. Mitchell visited with her husband over the phone. She spoke the sentiments of most every young mom when she said, "We've had a *great* day! He ran out of energy before I ran out of patience."[1465]

Partisan Pledge Althea Hall's five-year-old granddaughter, Priscilla, may have hit on a new idea for the GOP. While reciting the "Pledge of Allegiance," she said, "I pledge allegiance to the flag and to the Republican for which it stands."[1466]

Pastoral Epistles The following letters were submitted by children to various pastors: Dear Pastor, I know God loves everybody but he never met my sister (Arnold, age eight, Nashville). . . . Dear Pastor, I liked your sermon on Sunday. Especially when it was finished (Ralph, age eleven, Akron). . . . Dear Pastor, Please pray for our Little League team. We need God's help or a new pitcher (Alex, age ten, Raleigh). . . . Dear Pastor, My father says I should learn the Ten Commandments, but I don't think I want to because we have enough rules already in my house (Josh, age ten, South Pasadena). . . . Dear Pastor, Who does God pray to? Is there a God for God? (Chris, age ten, Titusville). . . . Dear Pastor, I would like to go to heaven someday because I know my brother won't be there (Stephen, age eight, Chicago). . . . Dear Pastor, I think a lot more people would come to your church if you moved it to Disneyland (Loreen, age nine, Tacoma). . . . Dear Pastor, My mother is very religious. She goes to play bingo at church every week, even if she has a cold (Annette, age nine, Albany).[1467]

Pastoral Relocation Upon arriving at his new place of ministry, the pastor received a call from his predecessor. The former pastor congratulated his replacement and wished him well. He then said, "When your honeymoon is over and things start going south, look inside the middle drawer of your desk. I've left you three envelopes. Read them in chronological order when things get tough." The new pastor nearly forgot about those envelopes until some of the ladies called him on the carpet. He opened the first envelope and it's brief message exhorted him to blame everything on the old pastor. It said, "I'm in another church in another state, so just tell them it's all my fault." The strategy worked and everything was smooth for a season. When the deacons got in an uproar and things were once again looking grim, the pastor pulled out the second envelope. This time the former pastor encouraged him to blame all of their ills on the denomination. He said, "They're big and hard to reach so just say they are the reason for our conflicts." Surprisingly, the strategy once again worked. The church calmed down and all went well until the pot got stirred up again. This time the pastor turned to the last envelope with great confidence. He tore it open and read, "Start preparing three envelopes."[1468]

Pastor Appreciation It's important to know this is really a true story. A Methodist minister received a call requesting that he make a particular hospital visit. The woman explained the patient was her mother and she really needed a minister right away. The minister agreed to make the visit and asked for the patient's name. He recognized the last name as a prominent family in the Baptist church. The minister said, "Your mother is a Baptist, and I am a Methodist pastor. Listen, I know the Baptist minister, so let me call him and tell him about your mother." The woman anxiously replied, "Oh, no! Mother has a contagious disease and we love our pastor and we don't want him to catch it. That's why we want you to go."[1469]

People Pleaser You may have heard about the minister who came to a church in view of a call. The vote was ninety-seven in favor of his coming and three were opposed to the calling. He felt as though a 3 percent opposition was minimal so he accepted the pastorate. Immediately upon his arrival, he made a commitment to win over his three opponents. In fact, it became an obsession. He spent an inordinate amount of time with these people and did everything he could to win their favor. A year later the church decided their pastor was not performing his duties well enough to continue so they called for a vote of confidence. The vote to fire him ended up being ninety-seven in favor of his termination and three opposed to it.[1470]

Performance Review The boss let Jacobs know exactly what he thought of his work. He said, "Jacobs, it's obvious you have two problems. First, you take no pride in your work. Second, you have absolutely no reason to!"[1471]

Pessimist A full-blown pessimist wrote this special addendum on his medical bracelet: "In case of an accident, I'm not surprised."[1472]

Planning Eight-year-old Myles had never earned a trip to the time-out chair, but one morning during Sunday school he asked his teacher a rather unusual question. After arriving early, he approached his teacher and asked, "Can I sit in the time-out chair until class starts so I won't have to sit in it later if I get in trouble?"[1473]

Political Speech While working the campaign trail, one political candidate found himself speaking to an exceptionally noisy crowd. After several minutes of trying to speak over the noise, he addressed the people with his plea, "Please help me out. You're so loud I can't hear a word I'm saying!" From the lively crowd someone shouted back, "Don't worry, you're not missing much!"[1474]

Politicians A young farm girl was out milking the family cow when a stranger approached the house and asked to speak with the girl's mother. The girl yelled to her mother, "There's a man here to see you." The mother hollered back, "Haven't I told you not to talk with strangers? Get in this house right now." The girl shouted, "But Momma, this man says he's a congressman." The mother then stepped onto the porch and said, "In that case, bring the cow in with you."[1475]

Politicians Congressman J. C. Watts told about his son's insight into politics. Trey, the congressman's son, was chosen as "Cubby of the Year" in his church's Awana program when he was just five years old. During that year, Trey completed three books when most of his peers just finished the allotted one book. Mrs. Watts bragged about her son and told him, "Trey, when you grow up, you're going to be a genius." He replied, "When I grow up I don't want to be a genius. I want to be a congressman like Daddy."[1476]

Politics As the little boy watched TV with his father, he saw a political advertisement come across the screen. He then turned to his dad and asked, "Did you say wrestling is fake and politics are real, or was it the other way around?"[1477]

Politics A very rude and abrasive man kept heckling a candidate during a campaign speech. At the conclusion of his speech, the congressman appealed for voter support. The heckler shouted, "I wouldn't vote for you if you were St. Peter!" The incumbent shot back, "If I were St. Peter, you wouldn't be in my district."[1478]

Politics Today's political arena could learn a thing or two from a man who never made it to the White House. In 1952, Adlai Stevenson cautioned his fellow Democrats with these famous words, "Better we lose the election than mislead the people." It was the honest wit of this man that stirred America's political scene a half-century ago. On one occasion, a supporter assured Stevenson that he had the vote of "every thinking voter." He humorously replied, "That's not enough . . . I need a majority."[1479]

Politics When speaking about Washington, D.C., Harry Truman once said, "If you really want a true friend in this city . . . go buy a dog."[1480]

Popular Diet Grandma LaMance took her granddaughter, Barbara, out to eat for her fifth birthday. As they began to look through a menu together, Mrs. LaMance asked Barbara what see wanted for lunch. The little girl thought for a few moments then replied, "Oh, let's have something that isn't good for me."[1481]

Prayer A couple with sporadic church attendance had been asked by their pastor to host a visiting minister for lunch. The couple obliged and put together a very special meal for the guest preacher. When they all sat down to eat, the little boy, who was accustomed to diving right in, immediately reached for the mashed potatoes, but because the minister was present, his mother gently stopped his hand and bowed her head in hopes he would follow her example. The boy caught on quickly. He looked around the table and saw that all of the adults were bowing their heads and closing their eyes. He was the only child present and he wanted to impress everybody so just as his father was about to say the blessing, the little boy belted out, "Hey Dad, can I be the one who talks to the plate?"[1482]

Prayer An eight-year-old boy came home with a smile on his face and a stuffed animal in his hand. He eagerly explained to his parents that he had won the toy at school during their Valentine party. He said, "The teacher put all of our names together, and then picked my name from the pile." He then confessed, "But I cheated." With a guilty look he said, "I prayed."[1483]

Prayer Barbara Kerby has written a humorous reflection about her first experience of driving. Barbara's father took her to the high school parking lot for driving lessons. For this particular lesson, Barbara's three-year-old sister rode along in the backseat. While trying to negotiate a turn, Barbara hit the curb. From the backseat she heard a small voice say, "God is great, God is good, let us thank him for our food." Barbara slammed on the brakes, turned around to the backseat and yelled, "What are you talking about?" Her little sister replied, "Your driving is scaring me, and that's the only prayer I know."[1484]

Prayer Corrie ten Boom wrote of a little boy whose mother heard him reciting the alphabet while sitting in the corner of his room. His mother asked, "What are you doing?" He replied, "Mom, you told me to pray, but I have never prayed in my life and I don't know how. So I gave God the whole alphabet and asked him to make a good prayer of it."[1485]

Prayer List Lorena Workman's granddaughter was saying her prayers before going to sleep. The little girl prayed about her grandpa's recovery from surgery and her aunt's recent injury. She then turned to her grandmother and asked, "Grandma, your cold isn't worth praying about, is it?"[1486]

Preaching After resigning his pastorate to go lead another church, this pastor was approached by an endearing older member of the congregation. She wept over the pastor's decision to leave and said, "Things will never be the same." The minister tried to console her by saying, "Don't worry, I'm confident God will send you a new pastor who is better than me." She continued to sob and replied, "That's what the last three pastors have said, but they just keep getting worse."[1487]

Preaching A young pastor was gloating with pride over the large crowd in his sanctuary. On this Sunday night the church was packed to see the Christmas play. While the pastor was savoring the moment, a young boy stepped behind him. The youngster was amazed by the crowd as well. As the two stood by each other taking in the crowded view, the little boy revealed a very humbling truth. He said, "Preacher, have you ever noticed that we have our largest crowds when you're not scheduled to preach?"[1488]

Preaching It was a typical church problem. This man couldn't sing a lick but he felt "called" to the choir. Several people gently suggested he might be better suited for some other area of ministry, but he thought it best to stay in the choir. The Minister of Music became very upset and confided in the pastor that he was going to resign if this man wasn't told to abandon the choir. Not wanting to lose his prized worship leader, the pastor approached this man about dropping out of choir. The man asked, "Why should I leave the choir?" The pastor replied, "Because a half-dozen people told me you can't sing." The off-key singer snorted, "So! I know fifty people who told me you can't preach!"[1489]

Preaching R. E. O. White described preaching as "a monstrous monologue by a moron to mutes." . . . One man described preaching as "the art of talking in someone else's sleep." . . . Buckner Fanning said, "When my deacons fall asleep while I'm preaching, I just see it as their vote of confidence that I won't say anything heretical."[1490]

Preaching The young pastor was anxious to get feedback on his sermons as he greeted the congregation after their morning worship service. Most of the comments were polite and noncommittal. One older woman, though, always gave him the same appraisal. She consistently said, "Pastor, that was a warm sermon." At first he took it in stride and felt certain she intended it as a compliment, but after several weeks he began to wonder why she kept telling him his sermons were "warm." Finally, he pressed her one Sunday and asked, "Mrs. Baxter, what exactly do you mean when you say, 'that was a warm sermon?'" She smiled and replied, "Pastor Collins, I thought you knew. Warm means, not so hot."[1491]

Preoperation Prayer Grandpa was going into surgery and his young great-granddaughter wanted to pray for him. She touched the hearts of all who heard her prayer and brought a smile to each stressed-looking face. She prayed, "Dear God, please take care of my 'ampie. His heart is sick and he needs to have an ice maker put in."[1492]

Pretense During the early years of Albert Einstein's career, he traveled extensively giving lectures on his innovative theories. Folklore says he was chauffeured by the same man for all of these engagements. After hearing the same lecture over one hundred times, the chauffeur told Einstein he could deliver the speech as well as the brilliant scientist. They agreed to see if he could do it, so Einstein dressed like a chauffeur and his driver took the podium. The lecture came off without a hitch . . . that is until they opened the floor for questions. One listener asked a very complex question about relativity. The chauffeur stood pensive for a moment, then replied, "That question is so easy, I'm going to let my chauffeur answer it."[1493]

Pride A very successful entrepreneur let his portfolio go to his head. He had all but conquered the business world so he felt he was ready to wrestle with God. He claimed he could do anything God could, so he challenged God to a contest. The Lord graciously accepted the wager and met him for a round of "creating." The man looked at all of creation and said, "I can do that!" God simply nodded and said, "Why don't we start out with my finest creation of all . . . man. I created man from the dust of the ground. Let's see if you can do that." The arrogant billionaire gave a cocky chuckle, then bent over to scoop some dirt. God calmly reached over to the stooping man and said, "You have to use your own dirt."[1494]

Pride One pompous candidate made a quick run through a nursing home in a final attempt to secure some last-minute votes. His bubble of pride was burst when he engaged a very witty retiree. As he approached her wheelchair, he extended his hand and asked in a very loud voice, "Do you know who I am?" She graciously took his hand, took a few seconds to examine his face, then replied, "No, but if you stop at that desk over there, they'll tell you who you are."[1495]

Procrastination A nostalgic, young man was going through some old relics in his parents' attic. He stumbled on his varsity letter jacket that he wore in high school ten years before. He tried it on, stuck his hands in the pockets, and to his surprise, he found and old claim ticket for some shoes that were to be repaired a decade ago. On a whim, he went to the shoe store and discovered that they were still in business. He then went inside and presented the ticket to see what the owner would say. The man silently took the receipt, looked it over, and then went to his cobbler's bench. He returned a few minutes later and mumbled, "They won't be ready until Friday."[1496]

Prodigal Son   This true story hails from Bari, Italy. It seems a wayward son went to snatching purses to finance his drug addiction. On August 10, 1995, he made a grave mistake. He sped down a crowded street on a motorcycle and snatched the purse of . . . his own mother. He apparently didn't recognize her from behind but she sure knew it was her boy. She was so angry that she immediately reported it to the police and he was arrested shortly thereafter.[1497]

Productivity   Fred was one of those guys who never came to work late and he never cut out early, but people frequently wondered what he did all day. After extensive research and evaluation by the boss, it was determined that Fred actually did very little work so he was fired. A few days later, one of Fred's colleagues stopped by to see the boss and said, "I'd like to apply for the vacancy that Fred left." The supervisor replied, "Fred didn't leave a vacancy!"[1498]

Progress Report   After he bombed an important test, Eddie's second-grade teacher sent home a progress report. His dad reviewed the teacher's assessment and then asked his son about the disastrous test. Eddie replied, "Dad, there were two answers to every question . . . mine and the right one."[1499]

Public Speaking   A minister was invited to be a guest speaker at a church banquet. The evening included a wonderful dinner prior to the minister's talk. At the head table, next to the minister, was the master of ceremonies. Just before the scheduled talk, the emcee looked out at all the people talking and laughing. He then turned to the minister and asked, "Are you ready to speak or should we let them enjoy themselves for a little while longer?"[1500]

Puppet Atheist   Two puppets were privately talking behind stage when one of them became very transparent with his doubts and said, "You know, sometimes I think there is no hand."[1501]

Quality Control   The following sign was posted in a farm equipment repair shop: "We do three types of jobs: cheap, quick, and good. You can have any two. A good quick job won't be cheap. A good job cheap won't be quick. A cheap job quick won't be good."[1502]

Real Revival During a community minister's breakfast, three pastors discussed the successes of their respective revival services. The Methodist minister boasted that they had received four new families during their revival. The Baptist pastor felt his church had done even better because six families joined their church. The Presbyterian cleric just smiled and said, "Our revival was better than both of yours combined. We lost ten of our most cantankerous families."[1503]

Receding Hairline The former high school class president brought his old schoolmates to their knees in laughter. Twenty-five years after graduating with a full head of hair, he was now sporting a growing forehead. He told the reunion participants, "You guys were right. Twenty-five years ago you selected me as the one 'Most Likely to Recede.'"[1504]

Recruitment An Army officer was recruiting some young men to join his airborne battalion. One new recruit was very resistant and shared some strong points of contention. He first explained he did not want to parachute because the chute might not open. The officer quickly noted that the percentage of failure was minuscule and then pointed out that such concern was unfounded because every jumper would also have a reserve chute. The recruit then complained about landing in obscure places where he would have to walk great distances after landing. The officer countered with the guarantee that trucks would pick them up so that he wouldn't have to make any long hikes. Realizing his fears were dispelled, the young man agreed to become a paratrooper. On his first jump, the main chute didn't open. He quickly struggled to cut open his reserve chute but found that it wouldn't open as well. He then looked down at the rapidly approaching ground and grumbled, "I bet he was lying about the trucks too."[1505]

Red-Letter Edition Little Charlie was accustomed to having his grandmother read the Bible whenever he visited. As they sat together and looked at God's Word, Mrs. Babb reminded her grandson that the red words were those spoken by Jesus. One night when he and his parents were on vacation at a motel, Charlie found a Gideon Bible that was not a red-letter edition. He thumbed through the pages, then gently laid it back on the table and said, "Jesus didn't say nothing in that Bible!"[1506]

Relief Pitcher A pitcher was struggling on the mound. His opponent's score was increasing so dramatically that the coach motioned to the bullpen and made his way out to the mound. The persistent pitcher didn't want to head for the showers so he asked the coach if he could stay in the game. The coach pointed out the score and the fact that the bases were once again loaded. The determined hurler said, "Yeah, but I struck this guy out last time he was up." The coach quietly took the ball out of his pitcher's glove and replied, "I know son, but that's the only out we have in this inning."[1507]

Repititious Prayers Lorene Workman's granddaughter came over to spend the night. The next morning as they were talking, Workman asked her grandchild if she said her prayers last night before going to sleep. The little girl replied, "No, Granny. I got down on my knees to pray, but I got to thinking that God might be tired of hearing the same old prayer every night, so I crawled into bed and told him about Little Red Riding Hood.[1508]

Resolutions Darrell was hard at work on his computer when his wife walked into the room. It was late and she wondered what was causing him to spend so much time at the keyboard. Darrell explained, "I'm making a list of all the things I ought to do before I die. It's my 'oughto-biography.'"[1509]

Response Time Seth came into the house with his new pants dirty and torn. His mother looked at the four-year-old's damaged clothes and sighed, "Seth, did you fall down with your new pants on?" The little guy quickly replied, "Yes, Mommy, there wasn't time to take them off."[1510]

Role Model Several years ago, Grey Baker took his three-year-old grandson along for a round of golf. Little Trevor seemed to enjoy it so his grandpa bought him a set of play clubs. During an ensuing family cookout, Trevor told everyone to watch him play golf. He swung the golf club, said a bad word, and then threw his club in the tree.[1511]

Romance An older couple had been married for many years. One day as they were traveling down a beautiful and romantically inspiring road, the woman turned to her husband and said, "Sweetheart, have you noticed how we don't sit close together any more?" The old man tightened his grip on the steering wheel, tensed up his jaw, and replied, "I ain't never moved!"[1512]

Romance The man knew he wasn't very romantic and had been recently convicted of his inattentiveness to his wife's need for romance. He made a commitment to change and started out by buying his wife some flowers on the way home from work. He wanted to really impress her so he went to the front door and rang the doorbell. When she opened the door, he just stuck out the flowers and gave her a big smile. His wife stepped back, sized up the situation, and then said, "What a fine day this has been. Rachel came home from school sick, Daniel broke a window with his baseball, the microwave won't work, and now you come home drunk!"[1513]

Rope Meter Ethan's mom laid down the law. She said, "I'm about at the end of my rope so you better behave or I'll pull out daddy's belt and use it on you." Ethan clearly understood the magnitude of his mom's declaration and learned the importance of reading her mood. The next day when Ethan woke up, the first thing he did was ask, "Mommy, where are you on your rope today?"[1514]

Sabbath Rest After working hard all day on Sunday, a pastor cherished his Monday of rest. When he returned to the office on Tuesday, he was scolded by a church member who claimed to have a pressing need while he was relaxing at home. She chided, "The devil never takes a day off!" The minister then calmly replied, "So, if I didn't take a day off I'd be just like him, wouldn't I?"[1515]

Safety Paul Delago and his wife have routinely drilled their children about proper safety procedures. Their discussions include things like seat belts, house fires, and responses to strangers. During one drill, Paul asked four-year-old Maria what she would do if a stranger asked her to get in his car. She proudly replied, "I would buckle up!"[1516]

Safety Some stores are filled with gadgets, gizmos, and weaponry for protecting yourself. Spray this, shoot that, and never be caught without it. Helen Mundis has taken a different approach. She says, "If you want to be safe on the streets at night, carry a projector and slides of your last vacation."[1517]

Salvation Paul Stripling has served as the director of missions in the Waco Association of Texas. On one occasion a woman asked him if he was a minister. He affirmed he was, then she asked to what denomination he belonged. When he told her Baptist, she railed, "Oh, so you're one of that narrow-minded bunch who thinks they are the only group that's going to make it to heaven!" Stripling diplomatically replied, "Lady, I am more narrow-minded than that. I'm not sure all of our group will make it."[1518]

Santa Claus John was still shaking his head in disbelief over the recent purchase of some very expensive skates for his oldest son when his youngest son approached him about the possibility of also getting some fancy skates like his brother. Remembering that Christmas was a few months away, John thought he would stall his son by suggesting he put it on his list for Santa. His little boy pointed down at the skates he was wearing and emphatically said, "No way! Who do you think brought me these cheap old plastic skates last year?"[1519]

Santa Claus Nobody is exempted from the antics of Dennis the Menace, even Santa Claus. In one of his comic strips, Hank Ketcham has his famous animated character sitting on the lap of Santa. Dennis is shown whispering into his ear, "Do you believe in yourself?"[1520]

School When Chase returned home from his first day of kindergarten, his mother asked how he liked school. Chase gave her an answer that represents most students of any age. He said, "It's fine, but not something you'd want to do every day."[1521]

School Learning Several weeks into the semester, Susan Moser asked her first-grade son for his evaluation of school. He said, "Oh, I love school. It's great!" After a brief pause he added, "Well, except for one thing. I don't really like it when Mrs. Decker tries to teach us stuff."[1522]

School Supplies A high- school student returned from the first day of school and began to share with his parents the various supplies he needed for his classes. He began his list with a protractor and compass for geometry. For English he needed a dictionary, and biology required a dissecting kit. He told his parents the coach makes everybody buy the school-colored gym uniform and then he noted, "And for Driver's Ed I need a car."[1523]

Secretarial Smile Doris Johnson got an unexpected job evaluation from a first-grader who was enrolled in the school where she worked. She had previously shared the job with a very pleasant and vivacious woman named Julie. When Julie quit, Doris became the full-time secretary. A little boy noticed this change and came by every day at noon for a whole week. He'd walk in, look over the counter, seem a bit confused, then quietly leave the office. Finally, Doris asked him if he needed some help. This little first-grader simply inquired, "Where's the *nice* secretary?"[1524]

Secret of Life Charlie Brown's sister, Sally, approached her brother and declared, "I think I've discovered the secret to life—you just hang around until you get used to it."[1525]

Selective Memory In one of Charles Schulz's *Peanuts* classics, Linus tells Charlie Brown about his dad's basketball career in high school. Linus notes, "He said he can't remember ever losing a game." Charlie Brown is very impressed and says, "They must have had a great team." Linus replies with reality, "No, he has a terrible memory!"[1526]

Self-Control Two cowboys and an Indian had been riding hard all day. There had been no time for lunch and dinner was still about an hour away. The two cowboys began talking about the big meals they were going to eat once they got to town. The Indian didn't enter the conversation so they asked him, "Aren't you hungry?" The Indian shrugged his shoulders and said, "No." When the threesome arrived at their destination, they ordered large meals and started filling their empty stomachs. The Indian ate faster than the other two and reached for any food that wasn't nailed to the table. The cowboys laughed and reminded him that less than an hour ago he said he wasn't hungry. The Indian poetically said, "Not wise to be hungry then. No food."[1527]

Self-Help A man entered his local bookstore with a new resolve to change his life. He confidently walked to the counter and asked, "Where are your self-help books?" The gum-chewing clerk popped back, "If I told you that, it would defeat the purpose, wouldn't it?"[1528]

Self-Help A world-renowned self-help author came to a highly publicized book signing for his latest tome. He applied the principles of his self-help philosophy by not signing a single book. He simply had each buyer sign the book themselves.[1529]

Semantics The church secretary answered a most unusual call. The caller asked if he could speak to "the head hog." She quickly defended the dignity of her boss and replied, "Our pastor is held in the highest of esteem around here and we address him as Reverend H. C. Harold. And currently, Reverend Harold is out of the office." The man then responded, "Well, I just learned about your new building program and my CPA recommended a donation of $100,000 to provide a good tax shelter for me." The secretary quickly responded, "Oh, wait a minute, I believe I see the fat pig coming down the hall right now."[1530]

Senior Softball Randy Hawkins was playing softball in his forties while most of his teammates were considerably younger. During one particular game, Hawkins was playing third base when a line drive was hit over his head. He jumped as high as he could but couldn't quite get a glove on it. At the end of the inning, when everyone was heading to the dugout, the left-fielder caught up with Randy and said, "That much," while holding his thumb and forefinger a couple of inches apart. The older third baseman replied, "I know, I almost had it!" His young outfield friend shot back, "No, I mean that's how far you got off the ground."[1531]

Sermon Helps The young minister's son was intrigued by what his father did every Sunday morning during the offertory. Finally he asked, "Daddy, why do you always close your eyes when Mrs. Feldon plays the organ and those mean-looking men make everybody put money in their wood Frisbees?" The pastor told his son he was praying. He said, "I ask God to make me a good preacher." The little guy solemnly asked, "So why doesn't he?"[1532]

Sex Education Lynn Aseltine was on her way to the mall when her five-year-old son noticed the colorful paint on an adult bookstore. David asked his mother, "What do they do in there?" Lynn took a deep breath and tried to explain that some people do things other than what God wants. She then rambled on about how important it is to always obey God. David seemed satisfied with his mother's extensive answer. Later on, David rode down the same road with his father. Upon seeing the same place he asked, "Daddy, what do they do in that store?" His dad wisely and honestly replied, "I don't know, David. I've never been in there." David quickly said, "You can ask Mommy. She knows all about it."[1533]

Sharing While engaged in an argument with her husband, a woman vented her intense displeasure with his consistent use of *my* house, and *my* car, and *my* children. She yelled, "I'm your wife and we share everything. You should be saying *our!*" Without saying a word, he continued looking under the bed for something. She got very exasperated and shouted, "What are you looking for now?" He coolly replied, "*our* shoes!"[1534]

Shopping Two men were off-shore fishing when they were caught by a sudden and fierce storm. The waves flipped their boat and they were both thrown into the water. As they hung on to some capsized cargo and tried to figure out what they were going to do, one man said, "You got admit, though, this sure beats shopping."[1535]

Sibling Rivalry Two children flew into the room in an obvious uproar as both were seeking advocacy from their dad. Each one was trying to drown out the other as they simultaneously shared their side of the story. The father yelled for a truce, then asked the younger boy for his explanation of the problem. He shouted, "It all started when Michael hit me back."[1536]

Siblings An older brother always made fun of his younger siblings. The elder son prided himself in being so much smarter than his "dumb" little sister and brother. One of his favorite tricks was to make fun of them in front of his friends by offering them the choice between a nickel or a dime. He would hold out his hand with a nickel and a dime then tell them to pick which one they wanted. Each time the two little kids would go for the nickel. The young teen would then die laughing with his friends. One friend had seen the trick a dozen times so he pulled the two little kids aside and asked why they always chose the nickel. Their response was priceless. With a mischievous smile they agreed, "If we picked the dime he would quit giving us all of those nickels."[1537]

Sinful Nature A conscientious Bible teacher was trying to teach his class of small children about the nature of sin. He hit a snag when he started telling them we are all born in sin. One little girl gave him a puzzled look, then said very seriously, "I wasn't born in sin. I was born in November."[1538]

Single Request John Fettermam told of an interesting memorial service for an elderly woman who had never married. In her instructions for the funeral she insisted that no men were to be used as pallbearers. She wrote, "They wouldn't take me out while I was alive; I don't want them to take me out when I'm dead."[1539]

Sin of Omission One little boy gave an interesting answer when his Sunday school teacher was talking about the difference between sins of commission and sins of omission. Derek explained to his teacher that the sins of omission are "those sins that we want to do but we just haven't gotten around to yet."[1540]

Sleeping Disorder Did you hear about the dyslexic insomniac agnostic? He stayed awake all night wondering if there really is a dog.[1541]

Snoring A distraught man sought medical help for his problem with snoring. The physician asked if this snoring was causing friction in his marriage. The man replied, "No, it's primarily just an embarrassment for my wife. The real problem is the distraction it creates for our pastor."[1542]

Soap Operas A husband scolded his wife for watching "trash TV" when he entered the room and heard Jerry Springer. She felt vindicated from her husband's remarks when she snapped back, "I'm *not* watching Jerry Springer. I'm watching *As the World Turns* and they're watching Jerry Springer!"[1543]

Social Security Two young children were riding in the backseat of their grandparents' car when Grandpa pulled into a parking lot of the local Social Security office. They had heard the name mentioned many times before so they were intrigued by the opportunity to actually see the building. Grandma stayed in the car with the kids while Grandpa walked into the building. As they waited in the car she overheard her oldest grandson explain the situation to his little sister. He said, "I'm not sure, but I think that's where Grandma and Grandpa get their allowance."[1544]

Special Funeral A distraught lady approached a Baptist minister about conducting a funeral for her dog. With great dignity, the pastor said he would not be able to assist the woman but suggested she contact a Pentecostal minister instead. The grieving pet lover then requested his help with one other item of business. She asked, "How much should I pay this Pentecostal minister for conducting my dog's funeral? Do you think $500 is enough?" The minister quickly changed his position and replied, "Oh, madam, why didn't you tell me your dog was Baptist?"[1545]

Special Music Four-year-old Delanee was making quite an impression on her grandmother during the time of congregational singing. They weren't seated next to each other, but Delanee's granny could see her singing away on a rather difficult hymn. After the service, Mrs. Marriot complimented her granddaughter for being able to sing such a difficult song. Little Delanee replied, "I didn't know any of the words in the song, so I just sang 'Jingle Bells.'"[1546]

Speeding As the policeman wrote out a speeding ticket the driver remarked, "I wouldn't have been speeding if I'd known you were hiding by that overpass."[1547]

Spiritual Checkup A pediatrician tried to make his check-ups as enjoyable as possible. With one little four-year-old girl he looked into her ears and asked, "Do you think I'll find Big Bird in here?" The girl didn't say a word. He then used a tongue depressor to gaze down her throat. This time he asked, "Do you think I'll see Cookie Monster down there?" The girl remained silent. When he placed the stethoscope to her chest he asked, "Do you think I'll hear Barney in there?" This time the girl spoke up. She replied, "Oh, no! Jesus is in my heart. Barney is on my underwear."[1548]

Spiritual Growth On the way home from church, a pastor's young boy asked his father, "How do you spell 'God?'" The pastor was thrilled that his son was showing signs of spiritual interest. He spelled out G-O-D and anxiously waited for his son's next theological question. The little boy then asked, "How do you spell 'Zilla?'"[1549]

Spiritual Laws One young child put a new twist on Bill Bright's Four Spiritual Laws. During a children's sermon the pastor asked his little listeners, "What must you do to receive God's forgiveness of your sins?" A child quickly declared, "First of all, you have to sin."[1550]

Stealing Those who steal aren't too bright and here's some evidence to prove it: A burglar in New Jersey stuck a piece of paper in the lock of an office building so he could later return for the heist. The police had no problem locating the thief because the paper he used was a parking ticket that clearly identified who he was and where he lived. . . . A twenty-two-year-old man in Wichita, Kansas, got arrested for trying to pass counterfeit money at an airport hotel. The counterfeit loot was two $16 bills. . . . Policemen in Rhode Island knew they had apprehended the right suspect when it came time to post bail. The man was charged with a string of vending machine robberies and paid his $400 bail entirely in quarters.[1551]

Stewardship Campaign The pastor was fully expected to deliver a moving stewardship sermon as the church prepared to launch their new building program. Everyone knew it was a big step of faith to raise that much money, so you can imagine their utter surprise when he stepped to the pulpit and proclaimed, "We already have all the money we need to complete our new building." He then added, "There is just one problem . . . most of it is still in your pockets."[1552]

Sunday School The little boy asked his father, "Dad, did Grandpa make you go to Sunday school when you were my age?" The man replied, "He sure did. We went every Sunday." The little guy then remarked, "Well, I bet it won't do me any good either."[1553]

Swedish Diet On a long, transatlantic flight, a gentlemen noticed an adjacent passenger pouring salt and pepper all over her dessert. Knowing that she was from a foreign country, the man assumed she didn't realize what she was doing. He quickly tried to stop her and said, "Madam, you don't need to do that. That's your dessert." The very attractive and shapely Swedish woman remarked, "Oh yes I do. It keeps me from eating it."[1554]

Sweet Evangelism The pastor was presenting his sermon on evangelism to the children. He had a fishing pole and had already talked about different types of bait that will attract fish. He then turned to the Lord's proclamation for each of us to be fishers of men. Looking for an answer from the children, he asked, "If I was going to fish for men, what kind of bait do you think I should use?" Without hesitation, a young boy shouted out, "Donuts!"[1555]

Sweet Tooth While shopping at the grocery store, Louise Henry observed a college student with a serious sweet tooth. The man was buying a bag of cookies plus ingredients to make cookies. The congenial clerk asked if he was buying the cookies in case his homemade treats didn't turn out. The coed replied, "No, they're for me to eat while I'm waiting for the others to bake."[1556]

Sympathy While lying in bed with his broken leg from a one-day ski trip, Allen read through his mail. One card hurt him more than his leg. It was a sympathy card from his boss that read, "I'm sorry you broke your leg while staying home sick with the flu."[1557]

Tactful Termination It has to be the most tactful method by which anybody has ever been fired. The boss delivered a pink slip to an unnecessary worker by saying, "Son, I don't know how our company could make it without you, but starting Monday we're going to try."[1558]

Taxes A terminally ill man knew he wouldn't live much beyond April fifteenth so he used his death as a protest against the IRS. On his tax return he answered, "You are!" to the question that asked, "Who are your dependents?" He then gave the executor of his estate a large envelope addressed to the IRS. He said, "When I die, put my ashes in this envelope, mail it to the IRS, and include a note that says, 'Now you have everything.'"[1559]

Teenager After a severe blizzard, a father called home to check on his family. The teenage son answered the phone and the father could hear the TV blaring in the background. The dad asked, "Where's your mother?" The teen explained, "She's outside shoveling snow." The father admonished his son for letting his mother work outside while he watched TV inside. He gruffly asked, "Why aren't you out there helping her?" The teen answered, "Because Grandma's using the other shovel."[1560]

Teenagers A teenage boy said, "No one is going to tell me what to do. I'm going to join the Marines!"[1561]

Teenagers Is it easier to be a teenager than the parent of one? Legend has it that one day Peter passed by a blind man and healed him. He later saw a demoniac and set him free. When he met an obstinate sinner he prayed for the man and he received Christ. He then saw a man crying so he knelt down to ask about his problem. The man said he was the father of a teenager. All Peter could do was sit down and weep with him.[1562]

Teenagers Parents of teenagers often worry about their children when they go out with their friends. A recent survey shows their fears are unfounded. Researchers asked teens from across the country, "What do you do when you go out?" These pollsters were astonished to find that 100 percent of all teenage respondents said that when they go out they do "nothing."[1563]

Television Six-year-old Myles started making some rather unusual observations about divorce. After sharing his unorthodox thoughts, his father asked, "Who's been telling you all of this stuff?" He replied, "Nobody...I guess I've just been watching too much TV."[1564]

Telling Time A mother had been working with her young son teaching him to tell time with a nondigital clock. For several days they had been talking about the "small hand" and the "big hand." When she heard him walk into the kitchen where they have a clock with hands, she called out from the other room, "Cameron, what is the little hand on?" He yelled back, "A chocolate chip cookie."[1565]

Temptation A young couple was struggling with their finances. In an effort to get a better handle on their spending, they agreed that whenever they were tempted to make an impulsive purchase they would say, "Get behind me Satan." One evening the wife came home with a very elegant dress that was obviously not a budgeted item. She proudly modeled it for her husband and asked him what he thought. He noted its beauty but wondered why his wife had not adhered to their little agreement. He said, "I thought we agreed that whenever we are tempted to make an impulsive purchase we would say, 'Get behind me Satan.' Did you forget to do that?" The wife replied, "Oh no, I did that just like we agreed." The husband then asked, "Well, what happened this time?" She confessed, "He said it looks good from back here too!"[1566]

Ten Commandments A gregarious minister was out inviting people to church when he came upon a man who said he had no interest in coming to church. The minister asked if there was some particular reason he didn't care for church. The man answered, "Oh, yeah . . . there are too many rules at church." The minister sarcastically replied, "I know what you mean. Don't steal, don't murder, love God, love your family . . . how could anyone handle that kind of pressure?"[1567]

Ten Commandments While fishing off-shore in his small boat, a man fell overboard and immediately started to panic. Because he was alone, he quickly turned to God. He cried out, "Lord, please save me! If you'll just let me live I'll start keeping the Ten Commandments. Thou shalt not, uh, thou shalt not, uh . . . Oh God, if you'll just get me out of this mess I promise to learn the Ten Commandments."[1568]

Test Results A professor at the University of North Carolina had a unique method for accentuating test scores. If you recorded an A, he would give you a dime. A grade of B earned a nickel, and any C got a penny. Once while he was distributing the graded tests with their corresponding monetary reward, a below average student asked the prof, "So, how much do I owe you?"[1569]

Thanksgiving A grouchy, young man was confronted by his pastor for being so negative during the Thanksgiving season. The young man responded, "Preacher, what do I have to be thankful for? I don't even have enough money to pay all of my bills!" The wise pastor replied, "In that case, you should be thankful that you aren't one of your creditors."[1570]

Theological Debate While walking along the beach, a little boy found a dead seagull. He quickly ran over to his mother and pulled her out of the beach chair. He showed her the dead bird and asked, "What happened to him?" The woman explained, "He died and went to heaven." The little boy stared at this lifeless seagull for a few moments then asked, "And then God threw him back down?"[1571]

Tithing A father had been teaching his children about tithing long before they could understand what it meant. When his son, Myles, was eight years old he reminded his dad of how difficult this concept can be for a child. On this particular day, Myles's mother and sister were away at camp. As he and his father were preparing to leave for church, Myles's father told him to make sure he had his tithe for church. Five minutes later, he came into the bedroom and quietly said, "Daddy, Mommy never makes me wear ties to church."[1572]

Tongue Tied Those who knew Darrell best, knew his tongue was all but tied by the intense verbosity of his wife. The woman's continuous speech eliminated the possibility of Darrell saying much in her presence. Whether or not it was the inundation of her words that eventually killed him, Darrell died nonetheless. His oldest son, who worked in another state, flew home for his dad's untimely death. His younger brother, who had been with his father when he died, picked up his older brother at the airport. The older son asked, "Did Dad have any last words before he died?" Darrell's younger son simply replied, "Nope! Mom was with him till the end."[1573]

Tough Day A teenager named Alex meandered up to some friends he hadn't seen in a while and they asked, "How's it going?" He answered, "Not well. First I got tonsillitis, and then appendicitis. After that I ended up with pneumonia as well as bursitis." One friend compassionately touched his arm and said, "Wow, you really have had a tough time." Alex replied, "I'll say. That was the toughest spelling test I've ever had."[1574]

Tough Questions A sea captain discovered a new approach for giving promotions to his crewmen. Three men were up for promotion but the captain had only enough in the budget to give two of them a raise. He lined them up and said they would be evaluated on their response to just one question. To the first man he asked, "What ship sank on its maiden voyage in 1912?" The sailor quickly replied, "The *Titanic*, sir." To the second prospective promotee he inquired, "And how many people perished in that nautical disaster?" The man hesitantly guessed 1,503. The captain gave his approval then turned to the third man and asked, "What were their names?"[1575]

Truth Have you ever noticed how you can tell people there are more than 300,000 billion stars in the universe and they'll believe you, but tell them the paint is wet and they'll touch it to see if you're telling the truth?[1576]

Upward Mobility Complaining and materialism were escalating around the house so Dad sat his children down for a talk. He said, "Kids, you don't realize how good you have it. When I was a boy, I had to get up before daylight to deliver newspapers. I walked to school in the rain and snow, then worked at a grocery store after school. Even then, we didn't always have enough to eat." The three children's silence made him feel as though the needed message had gotten through until his little four-year-old said, "Boy, Dad, I bet your glad you live with us now."[1577]

Used Cars A little girl was curious about the destiny of old cars so she asked her mother, "What happens to old cars when they stop running?" The mother sarcastically replied, "Someone sells them to your father."[1578]

Vacation Bible School When Dorothy Gray's son was a little boy, she took him to Vacation Bible School. Upon returning from the first day, she asked him how he liked it. He said it was okay but he didn't want to go back. Gray curiously asked him, "Why?" The little guy replied, "I learned enough."[1579]

Vacation Mail As a couple sat on the beach at their vacation resort, the wife read a postcard their children had mailed to the hotel. It simply read, "Dear Mom and Dad, We're having a wonderful time. Glad you are there."[1580]

Vacation Packing Larry had done everything possible to pack their van for vacation. The cargo area was packed to the roof, the luggage rack was bulging, and the seating area hardly had any room for the kids to sit. When his wife walked out with two more suitcases and a large backpack, Larry snorted, "I thought we were going to get away from it all . . . not take it with us."[1581]

Vacation Planning One of four senior adult golfing buddies showed up at the clubhouse looking rather frustrated. His concerned cronies asked what was bothering him. The old man answered, "My wife and I can't agree on our vacation. I want to go to Florida and she wants to go with me."[1582]

Vacation Spending Fred and Oleta got a rather unusual note with their American Express statement. Whereas most credit card providers encourage their clients to use that charge account extensively while on vacation, the Murdocks got an entirely different message. Their monthly statement contained a special notice that simply read, "Please leave home without it!"[1583]

Vacation Stress Darrell was looking forward to a nice relaxing vacation. He only got two weeks a year so he wanted to make the most of his short break. As Darrell loaded the van, his wife began reading off their itinerary. She said, "Our total driving time will be 48 hours, time spent visiting with relatives should be around 125 hours, and seeing the sites will take nearly 30 hours." Darrell suddenly felt very stressed about their vacation. His wife accentuated his feelings by noting, "If we plan to do any relaxing we'll have to do it in a hurry."[1584]

Vacation Travel A young family set out on a long drive for their summer vacation. As is customary with small children, they soon began to ask, "Are we there yet?" After several unsuccessful attempts to communicate how far they must travel, the father became irritated and gave some stern instructions. He said, "We won't be there until it's dark so I don't want to hear anyone else ask, 'Are we there yet?!'" The car became very quiet for about fifteen minutes then the silence was broken when little Amy asked, "Is it dark yet?"[1585]

Vacation Travel While Charles was traveling with his six-year-old cousin, Larry, he became agitated by the constant repeating of that dreaded question, "Are we almost there?" Charles finally lost his patience and gruffly warned his little cousin, "Don't ask me that anymore! It will be a long time before we get there." After a few minutes of silence, little Larry asked, "Will I still be six when we get there?"[1586]

Wake-Up Call The pastor of a smaller church was known for calling attention to people who fell asleep during his sermons. One morning a deacon dozed off and the preacher stopped his message. He addressed the deacon's wife and said, "Mrs. Taylor, wake up your husband!" Mrs. Taylor shot back, "You wake him up . . . you put him to sleep!"[1587]

Wedding Cake Disaster A cake decorator in New Zealand was asked to include the reference to a Bible verse on the couple's wedding cake. They requested 1 John 4:18 because it states, "There is no fear in love, but perfect love drives out fear." Unfortunately, the cake decorator wasn't a Bible scholar so the cake ended up with a reference to John's gospel instead of his epistle. In beautiful print was "John 4:18." Had the decorator taken time to look up the verse this error would have been detected before the wedding. "You have had five husbands, and the man you now have is not your husband."[1588]

Wedding Cakes Sarah attended her first wedding when she was just four years old. As you can imagine, she asked a lot of questions. During the reception she wondered why there were two different cakes. Her mother explained one was a groom's cake and the other was a bride's cake. Sarah then remarked, "What's the matter, Mommy, haven't they learned to share yet?"[1589]

Wedding Invitations Little Alex was enthralled by the story of Jesus turning water into wine at a wedding. After Sunday school he quickly told the story to his father while they were waiting for the worship service to begin. Alex's dad listened intently then asked his son, "So what did you learn from all of that?" Alex excitedly replied, "I learned if you're having a wedding, make sure Jesus is there!"[1590]

Wedding Notes The couple was all excited about the big day of their wedding. Every detail had been planned with precision so when they finally arrived at the altar they were unusually relaxed. That is until the minister began to speak. He opened his Bible and discovered he had the wrong notes. He whispered to the bride and groom, "These are my notes for a funeral, not a wedding." He paused for a few moments and then mumbled, "Oh well, they're both pretty much the same."[1591]

Wedding Options Six-year-old Melissa was very excited about being at her first wedding. She closely observed every aspect of the service. When the pastor, groom, and groomsmen came in, she couldn't take her eyes off of them. Then the organ piped up and everyone looked to the back of the church. Melissa saw the bride then glanced back at all the men standing up front. She then whispered to her grandmother, "Does she get to take her pick?"[1592]

Wedding Vows Comic strip artist, Joe Martin, recently posed an interesting "what if." He wondered what weddings would be like if Regis Philbin had gone into the ministry. With creative artistic design, he drew a couple repeating their wedding vows. After the bride and groom said, "I do," Reverend Philbin asked, "Is that your final answer?"[1593]

Wedding Vows It was the strangest response a minister had ever seen at a wedding. He asked the groom, "Do you take this woman for better or for worse, for richer or for poorer, and in sickness and in health? The tentative young man replied, "Yes, no, yes, no, no, yes."[1594]

Weight Loss Harold's wife deflated his ego when she announced, "Harold dropped some weight . . . it dropped from his chest to his stomach."[1595]

Weight Watcher During the children's sermon, a pastor asked if they knew what happens when people go to the hospital. The little kids began to rattle off suggestions: that's where people go when they're sick, broken arms are repaired there, mommies get babies, and some people lose their tonsils at the hospital. One little boy held up his hand and declared, "The hospital is where you go to get a hipposuction."[1596]

Weighty Compliment A woman was pleased with the way a new sweater improved her figure. Her six-year-old son noted the sweater and said, "Mommy, that's a pretty sweater. You look like the Wheel of Fortune." She was touched by the compliment because she assumed he was equating her with Vanna White. She replied, "Thank you, Sweetheart, but I think you mean that I look like Vanna White." He answered, "No, Mom. I mean you look like the wheel."[1597]

Wise Men During a school play near London, three six-year-old boys acted out the role of the wise men. As they presented their gifts at the nativity scene, each boy stepped forward and stated what they were offering to Christ. The first held out his arms and said, "Gold." The second boy knelt down and said, "Myrrh." The last boy stepped forward and declared, "Frank sent this."[1598]

Wise Women Someone pondered what the first Christmas might have been like if wise women had come from the east instead of wise men. They would have asked for directions, made it to Bethlehem on time, helped with the delivery, cleaned up the stable, made a decent meal, and brought some practical gifts.[1599]

Women The following are "rules" from an undocumented fax. 1. The female always makes the rules. 2. The rules are subject to change at any time without prior notification. 3. No male can possibly know all the rules. 4. If the female suspects the male knows all the rules, she must immediately change some of the rules. 5. The female is *never* wrong. 6. If the female is wrong, it is because of a flagrant misunderstanding that was a direct result of something the male did or said that was wrong. 7. If rule #6 applies, the male must apologize immediately for causing the misunderstanding. 8. The female can change her mind at any given point in time. 9. The male must never change his mind without expressed, written consent from the female. 10. The female has every right to be angry or upset at any time. 11. The male must remain calm at all times, unless of course the female wants him to be angry or upset. 12. The female must under *no* circumstances let the male know whether or not she wants him to be angry or upset.[1600]

Women "There are two ways to handle women. Unfortunately, no one knows either one of them."[1601]

Work A college graduate landed a job just one week after commencement exercises. For five years he had known nothing but college life. On the second day of employment he showed up to work an hour late. The boss asked about his tardiness to which the new recruit seriously replied, "I forgot I had a job."[1602]

Work After a very difficult day at work, Fred told his wife, "I have a very responsible job. Every time something goes wrong . . . the boss thinks I'm responsible."[1603]

Work Robert Orben notes a worthy strategy for showing up to work each day. He says, "Every morning I get up and look through the *Forbes* list of the richest people in America. If I'm not there, I go to work."[1604]

Work The boss called in his small ban of misfit summer employees and said, "We're going to change the way we do things around here!" One kid replied, "Whoa, Dude, you mean we're supposed to do things around here?"[1605]

WWJD A little boy was in a heated argument with his sister about who was going to get the last brownie. His mother overheard the loud discussion in their kitchen and came in to resolve the conflict. Her two children were obviously very distraught about getting that final treat. Sensing the need to teach a deeper truth, the mom asked her children that ever-relevant question: "What would Jesus do?" The older sibling immediately answered, "That's easy, Jesus would just break the brownie and make five thousand more!"[1606]

WWJD Kevin and Ryan were anxiously waiting for their mother to fix some pancakes. As the wait went longer than expected, they began to argue over who would get the first pancake. Seizing a moment of opportunity, their mom said, "If Jesus were sitting here, he would say, 'Let my brother have the first pancake, I can wait.'" Five-year-old Kevin promptly turned to his three-year-old brother and said, "Ryan, you be Jesus!"[1607]

SOURCE INDEX

1. *HomeLife*, January 1997, p. 19

2. *The Pastor's Weekly Briefing*, Oct. 15, 1999

3. *The Index of Leading Cultural Indicators*, March 1993

4. *AFA Journal*, August 1997, p. 20

5. *World*, Nov. 2, 1996, p. 7

6. *Houston Chronicle*, Aug. 11, 1995, p. 1

7. Author's files

8. *SBC Life*, June/July 1998

9. Author's files

10. *Executive Speechwriter Newsletter*, Vol. 10, No. 4

11. *U.S. News & World Report*, Sept. 30, 1996

12. *Reader's Digest*, 1988

13. Author's files

14. "A Heart Like His," Max Lucado, *UpWords* Tape TS9702

15. *Houston Chronicle*, June 26, 1996, p. 2D

16. Ibid, April 19, 1999, p. 2C

17. Author's files

18. *Executive Speechwriter Newsletter*, Vol. 11, No. 3

19. Author's files

20. *Parade*, Oct. 12, 1997, p. 8

21. *Houston Chronicle*, May 21, 1996, p. 1B; June 17, 1996, p. 1C

22. Author's files

23. *Bits & Pieces*, Feb. 26, 1998, p. 3; *USA Today*, June 1, 2000, p. 8D

24. *People*, Oct. 30, 2000, p. 56

25. Author's files

26. *Preaching Today*, Tape 172

27. Author's files

28. Ibid

29. Ibid

30. Ibid

31. *On Mission*, May/June 1999

32. *Christian Reader*, March/April 1995, p. 35

33. *Bay Area Sun*, July 9, 1997

34. The Church Growth Institute, July 3, 1995, p. 1

35. *Kindred Spirit*, Summer 1996, p. 13

36. *Baptist Standard*, Sept. 9, 1998

37. *Pastor's Family*, Oct./Nov. 1997

38. *Houston Chronicle*, Sept. 23, 1997

39. *Houston Chronicle*, Dec. 3, 1998

40. Ibid, Oct. 8, 1997

41. Ibid, June 24, 1998, p. 5A

42. *Examiner*, Oct.7, 1999, p. 49

43. *Houston Chronicle*, Jan. 8, 1997, p. 9A

44. *Center for Science in the Public Interest*, Dec 1996

45. *Houston Chronicle*, June 14, 2000

46. *U.S. News & World Report*, June 17, 1996

47. *Houston Chronicle*, Dec. 24, 1997

48. Author's files

49. Ibid

50. Ibid

51. *Reader's Digest*, July 1993, p. 90

52. *U.S. News & World Report*, Dec. 9, 1996, p. 79

53. *World*, Nov. 2, 1996, p. 5

54. "Rediscovering the Church," John Ortberg, Part 2, Seeds Tape Ministry, Jan. 17, 1996

55. *The Making of a Godly Man,* John Trent, 1997, p. 1

56. *Emotions: Can You Trust Them?* James Dobson, 1981, p. 106

57. *Houston Chronicle,* May 2, 2000, p. 10A; *Reader's Digest,* Dec. 1998, p. 96; *Houston Chronicle,* Jan. 13, 2000, p. 3D

58. *Associated Press,* May 12, 1987

59. *Examiner,* Oct. 7, 1999, p. 49

60. *Houston Chronicle,* Sept. 18, 1999, p. 19A; Aug. 15, 1999, p. 1D; Sept. 6, 1999, p. 16A

61. Author's files

62. *Houston Chronicle,* April 28, 1999, p. 9D

63. Ibid, Oct. 14, 1997

64. Ibid, June 12, 1996, p. 24A

65. Ibid, Oct. 28, 1999, p. 4A

66. Ibid, Nov. 5, 1996, p. 2A

67. *World,* May 30, 1998, p. 8; *Houston Chronicle,* May 19, 1998, p. 7A

68. *Preaching Today,* James Boice, Vol. 168

69. *Fort Worth Star Telegram,* March 27, 1987

70. Author's files

71. *Houston Chronicle,* Dec. 3, 1995

72. Author's files

73. Ibid

74. "Attitudes," John Ortberg, Seeds Tape Ministry M9733

75. *Family Research Council,* Jan. 1997, p. 2; *Focus on the Family,* Oct. 1996; "What Jesus Would   Say to Jack Kevorkian," Lee Strobel, *Preaching Today,* Tape 160, *Houston Chronicle,* Dec. 7, 2000, p. 17A

76. "The Beast Within Us All," Max Lucado, Sept. 26, 1999

77. *World Book Encyclopedia,* 1995; *Houston Chronicle,* March 19, 1996, p. 2D

78. *Positive Living,* Sept./Oct. 1998, p. 30

79. *Who Switched the Price Tags?* Tony Campolo, 1986, p. 109

80. Author's files

81. *Houston Chronicle,* Sept. 29, 1997, p. 1A

82. Author's files

83. *Baptist Beacon,* June 22, 1995, p. 8

84. *Baptist Standard,* June 3, 1998, p. 3

85. Author's files

86. *Houston Chronicle,* Nov. 26, 1997, p. 21A

87. Author's files

88. Ibid

89. "Making Life Work," Bill Hybels, Seeds Tape Ministry, Dec. 21, 1997

90. *Houston Chronicle,* June 18, 1999, p. 11D

91. *Houston Chronicle,* Oct. 12, 1999, p. 1C

92. *Christian History,* Issue 33, p. 13

93. *Associated Press,* Sept. 14, 1992

94. Author's files

95. *Worship Leader,* March/April 1998, p. 18

96. *Christian Reader,* Sept. /Oct. 1988

97. *Houston Chronicle,* April 2, 1998, p. 4D

98. *Commission,* July 1996, p. 31

99. *Houston Chronicle,* Jan. 14, 2000, p. 1C

100. *Zondervan Publishing,* 1996

101. *Vital Ministry,* March/April 1999

102. *Printer's Press,* June 2000, p. 3

103. *Baptist Standard,* Dec. 4, 1996, p. 1

104. *Examiner,* May 7, 1998, p. 26

105. *Houston Chronicle,* Aug. 5, 1996, p. 7A

106. *Favorite Psalms,* John Stott, 1988, p. 38

107. "What Would Jesus Say To . . . Phil Jackson," Lee Strobel, Seeds Tape Ministry, July 6, 1997

108. *Houston Chronicle*, Jan. 6, 1997, p. 2A

109. *The Good Life*, Elizabeth Peale Allen, 1992, p. 2-3

110. Author's files

111. Ibid.

112. Ibid

113. *Inc.*, Oct. 1997, p. 113

114. Author's files

115. *Focus on the Family*, June 1999, p. 12

116. *Baylor Messenger*, Summer Edition, 1995, p. 4

117. *Houston Post*, Feb. 20, 1994, p. B-2

118. *Houston Chronicle*, March 24, 1996, p. 9D

119. Author's files

120. *AARP Bulletin*, Jan. 2000; *Reader's Digest*, Nov. 1998, p. 73

121. *Houston Chronicle*, June 22, 1996, "The Mini Page"

122. *Bits & Pieces*, June 19, 1997, p. 16-18

123. *Saturday Evening Post*, Jan./Feb. 1995, p. 44-45

124. Author's files

125. Ibid

126. Ibid

127. *Leadership Journal*, Spring 1993, p. 120

128. *Sermon Notes & Illustrations*, Jan. 1996

129. *Fresh Illustrations for Preaching & Teaching*, Edward Rowell, 1997, p. 159

130. Author's files

131. Ibid

132. *Houston Chronicle*, April 8, 1998, p. 2A

133. Author's files

134. *Parade*, Dec. 31, 1995, p. 8

135. *World*, April 3, 1999, p. 18

136. *Baptist Standard*, Feb. 5, 1997, p. 12; "Walking in the Light," John Ortberg, Seeds Tape Ministry, May 8, 1996

137. *Houston Chronicle*, June 29, 1996, "The Mini Page"

138. "Over The Top," Zig Ziglar, 1994

139. *Baptist Standard*, March 13, 1996, p. 5

140. *Up Words*, Max Lucado, Spring 2000

141. "One-on-One with Ken Blanchard," Leadership Summit, Willow Creek Association, Aug. 1995

142. *The Promise Keeper*, Jan./Feb. 1999, p. 1

143. *Reader's Digest*, Aug. 1997

144. *Christian History*, Family Tree, Undated Volume

145. Keith Thomas, 1997 SBC Pastor's Conference, Dallas, Texas

146. *A 3rd Serving of Chicken Soup for the Soul*, Jack Canfield and Mark Hansen, 1996, p. 196

147. *Houston Chronicle*, Nov. 26, 1997

148. *Houston Chronicle, Family Circus*, Dec. 23 1988

149. *Chicken Soup for the Christian Soul*, Jack Canfield & Mark Hansen, 1997, p. 11

150. *The Citizen*, Dec. 4, 1996

151. *Houston Post*, Dec. 25, 1992

152. *Houston Chronicle*, Dec. 16, 1989

153. Author's files

154. Ibid, Dec. 29, 1998

155. *Fruit of the Spirit*, Ron Hembree, 1969, p. 89

156. *Houston Chronicle*, Dec. 19, 1991, p. 2A; Telephone Interview, Oct. 2, 1996

157. Ibid, Dec. 4, 1996

158. Ibid, Dec. 5, 1996, p. 6A

159. *Christmas Stories for the Heart*, Alice Gray, 1997, p. 21

160. *Houston Chronicle*, July 30, 1989, p. 1E; *USA Today*, Dec. 24, 1996, p. 1-2

161. *NEWSLETTER Newsletter*, March 2000, p .6

162. Contributed by Philip Riegel

163. *Houston Chronicle*, June 5, 1996, p. 1A

164. Ibid, Sept. 28, 1996, p. 8E

165. Author's files

166. Barna Research Council, 1991

167. Carl Dudley, professor of church and community at McCormick Theological Seminary

168. Author's files

169. Win Arn, Church Growth Specialist

170. *On Mission*, May/June 1999, p. 11

171. *Houston Chronicle*, Jan. 30, 1999

172. *Decision*, Nov. 1999, p. 20; *Houston Chronicle*, Jan. 22, 2000, p. 8E

173. *Margin,* Richard Swenson, 1992, p. 48

174. CNN, Aug. 4, 1999; *Houston Chronicle*, Aug. 5, 1999, p. 3A

175. *Inc.* 500, 1997, p. 62

176. *Parade*, May 17, 1998, p. 10

177. Author's files

178. Ibid

179. Ibid

180. *Reader's Digest*, May 1989, p. 48

181. *Saturday Evening Post*, March/April 1998, p. 38; *Houston Chronicle*, March 24, 1998, p. 17A

182. *What Every Mom Needs,* Elisa Morgan and Carol Kuykendall, 1995, p. 33

183. *Houston Chronicle*, Feb. 29, 2000, p. 19A

184. Author's files

185. *Therefore . . .*, May 1996, p. 1

186. *Saturday Evening Post*, March/April 1998

187. *NEWSLETTER Newsletter*, July 1996, p. 2

188. *Moody*, July/August 1998, p. 32

189. *Houston Chronicle*, Mini Page, June 27, 1998

190. *Bits & Pieces*, Aug. 14, 1997, p. 8; *Houston Chronicle*, July 17, 1996, p. 2B

191. *The 100: A Ranking of the Most Influential Persons in History,* Michael Hart, 1978, p. 349–354

192. *The Book of Acts*, BaptistWay Bible Study for Texas, 2000, p. 46

193. Author's files

194. *Houston Chronicle*, Dec. 10, 1995, p. 31A; Mexico Consulate, Telephone Interview, May 2000

195. *Your Church on Mission with God*, Nov. 12, 1999, p. 1

196. *NEWSLETTER Newsletter*, Aug. 1996

197. Author's files

198. *Have A Good Day*, April 1994, p. 1

199. Author's files

200. *Facts & Trends*, Nov. 1995, p. 6

201. *Houston Chronicle*, Oct. 1, 1999, p. 1A; Oct. 13, 1999, p. 7A

202. *Prevention*, Oct. 1998, p. 38

203. Ibid, Oct. 1998

204. Author's files

205. *Better Families*, Oct. '96

206. *Houston Chronicle*, April 26, 1998

207. *Facts & Trends*, Oct. 1996

208. Author's files

209. "The Jesus I Love to Know," Joseph Stowell, Willow Creek Association, Aug. 23, 2000

210. *Who Switched the Price Tags,* Tony Campolo, 1986

211. *Chicken Soup for the Soul,* Jack Canfield and Mark Hansen, 1993, p. 35

212. *Houston Chronicle*, Oct. 27, 1996, p. 16B

213. Author's files

214. *Reader's Digest*, Oct. 1998, p. 122

215. *San Antonio Express-News*, April 22, 1997, p. 9E

216. *Houston Chronicle*, Nov. 3, 1988, Special Five-Part Series, "Willie: An Autobiography"

217. "People Count," Calvin Miller, SBC Home Mission Board, 1996

218. *People*, Dec. 21, 1988, p. 91; *Houston Chronicle*, Sept. 26, 1998, p. 21A

219. *Parade*, Dec. 29, 1996, p. 16

220. *Houston Chronicle*, April 23, 1998, p. 10A

221. *Passages of Light,* A Guidepost Devotional, 1995, p. 9–10

222. *Houston Chronicle*, Aug. 20, 1998

223. *Humor for Preaching & Teaching,* Ed Rowell, 1996, p. 10

224. *Communication Solutions*, 1999

225. *Houston Chronicle*, April 6, 1998, p. 2A

226. Author's files

227. Ibid

228. *Working Well,* July 1995, p. 3

229. *Houston Chronicle*, Nov. 7, 1996, p. 9A

230. *Leadership*, Spring 1994, p.118

231. *Houston Chronicle*, Dec. 19, 1998, p. 1A, 1B

232. Author's files

233. *Houston Chronicle*, May 28, 1997, p. 1D

234. *Wall Street Journal*, Sept. 17, 1999, p. W5

235. *Reader's Digest*, April 1993, p. 96–98

236. Author's files

237. Ibid

238. *Houston Chronicle*, Dec. 3, 1995, p. 12

239. Author's files

240. Ibid

241. *Reader's Digest*, 1987

242. *Stories for the Heart,* Alice Gray, 1996, p. 46

243. *Guideposts*, May 1993, p. 27

244. *Houston Chronicle*, June 6, 1998

245. *Christian Reader*, May/June 1996

246. *Heaven: Your Real Home,* Joni Eareckson Tada, 1995, p. 76

247. Richard Couey, General Session, Baylor Ministers Conference, 1994; *The World Almanac*, 1993, p. 184

248. *Printer's Press*, Aug. 1999, p. 3

249. *Leadership*, Spring 1999

250. *Houston Chronicle*, June 5, 1996, p. 5A

251. Ibid, Dec. 22, 1999, p. 2A

252. Author's files

253. *New Man*, March/April 1997, Cover Story

254. *Shepherding the Sheep in Smaller Churches,* Paul Powell, 1995, p. 34

255. Author's files

256. Ibid

257. *Brian's Lines*, Nov./Dec. 1996

258. Author's files

259. Ibid

260. Ibid

261. *Parade*, Jan. 5, 1997, p. 22; *Houston Chronicle*, April 27, 1997, p. 20A

262. *The Good Life,* Elizabeth Peale Allen, 1992, p. 10

263. *The 911 Handbook,* Kent Crockett, Hendrickson Publishers, 1997, p. 212–213

264. *Houston Chronicle*, Jan. 4, 1998, p. 2A

265. Ibid, Sept. 22, 2000, p. 26A

266. Adapted from *The 911 Handbook,* Kent Crockett, Hendrickson Publishers, 1997, p. 217

267. *Houston Chronicle*, Feb. 18, 1999, p. 6A

268. *Houston Chronicle*, Jan. 5, 1997, p. 8F; *Executive Speechwriter Newsletter*, Vol. 11 No. 3

269. *Financial World*, Dec. 5, 1995

270. *Who Switched the Price Tags?*, Tony Campolo, 1986, p. 58–59

271. *Houston Chronicle*, June 26, 1996, "This Week", p. 5

272. Ibid, Oct. 14, 1996

273. *Baptist Standard*, Nov. 13, 1996

274. *The Financial Ten Commandments*, Bill Hybels, Seeds Tape Ministry

275. *Parade*, Sept. 28, 1997

276. *Promise Keepers Newsletter*, 1997

277. *Houston Chronicle*, Oct. 14, 1999, p. 2D

278. *Minister's Family*, Winter 1999–2000, Frank Pollard, p. 8

279. *Houston Chronicle*, Oct. 28, 1999, p. 4

280. Houston Public Library Reference Center, "Making the Most of Your Marriage," John Ortberg, Seeds Tape Ministry, Feb. 7, 1999

281. *Houston Chronicle*, July 21, 1998, p. 7B

282. *Reader's Digest*, March 1995, p. 38

283. Author's files

284. *Houston Chronicle*, Oct. 25, 1999, p. 7D

285. *Inc.*, Special Issue, June 18, 1996

286. *Parade*, Dec. 13, 1998

287. *Houston Chronicle*, May 12, 1998

288. *Parade*, Dec. 31, 1995, p. 11

289. *Beaumont Enterprise*, July 24, 2000

290. Author's files

291. *Houston Chronicle*, Sept. 16, 1996, p. 1A; *Parade*, Sept. 29, 1996, p. 16

292. *Reader's Digest*, April 1994; *U.S. News & World Report*, Dec. 9, 1996

293. *Houston Chronicle*, Nov. 22, 1998

294. *Inc.*, Jan. 1999, p. 60

295. *Parade*, Dec. 15, 1996, p. 16

296. Author's files

297. *Houston Chronicle*, Jan. 17, 1997

298. *Beaumont Enterprise*, Oct. 29, 2000

299. *Margin*, Richard Swenson, 1992

300. *People*, Oct. 30, 2000

301. *Houston Chronicle*, Dec. 1, 1998, p. 2D

302. *The Minister's Family*, Summer 1997

303. *Reader's Digest*, Dec. 1995

304. *Houston Chronicle*, Oct. 5, 2000

305. *Prevention*, March 1997

306. *Houston Chronicle*, Aug. 22, 1998

307. Ibid, Feb. 4, 1999

308. *HomeLife*, Jan. 1999; *U.S. News & World Report*, Nov. 22, 1999

309. *Houston Chronicle*, Nov. 1, 1999

310. *The 1997 Illustrated Calendar of Fat*

311. *Parade*, Dec. 28, 1997, p. 11

312. *Houston Chronicle*, June 23, 1999, p. 2A

313. *USA Today*, Jan. 29, 1999, p. 17F, 21F

314. *U.S. News & World Report*, Dec. 9, 1996, p. 17

315. *Houston Chronicle*, Feb. 6, 2000, p. 20A

316. *A 3rd Serving of Chicken Soup for the Soul*, Canfield and Hansen, Health Communications, 1996, p. 235–6

317. Author's files

318. *U.S. News & World Report*, Aug. 30, 1999, p. 41

319. *Executive Speechwriter Newsletter*, Vol. 10 No. 4

320. *Barna Research Group*, May 2000

321. *Commission*, July 1998, p. 14

322. *Brian's Lines*, Sept./Oct. 1996

323. *The 7 Habits of Highly Effective Families*, Stephen R. Covey, 1995, Tape 4

324. *Beaumont Enterprise*, Aug. 23, 2000; *Houston Chronicle*, Aug. 16, 2000, p. 11B

325. Author's files

326. *Reader's Digest*, Oct. 1995, p. 157

327. *Companion to Baptist Hymnal,* William Reynolds, 1976, p. 24; *Handbook to The Baptist Hymnal,* Wesley Forbis, ed., 1992, p. 81; *World,* Sept. 27, 1997, p. 25

328. *HomeLife,* Jan. 1997, p. 9

329. *Baptist Standard,* July 3, 1996, p. 5

330. *Houston Chronicle,* Jan. 12, 2000, p. 9D

331. Ibid, Aug. 15, 1996, p. 2D

332. Author's files

333. *SBC Life,* May 1999, p. 15

334. *I Still Do,* Dennis Rainey, *FamilyLife,* Oct. 1999, *Pastor's Weekly Briefing,* Dec. 29, 2000

335. *Light,* March/April 1999, p. 3

336. *Athens Daily News,* March 16, 1997, Contributed by Tracy Sims

337. Author's files

338. *U.S. News & World Report,* Sept. 8, 1997

339. *Examiner,* Aug. 13, 1998, p. 24; *Houston Chronicle,* May 3, 1998, p. 1F; "God's Word for the Weary," Max Lucado, May 10, 1998

340. *U.S. News & World Report,* Sept. 9, 1996, Cover Story

341. *The Ethics & Religious Liberty Commission,* Feb. 1999

342. *Parade,* Nov. 9, 1997

343. *Reader's Digest,* Nov. 1989, p. 207

344. *Baptist Standard,* Dec. 4, 1996, p. 1

345. *Focus on the Family,* March 1997, p. 19

346. *U.S. News & World Report,* Jan. 22, 1996, p. 22

347. *The Good Life,* Elizabeth Peale Allen, 1992, p. 8

348. *Beaumont Examiner,* May 4, 2000, p. 55

349. *Moody,* July/Aug. 1996, p. 40

350. *Houston Chronicle,* July 20, 1999, p. 2D

351. "Stress and the Heart," Dr. Michael Jacobson, Oct. 1996

352. *Houston Chronicle,* March 27, 1996, p. 9A

353. *Houston Chronicle,* John Lopez; *Compassion International Newsletter,* Positive Living, Sept./Oct. 1995, p. 13

354. Doug Fields, Saddleback Valley Community Church, July 20, 1997

355. *Dr. James Dobson's Bulletin,* Nov. 1997, p. 1

356. *Reader's Digest,* Nov. 1989, p. 142

357. *Parade,* Oct. 3, 2000, p. 4

358. *Stories for the Heart,* Alice Gray, 1996, p. 50–53

359. *Too Old Too Soon,* Doug Fields, 1991, p. 179

360. *Saturday Evening Post,* March/April 1998, p. 46

361. *Focus on the Family,* Dec. 1999, p. 24

362. Author's files

363. Ibid

364. *Houston Chronicle,* July 14, 1998, p. 2A

365. *Pastoral Letter,* Paul Powell, Jan. 1996, p. 2

366. *SBC Life,* Feb./March 1997, p. 22; *Bits & Pieces,* Dec. 5, 1996

367. *Wizard of Id,* Oct 9, 1997

368. Author's files

369. Ibid

370. *Houston Chronicle,* Dec. 31, 1995, p. 15A

371. Ibid, April 10, 1998, p. 1B

372. *Journal of Medical Ethics,* Feb. 1999

373. Adapted from *Executive Speechwriter Newsletter,* Vol. 11, No. 6

374. *Leadership,* Spring 1995, p. 74

375. *Baptist Standard,* Sept. 11, 1996, p. 1

376. *Christian Reader,* Sept./Oct. 1991, p. 61

377. *A Heart Like His,* Rebecca Pippert, 1996, p. 125–6

378. Author's files

379. *One Thousand Evangelistic Illustrations,* Aquilla Webb, 1921, p. 91; *The Timetables of History,* Bernard Grun, 1982, p. 374

380. *The Gospel of Matthew,* Vol. 1, William Barclay, 1975, p. 269

381. *Stories for the Heart,* Alice Gray, Vision House Publishing, 1996, p. 114

382. *The Greatest Lesson I've Ever Learned,* Bill Bright, 1991, p. 122–129

383. *Commission,* Oct. 1996

384. *Moody,* May/June 1998, p. 72

385. Ibid, July/Aug. 1996, p. 48

386. *Beaumont Enterprise,* Aug. 9, 2000, p. 1C

387. *Evangelism Today,* Vol. 2, 1997

388. *Decision,* July/Aug. 2000, p. 9

389. *Crossroads,* Vol. 1, No. 1, p. 1

390. *Houston Chronicle,* April 28,1996, p. 9D

391. *Beaumont Enterprise,* Oct. 14, 2000, p. 1B

392. "Love of Another Kind: No Greater Love," Bill Hybels, Seeds Tape Ministry, Oct. 16, 1994; *The Encyclopedia of Religious Quotations,* Frank Mead, 1965, p. 189

393. Author's files

394. Ibid

395. Ibid

396. Ibid

397. Leighton Ford Leadership Development Conference, 1991

398. *Houston Chronicle,* April 1, 1989, p. E-2

399. Author's files

400. *Reader's Digest,* Dec. 1993, p. 25

401. *U.S. News & World Report,* Feb. 24, 1997, p. 15 ; Sept. 15, 1997, p. 10

402. Ken Olan, Houston, Texas, Fall 1997; *Better Families,* Oct. 1997, p. 1; *A 2nd Helping of Chicken Soup for the Soul,* Jack Canfield and Mark Hansen, 1995, p. 253

403. *U.S. News & World Report,* Dec. 23, 1996, p. 18; *Saturday Evening Post,* July/Aug. 1997, p. 32

404. *Houston Chronicle,* Dec. 23, 1999, p. 6

405. Milton Cunningham, Baylor Ministers Conference, 1994

406. *Lord, Is It Warfare?,* Kay Arthur, 1993, p. 219–220

407. *God's Vitamin C for the Spirit,* Kathy and Larry Miller, 1996, p. 55

408. *The Root of the Righteous,* A.W. Tozer, 1986, p. 156

409. *I'm So Glad You Told Me What I Didn't Wanna Hear,* Barbara Johnson, 1996, p. 157

410. *Bits & Pieces,* Dec. 30, 1999, p. 14

411. Author's files

412. *Baptist Standard,* June 3, 1998, p. 12

413. *Bits & Pieces,* March 28, 1996, p. 15–17; *Houston Chronicle,* Oct. 12, 1997, p. 1F

414. Author's files

415. Ibid

416. *The Vision of His Glory,* Anne Graham Lotz, 1996, p. 81

417. *Houston Chronicle,* July 7, 2000, p. 15A

418. *USA Today,* Dec. 29, 1995, p. 2D

419. *Houston Chronicle,* Sept. 11, 1998, p. 5A

420. *Too Old Too Soon,* Doug Fields, 1991

421. Contributed by Alvin Reid

422. An Interview with Dr. Henry Cloud, Seeds Tape Ministry, May 11, 1997

423. *USA Weekend,* Feb. 24, 1995

424. *People*, Oct. 12, 1998, p. 170; *Houston Chronicle*, Sept. 27, 1998, p. 10A

425. *Houston Chronicle*, July 7, 1999, p. 2D

426. Author's files

427. *Houston Chronicle*, April 16, 1998

428. *American Family Association Journal*, April 1999, p. 24

429. *Life@Work*, Sept. 1998, p. 9

430. *Hollywood vs. Religion*, Michael Medved, 1994

431. Author's files

432. Ibid

433. *It Was Fire When I Lay Down on It*, Robert Fulghum, 1989

434. *Pastor to Pastor*, Vol. 28

435. Author's files

436. *Houston Chronicle*, June 25, 1996, p. 4B

437. *Bits & Pieces*, Sept. 9, 1999, p. 12

438. *Ambassador Speaker Bureau*, 1997, p. 17

439. *Better Families*, March 1996, p. 2

440. *Better Families*, Jan. 1996, p. 1

441. *World*, May 17, 1997, p. 23

442. *Houston Chronicle*, Sept. 8, 1998, p. 2D

443. *Beaumont Examiner*, April 23, 1998, p. 26

444. *Focus on the Family*, June 1989, p. 15

445. Author's files

446. Ibid

447. Ibid

448. *Health Watch, Christian Brotherhood Newsletter*, Feb. 1998

449. Contributed by Travis Hart

450. *The Olympic Factbook*, Rebecca Nelson and Marie MacNee, 1996, p. 629–30

451. *USA Today*, July 5, 1996, "Life" p. 1

452. Author's files

453. *Reader's Digest*, April 1999, p. 137

454. Ibid, Dec. 1995, p. 99

455. *Houston Chronicle*, Dec. 29, 1998, p. 2D, *Communication Briefings*, Vol. XVI, No. 1, p. 8

456. Author's files

457. *The 911 Handbook*, Kent Crockett, Hendrickson Publishers, 1997, p. 43

458. "The Father Heart of God," Jim Nicodem, *Preaching Today*, Tape 152

459. *Servant Leadership*, June 1998, p. 1

460. "The Blessing of Forgiveness," *Pastor to Pastor*, Vol. 43

461. *Today's Christian Woman*, July/Aug. 1992, p. 19

462. Author's files

463. "Searching for Eagles," John Maxwell, *Injoy*, Jan. 1995; *Houston Chronicle*, July 9, 1995, p. 29

464. *Houston Chronicle*, Sept. 10, 1997, p. 2D

465. *Death from the Other Side*, Paul Powell, 1995, p. 12

466. *Focus on the Family*, Jan.1999

467. *SALT*, 1998, Vol. 8, No. 2

468. *Houston Chronicle*, June 19, 1999; *World*, June 19, 1999, p. 32; *USA Weekend*, May 14, 1999, p. 4; *Family News Report* from Dr. James Dobson, April 1999, p. 5

469. *World*, Oct. 13, 1997, p. 10

470. Author's files

471. *No Greater Sacrifice*, Ray Boltz, 1996

472. *Stories For The Heart*, Alice Gray, 1996, p. 67–68

473. *Preaching Today*, Tape 156, *Baptist Standard*, Sept. 11, 1996, p. 12, *The Deacon*, Oct.–Dec. 1996, p. 44

474. *SBC Life*, May 1999, p. 6

475. *Financial Ink*, April 1999, p. 2; *Houston Chronicle*, April 13, 1999, p. 1C

476. *God's Vitamin "C" for the Spirit,* Kathy and Larry Miller, 1996, p. 271

477. *Leadership Journal,* Spring 1999, p. 75

478. Ken Olan, Houston Conference, Texas, Fall 1997

479. Author's files

480. *Better Families,* May 1997, p. 2

481. *Minister's Personal Management Manual,* Truman Brown, 1988, p. 4

482. *Fire In My Bones,* Fred Wood, Broadman Press, 1959, p. 116

483. *Times of Discovery,* July 1996, p. 1

484. Author's files

485. *Family Research Council Washington Watch,* Dec. 4, 1995, p. 4

486. Author's files

487. *Today in the Word,* Oct. 1996, p. 26

488. *Breaking the Surface,* Greg Louganis, 1995, p. 37–38, 186–187

489. Author's files

490. Ibid

491. *Houston Chronicle,* Feb. 28, 1997, p. 19A

492. *Houston Chronicle,* Oct. 23, 1999, p. 12A

493. *The Ten Commandments,* Schlessinger & Vogel, 1998, p. 183

494. *Houston Chronicle,* July 11, 1998, p. 4A; July 12, 1998, p. 8A

495. "Rediscovering the Church: How to Speak to Seekers," Lee Strobel, March 13, 1996, Seeds Tape Ministry; *Baptist Standard,* Oct. 9, 1996, p. 5

496. *Learn to Dance the Soul Salsa,* Leonard Sweet, 2000

497. *All the Promises of the Bible,* Herbert Lockyer, 1962, p. 10

498. *HomeLife,* July 1995, p. 10

499. Parade, 12/19/99, p. 9

500. Author's files

501. *Bits & Pieces,* Oct. 14, 1993, p. 1

502. *Houston Chronicle,* Jan. 18, 1998, p. 12A

503. *Prevention,* Aug. 1998, p. 40

504. Author's files

505. *Houston Chronicle,* Jan. 18, 1998, p. 19A

506. *Imprimis,* July 1997, p. 1

507. Author's files

508. *Executive Speechwriter Newsletter,* Vol. 14, No. 5

509. *Reader's Digest,* April 1993, p. 151

510. Author's files

511. *World,* March 1, 1997, p. 26

512. *Houston Chronicle,* July 13, 1995, p. 10A

513. Author's files

514. *Houston Chronicle,* Feb. 11, 2000, p. 11A

515. Ibid, June 19, 1989, p. 2A

516. Ibid, Jan. 3, 2000, p. 8A

517. Author's files

518. *Modern Maturity,* Jan./Feb. 1997

519. Author's files

520. Ibid

521. *Pastor's Update on Foreign Missions,* May 1996, p. 4

522. "ESPN SportsCentury," *Houston Chronicle,* Sept. 12, 1999, p. 10

523. *Houston Chronicle,* Sept. 25, 1999, p. 1E

524. Author's files

525. *The Minister's Family,* Fall 1998, p. 30

526. *Houston Chronicle,* Oct. 21, 1999, p. 7; *The Pastor's Weekly Briefing,* Focus on the Family, Oct. 15, 1999, p. 1; *SEEDS,* 1999

527. *Texas Magazine,* Feb. 5, 1989

528. *Houston Chronicle,* Nov. 1, 1996, p. 24A

529. *Today's Christian Woman,* Sept./Oct. 1999, p. 36

530. *A 3rd Serving of Chicken Soup for the Soul,* Jack Canfield and Mark Hansen, 1996, p. 12

531. *Houston Chronicle,* June 22, 1996, p. 2D

532. Ibid, April 1, 2000, p. 14A

533. *Into Thin Air,* Jon Krakauer, 1997, p. 278

534. Leighton Ford Leadership Development Conference, 1991

535. *Houston Chronicle,* Aug. 14, 1997, p. 2A

536. *SBC Life,* April 1997, p. 14

537. Author's files

538. *Moody,* Sept./Oct. 1996, p. 6

539. Author's files

540. *Houston Chronicle,* June 18, 1998, p. 6A

541. Ibid, June 13, 2000

542. Author's files

543. *Houston Chronicle,* June 15, 1996, p. 3E

544. *U.S. News & World Report,* Sept. 15, 1997

545. *Beaumont Enterprise,* July 11, 2000

546. *U.S. News & World Report,* July 14, 1997

547. *SBC Life,* Sept. 1996, p. 4

548. *HomeLife,* July 1998, p. 66

549. Author's files

550. *A 3rd Serving of Chicken Soup for the Soul,* Jack Canfield and Mark Hansen, 1996, p. 186

551. *Houston Post,* April 9, 1995, p. A-31; *Parade,* May 19,1996, p. 10

552. *Zinger,* Paul Azinger with Ken Abraham, 1995, p. 250–251

553. *The Vision of His Glory,* Anne Graham Lotz, 1996, p. 225

554. Author's files

555. *Harper's Index,* Oct. 1995

556. *Houston Chronicle,* Aug. 18, 1999

557. *Great Illustrations,* 1991

558. Author's files

559. Author's files

560. *Foxe's Christian Martyrs of the World,* John Foxe, 1989, p. 5

561. *Church Administration,* Oct. 1995, p. 37

562. *Parade,* June 28, 1998, *Houston Chronicle,* Oct. 25, 1998

563. *United Way,* Dec. 1997

564. *Baptist Standard,* July 30, 1997

565. *U.S. News & World Report,* March 2, 1998, p. 9

566. "Rediscovering the Church: How Christians Should Relate to Government," John Ortberg, Seeds Tape Ministry, Feb. 7, 1996

567. *U.S. News & World Report,* Jan. 27, 1997, p. 26

568. *Communication Briefings,* Vol. XVI, No. 1, p. 7

569. *Living on the Ragged Edge,* Charles Swindoll, 1985, p. 77

570. "Passion of the Gospel," Tony Evans, Sept. 1999

571. Author's files

572. *Seven Promises of a Promise Keeper,* Al Janssen and Larry Weeden, 1994, p. 197; Ligonier Conference, Orlando Florida, Feb. 1992

573. Author's files

574. Ibid

575. Ibid

576. Ibid

577. Ibid

578. Billy Graham Evangelistic Association, Feb. 1998, p. 3

579. *Commission,* Sept. 1997

580. "The Power to Overcome Apathy," Bill Hybels, Seeds Tape Ministry, Nov. 19, 1995

581. *Light,* Fall 1999

582. *U.S. News & World Report,* Dec. 2, 1996, p. 13; *Houston Chronicle,* Nov. 25, 1996, p.2A, Nov. 22, 1996, p. 10A; *Family*

583. *Research Council,* Jan. 1997, p. 2 *Executive Speechwriter Newsletter,* Religion and Philosophy

584. "Stop Dreaming/Start Planning," Sept./Oct. 1999, p. 1

585. "Accept No Substitutes," Rick Warren, Saddleback Church

586. *Parade,* April 19, 1998

587. *Associated Press,* April 8, 1998

588. *Houston Chronicle,* Dec. 10, 1999, p. 3C

589. *Beaumont Examiner,* April 20, 2000, p. 49

590. Author's files

591. *HomeLife,* Oct. '96, *U.S. News & World Report,* Nov. 11, 1996

592. *Houston Chronicle,* May 31, 1998

593. *Living Obediently,* Brian Harbour, 1992, p. 36; *Lady of Courage,* Ann Hughes, 1987, p. 24

594. *Houston Chronicle,* Nov. 2, 1999, p. 1A

595. Author's files

596. *The Citizen,* March 27, 1996, p. 2

597. *Inc.,* Jan. 1999, p. 64, 70

598. *Knight-Ridder Tribune News,* 1989

599. *Houston Chronicle,* March 28, 1998

600. Author's files

601. *World,* March 8, 1997, p. 26

602. *The Ten Commandments,* Schlessinger and Vogel, 1998, p. 256

603. Author's files

604. *Reminisce Extra,* Dec. 1994, p. 61

605. Author's files

606. Ibid

607. *Houston Chronicle,* Aug. 23, 1999

608. *Pastor's Weekly Briefing,* Jan. 28, 2000; *Houston Chronicle,* March 1, 2000, p. 5A

609. *Houston Chronicle,* April 30, 1997, p. 7A

610. *NEWSLETTER Newsletter,* July 1996, p. 2

611. *Sermon Notes & Illustrations,* Aug. 1995

612. *More Than a Carpenter,* Josh McDowell, 1977, p. 107–8

613. Author's files

614. "What Jesus Would Say to Larry King," Lee Strobel, Seeds Tape Ministry M9730

615. *Houston Chronicle,* Aug. 19, 1999, p. 9A

616. *American Family Association Journal,* July 1997, p. 3; *Houston Chronicle,* July 12, 1997, p. 1E

617. *Commission,* Jan. 1998, p. 24

618. *Houston Chronicle,* May 2, 1995, p. 7A

619. *Vital Ministry,* July/Aug. 1999

620. Author's files

621. *Houston Chronicle,* June 30, 1996, p. 4A; *Houston Post,* March 10, 1995, p. A–23; Houston Museum of Medical Sciences

622. Author's files

623. *San Antonio Express-News,* Feb. 18, 1997, p. 9E; *Houston Chronicle,* May 22, 1998, p. 40A

624. *HomeLife,* April 2000, p. 31

625. Author's files

626. *World,* Jan. 31, 1998, p. 16

627. *Parade,* Sept. 13, 1998, p. 15

628. "Yea God . . . For Being An Equal Opportunity Employer," John Ortberg, Seeds Tape Ministry, Feb. 5, 1995

629. *Parade,* May 31, 1998

630. *The Fellowship,* Aug. 1990

631. *Parade,* July 5, 1998

632. *Imprimis,* Sept. 1997

633. *Parade,* Dec. 22, 1996, p. 13

634. Author's files

635. Ibid

636. Ibid

637. *Bits & Pieces,* May 22, 1997, p. 9

638. *Into Thin Air,* Jon Krakauer, Villard Books, 1997

639. *People Weekly,* Aug. 21, 1995, p. 90

640. *Newsweek,* Aug. 6, 1990

641. Author's files

642. Ibid

643. *Houston Chronicle,* Jan. 30, 1999

644. *The Purpose Driven Church,* Rick Warren, 1995, p. 57

645. *Time,* May 2, 1996, p. 28

646. *Houston Chronicle,* March 6, 1996, p. 8C

647. *Inc.,* Sept. 1996, p. 11

648. *Houston Chronicle,* March 23, 1999, p. 2D

649. Author's files

650. Ibid

651. Ibid

652. Ibid

653. *Houston Chronicle,* Jan. 17, 1999, p. 1G

654. *The Purpose Driven Church,* Rick Warren, 1995

655. *Houston Chronicle,* Jan. 15, 1999, p. 2A

656. Ibid, Dec. 8, 1991, p. 1G; Dec. 19, 1998, p. 10E

657. *Prevention,* Oct. 1998, p. 46

658. *Houston Chronicle,* Aug. 29, 1996, p. 10A; Sept. 27, 1996, p. 4A

659. *A 3rd Serving of Chicken Soup for the Soul,* Jack Canfield and Mark Hansen, 1996, p. 61–64

660. *Positive Living,* Sept./Oct. 1995, p. 15

661. *Wind & Fire,* Bruce Larson, 1984, p. 167

662. Author's files

663. *The Family Book of Christian Values,* Stuart and Jill Briscoe, 1995, p. 42

664. *Family Research Council,* Jan. 1997, p. 3

665. *Passages of Light,* A Guidepost Devotional, 1995, p. 2–3

666. *Parade,* May 10, 1998, p. 10

667. *Houston Chronicle,* Nov. 16, 1998, p. 9A

668. Ibid, April 11, 1998, p. 22A

669. Author's files

670. *Bits & Pieces,* July 16, 1998, p. 16

671. *Houston Chronicle,* April 4, 2000, p. 13A

672. *San Antonio Express-News,* Feb. 21, 1997, p. 9G

673. *Reader's Digest,* Aug. 1999, p. 101

674. *Houston Chronicle,* May 21, 1998, p. 2D

675. *The National Gambling Impact Study Commission,* 1999 *Leadership,* April 1999, p. 9; *Houston Chronicle,* March 19, 1999, p. 2A

676. *The Ten Commandments,* Schlessinger and Vogel, 1998, p. 285

677. *Houston Chronicle,* July 7, 1999

678. Ibid, Jan. 9, 2000, p. 7D

679. *Parade,* Dec. 27, 1998, p. 16

680. Author's files

681. *Pastor to Pastor,* Vol. 41, *Focus on the Family*

682. *Houston Chronicle,* Jan. 7, 1999, p. 7A

683. "How To Triumph Over Temptations," D. Z. Cofield, *Preaching Today,* Tape 181

684. *Focus on the Family,* Aug. 1995, p. 3

685. *Baptist Standard,* Sept. 9, 1998

686. *Just As I Am,* Billy Graham, 1997, p. 714

687. Author's files

688. Ibid

689. *Homemade,* March 1992

690. *Houston Chronicle,* April 27, 1998

691. Ibid, Nov. 15, 1986

692. Ibid, July 23, 1995, p. 3G; Grand Forks Chamber of Commerce, April 1998

693. *USA Weekend*, Sept. 8, 2000

694. Author's files

695. *SBC Life*, May 1999

696. *The Ten Commandments*, Schlessinger and Vogel, 1998, p. 223

697. *Facts & Trends*, Nov. 1995, p. 6

698. Author's files

699. Ibid

700. Ibid

701. *Associated Press*, Nov. 29, 1995

702. *Commission*, Dec. 1996, p. 17

703. *The Messenger*, Jan. 1997, Editorial

704. *Living Above the Level of Mediocrity*, Charles Swindoll, 1987, p. 158

705. *Facts & Trends*, April 1999, p. 8; *SBC Life*, May 1999, p. 3

706. *San Antonio Express-News*, Feb. 5, 1998, p. 8F

707. *Houston Chronicle*, June 24, 1996, p. 9A

708. *Examiner*, April 29, 1999, p. 38

709. Author's files

710. Ibid

711. *Commission*, Sept. 1997

712. "Truths That Transform," John Ortberg, Seeds Tape Ministry M9948

713. *Prevention*, Aug. 1997, p. 24

714. Author's files

715. *Today's Christian Woman*, Jan./Feb. 1999, p. 50

716. Author's files

717. *Baptist Beacon*, May 23, 1996, p. 5

718. *American Health*, Dec. 1992, p. 46

719. Author's files

720. *A 2nd Helping of Chicken Soup for the Soul*, Canfield and Hansen, 1995, p. 191

721. Author's files

722. *Houston Chronicle*, Sept. 16, 1997, p. 10A

723. "How to Get Commitment for Ministry," John Maxwell, *The Pastor's Update*, April 1991

724. *Houston Chronicle*, June 15, 1999, p. 4A

725. *Vital Ministry*, March/April 1999

726. *Just for the Health of It*, Patty Wooten, R.N., Contributed by Brett Kays, 1999

727. Author's files

728. Ibid

729. Ibid

730. *Humor Connection*, Vol. 1013, 1996

731. *Better Families*, Aug. 1996, p. 2

732. *Houston Chronicle*, April, 23, 2000, p. 24A

733. *World*, Feb. 13, 1999, p. 12

734. "Rediscovering the Church: Embracing or Excluding People," Dieter Zander, Seeds Tape Ministry, Feb. 21, 1996

735. *Commission*, July 1990

736. "Ask Annie," North American Mission Board of the Southern Baptist Convention, Undated Material

737. *Christian Reader*, Jan./Feb. 1990, p. 49

738. Author's files

739. *Beaumont Enterprise*, Jan. 10, 2000, p. 2C

740. *Houston Chronicle*, Oct. 17, 1998, p. C1

741. Author's files

742. *Leaders*, Warren Bennis, Harper&Row, 1985, p. 76

743. Author's files

744. *U.S. News & World Report*, Dec. 22, 1997

745. *Associated Baptist Press*

746. *Parade*, April 18, 1999, p. 4

747. *Living Obediently,* Brian Harbour, 1992, p. 101; Personal Interview with Rob McConnell, M.D., Fall 1999

748. *Baptist Standard,* March 18, 1998, p. 8

749. Author's files

750. *SBC Life,* Sept. 2000, p. 5

751. *Parade,* July 19, 1998, p. 9

752. *U.S. News & World Report,* Dec. 22, 1997

753. Author's files

754. *Houston Chronicle,* Dec. 4, 1996

755. *SBC Life,* Sept. 1997, p. 13; *AFA Journal,* Jan. 1998, p. 1; *World,* Nov. 22, 1997, p. 19; *Houston Chronicle,* Nov. 9, 1997, p. 4A

756. *Leadership,* May 1999, p. 4, *SBC Life,* May 1999, p. 15

757. *Baptist Standard,* May 22, 1996, p. 1

758. Author's files

759. *SBC Life,* June/July 1998, p. 15

760. *Beaumont Enterprise,* Oct. 23, 2000, p. 11A

761. *Chicken Soup for the Christian Soul, Jack* Canfield and Mark Hansen, 2000, p. 104

762. *Dr. Dobson Answers Your Questions,* James Dobson, 1982, p. 355

763. *A 3rd Serving of Chicken Soup for the Soul,* Jack Canfield and Mark Hansen, 1996, p. 322–325

764. *AFA Journal,* June 1999

765. *Stories of Christmas Carols,* Ernest Emurian, 1967, p. 73

766. *Investing for the Future,* Larry Burkett, AudioBook, 1992

767. *Parade,* Sept. 10, 1995, p. 12

768. Author's files

769. *SBC Life,* Aug. 1995, p. 11

770. *Executive Speechwriter Newsletter,* Vol. 10 No. 4

771. *Houston Chronicle,* Aug. 19, 1990

772. *Moody,* July/Aug. 1997, p. 36

773. Author's files

774. *Yeager: An Autobiography,* Chuck Yeager, 1985 p. 129–31; *Houston Chronicle,* Oct. 13, 1997, p. 3A, Oct. 15, 1997, p. 10A

775. Houston Public Library Research Service; *The World Almanac,* 1993, p. 857

776. *Bits & Pieces,* March 27, 1997, p. 8

777. Author's files

778. "Over The Top," Zig Ziglar, 1994

779. Author's files

780. *Focus on the Family Bulletin,* Dec. 1999, p. 1

781. *Baptist Standard,* Mark Bumpus, Oct. 6, 1999, p. 14

782. *Parade,* Feb. 5, 1989, Intelligence Report

783. *Houston Chronicle,* April 24, 1999, "The Mini-Page", p. 4

784. *Pulpit Helps,* July 1999, p. 6

785. *AFA Journal* June, 1996

786. *Dr. James Dobson's Bulletin,* March 1997, p. 1

787. *Houston Chronicle,* Sept. 26, 1996, p. 9D

788. Ibid, Aug. 23, 1995, p. 1D

789. *Dr. James Dobson's Bulletin,* June 1998, p. 1

790. *Moody,* July/Aug. 1999, p. 40

791. Author's files

792. Ibid

793. *Decision,* June 1996

794. Author's files

795. Ibid

796. *Times of Discovery,* Mart De Haan, Dec. 1995, p. 1

797. Author's files

798. *Houston Chronicle,* May 7, 1999, p. 27A

799. Ibid, May 10, 1996, p. 2A; *Houston Post,* Jan. 3, 1994, p. A-8

800. *Rev.,* July/Aug.2000, p. 72

801. *Focus on the Family Bulletin*, Dec. 1995, p. 1

802. Author's files

803. Ibid

804. *Be All You Can Be,* John Maxwell, 1987, p. 18

805. *Parade*, Sept. 22, 1996, p. 20

806. Excerpts from *For the Love of the Game: My Story,* Michael Jordan, 1999; *World,* Jan. 23, 1999, p. 9, 27

807. Author's files

808. Ibid

809. Ibid

810. *Houston Chronicle*, May 28, 1998, p. 1A

811. Ibid, March 4, 1997, p. 1C; April 16, 1997, p. 1F; May 18, 1997, p.2D

812. *Moody*, Jan./Feb. 1999, p. 73

813. *The Best of Grandparents' Brag Board*, Judy Pregel and Robin Riley, 1993, p. 46

814. *Houston Chronicle*, July 6, 2000, p. 15A

815. *Decision*, Dec. 1995, p. 3

816. "Pieces of Passion," Max Lucado, *Up Words,* Nov. 7, 1999

817. *Houston Chronicle*, April 2, 2000, p. 16B; *Beaumont Journal*, April 6, 2000, p. 12

818. *Houston Chronicle*, May 18, 1998, p. 5B

819. Ibid, May 31, 1997

820. *SBC Life*, Oct. 1996

821. *Filled and Free*, Beth Moore, 1996, p. 3

822. *Pastor to Pastor*, "The Persecuted Church Fact Sheet," p. 2; *Reader's Digest*, Aug. 1997, p. 54

823. *Coral Ridge Ministries*, April 1999

824. *Houston Chronicle*, Feb. 21, 2000, p. 1C; Feb. 28, 2000, p. 2B

825. *50 Great Success Stories,* Joe Ford, 1995, p. 1

826. *Houston Post*, Oct. 23, 1993

827. Author's files

828. *Houston Chronicle*, "The Mini Page," June 27, 1998

829. *Houston Chronicle*, Dec. 1, 1999, p. 4D

830. Ibid, Sept. 9, 1998, p. 5B

831. Ibid, July 27, 1996, p. 4B

832. Ibid, Dec. 28, 1997, p. 21A

833. Ibid, March 14, 1996, p. 12B

834. *Reader's Digest*, Dec. 1996

835. *Praying to the God You Can Trust,* Leith Anderson, 1998, p. 56

836. Author's files

837. *The Winning Attitude,* John Maxwell, 1992, p. 122

838. Author's fiels

839. Ibid

840. *Commission,* March 1999, p. 3

841. *Bits & Pieces*, June 20, 1996, p. 1

842. *Houston Chronicle*, Oct. 13, 1998, p. 2C

843. *U.S. News & World Report*, May 12, 1997, p. 22–23

844. *Houston Chronicle*, Oct. 14, 2000, "The Mini Page"

845. *SBC Life*, April 1997, p. 12

846. *USA Today*, Jan. 29, 1999, p. 1A; *Inc.,* Technology 1998, No. 4, p. 25

847. *U.S. News & World Report*, Feb. 10, 1997, Cover Story

848. Author's files

849. *Chicken Soup For The Soul,* Jack Canfield and Mark Hansen, 1993, p. 69–71

850. Author's files

851. *Houston Chronicle*, May 22, 1998

852. Ibid, Nov. 5, 1996, p. 2A

853. Author's files

854. *Parade*, Aug. 23, 1998

855. *MissionsUSA*, Jan./Feb. 1997

856. *The Commission*, Oct. 1996

857. "The Power to Overcome Apathy," Bill Hybels, Seeds Tape Ministry, Nov. 19, 1995

858. *Parade*, Aug. 17, 1997

859. *Houston Chronicle*, Nov. 20, 1997

860. *Your Church on Mission*, Oct. 1999; *Pulpit Helps*, April 2000, p. 20

861. "Rediscovering The Church," John Ortberg, Seeds Tape Ministry, Feb. 28, 1996

862. *Saturday Evening Post*, Sept./Oct. 1997, p. 34

863. Author's files

864. *Houston Chronicle*, Oct. 22, 2000, p. 2E

865. *Fort Worth Star-Telegram*, May 25, 1987

866. *Commission*, Dec. 1996, p. 3

867. *Parade*, Dec. 1, 1996, p. 18

868. *Houston Chronicle*, Oct. 3, 1996, p. 26A

869. Ibid, Nov. 22, 1996, p. 2A

870. *Beaumont Examiner*, March 26, 1998, p. 26

871. *The Applause of Heaven*, Max Lucado, 1996, p. 20–21

872. Author's files

873. *Celebration of Discipline,* Richard Foster, 1988, p. 34

874. *Baptist Beacon*, Aug. 29, 1996, p. 5

875. *A 2nd Helping of Chicken Soup for the Soul,* Jack Canfield and Mark Hansen, 1993, p. 32

876. Author's files

877. Ibid

878. Ibid

879. *Pastor's Update*, Fuller Seminary, Nov. 1997

880. *Beaumont Enterprise*, Oct. 14, 2000, p. 3D

881. *Houston Chronicle*, May 3,1997, "The Mini Page", p. 4

882. Author's files

883. "Christianity Illustrated: What Makes Prayer Powerful," John Ortberg, Seeds Tape Ministry C9820

884. *Christian Reader*, March/April 1997, p. 27

885. Author's files

886. *Houston Chronicle*, Feb. 5, 1990

887. *The Minister's Family*, Summer 1998

888. *Pastor's Update on Foreign Missions*, June 1996, p. 4

889. Author's files

890. "Yea God...For Being An Equal Opportunity Employer," John Ortberg, Seeds Tape Ministry, Feb. 5, 1995

891. Author's files

892. *Times of Discovery*, Jan. 1998, p. 1

893. Author's files

894. Ibid

895. Ibid

896. "The Call and Character of Elders," Max Lucado, *UpWords,* Tape T0198

897. *Reader's Digest*, July 1993, p. 88

898. Author's files

899. Ibid

900. *Houston Chronicle*, Nov. 12, 1995, p. 14B

901. Ibid, Oct. 29, 1999, p. 2B

902. Ibid, Jan. 29, 1997, p. 5A

903. *Houston Chronicle*, June 29, 1998, p. 6A

904. *God's Vitamin "C" for the Spirit,* Kathy and Larry Miller, Starburst Publishers, 1996, p. 23

905. *First Things First*, Stephen Covey, 1994, p. 88

906. *The Criminal Justice Institutes' 1996 Corrections Yearbook; Houston Chronicle*, Jan. 10, 1998

907. *Houston Chronicle*, Dec. 29, 1996, p. 21A

908. Author's files

909. *The Paradox Principles,* The Price Waterhouse Change Integration Team, 1996, p. 105

910. *Houston Chronicle,* May 13, 1996, p. 8A

911. Ibid, Jan. 15, 1999

912. Author's files

913. Ibid

914. *People,* July 24, 1995, p. 160–162

915. *Decision,* Feb. 1998, p. 2

916. *Christian Reader,* Jan./Feb. 2000, p. 79

917. *Newsweek,* Dec. 11, 1995, p. 50

918. *Ministry Management,* Vol. 2, No. 1, p. 1

919. *Why America Doesn't Work,* Chuck Colson and Jack Eckerd, 1991, p. xi

920. *AFA Journal,* July 1999, p. 13

921. *Maybe (Maybe Not),* Robert Fulghum, 1993, p. 133–138

922. Author's files

923. *Houston Chronicle,* Aug. 27, 1998, p. 22A

924. *NEWSLETTER Newsletter,* March 1995

925. *Focus on the Family,* Jan. 1988, p. 7

926. *Houston Chronicle,* March 22, 1998, p. 2G

927. Author's files

928. "How to Select a Supporting Cast," John Maxwell, Sept. 1995, *Injoy Life Club; The Twenty-Third Psalm,* Charles Allen, 1961, p. 30

929. Author's files

930. Ibid

931. *AFA,* May 1998, p. 17

932. Author's files

933. *Christian Reader,* March/April 1997

934. *HomeLife,* Aug. 1997, p. 13; *21st Century Acts,* July 1997, p. 1

935. *Houston Chronicle,* May 23, 1999, p. 21A

936. Ibid, April 18, 1996, p. 23A

937. *Decision,* June 1996, p. 11

938. Author's files

939. *God's Vitamin "C" for the Spirit,* Kathy Miller, 1996, p. 31–32

940. *HomeLife,* Jon Walker's Editorial, Feb. 1997, p. 3

941. "R.E.S.P.E.C.T . . . Give This to Your Family," Dan Yeary, North Phoenix Baptist Church

942. *U.S. News & World Report,* Oct. 21, 1996, p. 30

943. *Houston Chronicle,* July 7, 2000, p. 15A

944. Ibid, Oct. 20, 1999, p. 4A

945. Ibid, April 27, 2000, p. 18A

946. *Houston Chronicle Zest,* Dec. 22, 1996, p. 9

947. Author's files

948. Houston's Library Resource Center, Jan. 1997

949. *Houston Chronicle,* Feb. 18, 1999, p. 6A

950. Ibid, June 28, 1999, p. 5A

951. *Insights for Pastors,* IMB/SBC, Oct. 1999, p. 2

952. *Houston Chronicle,* Oct. 20, 1996, p. 4A

953. *Decision,* Nov. 1998, p. 25

954. *Firefall: How God Has Shaped History through Revivals,* Malcolm McDow and Alvin Reid, 1997, p. 280–1

955. *Houston Chronicle,* May 12, 1996, p. 16B

956. *Promise Keeper,* Nov./Dec. 1999, *Leadership,* May 2000

957. Author's files

958. Ibid

959. Ibid

960. Ibid

961. Ibid

962. Ibid

963. Ibid

964. *Beaumont Examiner*, March 19, 1998, p. 26

965. *Parade*, Oct. 4, 1998, p. 24

966. *Christian Reader*, May/June 1996, p. 46

967. *Bits & Pieces*, March 27, 1997, p. 12

968. *Baptist Beacon*, Feb. 12, 1996, p. 2

969. *Houston Chronicle*, Oct. 6, 1997, p. 4A

970. Ibid, July 12, 1995, p. 3B; *Baptist Standard*, Aug. 23, 1995, p. 9

971. *Houston Chronicle*, July 21, 1999, p. 14A; Personal Interview with Bill Cook, Licensed Pilot

972. *Living Abundantly*, Brian Harbour, 1992, p. 25

973. *Houston Chronicle*, Aug. 16, 2000, p. 5A

974. *Moody*, Nov./Dec. 1997, p. 45

975. *Houston Chronicle*, May 28, 1996, p. 14A

976. *Raising Positive Kids in a Negative World*, Zig Ziglar, 1989, p. 45–46

977. "What Is The Good Life," David Davis, Bellaire, Texas

978. *A 2nd Helping of Chicken Soup for the Soul*, Canfield and Hansen, 1995, p. 12

979. Author's files

980. Ibid

981. Ibid

982. *Houston Chronicle*, June 26, 1999, p. 19A

983. Ibid, April 1, 1998, p. 6A

984. Ibid, Oct. 13, 1998, p. 1A

985. *Bits & Pieces*, Nov. 5, 1998, p. 19

986. *Christian Reader*, Sept./Oct. 1991, p. 17; *The Promise Keeper*, May 1999, p. 6

987. *U.S. News & World Report*, March 17, 1997, p. 34

988. *Baptist Beacon*, Jan. 30, 1997

989. Author's files

990. "What God Would Say To . . . Bill Gates," Lee Strobel, Seeds Tape Ministry, Aug. 13, 1995; *Reader's Digest*, March 1993, p. 112

991. *Leadership*, Sept. 1999, p. 7

992. *Living Expectantly*, Brian Harbour, 1990, p. 13

993. *The Twenty-Third Psalm*, Charles Allen, 1961, p. 15

994. *U.S. News & World Report*, June 17, 1996, p. 25

995. Author's files

996. *Fire In My Bones*, Fred Wood, Broadman Press, 1959, p. 118

997. *U.S. News & World Report*, Dec. 22, 1997

998. *Focus on the Family Bulletin*, April 1998, p. 1

999. Innovative Church Growth Conference, Glorieta, New Mexico, May 1999

1000. Author's files

1001. Ibid

1002. Ibid

1003. *Restoring Your Spiritual Passion*, Gordon MacDonald, 1986, p. 215

1004. "The Words That Changed the World," Max Lucado, UpWords T0698

1005. *God's Vitamin "C" for the Spirit*, Kathy and Larry Miller, 1996, p. 20

1006. Author's files

1007. Ibid

1008. *Institute of Medicine*, Nov. 1996

1009. *SBC Life*, June 1996

1010. *World*, Jan. 22, 2000

1011. *SBC Life*, Oct. 2000

1012. *Houston Chronicle*, Feb. 10, 1999, p. 12A; Feb. 15, 1999, p. 2A

1013. "Marriage Intimacy," Randall Williams, Bay Area First Baptist

Church; *U.S. News & World Report*, 1995

1014. *Washington Times*, Oct. 19, 1997

1015. *Pastor's Update On Foreign Missions*, June 1996, p. 2

1016. *Houston Chronicle*, April 17, 1998, p. 2A

1017. Ibid, Sept. 15, 1996, p. 17B

1018. *Reader's Digest*, March 1995, p. 86

1019. *Houston Chronicle*, April 8, 1997, p. 2A

1020. Ibid, Jan. 12, 1998, p. 1C

1021. *Beaumont Examiner*, Oct. 12, 1999, p. 49

1022. *Houston Chronicle*, May 14, 1999, p. 3D

1023. *Examiner*, July 16, 1998, p. 26; *Houston Chronicle*, March 27, 1997, p. 4A; *Houston Chronicle*, Jan. 31, 1999, p. 4A; *Parade*, Dec. 28, 1997, p. 6

1024. *Houston Chronicle*, Feb. 3, 1997, p. 12A

1025. Author's files

1026. Ibid

1027. *Houston Chronicle*, Sept. 13, 1999, p. 15A

1028. Author's files

1029. *U.S. News & World Report*, Oct. 23, 1995, p. 98

1030. *U.S. News & World Report*, Feb. 3, 1997

1031. *Holy Humor*

1032. *Houston Chronicle*, Jan. 22, 1999

1033. Ibid, Dec. 21, 1997

1034. *Prevention*, Oct. 1997

1035. *Houston Chronicle*, April 16, 1997

1036. *U.S. News & World Report*, Sept. 2, 1996

1037. *Archives of Pediatrics and Adolescent Medicine*, 1997

1038. *Therefore . . .*, March 1998

1039. Author's files

1040. Ibid

1041. Ibid

1042. *Journal of the American Medical Association*, 1996; *Prevention*, Oct. 1993, p. 118

1043. *Bits & Pieces*, Dec. 5, 1996, p. 2

1044. "Pray at Your Own Risk," Bill Hybels, Seeds Tape Ministry, March 16, 1997

1045. *Beaumont Enterprise*, June 6, 2000, p. 5C

1046. *Mirror, Mirror on the Wall: Discovering Your True Self through Spiritual Gifts*, Ken Hemphill, 1992, p. 145

1047. *A 3rd Serving of Chicken Soup for the Soul*, Jack Canfield and Mark Hansen, 1996, p. 239

1048. *Serving God Discovering & Using Your Spiritual Gifts*, Ken Hemphill, 1995, Lesson Three

1049. Author's files

1050. *Daily Bread*, May 20, 1997

1051. *Houston Chronicle*, Jan. 3, 1999, p. 15A

1052. Ibid, April 5, 1998, p. 5D

1053. Ibid, Dec. 31, 1995, p. 15A

1054. *Pastor's Weekly Briefing, Focus on the Family*, Feb. 11, 2000, p. 2

1055. *Houston Chronicle*, Dec. 29, 1996, p. 21A

1056. *Reader's Digest*, May 1999, p. 126

1057. *World*, Oct. 12, 1996, p. 9

1058. *Houston Chronicle*, Oct. 12, 1997, p. 34A

1059. Ibid, April 29, 2000, p. 2A

1060. *Reader's Digest*, May 1999, p. 98; *Leadership*, May 2000, p. 11

1061. *Margin,* Richard Swenson, 1992, p. 58,107

1062. *Working Well*, May 1995, p. 1

1063. *Houston Chronicle* Aug. 17, 1996

1064. Ibid, Jan. 6, 1999, p. 7A

1065. *Positive Living*, Jan./Feb. 1997, p. 29

1066. Author's files

1067. Ibid

1068. Ibid

1069. Ibid

1070. *Houston Chronicle*, Aug. 11, 1998, p. 2A

1071. *Maybe (Maybe Not): Second Thoughts from a Secret Life*, Robert Fulghum, 1993, p. 83

1072. *The Success Journey*, John Maxwell, Thomas Nelson Publishers, 1997, p. 1

1073. Author's files

1074. Ibid

1075. *The Finishing Touch*, Charles Swindoll, 1994, p. 60

1076. Author's files

1077. Ibid

1078. *Houston Chronicle*, April 22, 1998, p. 11B

1079. *USA Weekend*, July 7, 2000

1080. *Houston Chronicle*, Feb. 1, 1999

1081. Ibid, Sept. 29, 1996, p. 6A

1082. Ibid, July 20, 1996, p. 16A; Sept. 2, 1996, p. 24A

1083. *Parade*, Jan. 5, 1992, p. 2

1084. *Pastor's Weekly Briefing*, March 3, 2000, p. 1; *AFA Journal*, March 2000, p. 5

1085. *Houston Chronicle*, Oct. 24, 1998

1086. *HomeLife*, Nov. 1998, p. 14

1087. *Houston Chronicle*, June 22, 1996, p. 1E; *Decision*, Feb. 1987, p. 4

1088. *World*, Feb. 22, 1997, p. 22

1089. *Vital Ministry*, July/Aug. 1999, p. 18

1090. *Houston Chronicle*, July 15, 2000, p. 24A

1091. Ibid, April 8, 1998

1092. *Bits & Pieces*, March 2, 1995, p. 1

1093. *Reader's Digest*, Feb. 1994

1094. *Bits & Pieces*, April 24, 1997, p. 18

1095. *Fortune*, June 27th, 1994

1096. *Parade*, Sept 21, 1997

1097. *The People Puzzle*, Morris Massey

1098. *U.S. News & World Report*, July 1, 1996

1099. *Better Families*, Jan, 1996, p. 1

1100. *AFA Journal*, July 1996; *Houston Chronicle*, July 30, 1996, p. 8A; *NEWSLETTER Newsletter*, Aug. 1996

1101. *Reader's Digest*, Oct. 1995, p. 158

1102. *Houston Chronicle*, Feb. 4, 1999

1103. *HomeLife*, May 1997, p. 47

1104. *Garfield*, by Jim Davis, Jan. 25, 1997

1105. *Baptist Standard*, May 28, 1997

1106. Houston Public Library Research Center, January 1998

1107. *San Antonio Express-News*, July 28, 1998, p. 8E

1108. *Houston Chronicle*, Oct. 27, 2000, p. 31A; Oct. 28, 2000, p. 40A

1109. Author's files

1110. *Reader's Digest*, Sept. 1998, p. 222

1111. *SBC Life*, April 1997, p. 9

1112. *Athens Daily News*, May 11, 1997, p. 2A, Contributed by Tracy Sims

1113. *Stories for the Heart*, Alice Gray, 1996, p. 62

1114. *Reader's Digest*, Nov. 1994, p. 174

1115. *Houston Chronicle*, May 27, 1997, p. 8A

1116. *The Timetables of History*, Bernard Grun, 1982, p. 278; *NEWSLETTER Newsletter*, Nov. 1999, p. 6

1117. *Handbook to The Baptist Hymnal*, Wesley Forbis, ed., 1992, p. 197

1118. *Parade*, Oct. 7, 1997

1119. *U.S. News & World Report*, Sept. 23, 1996

1120. Author's files

1121. *Reader's Digest*, June 1996, p. 33

1122. *Don't Sweat The Small Stuff*, Richard Carlson, 1997

1123. *Race Relations*, Texas Baptist Christian Life Commission

1124. *Houston Chronicle*, Oct. 28, 1995, p. 4E

1125. *Stories For The Heart*, Alice Gray, 1996, p. 91

1126. *USA Today*, April 13, 1989, "Life" 4D

1127. Author's files

1128. *NEWSLETTER Newsletter*, Oct. 2000

1129. *Houston Chronicle*, Jan. 10, 1998

1130. Author's files

1131. *U.S. News & World Report*, March 16, 1998, p. 84

1132. *Bits & Pieces*, Nov. 7, 1996, p. 20

1133. "Loving Christ," Joseph Stowell, Seeds Tape Ministry, C9834

1134. *Houston Chronicle*, May 5, 1999, p. 10A; *Baptist Standard*, May 5, 1999, p. 5

1135. *Commission*, April 1989, Global Glimpses

1136. "Things and People Can Be Redeemed," Jim Moore, *Houston Chronicle*, Oct. 9, 1997, p. 31A

1137. God's Vitamin "C" for the Spirit, Kathy and Larry Miller, 1996, p. 10

1138. *Houston Chronicle*, Dec. 28, 1996, p. 8E

1139. *Your Church on Mission with God*, Oct. 2000, p. 2

1140. *Bits & Pieces*, Feb. 27, 1997, p. 12

1141. Author's files

1142. Ibid

1143. *Prevention*, Oct. 1993, p. 54

1144. *Parade*, March 3, 1996, p. 14

1145. *And God Wants People,* Mary Lou Lacy, 1962, p. 35

1146. Author's Personal Life; *Today's Better Family*, Fall 1993, p. 37

1147. *Bits & Pieces*, Jan. 27, 2000, p. 4

1148. *Houston Chronicle*, Nov. 18, 1997, p. 3A

1149. *Houston Chronicle*, Dec. 7, 1999, p. 2A

1150. *Baptist Standard*, April 2, 1997, p. 7

1151. *U.S. News & World Report* July 1, 1996

1152. *Houston Chronicle*, April 30, 1999, p. 1A

1153. Ibid, April 17, 1998

1154. *World Vision Today*, Summer 1999

1155. Author's files

1156. Ibid

1157. *Houston Chronicle*, July 23, 1999, p. 5F

1158. Author's files

1159. Brad Creed, Baylor University Ministers Conference, 1994

1160. Author's files

1161. *Executive Speechwriter Newsletter*, Vol. 11, No. 3

1162. *Church Planting for a Greater Harvest*, Peter Wagner, 1990, p. 141

1163. *Barna Research Group*, 1999

1164. *21st Century Acts*, June 1997, p. 4; *Houston Chronicle*, Nov. 2, 1996, p. 1E

1165. *Houston Chronicle*, June 29, 2000

1166. *Therefore . . .*, April 2000, p. 1–5; *Pulpit Helps*, April 2000, p. 20

1167. *Making Love Last Forever,* Gary Smalley, 1996, p. 5–6; *Houston Chronicle*, Dec. 22, 1997, p. 2C

1168. *Houston Chronicle*, Sept. 29, 1997, p. 10A

1169. *Parade*, Aug. 23, 1998, p. 6

1170. *Houston Chronicle*, Dec. 29, 1999, p. 19A

1171. *O'Jerusalem*, Larry Collins and Dominique Lapierre, 1972

1172. *Leadership Journal*, Winter 1995, p. 38

1173. *Parade*, Sec. 31, 1995, p. 12

1174. *Moody*, July/Aug. 1996, p. 39

1175. *The Complete Financial Guide for Young Couples*, Larry Burkett, AudioBook, 1993; *Houston Chronicle*, June 20, 1995, p. 4A; "Proven Principles for Successful Stewardship," John Maxwell, 1994, Tape 2

1176. *Bits & Pieces*, Dec. 5, 1996, p. 21

1177. Author's files

1178. *Houston Chronicle*, Jan. 18, 1998, p. 14B

1179. *The One Minute Manager to Work*, Ken Blanchard; 1995, *Houston Chronicle*, Dec. 29, 1998, p. 3D

1180. *UpWords*, Max Lucado, Tape T1197

1181. *Inc.*, March 1993, p. 46

1182. *Bits & Pieces*, Jan. 14, 1999, p. 5

1183. *Houston Chronicle*, April 16, 1998

1184. Author's files

1185. *Houston Chronicle*, Sept. 24, 1998

1186. Author's files

1187. *Houston Chronicle*, March 9, 1999, p. 5B

1188. *U.S. News & World Report*, Sept. 2, 1996, p. 20

1189. *Moody*, March/April 1998, p. 46; *Baptist Standard*, March 12, 1997, p. 8

1190. *Newsweek*, June 3, 1991, p. 56

1191. *Parables*, Dec. 1995; *Houston Chronicle*, Dec. 3, 1995

1192. Author's files

1193. Ibid

1194. Ibid

1195. *Mature Living*, July 1996, p. 7

1196. *NEWSLETTER Newsletter*, Sept. 1994

1197. Adapted from *Pulpit Resource*, Vol. 28, No. 3, p. 30

1198. Author's files

1199. *New Man*, March/April 1997, p. 98

1200. *Houston Chronicle*, Oct. 4, 1999, p. 30A

1201. Ibid, Oct. 30, 1999, p. 1E

1202. *Bits & Pieces*, Undated File

1203. *Pastor's Update on Foreign Missions*, April 1996, p.

1204. *Better Families*, Nov. 1995, p. 1; *Pastor's Update*, Nov. 1991, p. 4

1205. *SBC Life*, Charles Lowery, Nov. 1998, p. 16

1206. *Saturday Evening Post*, May/June 1993, p. 37

1207. *Humor for Preaching & Teaching*, Ed Rowell, 1996, p. 8

1208. *Sermon Notes & Illustrations*, Aug. 1995

1209. *Preacher Joke-a-Day Calendar*, Sept. 18, 1998

1210. *Christian Reader*, July/Aug. 1997, p. 12

1211. *Christian Reader*, March/April 1995, p. 68

1212. *911 Handbook*, Kent Crockett, Hendrickson Publishers, 1997, p. 150

1213. *U.S. News & World Report*, April 27, 1998, p. 76

1214. *Reminisce*, May/June 1995, p. 61

1215. Contributed by Tom Meador

1216. *Reader's Digest*, May 1999, p. 110

1217. Adapted from Max Lucado, "Fire from Heaven," Part 8, March 26, 2000

1218. *Christian Reader*, March/April 1997, p. 80

1219. Ronnie Burke, Westgate Memorial Baptist Church, Feb. 5, 2000

1220. *Reader's Digest*, Oct. 1995, p. 78

1221. Adapted from *NEWSLETTER Newsletter*, July 1996, p. 3

1222. "Withholding the Blessing," John Morgan, Sagemont Church, Nov. 24, 1996

1223. *Sermon Notes & Illustrations*, Jan. 1996

1224. *Bits & Pieces*, July 17, 1997, p. 9

1225. *Christian Parenting Today*, July/Aug. 1991, p. 59

1226. Adapted from *Parade*, April 30, 2000, p. 13

1227. *Positive Living*, Jan./Feb. 1999, p. 39

1228. *Executive Speechwriter Newsletter*, Vol. 10, No. 3

1229. *Humor Connection*, Vol. 1013, 1996

1230. *Stand Firm*, Aug. 1997, p. 3

1231. Author's files

1232. "Christianity Illustrated," John Ortberg, Seeds Tape C9816

1233. *Houston Chronicle*, Nov. 12, 1995

1234. *Bits & Pieces*, Nov. 6, 1997, p. 7

1235. *Christian Reader*, Sept./Oct. 1999, p. 9

1236. *Executive Speechwriter Newsletter*, Vol. 11, No. 3

1237. Adapted from *Reader's Digest*, Nov. 1998, p. 62

1238. *Today's Christian Woman*, July/Aug. 1992, p. 19

1239. *Sermon Notes & Illustrations*, Oct. 1995

1240. Adapted from *The Best of Grandparents' Brag Board*, Judy Pregel and Robin Riley, 1993, p. 13

1241. *Houston Chronicle*, Jan. 4, 1997, p. 7E

1242. Ibid, Dec. 30, 1999, p. 4A

1243. "Revelation: The Truth About Armageddon," John Ortberg, Seeds Tape Ministry C9917

1244. *Humor with a Halo*, Al Fasol, 1991, p. 16–17

1245. *Best of Grandparents' Brag Board*, Judy Pregel and Robin Riley, 1993, p. 67

1246. *Today's Christian Woman*, July/Aug. 1992, p. 19

1247. *HomeLife*, July 1995, p. 63

1248. *Executive Speechwriter Newsletter*, Vol. 14, No. 5

1249. KSBJ, Buddy Holiday

1250. *While Shepherds Washed Their Flocks*, Liz Higgs, 1998, p. 81

1251. *Positive Living*, Sept./Oct. 1997, p. 19

1252. *Humor with a Halo*, Al Fasol, 1991, p. 25–26

1253. *Bits & Pieces*, Dec. 30, 1999, p. 5

1254. *Reader's Digest*, Dec. 1996, p. 140

1255. *Parade*, Oct. 4, 1998, p. 28

1256. *Humor Connection*, Date Unknown

1257. *NEWSLETTER Newsletter*, Aug. 1999, p. 6

1258. *Preacher's Joke a Day Calendar*, Oct. 9, 1998

1259. Ibid, Sept. 25, 1998

1260. *Christian Reader*, May/June 1996, p. 73

1261. *Reader's Digest*, June 1994, p. 72

1262. *Living Abundantly*, Brian Harbour, Broadman, 1992, p. 103

1263. *Houston Chronicle*, Dec. 10, 1995, p. 6G

1264. Dr. Richard Couey, Baylor University Ministers Conference, 1994

1265. Ibid

1266. *Saturday Evening Post*, July/Aug. 1999, p. 23

1267. Adapted from *Great Stories*, Vol. 5, Issue 19, p.10

1268. "What's a Christian to Believe?" Skip Smith, Sagemont Church, Nov. 24, 1996

1269. *Sermon Notes*, Promotional Materials

1270. Author's files

1271. *Bits & Pieces*, March 28, 1996, p. 10–11

1272. Adapted from *Reader's Digest*, April 1994, p. 84

1273. *Inc.*, Dec. 1995, p. 13

1274. *Brian's Lines*, March/April 1999

1275. *Executive Speechwriter*, Vol. 10, No. 3

1276. *Houston Chronicle*, Nov. 8, 1999, p. 8C

1277. *Parade*, Sept. 21, 1997, p. 20

1278. Contributed by Parker Williams

1279. *Reader's Digest*, Oct. 1998, p. 121

1280. Adapted from the *Houston Chronicle*, April 22, 1998, p. 11D

1281. *Houston Chronicle*, Nov. 8, 1998, p. 12F

1282. "Leadership Servanthood," John Ortberg, Seeds Tape Ministry, Aug. 6, 1997

1283. Promise Keeper's Conference, Houston, Texas, Aug. 22, 1998

1284. John Morgan, Sagemont Church

1285. *Bits & Pieces*, Vol. M, No. 1, p. 22

1286. *Houston Chronicle*, Sept. 27, 1996, p. 9D

1287. Ibid, Jan. 18, 1997, p. 7E

1288. *Preaching Today*, Tape 156

1289. *Houston Chronicle*, June 26, 1996, p. 8D

1290. Ibid, "Non Sequitur," April 23, 1998

1291. *World*, Feb. 27, 1999, p. 34

1292. *Close to Home*, John McPherson, Aug. 28, 1997

1293. *Reader's Digest*, Jan. 1995, p. 82

1294. Author's files

1295. *Reader's Digest*, Jan. 1989, p. 202

1296. *Mature Living*, July 1996, p. 6

1297. "When It's Not Easy to Love," Max Lucado, *UpWords*, Aug. 1, 1999

1298. *Christian Reader*, Jan./Feb. 1997, p. 69

1299. *Reader's Digest*, Date Unknown

1300. Author's files

1301. *Executive Speechwriter Newsletter*, Vol. 12, No. 3

1302. *SBC Life*, Charles Lowery, Feb./March 1996, p. 4

1303. Author's Personal Life, Fall 1998

1304. *Brian's Lines*, May/June 1996

1305. *Christian Reader*, Sept./Oct. 1998, p. 10

1306. *Today's Christian Woman*, March/April 1999, p. 34

1307. Contributed by G. W. McNeese

1308. Charles Lowery, *SBC Life*, June/July 1999, p. 24

1309. *Saturday Evening Post*, April/March 1999, p. 40

1310. Author's files

1311. *Executive Speechwriter Newsletter*, Vol. 14, No. 4

1312. *Houston Chronicle*, Nov. 30, 1998, p. 8C

1313. *Reader's Digest*, Dec. 1996, p. 201

1314. *Saturday Evening Post*, Nov./Dec. 1996, p. 72

1315. *Positive Living*, July/Aug. 1998, p. 8

1316. *Reader's Digest*, Date Unknown

1317. Sandi Lewis in Concert, Westgate Memorial Baptist Church, Aug. 1999

1318. *Chicken Soup for the Soul*, Jack Canfield and Mark Hansen, 1993, p. 74

1319. Author's files

1320. *Humor with a Halo*, Al Fasol, 1991, p. 76–77

1321. *Houston Chronicle*, Feb. 25, 1996

1322. *Reader's Digest*, May 1993, p. 83

1323. *Mature Living*, June 1992, p. 49

1324. *Houston Chronicle*, March 6, 1996, p. 11D

1325. "Ten Values That Build Strong Families," Part 5, Rick Warren,

The Encouraging Word; Parade, Spring 2000

1326. *Living Abundantly,* Brian Harbour, 1992, p. 55

1327. *Houston Chronicle,* June 13, 1996, p. 10A

1328. *Executive Speechwriter Newsletter,* Vol. 12, No. 3

1329. *Humor Connection,* Vol. 1003, 1993

1330. Author's files

1331. *Bits & Pieces,* Dec. 4, 1997, p. 2

1332. *Houston Chronicle,* May 31, 1997, p. 4E

1333. Author's files

1334. *Bits & Pieces,* Nov. 6, 1997, p. 18

1335. *Rotarian,* June 1993, p. 56

1336. *Saturday Evening Post,* May/June 1999, p. 34; *Houston Chronicle,* Dec. 1, 1999, p. 9D

1337. *Reader's Digest,* June 1988, p. 147

1338. *Christian Reader,* Oct. 1990, p. 31

1339. *Holy Humor,* Cal and Rose Samra, 1996, p. 22

1340. Author's files

1341. *Executive Speechwriter Newsletter,* Vol. 8, No. 1

1342. *Positive Living,* July/Aug. 1997, p. 39; *Bits & Pieces,* May 22, 1997, p. 10

1343. *Houston Post,* March 15, 1995, p. B–2

1344. *Rotarian,* July 1993, p. 56

1345. *Houston Chronicle,* July 6, 1999, p. 7D

1346. *Leadership,* Aug. 31, 1996, p. 18

1347. Author's files

1348. *Executive Speechwriter,* Vol. 10, No. 3

1349. *Reader's Digest,* Dec. 1996, p. 202

1350. *Positive Living,* March/April 1995, p. 30

1351. *Executive Speechwriter Newsletter,* Vol. 10, No. 4

1352. *Houston Chronicle,* May 17, 1997, p. 4E

1353. *The Best of Grandparents Brag Board,* Judy Pregel and Robin Riley, 1993, p. 62

1354. *Reader's Digest,* March 1995, p. 88

1355. *Positive Living,* March/April 1997, p. 8

1356. *Positive Living,* Jan./Feb. 1997, p. 25

1357. Author's files

1358. *Executive Speechwriter Newsletter,* Vol. 11, No. 5

1359. *Houston Chronicle,* May 5, 1999, p. 7D

1360. Ibid, Feb. 19, 1997, p. 3D

1361. "Learning to Listen to God," Max Lucado, *Up Words,* Aug. 24, 1997

1362. *Reader's Digest,* July 1999, p. 145

1363. *Positive Living,* May/June 1998

1364. *Saturday Evening Post,* March/April 1999, p. 33

1365. "Christianity Illustrated," John Ortberg, Seeds Tape Ministry C9819

1366. "Thirty Seconds into Eternity," Ray Jones, North American Mission Board, Summer 2000

1367. *Saturday Evening Post,* July/Aug. 1996, p. 6

1368. *Reader's Digest,* Oct. 1993, p. 130

1369. *Rotarian,* June 1993, p. 56

1370. *Executive Speechwriter Newsletter,* Vol. 11, No. 6

1371. *NEWSLETTER Newsletter,* Dec. 1998, p. 6

1372. *Reader's Digest,* April 1999, p. 86

1373. *Houston Chronicle,* Aug. 7, 1996, p. 10D

1374. *Reader's Digest,* March 1995, p. 67

1375. "Unshakable Confidence," John Burke, Seeds Tape Ministry, June 19, 1996

1376. *Christian Reader,* Jan./Feb. 1992, p. 25

1377. *Humor Connection,* Vol. 1013

1378. Adapted from Seven World's Publishing, May/June 1991

1379. Author's files

1380. Adapted from *Reader's Digest,* Dec. 1996, p. 201

1381. *Positive Living,* March/April 1995, p. 7

1382. Contributed by Craig McGregor

1383. Promise Keeper Moment, KSBJ, Houston, Texas, 7/3/00

1384. *NEWSLETTER Newsletter,* March 1999, p. 7

1385. *Houston Chronicle,* Nov. 1, 1995, p. 13D

1386. *Humor with a Halo,* Al Fasol, 1991, p. 60

1387. *Reader's Digest,* Oct. 1998, p. 120

1388. Charles Lowery, *SBC Life,* Feb./March 1997, p. 23

1389. *Positive Living,* March/April 1996, p. 39

1390. *Leadership,* Oct. 26, 1993, p. 17

1391. *Holy Humor,* Cal and Rose Samra, 1996, p. 42

1392. Author's files

1393. Contributed by Milton Bailey

1394. Author's Personal Experience, April 2000

1395. Contributed by Loretta Reynolds

1396. *Reader's Digest,* Oct. 1993, p. 59

1397. *HomeLife,* Feb. 1997, p. 63

1398. *Reminisce,* May/June 1998, p. 61

1399. Author's files

1400. *Humor for Preaching & Teaching,* Ed Rowell, 1996, p. 83

1401. *Reader's Digest,* Sept. 1994, p. 32

1402. *Best of Grandparents' Brag Board,* Judy Pregel and Robin Riley, 1993, p. 61

1403. *Christian Reader,* Sept./Oct. 1999, p. 10

1404. *Houston Chronicle,* Oct. 3, 1997, p. 6D

1405. *Bits & Pieces,* Dec. 5, 1996, p. 10

1406. *Reminisce,* Jan./Feb. 1997, p. 61

1407. *Christian Reader,* March/April 1995, p. 68

1408. *Church Editor,* Sept. 1995, p. 2

1409. *Reader's Digest,* Oct. 1998, p. 127

1410. *Today's Christian Woman,* Sept./Oct. 1996, p. 41

1411. Author's files

1412. *Youth Specialties,* Oct. 29, 1999

1413. *Houston Chronicle,* June 17, 1998, p. 11D

1414. Ibid, Jan. 9, 2000

1415. *Reader's Digest,* Feb. 1994, p. 66

1416. Author's files

1417. Family Life Marriage Conference, Houston, Texas, Oct. 23, 1999

1418. *Preacher's Joke-a-Day Calendar,* Aug. 14, 1998

1419. *Reader's Digest,* May 1999, p. 77

1420. Ibid, Nov. 1995, p. 156

1421. *Mature Living,* July 1996, p. 6

1422. *Houston Chronicle,* April 24, 1996, p. 6D

1423. "Being an Attractive Wife," Randall Williams, Bay Area First Baptist Church

1424. *Reader's Digest,* April 1993, p. 86

1425. *Christian Reader,* May/June 1996, p. 58

1426. *Happy Clergy,* Herb Walker, 1997, p. 27

1427. Author's files

1428. *Reader's Digest,* Nov. 1993, p. 38

1429. *Leadership Journal,* Fall 1994, p. 110

1430. *Brian's Lines,* Jan./Feb. 1999

1431. *Executive Speechwriter Newsletter,* Vol. 11, No. 6

1432. *Reader's Digest,* Sept. 1993, p. 45

1433. *Reader's Digest,* Oct. 1994, p. 48

1434. *Best of Grandparents' Brag Board*, Judy Pregel and Robin Riley, 1993, p. 75

1435. *Saturday Evening Post*, Sept./Oct. 1998, p. 66

1436. *Houston Chronicle*, June 26, 2000, p. 8C

1437. Adapted from *Reader's Digest*, Feb. 1994, p. 94

1438. *Reader's Digest*, Oct. 1995, p. 114

1439. *Houston Chronicle*, Feb. 4, 2000, p. 12D

1440. *Daily Walk*, Jan. 21, 1994

1441. Richard Jackson, Westgate Memorial Baptist, Feb. 6, 2000

1442. *Houston Chronicle*, July 31, 1996, p. 6D

1443. Author's files

1444. *The Happy Clergy*, Herb Walker, 1977, p. 25

1445. *Pastor's Family*, Oct./Nov. 1997, p. 31

1446. *James Dobson's Bulletin*, June 1998, p. 1

1447. *Humor for Preaching & Teaching*, Edward Rowell, 1998, p. 27

1448. *Houston Chronicle*, Oct. 29, 1997, p. 8D

1449. *Homeward Bound*, March 1999, p. 2

1450. *Guideposts*, Aug. 1995, p. 13

1451. *Reader's Digest*, March 1999, p. 62

1452. *Bits & Pieces*, July 17, 1997, p. 22

1453. *San Antonio Express-News*, June 27, 1999, Insight

1454. *Sermon Notes*, May/June 1997

1455. *Christian Reader*, Sept./Oct. 1998, p. 10

1456. *Holy Humor*, Cal and Rose Samra, 1996, p. 6

1457. *Houston Chronicle*, July 14, 1995, p. 7D

1458. *Parade*, Dec. 31, 1995, p. 18; *Houston Post*

1459. *Examiner*, Sept. 24, 1998, p. 26

1460. Adapted from the *Houston Chronicle*, June 28, 1996, p. 9D

1461. *Scope*, Vol. 8, No. 16, 1998

1462. *Living Obediently*, Brian Harbor, 1992, p. 56

1463. *Positive Living*, March/April 1999, p. 39

1464. *A 2nd Helping of Chicken Soup for the Soul*, Jack Canfield and Mark Hansen, Health Communications, 1995, p. 88

1465. *Houston Chronicle*, Feb. 22, 2000, p. 11D

1466. *Best of Grandparents' Brag Board*, Judy Pregel and Robin Riley, 1993, p. 46

1467. *Pulpit Helps*, Feb. 2000, p. 19

1468. *Holy Humor*, Cal and Rose Samra, 1996, p. 176

1469. *Humor with a Halo*, Al Fasol, 1991, p. 51

1470. Phil Lineberger, Baylor Ministers Conference, 1994

1471. *Saturday Evening Post*, March/April 1993, p. 34

1472. Leighton Ford Leadership Development Conference, 1991

1473. Author's Personal Life, July 11, 1999

1474. *Saturday Evening Post*, Nov./Dec. 1999, p. 34

1475. *World*, May 17, 1997, p. 30

1476. 1997 SBC Pastors' Conference, Dallas, Texas

1477. *Parade*, April 16, 2000, p. 22

1478. *Positive Living*, Sept./Oct. 1996, p. 5

1479. *Houston Chronicle*, Feb. 1, 2000, p. 17A

1480. "Living in Little Communities," Bill Hybels, Seeds Tape Ministry, Sept. 17, 1995

1481. *Best of Grandparents' Brag Board*, Judy Pregel and Robin Riley, 1993, p. 67

1482. *Humor with a Halo*, Al Fasol, C.S.S. Publishing, 1991, p. 18

1483. *Humor for Preaching & Teaching*, Ed Rowell, 1996, p. 135

1484. *Parade*, Oct. 1, 2000, p. 16

1485. *Clippings from My Notebook*, Corrie ten Boom, 1982, p. 16

1486. *Best of Grandparents' Brag Board*, Judy Pregel and Robin Riley, Convention Press, 1993, p. 17

1487. *Sermon Notes & Illustrations*, April 1995, p. 18

1488. *Humor with a Halo*, Al Fasol, 1991, p. 15

1489. *Christian Index*, Jan. 28, 1999, p. 10, Contributed by Tracy Sims

1490. Author's files

1491. *Christian Reader*, July/Aug. 1994, p. 26

1492. *Aha!!!*, Oct. 1998, p. 12

1493. "Christianity Illustrated," John Ortberg, Willow Creek Church, March 25, 1998

1494. Max Lucado, *UpWords*, Dec. 1999, Tape T2099

1495. *Reminisce*, March/April 1997, p. 61

1496. "Living Now," John Ortberg, Seeds Tape Ministry, Aug. 24, 1997

1497. *Houston Chronicle*, Aug. 11, 1995, p. 22A

1498. *Living Obediently*, Brian Harbour, 1992, p. 97

1499. *HomeLife*, July 1996, p. 63

1500. *Holy Humor*, Cal and Rosa Samra, *Guidepost*, 1996, p. 56

1501. 'Evolution or Creation: Which Holds Up Under Scrutiny," Lee Strobel, Seeds Tape Ministry, April 27, 1997

1502. *Reader's Digest*, Feb. 1994, p. 127

1503. *Brian's Lines*, Sept./Oct. 1997, p. 23

1504. *Houston Chronicle*, April 3, 1996, p. 10D

1505. *Rotarian*, May 1998, p. 64

1506. *Mature Living*, Feb. 2000, p. 6

1507. "Fit or Fat? Let's Get Healthy!" Charles Lowery, March 1, 1998

1508. *Mature Living*, Feb. 2000, p. 6

1509. *Saturday Evening Post*, May/June 1999, p. 68

1510. *Mature Living*, April 2000, p. 6

1511. Contributed by Wayne Rouse

1512. Ibid

1513. Author's files

1514. Ibid

1515. *Baptist Standard*, Mark Harkrider, July 23, 1997, p. 5

1516. *Reader's Digest*, April 1994, p. 109

1517. *Bits & Pieces*, Sept. 19, 1996, p. 1

1518. *Baptist Standard*, Nov. 23, 1994, p. 4

1519. *Mission: Possible*, Young Life Banquet, Beaumont, Texas, Oct. 16, 2000

1520. *A 2nd Helping of Chicken Soup for the Soul*, Jack Canfield and Mark Hansen, 1993, p. 103

1521. *Positive Living*, Sept./Oct. 1998, p. 8

1522. *Today's Christian Woman*, Sept./Oct.1996, p. 41

1523. *Reader's Digest*, Sept. 1994, p. 113

1524. *Christian Reader*, Jan./Feb. 2000, p. 8

1525. *Peanuts*, Feb. 18, 1997

1526. *Houston Chronicle*, Jan. 11, 2000, p. 9D

1527. *Bits & Pieces*, Aug. 1993, p. 19

1528. *Positive Living*, Jan./Feb. 1997, p. 39

1529. *Parade*, May 10, 1998, p. 7

1530. Promise Keeper's Conference, Houston, Texas, Aug. 22, 1998

1531. *Reader's Digest*, Sept. 1998, p. 85

1532. Adapted from the *Bay Area Sun*, Oct. 15, 1997, p. 11

1533. *Focus on the Family*, Nov. 1999, p. 24

1534. *Positive Living,* Jan./Feb. 1999, p. 39

1535. Charles Lowery, Westgate Memorial Baptist Church Marriage Conference, Spring 1999

1536. *Reader's Digest,* Jan. 1999, p. 78

1537. Adapted from *Parish,* Sept. 1995, p. 2

1538. *Christian Reader,* July/Aug. 1997, p. 12

1539. *Humor for Preaching & Teaching,* Edward Rowell, Baker Books, 1996, p. 12

1540. *Living Obediently,* Brian Harbour, 1992, p. 97

1541. *Rotarian,* July 1992, p. 56

1542. *Preacher Joke-a-Day Calendar,* Oct. 26, 1998

1543. Adapted from *Houston Post,* March 7, 1995, p. A-15

1544. *Parade,* Aug. 15, 1999, p. 6

1545. Author's files

1546. *Best of Grandparents' Brag Board,* Judy Pregel and Robin Riley, 1993, p. 54

1547. *Houston Post,* Sept. 18, 1990

1548. *A 3rd Serving of Chicken Soup for the Soul,* Jack Canfield and Mark Hansen, 1996, p. 81

1549. *Reader's Digest,* Oct. 1994, p. 118

1550. *Sermon Notes & Illustrations,* Oct. 1994

1551. *Houston Chronicle,* Jan. 4, 1998, p. 10F; *Saturday Evening Post,* Sept./Oct. 1996, p. 32

1552. *Christian Reader,* Sept./Oct. 1998, p. 53

1553. *Humor Connection,* Vol. 1013, 1996

1554. Ibid, Vol. 1013

1555. *Positive Living,* May/June 1998

1556. *Reader's Digest,* Aug. 1999, p. 146

1557. *Houston Chronicle,* Sept. 28, 1999, p. 6D

1558. "Choosing Characters over Compromise," Rob Mahon, Hoffmantown Baptist Church, July 6, 1996

1559. *Executive Speechwriter Newsletter,* Vol. 11, No. 6

1560. *Reminisce Extra,* April 1994, p. 60

1561. *SBC Life,* Aug. 1995, p. 2

1562. Ibid

1563. *Positive Living,* Sept./Oct. 1996, p. 17

1564. Author's Personal Life

1565. *NEWSLETTER Newsletter,* July 2000, p. 6

1566. "Growing Toward Wholeness," John Ortberg, Seeds Tape Ministry, June 26, 1996

1567. *Ten Commandments,* Schlessinger and Vogel, 1998, p. 3

1568. *Beaumont Examiner,* July 8, 1999, p. 17

1569. *Reader's Digest,* Oct. 1993, p. 13

1570. *Brian's Lines,* Sept./Oct. 1997, p. 9

1571. *Scope,* Vol. 8, No. 16, 1998

1572. Author's Personal Experience, June 2000

1573. Charles Lowery, First Baptist Church, Beaumont, Texas, Oct. 12, 1992

1574. *Better Families,* Sept. 1997, p. 2

1575. "God's Top Ten Plus Two," Dan Yeary, North Phoenix Baptist Church, 1995

1576. *Leadership,* July 6, 1993, p. 6

1577. *Executive Speechwriter Newsletter,* Vol. 11, No. 6, p. 10

1578. *Bits & Pieces,* March 2, 1995, p. 16

1579. *Positive Living,* July/Aug. 1998, p. 8

1580. *Christian Reader,* July/Aug. 1994, p. 40

1581. *HomeLife,* May 1997, p. 63

1582. *Reader's Digest,* Feb. 1994, p. 98

1583. Ibid, Nov.1994, p. 174

1584. *Houston Chronicle*, July 1, 1996, p. 11D

1585. *Reader's Digest*, June 1998, p. 164

1586. *Christian Reader*, March 1990, p. 33

1587. Author's files

1588. *Holy Humor*, Cal and Rose Samra, 1996, p. 106

1589. *Humor for Preaching & Teaching*, Edward Rowell, 1996, p. 153

1590. *Sermon Notes*, May/June 1997, p. 14

1591. Author's files

1592. *Christian Reader*, May/June 1999, p. 27

1593. *Houston Chronicle*, Dec. 15, 1999, p. 9D

1594. *James Dobson's Bulletin*, Nov. 1997, p. 1

1595. *Houston Chronicle*, April 21, 1996

1596. *Christian Reader*, May/June 1999, p. 10

1597. *Reader's Digest*, Oct. 1993, p. 130

1598. *Executive Speechwriter Newsletter*, Vol. 14, No. 5

1599. "What the Bible Says About. . . Men and Women," John Ortberg, Seeds Tape Ministry, July 14, 1999

1600. Author's files

1601. Charles Lowery, FBC, Beaumont, Texas, Oct. 12, 1992

1602. *Reader's Digest*, May 1993, p. 101

1603. *Houston Chronicle*, Oct. 17, 1996, p. 8D

1604. *Better Families*, Nov. 1995, p. 2

1605. Adapted from the *Houston Chronicle*, May 28, 1996, p. 9D

1606. Adapted from "This We Believe," John Ortberg, Seeds Tape Ministry C9841

1607. *NEWSLETTER Newsletter*, June 1999, p. 7

MASTER INDEX

Note: Regular text = motivational section references
Bold = humorous section references